ROUTLEDGE LIBRARY EDITIONS: JAPANESE LINGUISTICS

Volume 4

COMPLEX PREDICATES IN JAPANESE

COMPLEX PREDICATES IN JAPANESE

CHIHARU UDA KIKUTA

LONDON AND NEW YORK

First published in 1994 by Garland Publishing, Inc.

This edition first published in 2019
by Routledge
2 Park Square, Milton Park, Abingdon, Oxon OX14 4RN

and by Routledge
52 Vanderbilt Avenue, New York, NY 10017

Routledge is an imprint of the Taylor & Francis Group, an informa business

© 1994 Chiharu Uda

All rights reserved. No part of this book may be reprinted or reproduced or utilised in any form or by any electronic, mechanical, or other means, now known or hereafter invented, including photocopying and recording, or in any information storage or retrieval system, without permission in writing from the publishers.

Trademark notice: Product or corporate names may be trademarks or registered trademarks, and are used only for identification and explanation without intent to infringe.

British Library Cataloguing in Publication Data
A catalogue record for this book is available from the British Library

ISBN: 978-1-138-36949-8 (Set)
ISBN: 978-0-429-40043-8 (Set) (ebk)
ISBN: 978-1-138-39419-3 (Volume 4) (hbk)
ISBN: 978-1-138-39430-8 (Volume 4) (pbk)
ISBN: 978-0-429-40131-2 (Volume 4) (ebk)

Publisher's Note
The publisher has gone to great lengths to ensure the quality of this reprint but points out that some imperfections in the original copies may be apparent.

Disclaimer
The publisher has made every effort to trace copyright holders and would welcome correspondence from those they have been unable to trace.

COMPLEX PREDICATES IN JAPANESE

CHIHARU UDA

GARLAND PUBLISHING, Inc.
New York & London / 1994

Copyright © 1994 by Chiharu Uda
All rights reserved

Library of Congress Cataloging-in-Publication Data

Uda, Chiharu, 1964–
  Complex predicates in Japanese / Chiharu Uda.
      p.   cm. — (Outstanding dissertations in linguistics)
  Includes bibliographical references and index.
  ISBN 0-8153-1698-4 (alk. paper)
    1. Japanese language—Verb phrase. 2. Japanese language—Passive
  voice. 3. Japanese language—Causative.   I. Title. II. Series.
  PL597.P52U33 1994
  495.6'5—dc20   93-45593
                                                                 CIP

Printed on acid-free, 250-year-life paper
Manufactured in the United States of America

Contents

Preface	ix
Acknowledgments	xi
List of Abbreviations and Symbols	xiii
Chapter 1: Introduction	1
Chapter 2: Theoretical Framework	7
2.1 Overview of Head-driven Phrase Structure Grammar	7
2.1.1 Linguistic Expression as Sign	7
2.1.2 Immediate Dominance Schemata	15
2.1.3 Lexical Rules	18
2.1.4 Control Structures	19
2.2 Semantic Roles and Thematic Role Types	24
2.2.1 Significance of Thematic Roles to Syntactic Issues	25
2.2.2 Problems with the Discrete Thematic Role Approach and the Relative Position Approach	27
2.2.3 Proto-Role Approach	29
2.3 Basic Sentence Structures and Configurationality of Japanese	32
2.4 Case Marking in Japanese	36
2.4.1 Case Marking Schemata in Japanese	36
2.5 Reflexive Binding in Japanese	40
2.5.1 Obliqueness Binding	40
2.5.2 *Zibun* Binding in Japanese	42
2.5.3 Obliqueness Binding for Japanese Reflexives	44
2.5.4 Thematic Binding for Japanese Reflexives	47
Chapter 3: Passive Constructions	65
3.1 Introduction	65
3.2 Three Types of Passive in Japanese	67
3.2.1 Direct Passives and Indirect Passives	67

	3.2.2 Possessive Passives	76
3.3	Previous Analyses of Passives in Japanese	80
	3.3.1 Transformational Approaches	82
	3.3.2 Lexicalist Approaches	84
	3.3.3 Movement Approaches: Without Verb Incorporation	87
	3.3.4 Movement Approaches: With Verb Incorporation	93
	3.3.5 Phrase Structure Approaches	99
	3.3.6 Summary of Previous Studies	103
3.4	Lexical Passives and Syntactic Passives	105
	3.4.1 Direct Passives as Lexical Passives	106
	3.4.2 Indirect Passives as Syntactic Passives	116
	3.4.3 Evidence for the Present Approach	119
3.5	Possessive Passives as Lexical Passives	130
	3.5.1 Evidence Against NP Movement in Possessive Passives	131
	3.5.2 The Lexical Rule for Possessive Passives	135
3.6	Double Passivization	142
3.7	On Case Distribution	144
3.8	Conclusion	150
	3.8.1 Independence and Interdependence of Morphology and Syntax	150
	3.8.2 Suppression of an Argument	151
	3.8.3 Uniformity in CONTENT	152

Chapter 4: Benefactive Constructions		173
4.1	Introduction	173
4.2	Syntactic Parallels between Passives and Benefactives	173
	4.2.1 Three Types of *Te-Moraw* Benefactives	174
	4.2.2 Do-Support Phenomena	179
4.3	Previous Analyses of *Te-Moraw* Benefactives	180
4.4	Analysis of *Te-Moraw* Benefactives Paralleling Passives	186
4.5	Evidence against the Parallelism	191
	4.5.1 Morpheme Order in Subject Honorification	191
	4.5.2 Semantic Properties of the Matrix Subject	198
	4.5.3 Implications of the Semantic Underspecification	205
4.6	Three Types of Japanese Benefactives	208
4.7	Conclusion	218

Chapter 5: Causative Constructions		229
5.1	Introduction	229

5.2	Two Types of Causatives in Japanese	230
	5.2.1 Intransitive-Based Causatives	231
	5.2.2 Transitive-Based Causatives	231
	5.2.3 *Wo*-Causatives and *Ni*-Causatives	234
5.3	Previous Analyses of Japanese Causatives	238
	5.3.1 Transformational Approaches	238
	5.3.2 Lexicalist Approaches	240
	5.3.3 Movement Approaches	241
	5.3.4 Argument Structure Merger Approaches	246
	5.3.5 Phrase Structure Approaches	248
5.4	Lexical Causatives and Syntactic Causatives	249
	5.4.1 *Wo*-Causatives as Lexical Causatives	250
	5.4.2 *Ni*-Causatives as Syntactic Control Structures	256
5.5	In Defense of the Present Approach	261
	5.5.1 Coerciveness and Self-Controllability	262
	5.5.2 Passivized Causatives and the Coercive Interpretation	266
	5.5.3 Biclausality of Causatives	269
5.6	More Supporting Evidence for the Present Approach	275
	5.6.1 Evidence from Do-Support	276
	5.6.2 Subject Honorification with Causatives	277
	5.6.3 Object Honorification with Causatives	283
5.7	A Third Type of Causatives	288
	5.7.1 Passive Causatives	289
	5.7.2 *Faire Par* Construction	291
	5.7.3 Causatives with the Function of Passives	293
	5.7.4 Passive-Type Causatives Based on a Transitive Verb	295
5.8	Conclusion	298

Chapter 6: Conclusion	315
Bibliography	327
Index	351

Preface

This is a very slightly revised version of my 1992 dissertation. The revision corrects the errors found in the original, provides more discussion, mainly in notes, on matters suggested by the comments I received, as well as updates the bibliography.

In the process of preparing this book, I came upon several issues which seem relevant, directly or indirectly, to the core argument of this work. Regretfully, however, I could not incorporate all those issues here due mainly to the limitation of time.

Among the recent works related to the subject matter dealt with in this book, I would particularly recommend readers to refer to Gunji (to appear) and to Washio 1993. The former presents a unification-based account of Japanese causatives subsuming both lexical and nonlexical approaches, while the latter explores the semantic continuum between passives and causatives in the framework of Jackendoff 1990.

Complex predicates involve a number of interesting topics, and different approaches reveal different aspects of language integrated in complex predicates. I hope this book will contribute to the elucidation of language in this sense, and encourage the readers to take interest in exploring the issues discussed here.

Acknowledgments

This book would not exist without the help and support of many people. My first and the deepest gratitude is due to my supervisor, Dr. Thomas E. Hukari. His comments always helped clarify my thoughts and led me in the right direction. His timely encouragement and support literally rescued me several times from the depth of despair during the course of writing the dissertation. I also owe a word of special appreciation to Dr. Leslie Saxon for her careful proofreading, valuable comments, and, most of all, for her very warm encouragement and support, which she was always ready to offer me.

My gratitude also goes to other members of my supervisory committee, Dr. Barry F. Carlson and Dr. Daniel J. Bryant. I would also like to express my sincere thanks to Dr. Joseph F. Kess, the Chair of the Department and my committee member, for all the support he has provided me ever since I decided to come to the University of Victoria.

I feel especially fortunate to have had Dr. Sige-Yuki Kuroda on my examination committee. His comments and criticism brought my attention to many potential problems for the issues dealt with in this work, and aroused my interest in pursuing them further.

I wish to thank all other faculty members of the Department. Thanks also to Ms. Darlene Wallace and Mrs. Gretchen Moyer of the Departmental office for their support.

I also have to acknowledge the great debts of gratitude that I owe to my teachers in Japan. Their support has made it possible for me to complete my programme in Canada. My special thanks are due first of all to Professor Ishiguro, whose guidance has been invaluable ever since I decided to major in linguistics. To Professor Kamaike, whose constant encouragement has been an immense support to me during the three years of my study in Canada. To Professor Tatsuki, who has kindly provided help in many ways both in Japan and in Canada.

It seems impossible to list the names of all the people whose friendship has helped me make it through. I particularly would like to thank all my friends in the Department, new and old. To Sandra, Andrea, Erica, Evan, Tadao, Norman, Chris and Forrester, Tracêl and Rudi, Yang Wei and Hongyan, Lin Hua, Suying, Xia, Shu-Chen.

Special thanks are also due to my friends in Japan: Kitabayashi-kun, Itô-kun, Tamai-kun, and Tomotsugu-san, among others. My deepest gratitude goes to my important friend Panna, who has constantly sent me power across miles to carry on with. Thanks also to my other friends in Malta: Lydia, Joe, and Mario.

I cannot finish my acknowledgments without mentioning the names of Dr. Shûichi Yatabe and Dr. Kazuhiko Fukushima, to whom I am especially indebted for the invaluable comments on the original dissertation, which helped me revise it into the present form.

Finally, this book is dedicated with my sincere gratitude and love to my mother and my late father, Yoshie and Shoichiro Uda.

List of Abbreviations and Symbols

AE	adverbial ending
ASP	aspectual inflection
BEN	benefactive
B-GROUND	BACKGROUND
CAS	causative
CAT	CATEGORY
COMP	complementizer
CONXT	CONTEXT
CONT	CONTENT
DES	desiderative
EXT-ARG	External-Argument
GEN	GENDER
GER	gerundive
HON (HN)	honorific
LOC	LOCAL
MOD	modal
NUM	NUMBER
OH	object honorification
PAS	passive
PHON	PHONOLOGY
PER	perfect (aspect) / PERSON
POT	potential
PRS	present
PST	past
SH	subject honorification
SUBCAT	SUBCATEGORIZATION
SYNSEM	SYNTAX-SEMANTICS
acc	accusative case
conj	conjunction
dat	dative case
dir	direction
fem	feminine
fin	finite (verb)

gen	genitive case
inst	instrumental postposition
loc	locative case
neut	neuter
nom	nominative case
psoa	parametrized state-of-affair
sing	singular
soa	state-of-affair
top	topic marker
Vform	verb form
¬	negation
A P B	A and B are connected in such a way that B's undergoing the given event necessarily entails that A is affected (cf. section 3.5.2).

I
Introduction

Being an agglutinative language, Japanese abounds in complex predicate constructions, which consist of a verb stem or gerund followed by another morpheme. Some such morphemes are bound forms and occur only adjacent to a verb stem, while others are free forms in the sense that they have a homophonous counterpart as a lexical verb. Complex predicates typically convey particular meanings concerning aspect, voice, modality, and so on, added to the lexical meaning of the stem/gerundive verb.

Japanese passives, *te-moraw* benefactives, and causatives that are examined in this dissertation also involve complex predicate structures. Passives and causatives use bound forms *(r)are* and *(s)ase*, which are attached to a verb stem. *Te-moraw* benefactives, on the other hand, use an auxiliary *moraw*,[1] which is homophonous with a lexical verb meaning 'to receive' attached to a gerundive verb. These three complex predicates are related to each other in that they all apparently alter the valency of the stem/gerundive verb.

The three complex predicates also show special interrelations among themselves. First of all, morphologically, the passive morpheme and the causative morpheme form a closed class. The initial consonants /s/ and /r/ are dropped when the verb stem ends in a consonant; this rule applies only to the suffixation of the passive/causative morpheme. Secondly, it has been observed that the syntactic properties of passives and *te-moraw* benefactives are very similar. At the same time, some scholars have analyzed *te-moraw* benefactives as polite causatives (Nakau 1973; see also section 4.5.2 below). In fact, as we will see later, the most natural paraphrase of subject honorification of a causative takes the form of a *te-moraw* benefactive (section 5.6.2). So it is part of our purpose to analyze the similarities and differences among passives, causatives, and *te-moraw* benefactives in a consistent way, and to clarify how the three complex predicates are related to each other. One of the recurring issues involving complex predicate constructions in general concerns monoclausality and biclausality. It has often been observed that complex predicate constructions reveal both monoclausal and biclausal properties. To put it differently, the question is whether the verb stem and the affixational morpheme as an amalgam head a clause, or whether each of them separately heads a clause.

Recent studies have attempted to reconcile such duality of complex predicate structures. Marantz's (1984) model posits a biclausal structure for a complex predicate (causative) before the operation called merger, and a monoclausal structure after merger. According to the mechanism of verb incorporation by Baker (1988), a lexical verb head is eventually raised to be incorporated into a passive/causative morpheme; so the complex predicate structure starts out as biclausal, with two verb heads, but the two verbs end in one amalgam.[2]

On the other hand, it has also been observed that morphological independence does not necessarily imply syntactic independence. Zubizarreta (1985, 1987) has claimed that Italian causatives are biclausal in one sense and monoclausal in another. Rosen (1989) has proposed a model where the argument structures of a causative verb and a lexical verb are merged together, though their morphological independence is maintained in syntactic mapping. These proposals imply that though Romance causatives are apparently periphrastic, they show significant monoclausal properties, for instance, concerning passivization and clitic climbing.

We adopt the insights of these predecessors and assume that the morphological properties of a morpheme and its syntactic function are two different matters, though morphological requirements may interact with syntax (cf. Borer 1990). Specifically, homophonous morphemes may have two functions: either as verbs or as derivational affixes.[3] That is, we assume as a working hypothesis that it is theoretically possible that one type of a morpheme, say, *(r)are*, is a verb, and another type of phonologically the same morpheme *(r)are* is a derivational affix. That they must be attached to the verb stem is a morphological requirement of these morphemes and is independent of their syntactic function. So the phonological identity of passive morphemes *(r)are* of different subtypes does not necessarily indicate that they are uniformly syntactic words or derivational affixes.

The main purpose of this book is to give an analysis of complex predicate constructions in Japanese in the framework of Head-driven Phrase Structure Grammar (HPSG). The most important aspect of HPSG for our purposes is that it is an information-based, multi-level theory. Language is considered as a sign, more precisely a feature structure (represented in the form of an attribute-value matrix (AVM) diagram), which conveys phonological, syntactic, and semantic information. Such pieces of information are sorted out and made simultaneously available. The information concerning the subcategorization of a predicate, for instance, is represented independently of the information concerning semantic roles specified by the predicate, but the two are co-present in the feature structure and can interact.

This organization of information in a feature structure will prove to be very effective in representing and analyzing the three types of complex predicate constructions in Japanese discussed in this book. As will be made clear in the course of discussion, it first of all enables us to factor out the complex linguistic facts into several levels of information, and to analyze them in their own proper domains. Furthermore, our approach provides a straightforward way to capture the common denominator among them, and at the same time refer to their differences, thus solving one of the long-standing issues in the analysis of Japanese passives and causatives.

This book is organized in the following way. Chapter 2 presents the theoretical framework as a basis of the following analyses. A synopsis of Head-driven Phrase Structure Grammar as laid out in Pollard and Sag 1994 will be given. Other assumptions crucial in the following discussion will also be presented, concerning thematic roles, reflexive binding, and case marking, among others. Chapters 3 through 5 discuss passive, benefactive, and causative constructions in this order. In chapter 3 passive constructions are examined. We follow Dubinsky 1989, Kubo 1990, and Terada 1990 in classifying Japanese passive constructions into three types: direct, possessive, and indirect passives. We will claim that the first two are lexical passives, while the last one is a syntactic passive. Chapter 4 will investigate *te-moraw* benefactives in comparison with passives. It will be shown that passives and *te-moraw* benefactives are syntactic parallels. Significant incongruities between the two constructions will also be discussed and will be accounted for without challenging their syntactic parallelism. We will propose that the benefactive relation is encoded in a MODAL feature, and seek support for this hypothesis in a more complete system of Japanese benefactive complex predicates, involving *te-yar* and *te-kure*. Chapter 5 gives an analysis of causative constructions, drawing on the results obtained in chapters 3 and 4. We will argue that *wo*-causatives are lexical causatives, while *ni*-causatives are syntactic causatives, which have a syntactic object control structure. Towards the end, a third type of causatives, passive-type causatives, will be identified based on the analysis of direct passives. Finally, chapter 6 gives a brief summary of the overall discussion.

Notes

1. Here and throughout the dissertation, we refer to a morpheme constituting a complex predicate with a gerundive verb as an *auxiliary*. For more discussion on this issue, see note 1 in section 4.2.

2. In an incorporation analysis, the complex predicate structure does not in fact have a monoclausal structure at any level of representation. Though the verb stem and the causative/passive morpheme are incorporated into one, a lower clause is still present, headed by traces.

3. Here and throughout this dissertation, we define a syntactic word as a morpheme which participates in a syntactic subcategorization. It subcategorizes for some arguments when it is a head (e.g., verb). A derivational affix is defined as a morpheme which cannot have a subcategorization frame on its own, but can alter the subcategorization frame of the verb stem it attaches to.

II
Theoretical Framework

This chapter briefly illustrates the theoretical framework this book is based on. We will first give an overview of the fundamental principles and the technical apparatus of HPSG as laid out mainly in Pollard and Sag 1987, 1994. We will also try to establish our assumptions on some of the issues which will bear an importance on the subsequent discussions. The issues include the concept of thematic roles, case marking and reflexive binding in Japanese.

2.1 Overview of Head-driven Phrase Structure Grammar

2.1.1 Linguistic Expression as Sign

One of the fundamental properties of HPSG is that it is a unification-based linguistic theory and, in this respect, it has much in common with Categorial Grammar (CG), Generalized Phrase Structure Grammar (GPSG), and Lexical-Functional Grammar (LFG). First of all, the syntactic theory is strictly nonderivational, in contrast with virtually any version of the Government-Binding (GB) Theory or Relational Grammar (RG). There is no notion of transformation, or movement. Nor are there any structural strata ordered according to the derivational history. The attributes of linguistic structure are related not by movement but by *structure-sharing*, a notion to be explained shortly.

HPSG is *monostratal*, but is a *multi-level* theory. [1] A linguistic expression, referred to as a *sign* in HPSG, is modelled in a system of *sorted feature structures*. (Moshier 1988; Pollard and Moshier 1990). A sign is represented as a feature structure whose attributes and values are arranged according to the principles of the theory. Each feature structure consists at least of such attributes as PHONOLOGY (PHON) and SYNTAX-SEMANTICS (SYNSEM), and is standardly represented in an attribute-value matrix (AVM) diagram. One could draw an analogy, say, between PHON and the PF of GB, but the analogy is not accurate. First of all, a sign can be of any size. All signs, be they sentences or words, have those attributes. Besides, more importantly, all the attributes are "co-present" in the sign. Unlike the levels D-structure, S-structure, LF, and PF in GB, there is no precedence relation among these attributes.

The following AVM diagrams exemplify the sorted feature structure representations for a verb *see*, a noun *cookie*, and a pronoun *she* (Pollard and Sag 1994, chap. 2):

(1) a. see

$$\begin{bmatrix} \text{PHON} \mid see \\ \text{SYNSEM} \mid \text{LOC} \begin{bmatrix} \text{CAT} \begin{bmatrix} \text{HEAD} & \text{verb[fin]} \\ \text{SUBCAT} & \langle \text{NP}_{[1]}, \text{NP}_{[2]} \rangle \end{bmatrix} \\ \text{CONTENT} \begin{bmatrix} \text{RELATION} & see \\ \text{SEER} & [1] \\ \text{SEEN} & [2] \end{bmatrix} \end{bmatrix} \end{bmatrix}$$

b. cookie

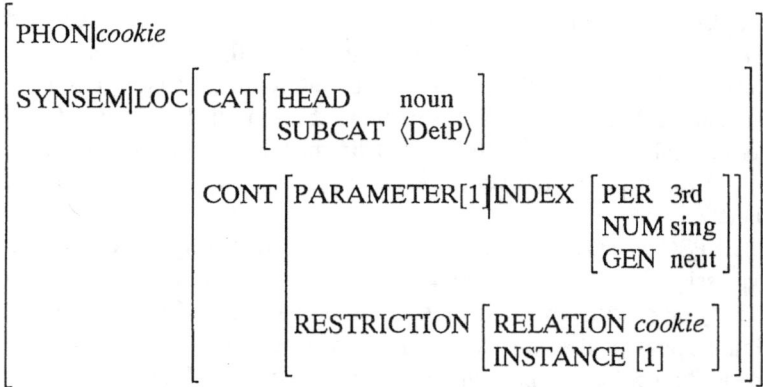

c. she

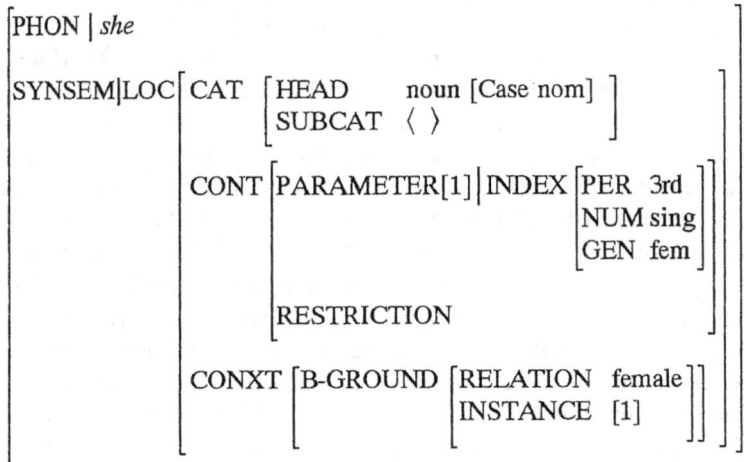

Note how the relevant information is organized in the feature structure. The PHON attribute specifies what phonological shape is taken by the given expression.[2] The SYNSEM feature has as its value the LOCAL (LOC) and, when necessary, the NONLOCAL features. The LOC feature is further sorted into the CATEGORY (CAT) and the CONTENT (CONT) features. The CAT feature comprises the HEAD feature and the SUBCAT feature, which specifies the basic syntactic properties of the sign such as the part of speech and the subcategorization. The CONTENT feature defines the (semantic) property of a sign. When a sign is a predicate, the CONTENT feature is its logical predicate-argument structure. The mechanism of these SYNSEM attributes will be further illustrated in the next section. The CONTEXT (CONXT) value contains certain context-dependent linguistic information such as deictic status, conventional implicature, etc. When the sign is not lexical but phrasal, it also bears the attribute DAUGHTERS (DTRS). The value of this attribute is a feature structure of sort *constituent structure* (*con-struc*) and it represents the immediate constituent structure of the phrase. The con-struc is of various subsorts depending on the types of daughters involved. Most of the studies in HPSG have focused on the constituent structure subsort *headed-structure* (*head-struc*), which is used in all endocentric (headed) constructions.

The feature structures used in HPSG are required to be both *totally well-typed* and *sort-resolved*. A feature structure is *well-typed* when the attributes that appear in it are appropriate for the sort label. A feature structure is *sort-resolved* when every attribute ends in a label which is the most specific in the sort ordering. For instance, the CASE attribute of a noun must end in a case value, NOM, ACC, etc.

HPSG does not use tree diagrams except as a short-hand representation. This is not simply a matter of representation. With other unification-based theories such as GPSG, HPSG takes the view that the role of linguistic theory is to give a precise specification of which feature structures are to be considered admissible. Tree-configurational notions are assumed not to play any significant role at all. Such configurational notions as government or c-command are excluded from the theory. Much of the burden is shifted instead to the lexicon, in particular the lexically specified SUBCAT value of a head, and the mechanism of structure-sharing (i.e., unification). For instance, assignment of case to complements is treated as part of subcategorization. The assignment of semantic roles to an argument is also carried out without a configurational mechanism. Binding and control theories are constructed based on the obliqueness of the arguments and the semantics of the verbs. In the next section we will illustrate in more detail the SYNSEM features to show how the mechanism of structure sharing works in various aspects of syntax and semantics.

2.1.1.1 The SYNSEM Features and Structure Sharing

2.1.1.1.1 The HEAD Feature

Now, take an example to see how a sentence is actually analyzed under this grammar. A simple sentence, *Felix chases Fido*, has a structure conventionally represented in a tree diagram as in (2):

(2)

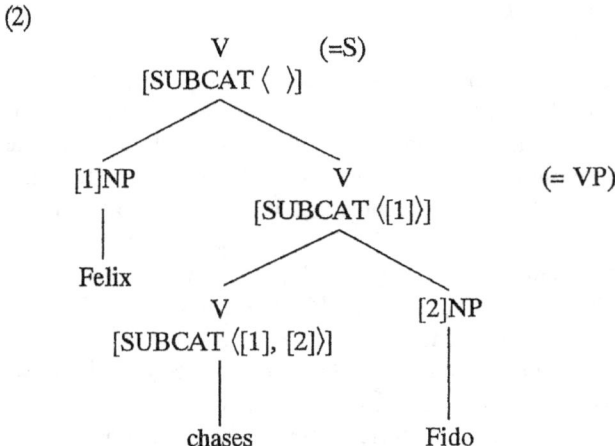

Note first of all that the whole clause (S) and its head (V) are of the same category. Namely, S is defined as a projection of V as in GPSG, rather than a projection of some functional category corresponding to CP, IP, etc. in GB Theory (Chomsky 1986). So S is defined as a V with a saturated SUBCAT list. We will still refer to this category as S, for simplicity's sake, as a notational variant. This categorial information is encoded in the HEAD feature attribute of a sign. In the given example the head verb is of the category V[fin] (=finite), a specification which is a part of its HEAD feature. The legitimate "percolation" of this feature between the head and its projection is guaranteed by the Head Feature Principle, stated in (3):[3]

(3) Head Feature Principle (Pollard and Sag 1994: chap. 2)

The HEAD value of any headed phrase is structure-shared with the HEAD value of the head daughter.

The effect of this principle is that a lexical head (V), its mother node (VP), and the top node (S) all share the same head feature. Structure-sharing, indicated by boxed numerals called *tags*, involves token identity of values, not just values which are structurally identical feature structures. As a result, it is guaranteed that the HEAD value of the entire phrase is token-identical to that of the lexical head.

2.1.1.1.2 The SUBCAT Feature

The second point to note with respect to the construction of a phrasal sign is the SUBCAT feature. The lexical specification for the SUBCAT feature is carried by verbs and other lexical items that head phrases. A bare common noun is subcategorized for a determiner phrase, and a lexical head verb is subcategorized for its complements, including the subject. The value of this feature is an ordered list, in which the items are ordered according to obliqueness, with more oblique elements appearing to the right of less oblique elements. The leftmost element always corresponds to the subject.

In the case at hand, the head verb *chases* is subcategorized for two NPs. The first one, tagged with [1], corresponds to the subject, while the second one, tagged with [2], corresponds to the direct object. Note also that the next node up, the mother node immediately dominating the head verb, has a SUBCAT feature with only one NP in its value, which corresponds to the subject NP. These states of affairs are governed by the Subcategorization Principle, one of the universal principles in HPSG theory, stated as follows:

(4) Subcategorization Principle (Pollard and Sag 1994)

In a headed phrase (i.e. a phrasal sign whose DTRS value is of sort *head-struc*), the SUBCAT value of the head daughter is the concatenation of the phrase's SUBCAT list with the list (in order of increasing obliqueness) of SYNSEM value of the complement daughters.

The Subcategorization Principle states that the SYNSEM value of a complement is structure-shared with the corresponding specification within the SUBCAT value of the sign which selects the complement. What that means in the present case is that the entire SYNSEM value of *Fido* is structure-shared with the rightmost item in the SUBCAT list of *chases*.[4]

Further, this principle works in much the same way as cancellation in Categorial Grammar in passing the SUBCAT specification upwards (cf. Dowty 1982). With this principle, the subcategorization requirements of the lexical head are checked off as they become satisfied by the complement daughters of its phrasal projections; at the same time, the SUBCAT elements themselves are token-identical to the

Theoretical Framework

SYNSEM values of the corresponding complements. Thus a grammatically complete phrasal projection has an empty SUBCAT list, or a *saturated* SUBCAT value. It is important to note, however, that HPSG does not require that every lexical sign end up in a saturated phrasal projection.[5]

Thus the Subcategorization Principle and the Head Feature Principle jointly guarantee that the syntactic and semantic information of the lexical head is in some sense respected in the sentence itself. To see the point, compare the feature structure of a VP *chases Fido* and that of the head verb *chases* represented in AVM diagrams below:[6]

(5)[7]

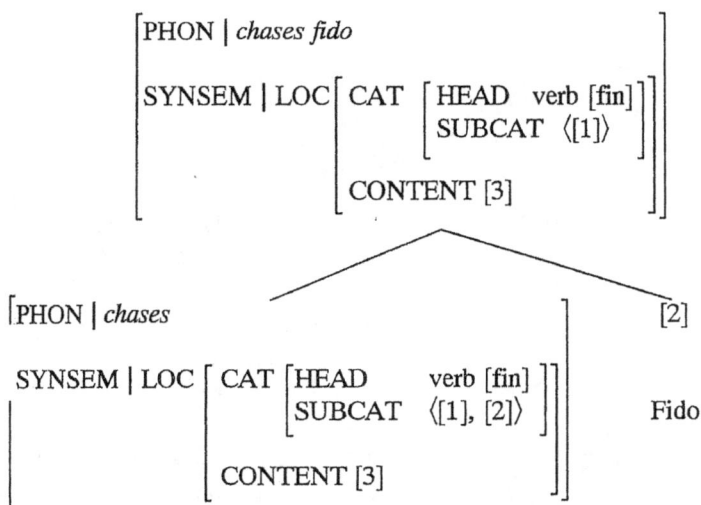

2.1.1.1.3 The Content Feature

PARAMETER features enter into another type of structure-sharing, which is typically observed in the operation of semantic role assignment. The tree diagrams and feature structures given above, however, are not adequate for illustrating this mechanism. Let us then look at the feature structures of *Fido* and *chases* with a slightly different use of tags. Despite the difference in tagging, the structure in (6-a) represents the same feature structure as (5):

(6) a. chases

$$\begin{bmatrix} \text{PHON} \mid \textit{chases} \\ \text{SYNSEM} \mid \text{LOC} \begin{bmatrix} \text{CAT} \begin{bmatrix} \text{HEAD} \quad \text{verb [fin]} \\ \text{SUBCAT} \ \langle \text{NP}_{[1][\text{3rd.sing}]}, \text{NP}_{[2]} \rangle \end{bmatrix} \\ \text{CONT} \begin{bmatrix} \text{RELATION } \textit{chase} \\ \text{CHASER} \quad [1] \\ \text{CHASEE} \quad [2] \end{bmatrix} \end{bmatrix} \end{bmatrix}$$

b. Fido

$$\begin{bmatrix} \text{PHON} \mid \textit{fido} \\ \text{SYNSEM}|\text{LOC} \begin{bmatrix} \text{CAT} \begin{bmatrix} \text{HEAD noun} \\ \text{SUBCAT} \quad \langle \ \rangle \end{bmatrix} \\ \text{CONT} \begin{bmatrix} \text{PARAMETER[2]} \mid \text{INDEX} \begin{bmatrix} \text{PER 3rd} \\ \text{NUM sing} \end{bmatrix} \\ \quad\quad\quad \textit{npro} \quad\quad\quad \textit{index} \\ \text{RESTRICTION} \begin{bmatrix} \text{RELATION } \textit{naming} \\ \text{BEARER} \quad [2] \\ \text{NAME} \quad\quad \textit{Fido} \end{bmatrix} \\ \quad\quad\quad\quad\quad \textit{psoa} \end{bmatrix} \end{bmatrix} \end{bmatrix}$$

The CONTENT value in HPSG is a *parametrized state of affair* (*psoa*), which is represented by a feature structure which specifies a relation, participating argument roles, and polarities.[8] The CONTENT value of a verb *chases* indicates that the verb makes reference to the *chase* relation, which involves the *chaser* and the *chasee* roles. A comment is in order. The CONTENT attribute, which will also be referred to as the semantic CONTENT feature in subsequent discussion, is a value of the SYNSEM feature; it encodes semantic information relevant to syntax. It is therefore a part of syntactic information, and is not to be understood as a variant of the conceptual structure in the sense of Jackendoff 1983, 1987, 1990.

Notice that the CONTENT value of the head verb contains the tags corresponding to the PARAMETERS of the NP arguments. The PARAMETER is a CONTENT attribute of an NP, and is indicated by a subscript put at the right of the NP in the SUBCAT list.[9] Semantic role assignment in HPSG is essentially the structure-sharing between a SUBCAT element's parameter and a semantic role value of the verb's CONTENT feature. The CONTENT value of a verb *chases* thus indicates that the verb makes reference to the *chase* relation, and the *chaser* role, for instance, is filled by the referential parameter of the least oblique (=subject) argument. This is essentially how semantic role assignment is effected in HPSG; it would, therefore, more appropriately be characterized as a lexically specified identification. Two points merit attention: First, the semantic (or thematic) roles are assigned not to the complements themselves but rather to their referential parameters. Second, the structure sharing for semantic role assignment is thus between parameters, in contrast to that for subcategorization, which is between entire SYNSEM values.

There is yet another important type of structure-sharing: coindexing. Coindexing in HPSG is literally structure-sharing between the INDEX values, which are borne by parameters. If an NP is referential, than any NP coindexed with it must have the same reference. However, coindexing of parameters (= structure-sharing of indices) and parameter identity (= structure-sharing of parameters) are to be distinguished. Coindexing is a crucial mechanism in the agreement theory, binding theory, and control theory of HPSG, and more will be said about it in the sections to follow.

2.1.2 Immediate Dominance Schemata

HPSG has a set of phrase structure "rules" called Immediate Dominance (ID) schemata. These schemata are analogous to X'-theory in GB Theory or ID rules in GPSG in that they serve as templates for permissible local phrase structures or configurations of immediate constituency.[10] Cross-theoretically, there has been assumed to be a small, universal set of disjunctive constraints on the immediate constituency of phrases that each language can take. In the X'-theory of GB, for instance, it is assumed that any phrasal projection should satisfy the following two highly schematic universal immediate dominance templates.[11]

(7) a. X" →   Y"   X'
                (specifier)

    b. X' →   X   Y"
                (complement)

ID schemata in HPSG formalize exactly the same kind of constraints. There are a few points of difference to note, however. First, they are stated in a universal principle, called the Immediate Dominance Principle (IDP). Second, they contrast with X'-theory in rejecting the concept of bar-level. Third, the ID schemata do not define grammatical properties, such as subject and object.

The Immediate Dominance Principle defines several schemata available in languages. The first two schemata, given in (8), roughly correspond to the X'-schemata of (7-a) and (7-b), respectively. They have the general form translated in the shape of a tree in (8-a) and (8-b), respectively.

(8) Immediate Dominance Principle (IDP)

The universally available options for a well-formed phrase are:

(Schema 1) a saturated ([SUBCAT < >) phrase with DTRS value of sort *head-comp-struc* in which the HEAD-DTR value is a phrasal sign and the COMP-DTRS value is a list of length one;

(Schema 2) an almost saturated (SUBCAT list of length one) phrase with DTRS value of sort *head-comp-struc* in which the HEAD-DTR value is a lexical sign.

a: Schema 1

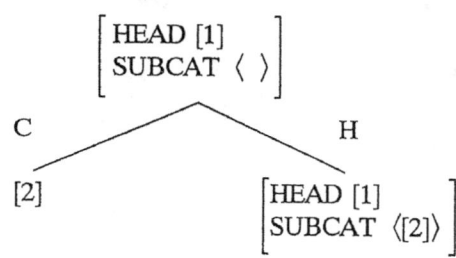

b: Schema 2

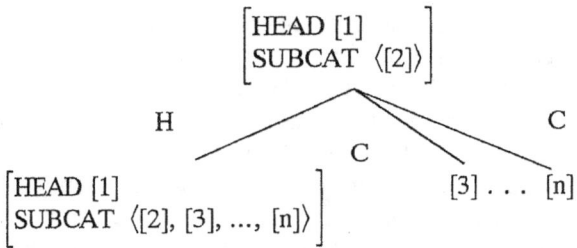

Schema 1 licenses a local phrase structure with a saturated mother dominating a phrasal head and a complement. Given the SUBCAT principle mentioned above, the complement is subcategorized for by its sister (head). The structures licensed by this schema include sentences (S → NP VP), "small clauses," and noun phrases consisting of a determiner and a nominal head (NP → Det N').

Schema 2, on the other hand, licenses a local phrase structure in which a mother subcategorizes for one argument and the head daughter is lexical. The number of (non-head) complement daughters can be zero or more. According to the SUBCAT principle, the structures licensed by schema 2 have the lexical head subcategorize for all the complement daughters as well as the one left in the mother's SUBCAT list.

Notice that no mention is made of the "bar level". The function of bar level is replaced in part by the degree of saturation of the subcategorization and by the distinction between lexical and non-lexical (phrasal). The maximal projection of, arguably, bar level 2, corresponds to a saturated phrasal category. The lexical category of bar level 0 is simply stated as a lexical category, which is not saturated. Categories of an intermediate level, presumably of bar level 1, are treated as unsaturated phrasal categories.

ID schemata themselves do not define the grammatical functions of the items. In X'-theory, such notions as specifier, subject, etc. are defined configurationally. Namely, the subject or specifier is defined as such by virtue of occupying a particular configurational position. ID schemata in HPSG do not play such a defining role. Most of the notions configurationally defined in GB, for instance, are lexically defined in terms of the position on the SUBCAT list of the lexical head. What ID schemata do is provide a constraint on the way they can be realized configurationally.[12]

2.1.3 Lexical Rules

HPSG utilizes lexical (redundancy) rules of various kinds. They are basically the functions which map one class of words to another. The postulation of lexical rules has been defended in lexicalist approaches for its advantage of simplifying the organization of the lexicon (Kaplan and Bresnan 1982). Lexical rules in HPSG are allowed to refer to some specific features, most typically the SUBCAT features. Some of the lexical rules have a function similar to metarules in Gazdar et al. 1985.

One of the lexical rules crucially relevant to the present study is the Passive Lexical Rule. The formulation of passives in HPSG is relational on the one hand and lexical on the other. The core operation affects the SUBCAT list. The Passive Lexical Rule for English, represented in (9), cyclically permutes the elements in the SUBCAT list. The input form's least oblique argument is dropped off and its parameter is reassigned to an optional PP[by]-phrase added at the end of the SUBCAT list (= the most oblique position.) The semantic content is simply carried over from the input form without change.

(9) Passive Lexical Rule[13]

$$\begin{bmatrix} \text{SYNSEM} \mid \text{LOC} \begin{bmatrix} \text{CAT} \mid \text{SUBCAT} \ \langle NP_1, NP_2, ... \rangle \\ \text{CONTENT [3]} \end{bmatrix} \end{bmatrix} \Rightarrow$$

$$\begin{bmatrix} \text{SYNSEM} \mid \text{LOC} \begin{bmatrix} \text{CAT} \mid \text{SUBCAT} \ \langle NP_2, ...PP[by]_1 \rangle \\ \text{CONTENT [3]} \end{bmatrix} \end{bmatrix}$$

This rule simply recapitulates the traditional wisdom that passive is an operation on grammatical relations, which promotes a non-subject argument to the subject status, at the same time as demoting the subject argument to the most oblique status, a view shared by such theories as Relational Grammar (Perlmutter 1978, 1983; Perlmutter and Postal 1983), GPSG (Gazdar et al. 1985), and the early versions of LFG (Kaplan and Bresnan 1982).[14] Different from Relational Grammar, HPSG takes a lexicalist view on passives in that this operation takes place in the lexicon.

Much argumentation supporting the relational and lexical views on passives has been given in the literature. The alternation of grammatical relations and the conformity to the general phrase structure schemata seem observationally and pre-theoretically correct.

No passives are formed without the alternation of grammatical relations between arguments, though it is still a matter of controversy whether promotion is more central than demotion or vice versa. (Perlmutter 1978; Perlmutter and Postal 1983; Comrie 1977; among others).

Though the treatment of passivization as a lexical process has found support in many theories, alternative syntactic approaches have also existed. One piece of evidence for the lexical treatment in HPSG is theory-internal. Note that on the syntactic level, the organization of feature structures as regulated by the mechanism of unification allows only unifying compatible pieces of information or adding compatible information, maintaining monotonicity. Thus feature values cannot be changed in order to achieve compatibility or for any purpose. Given this constraint, and given the characterization of passivization as a change in grammatical relations, it is obvious that passivization cannot be a syntactic process. Syntactic processes in HPSG, as in any unification-based theory, do not allow such radical changes of information.

Besides theory-internal motivation, other strong support for a lexicalist approach comes from observations about phrase structure. Note that under the lexical approach, the output form of the Passive Lexical Rule, namely, the passive participle in English, is treated simply as another type of lexical verb to be mapped onto syntax following exactly the same phrase structure schemata as active verbs. And in fact, there seems to be no language where passives occur in unique phrase structures. From these considerations Pollard and Sag 1994 concludes that passives should be obtained through a lexical rule which changes the grammatical relation among arguments.

2.1.4 Control Structures

This section briefly presents the control theory of HPSG, which provides the basis for our analysis of syntactic causatives. The HPSG control theory is based on coindexing between the unexpressed subject of a complement and a controller. The controller assignment is determined by semantic roles, rather than by configurational relations or by semantic types as in GPSG.

As mentioned above, HPSG posits no phonetically unrealized PRO in control structures, exemplified in (10):[15]

(10) a. Kim tried [to win].
    b. Terry promised [to go to England].
    c. Terry promised Lucie [to go to England].
    d. Terry persuaded Lucie [to go to England].
    e. Lucie wanted [to buy that house].

The matrix verbs of the sentences in (10) subcategorize for one or two NP complements and an unsaturated VP complement set off by the square backets. (11) gives a simplified SYNSEM value for the feature structure of the verb *persuade* (10-d):[16]

(11)
$$\begin{bmatrix} \text{SUBCAT} \langle \text{NP}[1], \text{NP}[2]. \text{VP}[\mathit{inf}]{:}[3] \rangle \\ \text{CONTENT} \begin{bmatrix} \text{RELATION} & \mathit{persuade} \\ \text{PERSUADER} & [1] \\ \text{PERSUADEE} & [2] \\ \text{SOA-ARG} \ [3] \begin{bmatrix} \text{RELATION} & \mathit{go} \\ \text{GOER} & [4] \end{bmatrix} \end{bmatrix} \end{bmatrix}$$

Similarly, raising verbs such as those involved in the sentences in (12) are assumed to subcategorize for an unsaturated VP complement, though their treatment is distinct from that of equi verbs in (10):

(12) a. Lucie seemed [to be happy].
    b. Kim believed John [to be honest].

This approach is in clear contrast with the GB approach where the matrix verb is subcategorized for a "full clause" or IP/CP. Notice that VP embedding is a legitimate possibility in HPSG because there is no analog of the *projection principle*. Once the obstacle posed by the projection principle is removed, VP embedding is motivated by the consideration of the locality of subcategorization in the following way. It has been observed that the grammaticality of a sentence is often sensitive to the categorial type of the embedded complement. Thus the grammaticality of the following sentences depends on the category of the embedded complement set off by square brackets (examples and their judgments from Pollard and Sag 1994, chap. 3):

(13) *a. I expect that island [PP off the route].
   *b. I expect that island [NP a good vacation spot].
    c. I expect that island [VP to be off the route].
    d. I expect that island [VP to be a good vacation spot].
    e. I expect that man [AP dead] by tomorrow.

(14) *a. I consider that island [PP off the route].
    b. I consider that island [NP a good vacation spot].
    c. I consider that island [VP to be off the route].
    d. I consider that island [VP to be a good vacation spot].
   *e. I consider that man [AP dead] by tomorrow.

Pollard and Sag 1994 argues that for the syntactic information about the complement phrases to be accessible, the matrix verb (*expect*, *consider* in the examples above) must select them, given the common assumption that subcategorization is local.

Let us turn to controller selection for the sentences in (10). "Control" in HPSG is effected by coindexing the controller and the unexpressed subject argument of the VP complement. Controller selection is based on the semantic class of a verb rather than on syntactic properties such as hierarchical structure or grammatical relations. This idea was originally suggested by Jackendoff 1972. The greatest advantage of the semantic account is that it captures the fact that the controller remains constant across different syntactic realizations of the same verb as illustrated in (15):

(15) a. Sandy promised Tracy to leave the party early.
    b. Sandy's promise to Tracy to leave the party early caused quite an uproar.
    c. The promise by Sandy to leave the party early caused quite an uproar.
    d. The promise that Sandy made, to leave the party early, caused quite an uproar.
    e. Sandy made Tracy a promise. It was to leave the party early.

Sag and Pollard 1991 proposes the following three classes of control verbs:

(16) *influence*-type [object control]:
order, persuade, bid, charge, command, direct, advise, convince, prompt, compel, push, encourage, exhort, urge, lead, ask, appeal (to), forbid, allow, permit, enable, cause, force, etc.

(17) *commitment*-type [subject control]:
promise, swear, agree, contract, pledge, vow, try, intend, refuse, choose, decline, decide, demand, endeavor, attempt, threaten, undertake, propose, offer, etc.

(18) *orientation*-type [subject control]:
want, desire, fancy, wish, ache, hanker, itch, long, need, hope, thirst, yearn, hate, aspire, expect, etc.

The semantic CONTENT value of all the verbs in the first class (16) consists of a relation of the *influence* type and three semantic roles, which are referred to as *influence*[17] (the agentive influencer), *influenced* (the recipient of the influence, typically animate), and *soa-arg* (the action for the influenced participant to perform). Similarly, the *commitment*-type verbs in (17) all involve a participant playing the *committor* role, an optional participant for the *commissee* role, and a *soa-arg*. The third class, (18), involves desire, expectation, or similar mental orientation toward a given soa, and is identified as *orientation* type. The participating roles are an *experiencer* and a *soa-arg*.

The semantic generalizations underlying the controller assignment are informally stated as in (19) (Sag and Pollard 1991, 66):

(19) Given a nonfinite VP or predicative complement C, whose semantic content C' is the soa-arg of a soa s whose relation is R, the unexpressed subject of C is linked to:

A. the influenced participant of s, if R is of influence type,
B. the committor participant of s, if R is of commitment type,
C. the experiencer participant of s, if R is of orientation type.

A more formal rendering of the control theory is as follows:

(20) HPSG control theory[18]

Given a soa: $\begin{bmatrix} \text{RELATION} \\ \text{SOA-ARG [EXT-ARG }_{refl}\text{ [INDEX [1]]]} \end{bmatrix}$

if R is of sort *influence, commitment*, or *orientation*, then the value of the *influenced, committor*, or *experiencer* role respectively is [INDEX [1]].

In the rule above, Ext-Arg (external argument) is a feature of content that picks out a particular role argument of a given soa as distinguished with respect to external relations such as control. In English the Ext-Arg is generally identified with the subject; that is, the controller corresponds to the unexpressed subject of the complement clause. In Tagalog, however, the controllee is identified as the *actor* rather than the subject; the Ext-Arg value is not the subject's parameter but rather that of the *actor* in the language (Kroeger 1991; Sag and Pollard 1991).

Given the rule (20), the controllee of the *influence*-type verb is coindexed with the *influenced* role argument (=object), while the controllee of the *commitment*-type verb is coindexed with the *committor* role argument (=subject), resulting in the controller contrast represented by *promise* and *persuade*. As the rule (20) is quite general, it applies not only to verbal constituents, but also to nominal constituents whose feature structure satisfies the description in (20).

The tree diagram in (21) and the feature matrix of the head verb in (22) show the basic representation of a control structure in HPSG:

(21)

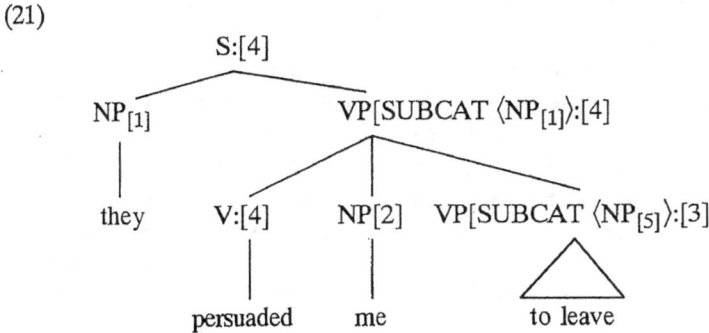

(22)
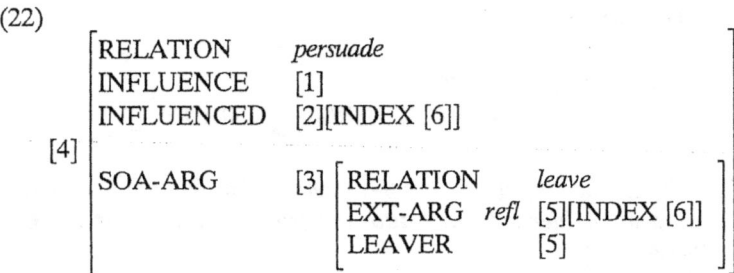

The matrix predicate *to persuade* is of *influence* type. It follows, therefore, given the control theory stated above, that the Ext-Arg of the embedded predicate, tagged with [5], is coindexed with the *influenced* argument, tagged with [2]. This coindexing relation defines the *influenced* argument [2] to be the controller.

2.2 Semantic Roles and Thematic Role Types

HPSG does not commit itself to any particular theory of thematic roles, even though such role labels as Agent, Experiencer, Theme, and the like are occasionally used. It explicitly rejects the idea that a small number of thematic roles can be meaningfully established for the entire vocabulary of a language. The rejection of thematic roles goes beyond the matter of labeling a particular role. Such a hypothesis as the Universal Thematic Alignment Hypothesis (UTAH) (Baker 1988), which is widely accepted in the current studies of GB, is therefore totally incompatible with the premises of HPSG. The most common practice in HPSG is to tentatively adopt the assumption in situation semantics that each semantic relation comes with a set of roles which are unique to that relation, termed *individual thematic roles* by Dowty 1989. Role type names such as Agent and Experiencer are used always with the understanding that the usage is only for the sake of familiarity.

As shown in the control theory given above, however, HPSG does not deny that semantic regularities can hold over certain semantic roles. In fact, thematic generalization over a certain class of verbs and their arguments figures prominently in our subsequent discussion of Japanese passives and causatives. So it seems essential for us to lay out our approach to thematic roles. Sag and Pollard 1991 refers to Ladusaw and Dowty 1988 as a view on this issue which HPSG is in sympathy with. This section briefly reviews the Proto-Role approach, proposed by Ladusaw and Dowty 1988 and Dowty 1991, in comparison with alternative views on thematic roles which have been assumed in the literature.

2.2.1 Significance of Thematic Roles to Syntactic Issues

It has been noticed for a long time that the arguments of predicates do not behave utterly idiosyncratically. Generalization over a set of arguments is possible, suggesting that arguments can be divided into several role-types, in which members share some significant syntactic and/or semantic properties. The term "thematic relations" is credited to Gruber 1965, but a similar idea can be traced back even to Pāṇini's concept *kārakas* (Dowty 1991). The idea of thematic roles/relations was elaborated particularly by Fillmore in his Case Grammar (Fillmore 1968), and by Jackendoff (Jackendoff 1972, 1987, 1990). Many current linguistic theories assume the concept of thematic roles/relations, and in some, the function of thematic roles is crucial.

The various approaches proposed so far in the literature can be classified into three types: (1) the Discrete Thematic Roles approach, (2) the Relative Position approach, and (3) the Macro (Proto) Role approach.[19] Among these, the Discrete Thematic Roles approach is the one which is implicitly assumed by most of the works referring to thematic roles and thematic hierarchy. In this approach, arguments are grouped into a certain number of role types such as Agent, Experiencer, Instrument, Theme, etc. Each role type is a discrete set, and the classification is unambiguous; i.e., Agent and Experiencer are different entities.

The class of generally-assumed thematic roles includes Agent, Patient, Theme, Goal, Source, Instrument, Locative, and Experiencer. It is also assumed by many that these thematic roles constitute a hierarchy of thematic prominence. A representative hierarchy, taken from Bresnan and Kanerva 1989 is given in (23):[20]

(23) Agent > Benefactive > Goal (Experiencer) > Instrument
 > Patient (Theme) > Locative

It is well known that the association between thematic roles and their syntactic realization (grammatical relation) is not arbitrary.[21] A hierarchical relation among thematic roles, in some form, was first suggested by Fillmore 1968 in drawing a generalization on subject selection. In a great many languages, the subject argument of a two-place predicate is usually the one which is higher than the other in the hierarchy. For instance, with a verb meaning "kick," the one who performs the action is very likely to be the subject, and the patient the object. There is not likely to be a verb, say, *hick*, which means the same as *kick* but has the subject corresponding to the patient, and the object to the agent.

The celebrated example *open* potentially selects Agent, Theme, and Instrument roles. Agent will be the subject whenever it appears. Instrument can be the subject only when Agent does not show up. Theme can be the subject only when it is the sole argument (cf. Jackendoff 1972, 43):[22]

(24) a. John opened the door with the key.
 b. The key opened the door (*by John).
 c. The door opened (*with the key).

Other syntactic phenomena that seem to refer to thematic roles include reflexive binding in some languages at least. For instance, in Marathi and Tagalog, the binder of a reflexive is restricted to the argument with the highest thematic role among the arguments of a predicate. The controllee in a control structure is also the argument with the highest thematic role in these languages (Joshi 1989; Guilfoyle, Hung, and Travis 1990; Kroeger 1991).

The distinction between unergativity and unaccusativity is assumed by many linguists to pertain to the distinction between Agent and Theme.[23] In a great many languages, for instance, passivization is possible only when there is an argument whose thematic role is Agent or something higher than Experiencer. So in Dutch, for instance, unergatives can undergo (impersonal) passivization, while unaccusatives cannot. Morphological causativization in some languages is possible only with unaccusative predicates (Rice 1991).

The predicates whose highest thematic role is not Agent but Experiencer (= psych predicates) are known to manifest many syntactic properties different from predicates with an Agent argument. Noncanonical case marking on the subject found across languages (i.e., "dative subject" in many instances) is often a characteristic of a predicate without an Agent argument. In the analysis of Italian psych predicates by Belletti and Rizzi 1988, it is crucial for them to distinguish between Experiencer and Theme, and the distinction is translated into syntax as the relative height of the structural positions the two arguments occupy. Specifically, Experiencer is higher than Theme.

The data of unaccusativity and psych predicates have focussed attention on the syntactic significance of thematic roles. The existence of thematic roles is so taken for granted now that it is almost standardly assumed in GB that the syntactic projection of arguments is directly based on the thematic roles and the hierarchy. This principle, stated by Baker 1988 as the Uniformity of Theta Assignment Hypothesis (UTAH), a descendant of the Universal Alignment Hypothesis (UAH) by Perlmutter and Postal 1984, is given in (25):

(25) The Uniformity of Theta Assignment Hypothesis (UTAH) (Baker 1988, 46)

Identical thematic relationships between items are represented by identical structural relationships between those items at the level of D-structure.

Notice that UTAH presupposes that thematic roles are unambiguous and discrete. UTAH entails that arguments of Theme role, for instance, are all mapped into an identical position specified for Theme in D-structure. It further implies that there is a separate slot in D-structure unique to each thematic role.

2.2.2 Problems with the Discrete Thematic Role Approach and the Relative Position Approach

In spite of the widespread belief in their existence, there is in fact no consensus about what thematic roles are, how many thematic roles should be assumed, nor how each thematic role should be defined. It is no clearer what the "correct" hierarchy is. In the absence of a clear definition of each thematic role, a distinction cannot be made easily between, say, Source and Agent for the italicized NPs in such sentences as follows:

(26) a. *John* gave the book to Mary.
    b. Mary got the book from *John*.
    c. Mary was given the book by *John*.

d. *That teacher* taught Kim English.
e. Kim learned English from *that teacher*.

f. *The chart* tells you that the GNP has dropped in these five years.
g. You can see from *this chart* that the GNP has dropped in these five years.

Even if role types were clearly distinguished, the hierarchical order would pose another vexing problem. The examples of the thematic roles and hierarchies proposed in the literature are enough to show the difficulty and implausibility of establishing a really dependable hierarchy.24

(27) a. Fillmore 1968:   Agent > Experiencer > Instrument > Object (=Theme) > Source > Goal > Location > Time

b. Jackendoff 1972:   Agent > Loc/Source/Goal > Theme

c. Larson 1988:   Agent > Theme > Goal > Oblique

d. Bresnan & Kanerva: Agent > Benefactive > Recipient/Experiencer
    1989   > Instrument > Theme/Patient > Locative

e. Grimshaw 1990:   Agent > Experiencer > Goal/Source/Location > Theme

f. Van Valin 1991:   Agent > Effecter > Experiencer > Locative > Theme > Patient

Realizing these fundamental problems, Grimshaw 1990 argues that particular thematic role types should not play a significant role in syntax. She claims instead that what is important is the relative prominence among arguments. According to her framework, an argument structure (a-structure) is an ordered list rather than a set. Arguments bear a specific thematic role, based on which they are ordered according to the thematic hierarchy given in (27-e) above. A similar view is taken in recent works on a-structure in LFG (Bresnan and Kanerva 1989; Alsina 1990). There are two differences to note, however. First, "ordered list" is not an accurate term for describing Grimshaw's (1990) organization of a-structure. It is not a matter of occurring either to the right or to the left. A-structure as conceived of by her is a "structured representation" with its own internal structure, analogous to the "embedding" of arguments. So the argument with a lower thematic role is actually located "lower" in the a-structure, represented with brackets as in (28):

(28) (Agent (Experiencer (Goal/Source/Location (Theme))))

Second, Grimshaw 1990 takes this ordered a-structure approach one step further and proposes that establishing the order is the sole function of the names of thematic roles. Once the order is fixed, the particular names lose their function. Hence the role names are not accessible in syntax; all that is accessible is the information about the relative order of the arguments reflecting thematic prominence.[25]

One of the problems with her Relative Order Approach is that relative order is sometimes not enough to make a necessary distinction. Namely, when a verb has only one argument, by definition, no relative prominence would result. This is not a welcome effect, however, because then no distinction can be made between unergative verbs and unaccusative verbs. The solution that she takes is rather *ad hoc*. The theme argument is put inside two sets of brackets, whereas the agent has only one set of brackets:[26]

(29) a.   *unergative*   b.   *unaccusative*
          (x)   ((x))
          Agent   Theme

Though this representation makes the distinction, it certainly reduces the appeal of Grimshaw's (1990) Relative Order approach, as it ends up recognizing an "absolute" difference in prominence between Agent and Theme.

2.2.3 Proto-Role Approach

Dowty 1991 rejects the system of discrete roles and proposes a theory in which the only roles are two cluster-concepts called Proto-Agent and Proto-Patient. A thematic role is defined as a set of entailments of a group of predicates with respect to one of the arguments of each. Some examples of the entailments that characterize the two Proto roles are listed in (30)--(31):

(30) Agent Proto-Role
   a. volitional involvement in the event or state
   b. sentience (and/or perception)
   c. causing an event or change of state in another participant
   d. movement (relative to the position of another participant)
   (e. exists independently of the event named by the verb.)

(31) Patient Proto-Role
   a. undergoes change of state
   b. incremental Theme
   c. causally affected by another participant
   d. stationary relative to movement of another participant)
   (e. does not exist independently of the event, or not at all.)

This idea is similar to but distinct from the feature decomposition of thematic roles suggested by Rozwadowska 1988 or Zaenen 1988. Dowty 1991 believes that the boundaries of these kinds of entailments may never be entirely clearcut. In this point, Dowty's Proto-Roles are distinct from the Macro-Roles of Foley and Van Valin 1984 and Van Valin 1991, too, where the two roles Actor and Undergoer are discrete categories.

Another point to note is that Proto-roles are higher-order generalizations about lexical meanings, and not statements about individual lexical meanings. Combinations of certain P-entailments correspond to the role types which have traditionally been recognized. For instance, Agent is volition + causation + sentience + movement, or in some cases, a combination of only some of these. Experiencer is sentience without volition or causation. Instrument is causation + movement without volition or sentience. Patient is causally-affected + change + Incremental Theme, while Theme can perhaps dispense with causally-affectedness.

Dowty 1991 suggests an argument selection principle. It says that the argument with the greatest number of Proto-Agent properties will be selected as the subject; the argument with the greatest number of Proto-Patient entailments will be selected as the direct object. As a corollary of this principle, if two arguments have approximately equal number of those entailments, then either or both may be lexicalized as the subject.

The idea of Proto-Roles gives an interesting explanation to the subject selection of psych predicates. As mentioned above, such doublets as *fear/frighten* can have either of the arguments as the subject. This suggests, given the above-mentioned corollary, that the two arguments are on a par in terms of the Proto-Role entailments. Thus compare a psych predicate pair such as follows:

(32) a. *x* fears *y*.
b. *y* frightens *x*.

(32-a) has an Experiencer subject, while (32-b) has a Stimulus or Theme subject. The Experiencer subject is sentient/perceiving, one of the entailments for a Proto-Agent. The Stimulus subject is not sentient, but causes some emotional reaction in the Experiencer, thus satisfying another one of the entailments (=causer) for a Proto-Agent. As the Experiencer is neither volitional nor causative, it is no more Proto-Agent-like than the Stimulus in this case.[27] As Croft 1986 observes, the Experiencer subject verbs of this class are always stative, while the Stimulus-subject verbs can be either stative or inchoative (causative). When the subject is the Stimulus and the verb is inchoative, the Experiencer is causally-affected (by the stimulus); i.e., the Experiencer has a Proto-Patient-like property.

Thus there seem to be various advantages to the Proto-Role Approach. In the following discussion we will assume the Proto-Role Approach. In representations, semantic roles will be given individually (e.g., *hitter* and *hittee* for a predicate *hit*). When generalization is necessary, Proto-Role types will be used. Traditional role names such as Agent, Experiencer, etc. are also used for the sake of familiarity when no confusion is likely to occur. These traditional roles are to be interpreted as representing a certain combination of Proto-Role entailments in the way suggested above. The labels are used simply to refer to the particular combination; no more importance is attached to the names of those role types. Other role types such as Influence, Committor, etc. are used for particular purposes, i.e., describing a control relation, when necessary. They should be interpreted in a similar way: these labels refer to a set of entailments of a group of predicates with respect to one of the arguments which share a certain significant semantic properties. It has to be kept in mind that we follow Dowty 1991 in taking the Proto-Agent/Proto-Patient distinction as a matter of degree. So, for instance, the distinction between Agent and Experiencer may be substantial, but is still a matter of degree. The consequence of this stance is that ambiguous cases between the two role labels are not eliminated.

2.3 Basic Sentence Structures and Configurationality of Japanese

In this section we will give a brief description of the major characteristics of Japanese constituent structures. The discussion will be focused on the structure of a sentence, case marking, and reflexive binding. All of these issues are extremely controversial not only in Japanese linguistics but also cross-linguistically, however, and a thorough investigation would be far beyond the scope of this section. The purpose of this section is, therefore, much more modest: we attempt to establish some crucial assumptions, or working hypotheses, to serve as a basis for the following chapters.

The basic word order of a Japanese sentence is almost uncontroversially SOV. The order of the subject and the object is not very rigid. The position of the verb, however, is strictly sentence final. The position of adjuncts is quite free so long as they occur preverbally. So all the sentences in (34) and in (34) are grammatical and mean the same, though (33-a) and (34-a) sound somehow unmarked. One might object to saying that they have the same meaning, but they are at least truth-functionally equivalent in that one cannot assert (33-a) and deny (33-b), for example:[28]

(33) a. Kyoko -ga   Syota -wo   home-ta.
              nom   acc   praise-PST
     b. Syota -wo   Kyoko -ga   home-ta.
              acc   nom   praise-PST
     'Kyoko praised Syota.'

(34) a. Kyoko -ga   kinoo   Syota -wo   home-ta.
              nom   yesterday   acc   praise-PST
     b. Kinoo Kyoko -ga   Syota -wo   home-ta.
     c. Kyoko -ga   Syota -wo   kinoo home-ta.
     d. Syota -wo   Kyoko -ga   kinoo home-ta.
     e. Syota -wo   kinoo Kyoko -ga   home-ta.

f. Kinoo   Syota -wo   Kyoko   -ga   home-ta.
'Kyoko praised Syota yesterday.'

As illustrated in the previous section, HPSG does not postulate individual phrase structure rules as do other phrase structure grammars such as GPSG. The role played by phrase structure rules in other frameworks is factored out in HPSG into the lexical information of subcategorization and the highly schematic templates called schemata in Immediate Dominance Principle. In this book we assume that Japanese can be described with the Schemata 1 and 2, repeated below:

(Schema 1) a saturated ([SUBCAT < >]) phrase with DTRS value of sort *head-comp-struc* in which the HEAD-DTR value is a phrasal sign and the COMP-DTRS value is a list of length one;

(Schema 2) an almost saturated (SUBCAT list of length one) phrase with DTRS value of sort *head-comp-struc* in which the HEAD-DTR value is a lexical sign.

Assuming Schemata 1 and 2 entails that we are adopting a configurational (= non-flat structure) approach to Japanese, counter to Pollard and Sag's (1994) suggestion that (relatively) free word order languages including Japanese and Korean might embody a schema 3 for a flat structure given below:

(Schema 3) a saturated ([SUBCAT < >]) phrase with DTRS value of sort *head-comp-struc* in which the HEAD-DTR value is a lexical sign.

Our stance on this point is in fact very tentative.

The "configurationality" of the Japanese language has been a controversial issue for at least the last twenty years.[29] The strongest argument for a flat structure (without VP node) comes from the (relatively) free order among the arguments and the apparent lack of evidence for the constituency of VP. Whitman 1986 and Speas 1990 carefully examine five major types of evidence that suggest the lack of the VP node, and conclude that none of them is compelling enough for one to abandon a non-flat structure, which they assume is unmarked crosslinguistically.

Support for the non-flat structure in HSPG is hard to come by. Most of the evidence in the literature comes from subject/object asymmetries analyzed in GB theory. They include such phenomena as binding, control, quantifier floating, etc. The difficulty is that the phenomena which are configurationally analyzed in GB usually find non-configurational (lexical, etc.) accounts in HPSG.[30] Consequently the argument for a non-flat structure does not have much force in it when translated into HPSG.

We still assume a non-flat structure for Japanese because (1) there is no strong motivation for a flat structure, as proved by Whitman 1986 and Speas 1990; (2) on the other hand, it is not clear if the arguments for a non-flat structure given by Hoji 1985, Saito 1985, and others can all really find a plausible account based on a flat structure; and (3) it is essential for us to assume a VP (i.e. a verbal category with an unsaturated SUBCAT list) in Japanese, as our analysis of *ni*-causatives in chapter 5 posits a VP-embedding structure.[31] So, even if Schema 3 were assumed, Schema 2 would still be necessary to accommodate the cases of VP-embedding.

Now, as mentioned above, Japanese usually allows the scrambling of arguments. Thus even though SOV is considered the unmarked word order of Japanese, O can precede S. Long distance scrambling, namely, scrambling of an argument out of a clause is also usually allowed.[32] However, scrambling seems sensitive to constituency. Thus an element cannot be freely scrambled out of an NP or PP. Compare the following cases of non-local scrambling:

(35) a. Kyoko -ga [[ie -ni i-ta] Syota] -wo home-ta.
            nom house at stay-PST acc praise-PST
   b. [Ie -ni i-ta] Syota] -wo Kyoko -ga home-ta.
*c. Ie -ni Kyoko -ga i-ta Syota -wo home-ta.
   'Kyoko praised Syota who was at home.'

(36) a. Kyoko -wa [Syota -ga sono hon -wo nakusi-ta] -to
            top nom that book acc lose-PST-COMP
   it-ta.
   say-PST
   b. Sono hon -wo Kyoko -wa [Syota -ga nakusi-ta] -to it-ta.
   'Kyoko said that Syota lost that book.'

Theoretical Framework

Though the order among nonhead arguments and adjuncts is relatively free, the order between head and nonhead elements is extremely rigid. Japanese is a strictly head-final language. This property is manifest in every level of structure and in every category of constituent: PP, AP, NP, and VP. In this sense, Japanese quite clearly conforms to the characteristics of SOV languages or head-final languages as suggested by Greenberg 1963. A postposition is preceded by a noun phrase in a PP; an adverb precedes an adjectival head in an AP; any noun modifiers including PP, AP, VP, or relative clauses precede a nominal head in an NP; all the arguments and adjuncts precede a verbal head in a VP.[33]

This head-final property is captured by the following L(inear) P(recedence) Rule (cf. Fukushima 1990):

(37) LP 1
    [ ] < HEAD

Given the Schemata 1 and 2 and the LP-Rule (37), a sentence like (38) will be analyzed as having the structure in (39). A tree structure is used for the sake of familiarity:

(38) Syota   -ga   Kyoko   -ni   hana   -wo   age-ta.
                 nom   dat   flower   acc   give-PST
     'Syota gave flowers to Kyoko.'

(39)

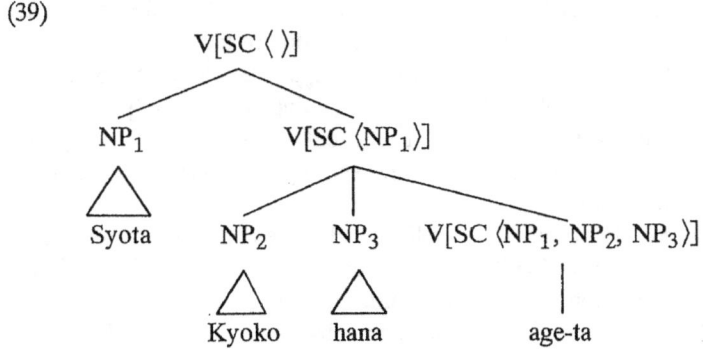

The top local tree instantiates Schema 1, and the second local tree Schema 2. The SUBCAT feature is lexically specified on the head verb *age* ('give'), and is matched with the complements by the Subcategorization Principle until it is saturated at the top node.

2.4 Case Marking in Japanese

Case has played an essential role in many analyses of passives, particularly in GB. The passive NP movement is often motivated by the lack of Case on the underlying object (Jaeggli 1986; Roberts, 1987; Miyagawa 1989a; Terada 1990; among others.)[34] In Japanese causatives, the case marking property has often been central in distinguishing between the two types of causatives: *ni*-causatives and *wo*-causatives (Kuno 1973; Terada 1990; among others.) Our approach to case marking is significantly different from the Case Theory in GB; no passivization is motivated by case, for instance. Our approach has much in common with Farmer 1980, 1984 in specifying case as a part of lexical information. As case marking is such a recurrent issue in Japanese linguistics and it is particularly so with passives and causatives, we find it necessary to lay out our approach to case marking in Japanese.

2.4.1 Case Marking Schemata in Japanese

Case is considered in HPSG as a part of the information given in the subcategorization of a predicate. Case is a head feature specified for an NP. Given the SUBCAT Principle, when a predicate is subcategorized for an NP with the case value, accusative, the feature has to be realized on one of its arguments, i.e., one of the complements has to receive an accusative case. That is, as explained above, the SUBCAT Principle guarantees that the SYNSEM value of the complements is structure-shared with the SUBCAT elements, and a head feature is part of a SYNSEM feature. This structure sharing provides the mechanism of case assignment.

Case specification, on the other hand, is lexically determined. It is encoded in the SUBCAT list of a predicate in the lexicon. If the encoding were done word by word, however, it would lead to a tremendous amount of redundancy, for obviously case specification is by no means arbitrary. In this section we will propose the basic case marking schemata in Japanese which serve to sanction the case marking on the arguments in SUBCAT lists.

In Japanese, the more oblique argument in a SUBCAT list of length two is usually specified to receive accusative case.35 There cannot be more than one accusative case NP per clause; the indirect object receives dative case, whether it functions as a Goal or Source argument. See the following pattern:

(40) a. Kyoko -ga   Syota -wo   home-ta.
           nom   acc   praise-PST
    'Kyoko praised Syota.'

   b. Kyoko -ga   Syota -ni   hon   -wo   age-ta.
            nom   dat   book   acc   give-PST
   *c. Kyoko -ga   Syota -wo   hon   -wo   age-ta.
            nom   acc   book   acc   give-PST
    'Kyoko gave a book to Syota.'

The distribution of nominative case in Japanese is in some sense similar to that of English. First of all, any finite clause has to have one nominative case NP.36 Second, the subject of a non-finite clause fails to receive nominative case:37

(41) a. Kyoko -ga Syota -wo   home-ta.
              nom   acc   praise-PST
   *b. Kyoko -ni Syota -wo   home-ta.
    'Kyoko praised Syota.'

(42) *a. Kyoko -ga   Syota -ga   soko-e   iku-yoo   susume-ta.
              nom   nom   there   go-MOD   recommend-PST
     b. Kyoko -ga   Syota -ni   soko-e   iku-yoo   susume-ta.
    'Kyoko recommended that Syota go there.'

Given this, we might assume that nominative case is assigned by Infl as is standard in GB, or following Pollard and Sag 1994 which suggests that the nominative case is related to the Vform feature V[fin].38 The prediction is that there should not be any nominative case in non-finite clauses. This prediction, however, fails with a desiderative construction such as follows:

(43) Kyoko -wa [Syota -ni uta ga/wo utatte] hosii.
　　　　top　　　　dat　song nom/acc sing-GER want
'Kyoko wants Syota to sing a song.'

Here, the direct object of the embedded gerundive (=non-finite) clause optionally gets nominative case. Whatever structural analysis is taken, the nominative case in question does not seem to depend on the finiteness of the predicate.

The distribution of the dative case is rather difficult to define. The thematic roles it covers, for instance, range from Agent, Experiencer, Goal (Benefactive), Source, Locative, and even to some kinds of Theme:

(44) a. *Syota* -*ni* piano -ga hik-e-ru.
　　　　　　　　dat　　　　nom play-POT-PRS
　　'Syota can play the piano.'

b. *Syota* -*ni* Eigo -ga wakar-u.
　　　　　　dat　English nom understand-PRS
'Syota understands English.'

c. Kyoko -ga *Syota* -*ni* hon -wo age-ta.
　　　　nom　　　　　dat book acc give-PST
'Kyoko gave a book to Syota.'

d. Kyoko -ga *Syota* -*ni* hon wo morat-ta
　　　　nom　　　　　dat book acc get-PST
'Kyoko got a book from Syota.'

e. Kyoko -ga *Syota* -*ni* tatak-are-ta.
　　　　nom　　　　　dat hit-PAS-PST
'Kyoko was hit by Syota.'

f. Kyoko -ga *Syota* -*ni* hon -wo yom-ase-ta.
　　　　nom　　　　　dat book acc read-CAS-PST
'Kyoko made Syota read a book.'

g. Kyoko ga *Syota* -*ni* hon -wo yomu-yoo
　　　　nom　　　　　dat book acc read-MOD

susume-ta.
recommend-PST
'Kyoko advised Syota to read a book.'

h. Kyoko -ga *Tokyo* -ni it-ta.
   nom   dat   go-PST
   'Kyoko went to Tokyo.'

i. Kyoko -ga *Syota* -ni at-ta.
   nom   dat   meet-PST
   'Kyoko met Syota.'

We argue that dative case is a default case in Japanese. It marks an NP which is subcategorized for by a predicate when it fails to be marked by either the nominative or the accusative case. We propose that a predicate is lexically specified whether it has accusative case to mark or not; a finite clause has to have at least one nominative case. As a negative requirement, the subject of a non-finite clause cannot be marked with nominative case. Default case cannot be assigned when there is a non-default case available.

The following shows the case marking schemata we propose:

(45) a. V[Vcase: +AC]:   <NP_1, NP_2[acc], ... >
     b. V[Vform: FIN]:   <NP_1[nom], ... >
     c. Default: Mark a non-case-marked argument with [dat]

The [Vcase] feature is specified for a transitive or ditransitive predicate, and the value [+AC] means that the predicate has accusative case to assign. It is important that the schemata in (45) apply in the given order. Thus, an accusative case marking precedes a nominative case marking. The nominative case marking scheme in (45-b) applies regardless of the [Vcase] attribute, but the predicate must be in the finite form. Any argument in the SUBCAT list that fails to get either accusative or nominative case will be given dative case by default.

Let us turn back to the examples of dative case in (44). The examples (44-a) and (44-b) are instances of non-canonical case marking. The dative case arguments in (44-c) and (44-d) are the indirect objects. In our account of case marking, the direct object gets accusative case, and the subject nominative case. It follows naturally that the indirect object is left with the default case, dative. The dative case on the passive agent in (44-e) will be discussed in the next chapter (section 3.7). To account for the dative case marking with control verbs (44-f) and (44-g),[39] and with the class of verbs of the type exemplified by (44-i), we stipulate that these verbs do not have a [Vcase] feature. Then only the schemata (45-b) and (45-c) provide the case specification to the arguments, i.e., nominative and dative, as desired. The case marker *ni* on a locative phrase in (44-h) may be considered a default case as well.[40]

Though our approach is still quite programmatic, we maintain it as a working hypothesis. The discussion of case marking in passives will provide support for this approach.

2.5 Reflexive Binding in Japanese

The last section of this chapter deals with reflexive binding in Japanese. We need to establish at least a rough definition of this property because reflexive binding forms a major part of the evidence that has traditionally been drawn upon in the discussion of passives and causatives, and because we do not assume the commonly accepted definition of reflexive binding in Japanese. A received view is that an anaphor is bound only by a grammatical subject in Japanese, and this property is very often used as a test of subjecthood. We claim instead that reflexive binding in Japanese is sensitive to thematic prominence. This view will prove essential in our discussion of causatives in chapter 5.

There have been three major types of approaches to reflexives. The configurational approach can be represented by the binding theory of GB (Chomsky 1981, 1986). Thematic approaches crucially refer to the thematic hierarchy (Jackendoff 1972; Wilkins 1988). The obliqueness approach is defended by Pollard and Sag (1987, 1992). In this section we compare the obliqueness approach and the thematic approach, and show that the latter is more appropriate in accounting for reflexive binding in Japanese.

2.5.1 Obliqueness Binding

Pollard and Sag 1992 argues extensively that the binding of anaphors should be treated not in terms of such configurational notions as c-command but in terms of the obliqueness hierarchy.[41]

Theoretical Framework

The intuitive idea defended by them is that an anaphor must be coindexed with a less oblique coargument, if there is one. More formally, it is stated based on the definition of the concept *o*-binding (Pollard and Sag 1992, 287):

(46) Definitions of Local O-Command and Local O-Binding

A *locally o-commands* B just in case the content of A is a referential parameter and either

   a. A precedes B on a SUBCAT list, or
   b. A locally o-commands some C that subcategorizes for B.

A *locally o-binds* B just in case A and B are coindexed and A locally o-commands B. If B is not locally o-bound, then it is said to be *locally o-free*.

(47) Principle A

A locally o-commanded anaphor must be locally o-bound.

One of the major consequences of these formulations of binding theory is that many of the instances of reflexives analysed in the literature turn out to be exempt from grammatical constraints on binding.[42] Namely, given (46) and (47) above, if an anaphor does not have a less oblique coargument, it does not have to be locally bound. Such "exempt anaphors" include the least oblique arguments (i.e., subjects) as well as the constitutents of an NP (i.e., the specifier of an NP) and the class of picture noun anaphors such as the *picture of himself*. In short, only non-subject co-argument anaphors are constrained by Principle A. So the reflexives in (48) are subject to the Principle A above, whereas those in (49) are all exempt from it. (Examples and their judgments are taken from Pollard and Sag 1992):[43]

(48) a. John$_i$ hates himself$_i$.
   *b. John$_i$ hates himself$_j$.
   *c. John$_i$'s mother hates himself$_i$.
   d. Mary$_i$ explained Doris$_j$ to herself$_{i/j}$.
   e. Dana$_i$ talked to Gene$_j$ about himself$_{i/j}$.

(49) a. A fear of himself$_i$ is John$_i$'s greatest problem.
  b. The picture of himself$_i$ in the museum bothered John$_i$.
  c. [Kim and Sandy]$_i$ knew that the journal had rejected each other$_i$'s papers.
  d. Mary$_i$ was well aware that, although everyone knew that the building had been designed by John and herself$_i$, only he would
  receive the professional recognition that would ensure his future in the field of achitecture.
  e. Jessie$_i$ knew full well that the local people would all feel that people like himself$_i$ were not to be trusted, let alone hired.
  *f. Himself$_i$ hates John$_i$.

Thus it is essential in their theory to distinguish between the exempt anaphors and the non-exempt anaphors. Exempt anaphors are not, however, completely unconstrained with respect to the choice of antecedent. They are constrained by extra-syntactic considerations. Pollard and Sag 1992 suggests two constraints on exempt anaphors: one to do with processing (intervention), and the other to do with discourse structure (point of view).

The importance of the latter has long been recognized and defended in such works as Kuno 1973, 1976a, 1983, 1987, Kuno and Kaburaki 1977, Sells 1987, Iida and Sells 1988, under such rubics as "empathy," or "logophoricity," as well. Simply put, a reflexive tends to take as its antecedent an NP whose referent is the individual from whose point of view the text is represented. According to Kuno 1976a, the subject tends to be the locus of such a point of view more than other arguments. When there is a topic NP, it supersedes the subject in setting the point of view.

2.5.2 *Zibun* Binding in Japanese

The Japanese reflexive *zibun* has been characterized as a subject-oriented, long-distance anaphor (McCawley 1976; Inoue 1976a; Katada 1991; Kuno 1973; Saito 1985; and others). The antecedent has to be a subject of some clause, and the domain of reflexivization does not have to be local. So when a sentence has an embedded clause, the antecedent of a reflexive is ambiguous. The antecedent, however, cannot appear in a clause lower than the clause where the anaphor appears. See the following examples:[44]

(50) a. Syota$_i$ -ga zibun$_{i/*j}$ -wo nagut-ta.
          nom   self   acc   hit-PST
     'Syota hit himself.'

*b. Zibun$_i$ -ga Syota$_i$ -wo nagut-ta.
    self   nom   acc   hit-PST
    'Syota hit himself.'

(51) a. Syota$_i$ -ga Kyoko$_j$ -wo zibun$_{i/*j}$ -no heya -de nagut-ta.
          nom   acc   self   gen room loc hit-PST
     'Syota hit Kyoko in his own room.'

   b. Syota$_i$ -ga Kyoko$_j$ -ni zibun$_{i/*j}$ -no hon -wo
           nom   dat   self   gen book acc
     watasi-ta.
     hand-PST
     'Syota gave his own book to Kyoko.'

(52) a. Syota$_i$ -wa Kyoko$_j$ -ga zibun$_{i/j}$ -no heya -ni
          top   nom self   gen room loc
     i-ta   -to   it-ta.
     be-PST COMP   say-PST
     'Syota said that Kyoko was in his/her own room.'

   b. Syota$_i$ -wa zibun$_{i/*j}$ -ga Kyoko$_j$ -no heya -ni
           top   self   nom   gen room loc
     i-ta   -to   it-ta.
     be-PST COMP   say-PST
     'Syota said that he was in Kyoko's room.'

*c. Zibun$_{i/j}$ -wa Syota$_i$ -ga Kyoko$_j$ -no heya -ni
    self   top   nom   gen room loc
    i-ta   to   it-ta.
    be-PST COMP   say-PST
    '(lit.) Self said that Syota was in Kyoko's room.'

Though either of the subjects can serve as the antecedent as shown in (52), if there are two or more reflexives in a simple clause, they have to be coreferential. In the following example, due to the function of the benefactive predicate *kure*, the direct object has to be coreferential with the matrix subject *Syota*; then accordingly, the other reflexive also has to be coreferential with it. If no such restriction is imposed, both of the reflexives can be coreferential with either *Syota* or *Kyoko*, but have to be consistent:[45]

(53) Syota$_i$ -wa Kyoko$_j$ -ga   zibun$_{i/*j}$ -wo   zibun$_{i/*j}$ -ni
            top   nom   self   acc   self   dat
     taisuru   hihan   kara   mamotte-kure-ta to   itta.
     against criticism from   defend-BEN-PST COMP say-PST
     'Syota said that Kyoko defended him from a criticism against him.'

2.5.3 Obliqueness Binding for Japanese Reflexives

Now, given the non-locality and subject orientation of *zibun*, Principle A presented above evidently cannot apply as it is to Japanese. Non-locality entails that the antecedent and the anaphor do not have to be co-arguments. The Principle A of Pollard and Sag 1992, however, would render all cases of long-distance anaphors exempt from the binding theory, since they are not locally o-commanded. Subject orientation means that relative position on the obliqueness hierarchy does not suffice. The antecedent not only has to be less oblique than the anaphor but has to be the least oblique argument. There are at least two ways to incorporate these facts into the obliqueness approach, each of which suffers from a serious problem, however.

First, if one takes non-locality seriously, one has to conclude that co-argument-hood is not a necessary condition on grammatical reflexivization in Japanese.

Suppose, for the moment, that locality is not a necessary condition in Japanese. As the Japanese reflexive binder is not only less oblique, but is the least oblique (subject), an antecedent of an anaphor would be defined as the least oblique argument appearing in the same SUBCAT list as the anaphor, or in a SUBCAT list of a predicate in a higher clause. This is actually a recapitulation of the received view of reflexive binding in Japanese. In the absence of the requirement of co-argument-hood, according to Pollard and Sag 1992, the class of exempt anaphors would include only a reflexive subject of a main clause. That is, different from English, no anaphors inside an NP will be exempt in Japanese.

This approach seems to lead to an incorrect prediction. There is a set of apparent counterexamples to the requirement of subject-orientation, as observed by McCawley 1976.[46] They are not reflexive subjects, as might be predicted, but reflexives which appear within NP. See the contrast between (54-a) and (54-b):

(54) *a. Zibun$_i$ -ga Kyoko$_i$ -wo kurusime-ta.
     self   nom   acc   suffer-PST
     '(lit.) Self troubled Kyoko.'

   b. [Zibun$_i$ -no orokasa] -ga Kyoko$_i$ -wo kurusime-ta.
     self   gen stupidity nom   acc   suffer-PST
     '(lit.) Self's stupidity troubled Kyoko.'

The subject anaphor in (54-a) is supposed to be an exempt anaphor; so its ungrammaticality must be explained by something other than the obliqueness binding theory.[47] The grammaticality of (54-b) is also quite unexpected. To allow the exemption of the anaphoric phrase in (54-b) in this context, one has to draw upon the concept of locality or co-argument-hood. However, this contradicts our initial hypothesis that locality is irrelevant in Japanese binding.[48]

The insistence on locality, on the other hand, faces another type of problem. If indeed, as Pollard and Sag 1992 assumes for English, only the antecedents and anaphors which are co-arguments are subject to a syntactic binding condition, the instances of long distance binding have to find an independent explanation. Reflexives within an NP will also be exempt anaphors, to be constrained by certain other principles, presumably based on the concept of point of view and the like. Long-distance binding may very well be constrained by a similar principle. Now, notice that the syntactic binding condition under this approach will not be a restrictive one, as local binding is only an option; long distance binding is always possible as long as a potential binder is available. Now, the problem is that, as local binding is not obligatory even when there is a local o-commander, all the reflexives are potentially exempt anaphors. In other words, the function of the obliqueness binding condition will be vacuous after all.

Fukushima 1990 follows Pollard and Sag in assuming obliqueness binding, ignoring the issue of locality,[49] in accounting for the contrast in reflexive interpretation in control structures:

(55) a. Syota$_i$ -ga Kyoko$_j$ ni [hon wo
nom dat book acc
zibun$_{i/j}$ -no heya -de yomu-yoo] tanon-da.
self gen room loc read-MOD ask-PST
'Syota asked Kyoko to read a book in his/her own room.'

b. Syota$_i$ -ga Kyoko$_j$ -ni [hon wo
nom dat book acc
zibun$_{i/j}$ -no heya -de yomu-to] yakusokusi-ta.
self gen room loc read-COMP promise-PST
'Syota promised Kyoko to read a book in his/*her own room.'

He draws on the obliqueness hierarchy in accounting for this contrast: When *zibun* is contained within a complement VP, its antecedent is either the controller of that complement VP, under the condition that the controller is less oblique than the VP,[50] or an argument less oblique than the controller. According to the control theory of Pollard and Sag (1994), the controller in (55-a) is coreferential with the dative phrase *Kyoko*, while the one in (55-b) is coreferential with the subject phrase *Syota*. So the former, an object control structure, has two possible antecedents of the reflexive in the complement VP; that is, either the dative object phrase, which is the controller, or the matrix subject, which is less oblique than the controller. In the latter, a subject control structure, on the other hand, the antecedent can only be the controller, i.e., subject, because it is the least oblique argument.

The problem of locality aside, this explanation surely works in these control structures, and the obliqueness hierarchy may seem to be a viable notion in determining a potential antecedent of a reflexive in Japanese. However, an account based on the obliqueness hierarchy does not have much force in a more general context of reflexive binding in Japanese. For, as has been observed, non-subjects in general are usually not allowed to bind reflexives in a simple clause in Japanese. Relative height in obliqueness is not a relevant notion:[51]

(56) a. Syota$_i$ -ga Kyoko$_j$ -ni hon -wo
    nom   dat   book acc
 [zibun$_{i/*j}$ -no heya] -de watasita.
  self   gen room   loc give-PST
 'Syota gave Kyoko a book in his/*her own room.'

 b. Syota$_i$ -ga Kyoko$_j$ -wo [zibun$_{i/*j}$ -no heya] -de
    nom   acc   self   gen room   loc
 sikat-ta.
 scold-PST
 'Syota scolded Kyoko in his/*her own room.'

What seems relevant is the notion "the least oblique" (= subject) rather than "less oblique."[52] Thus the obliqueness approach creates more problems than it solves. It can be maintained only by restricting the possible binder to the least oblique argument (=subject), and by removing the locality condition. But with these modications, it is not clear whether the obliqueness approach still maintains its original appeal. The next section will explore the possibility of an alternative approach based on the thematic hierarchy and the notion of "point of view" or "empathy." We will show that even if the problem could be entirely overcome, the obliqueness approach would be redundant in Japanese.

2.5.4 Thematic Binding for Japanese Reflexives

The possibility of a semantic/thematic account of binding was first suggested by Jackendoff 1972. He stated the condition as follows: A reflexive may not be higher on the thematic hierarchy than its antecedent (Jackendoff 1972, 148). This idea, which had been neglected to a degee under the influence of the configurational formulation of Binding Theory in GB, has been re-recognized recently due to the shift of attention in many linguistic theories toward thematic roles.

Wilkins 1988 re-assesses the advantages of explaining the distribution and the binding of the reflexives in terms of thematic structures. Mohanan 1990, Bresnan and Kanerva 1989, and Sells 1988 also defend thematic accounts of reflexives. It is also widely acknowledged that the antecedent of an anaphor has to be stated in thematic terms in such languages as Marathi (Joshi 1989).

A thematic explanation has been defended in Japanese linguistics as well. Such an account was first explicitly proposed by Inoue 1976a; this work was followed by Kitagawa 1981 and others. Rosen 1989 also claims that binding of *zibun* is sensitive not to grammatical subjecthood but to thematic prominence in an argument structure (see also Giorgi 1983-1984). A thematic account seems feasible in Japanese. Most of the instances of the grammatical subject as an antecedent can simply be reanalyzed in terms of the thematically most prominent argument, as the grammatical subject usually coincides with the thematically highest argument, as mentioned in section 3.2.1 above.[53] By thematically most prominent argument we mean an argument which has the largest number of Proto-Agent entailments. An agentive argument is a typical case. With an intransitive predicate, the sole argument will qualify. In the case of a multiclausal structure, we assume that the most prominent argument in any domain of argument structure is qualified as an antecedent, so long as it is in a clause higher than the anaphoric phrase. (57) gives the condition of *zibun* binding that we assume in this book.[54]

(57) *Zibun* binding (preliminary)

(i) The binder of a reflexive *zibun* must be the bearer of the most thematically prominent semantic role in a semantic CONTENT structure, where the most thematically prominent role is defined as the one carrying the greatest number of Proto-Agent role entailments (Dowty 1991; and also section 2.2.3 above).

(ii) The binder can be either in the same CONTENT structure as the reflexive or in a CONTENT structure inclusive of the one involving the reflexive phrase.

With this reanalysis in mind, let us look at some examples again. In all of these cases, the legitimate antecedents are in fact agentive:

(58) a. Syota$_i$ -ga   zibun$_{i/*j}$ -wo   nagut-ta.
            nom self   acc   hit-PST
    'Syota hit himself.'

b. Zibun$_{i/*j}$ -ga Syota$_i$ -wo nagut-ta.
   self   nom   acc hit-PST
   '(lit.) Himself hit Syota.'

(59) a. Syota$_i$ -ga Kyoko$_j$ -wo zibun$_{i/*j}$ -no heya -de
         nom   acc self   gen room loc
      nagut-ta.
      hit-PST
      'Syota hit Kyoko in his own room.'

   b. Syota$_i$ -ga Kyoko$_j$ -ni zibun$_{i/*j}$ -no hon -wo
         nom   dat self   gen book acc
      watasi-ta.
      hand-PST
      'Syota gave his own book to Kyoko.'

(60) Syota$_i$ -wa Kyoko$_j$ -ga zibun$_{i/j}$ -no heya -ni,
         top   nom self   gen room loc
      i-ta   to   it-ta.
      be-PST COMP say-PST
      'Syota said that Kyoko was in his/her own room.'

Thus the "grammatical subject (of any domain)" constraint and the "thematically most prominent (in any domain)" constraint make the same prediction as far as these examples go, and here they are on a par.

Recall the cases of reflexive binding in control structure discussed by Fukushima (1990). We argued above that his account lacks generality and that the principle of obliqueness binding does not generally hold in Japanese without significant modifications. The binding relation in question can be in fact be captured by stating that the potential antecedent is the least oblique argument in each SUBCAT domain. Then either the matrix subject or the subject argument of the controlled VP, which is coindexed (coreferential) with the controller, will be qualified as an antecedent, giving the desired effect. We would like to point out, however, that the data can also be easily accommodated by a thematic explanation. Recall the examples, repeated here for the sake of reference:

(55) a. Syota$_i$ -ga Kyoko$_j$ -ni [hon -wo
　　　　 nom　　　　 dat　 book　acc
　　zibun$_{i/j}$ -no heya -de yomu-yoo] tanon-da.
　　self　　 gen room　 loc　read-MOD ask-PST
　　'Syota asked Kyoko to read a book in his/her own room.'

　b. Syota$_i$ -ga Kyoko$_j$ -ni [hon -wo
　　　　 nom　　　　 dat　 book　acc
　　zibun$_{i/j}$ -no heya -de yomu-to] yakusokusi-ta.
　　self　　 gen room　 loc　read-COMP promise-PST
　　'Syota promised Kyoko to read a book in his/*her own room.'

(55-a) is an instance of object control structure, while (55-b) is an instance of subject control structure. According to the control theory of Sag and Pollard 1991 and Pollard and Sag 1994, only in (55-a) is the dative phrase *Kyoko* (= controllee) coreferential with the agentive participant of the lower predicate, *to read a book*. In (55-b), the agentive participant of the lower predicate is coreferential with the matrix subject *Syota*. Thus, reflexive binding by the dative phrase *Kyoko* is possible only in (55-a). The matrix subject *Syota* is the agentive participant of the higher predicate in each case, i.e., *to ask/ to promise*, hence qualified as the binder in each case. The problem of a contrast between reflexive binding in object control and subject control structures thus finds a simple solution in the thematic prominence approach without reference to the obliqueness hierarchy.

A stronger argument for a thematic prominence approach comes from reflexive binding in the context of psych predicates. It has been noted cross-linguistically that psych predicates present a set of apparent exceptions to syntactic binding principles (Jackendoff 1972; Belletti and Rizzi 1988). In Japanese as well, they are problematic in that the subject does not have to be the antecedent (McCawley 1976; Kitagawa 1981).

(61) a. [Zibun$_i$ -no orokasa] -ga Taroo$_i$ -wo kurusime-ta.
　　　 self　 gen stupidity nom　　　 acc trouble-PST
　　　 '(lit.) Self's own stupidity troubled Taroo.'

*b. [Taroo$_i$ -no orokasa] -ga zibun$_i$ -wo kurusime-ta.
      gen stupidity nom self acc trouble-PST
'Taroo's own stupidity troubled himself.'

(62) a. [Zibun$_i$ -ga oroka-da to-iu koto] -ga Taroo$_i$ -wo
       self nom stupid COMP thing nom acc
       kurusime-ta.
       trouble-PST
       '(lit.) The fact that self is stupid troubled Taroo.'

*b. [Taroo$_i$ -ga oroka-da to-iu koto] -ga zibun$_i$ -wo
    self nom stupid COMP thing nom acc
    kurusime-ta.
    trouble-PST
    'The fact that Taroo is stupid troubled himself.'

(63) a. [Zibun$_i$ -no koto] -ga Taroo$_i$ -wo kurusime-ta.
       self gen thing nom acc trouble-PST
       'Things about himself troubled Taroo.'

*b. [Taroo$_i$ -no koto] -ga zibun$_i$ -wo kurusime-ta.
    gen thing nom self acc trouble-PST
    'Things about Taroo troubled himself.'

In the a-sentences of the examples above, the reflexive is bound by the accusative phrase, which is unquestionably not a subject. As the b-sentences show, an argument inside an NP cannot serve as the antecedent whether it is an argument of a predicate (62-b) or the specifier of a head noun (61-b, 63-b).

The sentence in (61-a) is given above as (54-b) in the discussion of locality requirement. As suggested above, one might be tempted to attribute this exceptional behaviour of the reflexive to its not being a clausemate of the antecedent. In fact, if the reflexive is a co-argument of the antecedent, then the judgment reverses even if the predicate is the same; the intended binding is out in the a-sentence and is grammatical in the b-sentence.

(64) *a. Zibun$_i$ -ga   Taroo$_i$ -wo   kurusime-ta.
       self   nom   acc   trouble-PST
       '(lit.) Self troubled Taroo.'

   b. Taroo$_i$ -ga   zibun$_i$ -wo   kurusime-ta.
      'Taroo troubled himself.'

The binding pattern in (64) is just like the standard cases. The accusative reflexive phrase can be bound by the subject antecedent; the reflexive subject is ungrammatical. In other words, one might wish to argue that the exceptional behaviour of the a-sentences in (61)-(63) is due not to a property of psych predicates, but to a syntactic property of the reflexive, that it is not a co-argument of the antecedent.

This explanation does not go through, however. In (65), the reflexive cannot be bound by the accusative antecedent even though the examples have exactly the same syntactic structure as (61) and (63):

(65) *a. [Zibun$_i$ -no   imooto]   -ga   Taroo$_i$ -wo   kurusime-ta.
        self   gen   sister   nom   acc   trouble-PST
        '(lit.) Self's sister troubled Taroo.'

   b. [Taroo$_i$ -no   imooto]$_j$ -ga   zibun$_{*i/j}$ -wo   kurusime-ta.
                  gen   sister   nom   self   acc   trouble-PST
      '(lit.) Taroo's sister troubled him/herself.'

Thus, it is clear that the issue is not the co-argument-hood of the antecedent and an anaphor.

We suggest that what brings about this contrast is thematic properties of the psych predicate, and the animacy of the subject argument. It is generally agreed that a psych predicate subcategorizes for two arguments, standardly labeled as Experiencer and Theme. In the examples (61) through (63), the subject corresponds to the Theme argument and the direct object to the Experiencer argument. It is understandable that the Experiencer argument is closer to the Proto-Agent role: it is animate and sentient, though not volitional.[55] In other words, the Experiencer argument is thematically the highest, thus qualifying as the binder.

In (64) and (65), on the other hand, the subject is animate. The predicate in this structure, we claim, is not in fact a psych predicate which subcategorizes for a Experiencer argument and a Theme argument. The subject in these cases is closer to the Proto-Agent role than to the Proto-Patient role. Crucially, the animate subject is sentient and volitional; in short, close to an Agent. It is easily conceivable that it supersedes the direct object (Experiencer) in thematic hierarchy. Given this, it is a natural consequence that the a-sentences in (64) and (65) pattern with the other agentive sentences. The contrast between the b-sentences of (64) and (65) is also consistent with the present analysis; *Taroo* of (65-b) is an element within the subject NP and cannot be a binder, whereas that of (64-b) is an agentive argument of a matrix clause and thus can be a binder. The subject argument *Taroo -no imooto* 'Taroo's sister' as a whole can serve as a binder in (65-b) for the same reason as (64-b). This account is further confirmed by the fact that if the subject phrase of (65) is followed by *-no-koto* ('things about'), reflexive binding by the accusative phrase becomes possible. Compare (65) and (64) given above with (66) and (67), respectively:

(66) a. [[Zibun$_i$ -no imooto] -no koto] -ga Taroo$_i$ -wo
        self   gen sister gen thing nom   acc
    kurusime-ta.
    trouble-PST
    '(lit.) Things about self's sister troubled Taroo.'

*b. [[Taroo$_i$ -no imooto]$_j$ -no koto] -ga Zibun$_{i/j}$ -wo
    kurusime-ta
    '(lit.) Things about Taroo's sister troubled himself.'

(67) a. [[Zibun$_i$ -no koto] -ga Taroo$_i$ -wo kurusime-ta.
        self   gen thing nom   acc trouble-PST
    '(lit.) Things about self troubled Taroo.'

*b. [[Taroo$_i$ -no koto] -ga zibun$_i$ -wo kurusime-ta.
                gen thing nom self acc trouble-PST
    '(lit.) Things about Taroo troubled himself.'

This shift of grammaticality supports our claim that the "exceptional" binding phenomena are due to the semantic properties of the arguments. The head noun *koto* 'things' renders the subject argument inanimate, just as in the examples in (61)-(63). The accusative, Experiencer argument, then, naturally surpasses the subject argument in terms of thematic prominence, and qualifies as a binder.

Thus thematic prominence seems to be a very effective concept in accounting for reflexivization in Japanese. The cases of reflexive binding in psych predicates, which the concept "grammatical subject" fails to accommodate, and the shift of grammaticality depending on the semantic property of arguments are treated just as a normal case. Therefore, we conclude that the thematic prominence approach to reflexive binding is well-motivated in Japanese.[56]

The following repeats the preliminary form of the binding condition of *zibun* that we assume in the following discussion.

(57) *Zibun* binding (preliminary)

(i) The binder of a reflexive *Zibun* must be the bearer of the most thematically prominent semantic role in a semantic CONTENT structure, where the most thematically prominent role is defined as the one carrying the greatest number of Proto-Agent role entailments.

(ii) The binder can be either in the same CONTENT structure as the reflexive or in a CONTENT structure inclusive of the one involving the reflexive phrase.

The examination of reflexive binding in passives will lead to a slight modification of the condition (57). The present approach will prove particulary promising in the discussion of reflexive binding in causatives, where the "causee" argument shows both subject-like properties and object-like properties with respect to different tests. By accounting for reflexive binding in terms of thematic prominence rather than in terms of grammatical relation or obliqueness hierarchy, we will be able to analyze the causee argument consistently as an object.

In this section we have argued that a binder of *zibun* is not necessarily a syntactic subject, as has often been assumed in the literature, but is instead the thematically most prominent argument, whatever the grammatical relation it has. This assumption has a far-reaching effect in the following discussion, because reflexive binding no longer works as an identification test for the subjecthood of arguments. To be more precise, reflexive binding will not be able to test the syntactic monoclausality/biclausality of a complex predicate structure. In the discussion of causatives, we will show that this position is indeed on the right track.

Notes

1. The distinction between *level* and *stratum* is due to Ladusaw (1985).

2. The feature structures given above do not give an accurate phonological representation. It is customary in the current HPSG to use the word itself as a shorthand. The concept of PHON attribute is reminiscent of that of *signifiant* in the sense of Saussure.

3. This principle is a descendant of the Head Feature Convention in GPSG (Gazdar et al. 1985).

4. Note that one of the welcome consequences of making only the SYNSEM value be the target of structure sharing in the subcategorization operation is that the locality of subcategorization naturally falls out. It is generally assumed across theories that subcategorization is local; a head cannot specify its daughter's subcategorization frame, for instance. In Pollard and Sag 1987, the Locality Principle was explicitly introduced to that effect. However, in the present formulation, this effect is an automatic consequence, since the subcategorization does not induce a structure-sharing of DTRS attributes.

5. Note that one of the welcome consequences of making only the SYNSEM value be the target of structure sharing in the subcategorization operation is that the locality of subcategorization naturally falls out. It is generally assumed across theories that subcategorization is local; a head cannot specify its daughter's subcategorization frame, for instance. In Pollard and Sag 1987, the Locality Principle was explicitly introduced to that effect. However, in the present formulation, this effect is an automatic consequence, since the subcategorization does not induce a structure-sharing of DTRS attributes.

6. Here and throughout, all the irrelevant information is suppressed, for the sake of simplicity.

7. The Semantic Principle guarantees that the CONTENT value of the phrase is identical with its head in the absence of an adjunct (Pollard and Sag 1994; Sag and Pollard 1992). The Semantic Principle is stated as follows: In a headed phrase, the CONTENT value is token-identical to that of the adjunct daughter if the DAUGHTERS value is sort head-adj-structure, and with that of the head daughter otherwise. (Pollard and Sag 1994, chap. 1).

8. The polarity attribute is often suppressed, which can be interpreted as having the value *yes*.

9. Parameters are analogous to logical variables. They can also be considered as the HPSG analog of a reference marker in discourse representation theory (DRT) (Kamp 1984) or of a parameter introduced by an NP in situation semantics (Barwise and Perry 1983).

10. The term "configuration" here does not imply a tree type of phrase structure. What it refers to is the featural relation of the constituents.

11. The category-neutral X'-schemata were first proposed by Jackendoff 1977. Chomsky 1986 adopted the schemata to cover the projection of all lexical and functional categories in syntax. The schemata are widely accepted as standard in GB.

12. Other schemata proposed in Pollard and Sag 1994 include the one which licenses a "flat-structure" (Schema 3), and the one for "marker structure" (Schema 4). The former licenses a structure with a saturated mother immediately dominating a lexical head and other complements. When the mother is of category V (=S), this amounts to saying that there is no VP node dominating V. Pollard and Sag (1994) propose such a structure for languages with free word order, including Japanese. Configurationality has been a controversial issue in Japanese linguistics, and many arguments have been given for the configurational (= non-flat) structure. We do not follow Pollard and Sag's (1994) suggestion and assume Schema 1 and Schema 2 for Japanese as well. For more on this issue, see section 2.3 below.

The latter, the schema for marker structure, refers to structures with a complementizer, comparative words such as *than*, and a case-marking postclitic found in many languages including Japanese.

13. This rule is from Pollard and Sag 1987 with slight modification to adjust to the current model of HPSG (Pollard and Sag 1994). For instance, the SYNSEM attribute used to be separated into SYNTAX and SEMANTIC features in earlier models.

14. LFG has recently turned its attention from grammatical relations to thematic relations as the domain of operation of passivization. In the recent studies of LFG, passivization is analyzed as a "suppression" of an argument with the highest thematic role. The thematically highest argument is thus made unavailable for the subject, resulting in the apparent demotion and the promotion of arguments (Bresnan and Kanerva 1989; Alsina 1991).

15. Here, only VP complements are given as examples. The same analysis applies to (predicative) PP, AP, and NP complements.

16. The coindexing relation, which represents the control relation in HPSG, is suppressed here for the sake of simplicity. The discussion regarding this point follows later in this section.

17. HPSG takes a skeptical view about postulating a small inventory of semantic (thematic) roles. The notions *influence*, *committor*, *experiencer*, and the like always appear with a warning that they do not imply commitment to any particular thematic theories (Pollard and Sag 1987, 1994). Those notions are used simply as a convenient way of representing the semantic regularities that hold over the particular types of relations and soas in question. The issue of thematic roles will be discussed in the next section.

18. As the parameter feature *refl* indicates, the controlled element is considered an anaphor. This feature is introduced by the Principle of External Argument Reflexivity. Consequently, the binding theory also comes into play in determining the control relation. Reflexivity, however, is not crucial to the present study. Besides, as Pollard and Sag 1994 mentions, it is not clear whether the same type of reflexivity obtains in Japanese, in which the controllee may be an overt pronominal (Kuno 1976b).

19. We do not include the Individual Thematic Roles approach because (i) it does not presuppose the grouping of thematic roles, and (ii) as we argue here, it is compatible with any of the approaches to the role types. The Semantic Decomposition approach, or lexical conceptual structure approach, assumed by Jackendoff in his various works and by Van Valin 1991 among others, is not included either.

20. This hierarchy does not include Source. This role is usually ordered together with Goal.

21. Carter 1976 gives various "linking regularities" based on thematic roles.

22. There are a set of verb pairs which apparently pose problems to the principle of subject selection mentioned above, i.e., verbs of transaction: e.g., *buy/sell, give/get, send/receive*. These verb pairs describe the same situation with a different argument as the subject. In other words, either Source or Goal argument qualifies for the subject. Another example of an exception is the "psychological" predicate. The pairs *please/like, frighten/fear*, for instance, have the same truth value, with a different choice of the subject. The robust tendency for selecting

the higher argument as the subject, however, renders these exceptions almost negligible.

23. The unaccusative hypothesis was originally put forth by Perlmutter 1978. The fundamental idea is that superficially intransitive verbs can be classified into two classes: unergatives and unaccusatives. Syntactic behavior suggests that the surface subject of unergative verbs is an underlying subject, while the surface subject of unaccusative verbs is an underlying object. This idea has been developed in GB theory, particularly since Burzio 1986. It is a matter of controversy whether unergativity and unaccusativity should be defined in terms of semantics/thematic roles or whether it is purely a syntactic notion. Rosen 1984 and Dubinsky 1989, among others, take the latter view, but most of the recent studies in GB, particularly those which assume UTAH, take the former view (Burzio 1986; Baker 1988; Grimshaw 1990; Rice 1991; among others). For those who define unergativity and unaccusativity in terms of thematic roles, unergative verbs are the ones which take an Agent as their sole argument, while unaccusative verbs are the ones whose sole argument is a Theme.

24. Note that not all these linguists are proponents of the Discrete Thematic Roles approach.

25. Grimshaw's (1990) theory sets up another level of prominence relation, i.e., "aspectual prominence." We do not discuss this issue, but simply point out that this notion is incorporated into thematic theory in Proto-Role approaches.

26. It is not very clear what we find if the sole argument is Experiencer. Perhaps it has the same representation as (29-b).

27. The same point is independently discussed in Grimshaw 1990 as showing the motivation of positing the "aspectual prominence."

28. The accusative marker is spelled *wo* instead of *o* throughout this book. This practice, which follows Gunji 1987, is taken simply to avoid confusion with the honorific particle *o*. No theoretical implication is intended.

29. Arguments on this issue can be found in the following list of references, which is by no means exhaustive: for flat structure, Kuno 1973, Hinds 1973, Hale 1980, Farmer 1980, 1984; against flat structure, Hasegawa 1980, Hoji 1985, Saito 1985, Whitman 1986, Gunji 1987, Speas 1990.

30. In GB, a non-flat structure is further supported by considerations of UG. As a non-flat structure conforming to X'-theory

is so widely defended cross-linguistically that it is much more preferable, if it is possible, than a flat structure which is totally exceptional to X'-theory. But this line of argument does not have much force, either, in HPSG.

31. For arguments for the VP node in Japanese, see also Hasegawa 1980 and Gunji 1987.

32. We assume scrambling involves some kind of unbounded dependency. A different approach to scrambling is found in Gunji 1987, 1988 and other works based on his framework. Scrambling of a subject out of an embedded clause, crossing over the matrix subject is usually ungrammatical. This property has been analyzed in terms of a Feature Cooccurence Restriction by Fukushima 1989. Analyses in terms of the Empty Category Principle (ECP) will not easily work because Japanese generally does not demonstrate subject/object asymmetry with respect to the ECP. (On the ECP, see Chomsky 1981, Huang 1982, Lasnik and Saito 1984, among others.) We assume that the marginality of subject scrambling is simply a result of some restriction for parsing (for a different view, see Saito 1985, 1987).

33. Sige-Yuki Kuroda has pointed out the cases of nonfloating instances of the so-called floating quantifiers as a possible counterexample for the head-final property (p.c.). An example is *hon-ga 3-satsu* 'three book.' We do not think this is necessarily a counterexample. Even though *3-satsu* seems to modify the head noun *hon*, another analysis is possible in which the quantifier phrase is taken as adverbial. There seems to be a contrast in terms of definiteness between this type of postnominal quantifier and a quantifier in the form of an ordinary prenominal modifying phrase. Compare *3-satsu -no hon* 'three books' and *hon-ga 3-satsu* 'three books.' Suppose someone was looking for three books and he/she finally found all of them. He/she would say, "I found the three books." It seems more felicitous to use the prenominal quantifier phrase in this context. The postnominal quantifier phrase, on the other hand, seems felicitous in a context where he/she was looking for an indefinite number of books and he/she happened to find three. This issue is beyond the scope of this book, but see Fukushima 1989 for an adverb analysis of Quantifier Floating in HPSG.

34. We use Case in upper case when we refer to the abstract case (Structural or Inherent) as opposed to the morphological case only in the context of GB Theory (cf. Chomsky 1981; Marantz 1991).

35. Some transitive verbs idiosyncratically mark the object with dative case.

36. As is well known, however, Japanese is different from English in allowing more than one nominative case argument to appear in a single sentence.

37. There are many instances where the subject of an embedded clause can alternate between dative and nominative. It is a matter of debate whether the dative phrase is really the subject of the embedded clause or the object of the matrix clause. In the classical transformational analyses, these alternations are accounted for in terms of Equi NP deletion and Raising (Kuroda 1965a; Kuno 1973; Inoue 1976b; among others).

38. For analyses of case marking in Japanese within the framework of GB, see Takezawa 1987, Miyagawa 1990, and works cited there.

39. As we will argue in chapter 5, the *ni*-causative (44-f) shares the same structure as the control sentence (44-g).

40. Locative marker (dative case?) *ni* occurs with two types of locations: (1) the destination of a small set of "intransitive" verbs of directed movement such as *ik* ('go') and *kaer* ('return'); (2) the location of a small set of "intransitive" verbs of existence or stative action when the focus is placed on the location rather than on the action such as *ir* ('exist (animate)'), *ar* ('exist (inanimate)'), *nokor* ('remain'), *suwar* ('sit'), *tat* ('be built/stand'), *ne* ('lie down'). The location of a more dynamic activity is marked with *de*, though *ni* of the latter type and *de* can sometimes alternate with a slight semantic difference. What we suggest is that the locative phrase marked with *ni* is different from other "adjunctive" phrases in that it is an essential part of the semantics of the predicate. In that sense it may well be considered as a subcategorized element.

41. Detailed argument for the obliqueness approach in English is given in Pollard and Sag 1992. Here we will recapitulate the essential claim that they make and examine whether it can be extended to the Japanese cases.

42. A similar idea of exemption from binding theory is defended by Reinhart and Reuland 1991. Their analysis is an extension of the GB approach, but is not configurational.

43. The ungrammaticality of (59-f) is ascribed to the lack of a nominative case form of the reflexives. This point may be worth

elaboration, but we will leave this issue open. See Reinhart and Reuland 1991 for a different explanation.

44. In (60-a), the subject and the object can be scrambled.

45. This issue is discussed by Kuno 1987 together with related facts in terms of his *Ban on Conflicting Empathy Foci*. See also Pollard and Sag 1992.

46. As will be shown in chapter 5, causatives present another set of counterexamples to the claim of subject-orientation.

47. This problem cannot be ascribed to the lack of a nominative form of *zibun* phrase, as Pollard and Sag 1992 suggests for parallel English data. Different from English, Japanese reflexive *zibun* can appear as a nominative phrase as shown in the sentence (52-b).

48. Our account of reflexive binding based on thematic prominence does not refer to co-argument-hood or locality. The contrast in (54) is explained not in terms of co-argument-hood, but in terms of the semantic properties of arguments.

49. He does not even address the issue of locality and long-distance binding.

50. A complement VP is usually considered the most oblique among the arguments subcategorized for by a control predicate (see the SUBCAT list of (11) above). This condition becomes relevant when a control verb is passivized. Namely, the standard passive lexical rule of HPSG makes the original subject the most oblique argument (Pollard and Sag 1987). So when a subject-control verb is passivized, the controller becomes even more oblique than the VP complement, and hence cannot bind a reflexive phrase in the complement. In contrast, a controller can remain the binder after passivization with an object-control verb.

51. If the obliqueness binding of Pollard and Sag 1992 were to be more strictly followed, the reflexive phrases in (55) would all be exempt anaphors, as they occur inside an NP. It is in fact possible to construct a sentence with a reflexive phrase not inside an NP, and the grammaticality is exactly the same:

(i) a. Syota$_i$ -ga Kyoko$_j$ -ni [zibun$_{i/j}$ -wo semeru-yoo]
        nom   dat   self   acc blame-MOD

tanon-da.
ask-PST
'Syota asked Kyoko to blame him/herself.'

b. Syota$_i$ -ga Kyoko$_j$ -ni [zibun$_{i/*j}$ -wo semeru-to]
   nom   dat   self   acc blame-COMP
yakusokusi-ta.
promise-PST
'Syota promised Kyoko to blame him/*herself.'

52. Fukushima's 1990 condition on reflexive binding could be reformulated without referring to the obliqueness hierarchy. Namely, the potential antecedent is either the controller of VP or a subject argument. Then, as the controller informally corresponds to the subject argument of the VP after all, his account would achieve more generality. At the same time, however, it would fail to give enough support for the significance of the notion "less oblique" in Japanese reflexive binding.

53. The thematic prominence approach is closely related to the account of reflexive binding based on the notion point-of-view or empathy proposed by Kuno 1973, 1976a, 1983, 1987, Kuno and Kaburaki 1977, Iida and Sells 1988, Sells 1987, and many others. A commonly reached conclusion is that the antecedent of a reflexive is the NP whose referent is the individual whose point of view is represented in a given text. One supporting fact is that the antecedent is strictly animate. For another thing, a topic argument can be a binder besides a syntactic subject. A topic argument typically sets up the point of view of the text. The requirement on the consistency of referent, as observed in (53) above, is also a direct consequence of the viewpoint consistency. Thematic prominence can be understood as one facet of the point of view analysis. Simply put, the more prominent in the thematic hierarchy, the more likely to hold the point of view. In this regard, thematic prominence might be understood as a binding principle governing the cases of exempt anaphors in the sense of Pollard and Sag 1992, which further suggests that all instances of Japanese reflexive *zibun* are exempt anaphors in the sense of Pollard and Sag 1992 and are subject to more semantic/discourse oriented principle. It is plausible, but we do not pursue this possibility here, as it goes far beyond the scope of this book. We simply suggest that thematic prominence is one aspect of a more general principle constraining *zibun* binding in

Japanese. See also Iida 1992 for a detailed discussion of Japanese reflexives rich in highly plausible hypotheses and assumptions.

54. A slight modification will be added in section 3.4.3.2 below.

55. We ignore for the moment the "causative" property of the Theme argument that we discussed above in relation to subject selection of the psych predicates. Japanese is one of the languages that strongly prefer an animate subject to an inanimate one. This property may have some bearing on this issue.

56. Though there are more complex cases involving scrambling and *wh*-phrases, which we do not examine here, we believe that the thematic prominence serves to identify the potential binder in such cases as well.

III
Passive Constructions

3.1 Introduction

This chapter presents an HPSG analysis of Japanese passives. We will defend the approach in HPSG by showing that it can simultaneously accommodate both syntactic differences and semantic commonalities among different types of Japanese passive, thus resolving a long-standing problem in the studies of Japanese passives.

Passive constructions have been studied from various points of view. Crosslinguistically, it has been observed that a passive sentence usually has a corresponding active sentence with the same truth value, where the subject of a passive sentence corresponds to an object of an active sentence. The subject argument of an active sentence is expressed as an agentive (instrumental, locative, etc.) prepositional/postpositional phrase in the corresponding passive sentence in some languages, while some languages do not allow the argument in question to appear on the surface. These properties constitute a core part of the received universal characterization of passives in theory-neutral terms (Spencer 1991).

Japanese passives have provided an interesting case because (1) there seems to be more than one type of passive, though their morphological shape is identical, and (2) one type among them evidently goes counter to the universal characterization of passives mentioned above.

This situation has motivated some to postulate more than one syntactic type of passive in Japanese, but some have resisted the suggestion for two main reasons: morphological identity and semantic intuition. Morphologically speaking, there is no way to distinguish between the passive verbs of different types. Further, there is a certain kind of "passiveness" common to each type of passive, impressionistic as this statement is, which strikes any native speaker of Japanese strongly.[1]

Those holding these two main stances on this issue have been referred to as uniformists and non-uniformists (Howard and Niyekawa-Howard 1976). Uniform approaches start out with the assumption that the discrepancies between the two types are only a surface matter (Kuroda 1965a; Howard and Niyekawa-Howard 1976; Kuno 1983; Gunji 1987; Hasegawa 1988; Miyagawa 1989a; Kubo 1990; Terada 1990; among others). They attempt to capture a uniformity of passives in some level of derivation. Non-uniform approaches, on the other hand, posit distinct structures or derivations for each type of passive, regarding the morphological identity and intuitive commonality as inessential (Kuno 1973; Hasegawa 1981a).[2]

There seems to be a general trend favoring uniformist approaches;[3] most researchers attempt to achieve uniformity at some level of analysis, at least. However, researchers are still far from reaching a consensus on an analysis because, as we will see shortly, there are almost insurmountable syntactic differences among the different types of passives. So one of the fundamental questions recurring in the studies of Japanese passives has been how to achieve a uniform analysis in the face of the robust syntactic differences.

In this chapter we follow Dubinsky 1989, Terada 1990, and Kubo 1990 and assume that the Japanese passive consists of three types: direct, possessive, and indirect passives. We will further claim that the first two constitute a class of lexical passives, while the last one constitutes a class of syntactic passives. This claim entails two further claims: (1) The lexical (direct/possessive) passives are monoclausal, whereas the syntactic (indirect) passives are biclausal; and (2) The passive morpheme of the former is a derivational affix, while that of the latter is a syntactic verb. We will show that the syntactic differences among the different types of passive directly follow from the contrast pointed out in the above claims.

Uniformity in the analysis of passives, on the other hand, is achieved in the level of semantic CONTENT structure. The information-based nature of HPSG makes it possible for all types of Japanese passive to share essentially the same semantic CONTENT structure.

This chapter is organized in the following way. Section 3.2 gives a theory-neutral description of the three types of passive in terms of seven significant properties. We will survey previous studies of Japanese passives in section 3.3 to give the idea of how the problems concerning passives have been dealt with. Section 3.4 presents our analysis; direct and indirect passives will be examined first to show how the contrast between lexical passives and syntactic passives accounts for the seven distinctive properties. Possessive passives will then be analyzed. Finally case marking will be briefly discussed in section 3.7.

3.2 Three Types of Passive in Japanese

Japanese passives are composed of a verb stem followed by a bound morpheme *(r)are*.[4] It has commonly been observed that Japanese has two different types of passives with the same morphological shape: direct passives and indirect passives. Recent studies, especially since Terada 1990 and Kubo 1990, have identified a third type of passive, possessive passives, as a subtype of direct passives.[5] In what follows, we will first present the distinctive characteristics of direct passives and indirect passives which have been observed in the literature by various authors. Then a third type, possessive passives, which has recently been identified, will be examined in comparison with the other two types of passives.[6]

3.2.1 Direct Passives and Indirect Passives

Direct passives in Japanese can easily find correspondents in crosslinguistic studies of passives.[7] They typically have a corresponding active sentence. Observationally, the object of the active sentence corresponds to the subject of the passive sentence. No direct passive can be made from an intransitive verb. The truth value of the active sentence is maintained in the corresponding passive sentence. Following are examples of direct passives shown with their active counterpart:[8]

(1) a. John -ga Kyoko -wo nagut-ta.
              nom   acc   hit-PST
    'John hit Kyoko.'

   b. Kyoko -ga John -ni nagur-are-ta.
              nom   dat   hit-PAS-PST
    'Kyoko was hit by John.'

(2) a. Syota -ga Kyoko -ni hon -wo watasi-ta.
         nom   dat   book acc hand-PST
   'Syota handed the book to Kyoko.'

   b. Kyoko -ga Syota -ni hon -wo watas-are-ta.
         nom   dat   book acc hand-PAS-PST
   'Kyoko was handed the book by Syota.'

   c. Hon -ga Syota -niyotte Kyoko -ni watas-are-ta.
         nom   by   dat   hand-PAS-PST
   'The book was handed to Kyoko by Syota.'

As can be seen in (2), either the direct or the indirect object can be passivized in Japanese. The unpassivized object, i.e., the one which does not become the subject, maintains its original case, whether accusative or dative.

Indirect passives, on the other hand, go counter to most of the universal characterization of passives, and have provided a long-standing problem in characterizing the Japanese passive. First of all, they have no active counterpart. Further, the indirect passive can be based not only on transitive verbs but also on intransitive verbs. In fact, if an indirect passive sentence is compared with an active sentence sharing the same stem verb, the valency is increased by one in the passive form. That is, an indirect passive has one argument more than is subcategorized for by the stem verb. The following sentences exemplify the indirect passive:

(3) a. Syota -ga Kyoko -ni soko -e ik-are-ta
         nom   dat   there dir go-PAS-PST
   'Kyoko went there on Syota.'

   cf. Kyoko -ga soko -e it-ta
         nom   there dir go-PST
   'Kyoko went there.'

   b. Syota -ga Kyoko -ni eiga -wo mi-rare-ta.
         nom   dat   there acc see-PAS-PST
   'Syota was adversely affected by Kyoko's seeing a movie.'

cf. Kyoko -ga eiga   -wo mi-ta
          nom movie   acc see-PST
   'Kyoko saw a movie.'

The number of the arguments is not the only aspect in which the direct passives and indirect passives contrast. There are several syntactic or semantic differences recognized in the literature.

First of all, as the English glosses in the above examples suggest, indirect passives are characterized by a special obligatory connotation. That is, they are always accompanied by an implication that the matrix subject is adversely affected by the event denoted by the rest of the sentence, and for this reason this class of passive has been referred to as adversity passives since Kuno 1973.[9] It has been noticed that direct passives also tend to carry the adversity implication, but the implication is often cancellable. The examples in (4) demonstrate clear cases of neutral interpretation. Such neutral interpretation is unavailable with indirect passives:[10]

(4) a. Kyoko -ga John -ni   home-rare-ta.
            nom   dat   praise-PAS-PST
       'Kyoko was praised by John.'

    b. Sono hon   -ga   yatto   syuppans-are-ta.
       that book nom   finally publish-PAS-PST
       'The book was finally published.'

The second difference concerns a semantic requirement on the matrix subject. The matrix subject of indirect passives is restricted to animate NPs. An inanimate subject would be interpreted as metaphor, metonymy, or personification. No such restriction is imposed on direct passives. Sentence (4-b) above where the matrix subject is an inanimate entity *hon* 'book' is totally grammatical. This sentence contrasts with the following indirect passive (5-a), where the same inanimate matrix subject results in an ungrammatical sentence. Indirect passives must have an animate subject as in (5-b):[11]

(5) *a. Sono hon   -wa syuppansya -ni   betuno   hon   -wo
       that book top publisher   dat   different book acc

syuppans-are-ta.
publish-PAS-PST
'That book was adversely affected by the publisher's publishing a different book.'

b. Sono otoko -wa zyoosi -ni betuno otoko -wo
   that man top boss dat different man acc
   home-rare-ta.
   praise-PAS-PST
   'That man was adversely affected by his boss' praising a different man.'

The third difference concerns case marking on the agent phrase.[12] It is known that the agent phrase in Japanese passives is usually marked with the dative case *ni*, as illustrated by the examples given so far. The dative case, however, can alternate with an agentive postposition *niyotte*[13] or a source postposition *kara* in some cases but not in others. Terada 1990 and Kubo 1990 argue that the possiblity of alternation correlates with the distinction between the direct and indirect passives. According to them, the alternation is possible only with direct passives. The data given below seem to support their argument:[14]

(6) a. Kyoko -ga Syota -ni/-niyotte izime-rare-ta.
        nom   dat/by   bully-PAS-PST
   'Kyoko was bullied by Syota.'

   b. Sensei -ga seito -ni/-niyotte/-kara hihans-are-ta.
      teacher nom pupil dat/by/from   criticize-PAS-PST
   'The teacher was criticized by the students.'

(7) a. Syota -ga ame -ni/*-niyotte/*-kara hur-are-ta.
        nom rain   dat/by/from   fall-PAS-PST
   'It rained on Syota.'

   b. Syota -ga musuko -ni/*-niyotte/*-kara sin-are-ta.
        nom son   dat/by/from   die-PAS-PST
   'Syota's son died on him.'

   c. Syota -ga musuko -ni/*-niyotte/*-kara gakkoo -wo
        nom son   dat/by/from   school acc

yame-rare-ta.
quit-PAS-PST
'Syota's son quit school on him.'

d. Syota -ga Kyoko -ni/*?-niyotte/*-kara oogoe-de uta -wo
      nom   dat/by/from   loudly   song acc
utaw-are-ta.
sing-PAS-PST
'Kyoko sang a song loudly on Syota'

The sentences in (6) are direct passives, and those in (7) indirect passives. The agent phrases in (6) can be marked by either dative case *ni* or postposition *niyotte/kara*. Indirect passives, however, do not allow this alternation. As the sentences in (7) show, the agent phrase can only be marked with dative case *ni*.

The fourth point of difference is related to the third one. In Japanese passives, as well as in the passives of many other languages including English, the agent phrase is not an obligatory argument. The agent phrase can be omitted in some cases but, again, not in others. It has been observed that this optionality of the agent phrase correlates with the distinction between direct passives and indirect passives (Miyagawa 1989a; Kubo 1990; Terada 1990). That is, the agent phrase can be omitted only in direct passives. This observation holds true as the following data show:[15]

(8) a. Kyoko -ga izime-rare-ta.
           nom bully-PAS-PST
     'Kyoko was bullied (by someone.)'

     b. Sensei -ga hihans-are-ta.
        teacher nom criticize-PAS-PST
     'The teacher was criticized (by someone.)'

(9) *a. Syota -ga hur-are-ta.
            nom fall-PAS-PST
     'Syota had something (rain) fall on him.'

    *b. Syota -ga sin-are-ta.
            nom die-PAS-PST
     'Syota had someone die on him.'

*c. Syota   -ga   gakkoo   wo   yame-rare-ta.
           nom   school   acc   quit-PAS-PST
   'Syota had someone quit school on him.'

Thus, direct passives in (8) allow the omission of the agent phrase, while indirect passives in (9) do not.

The fifth difference pertains to reflexive binding. It has been pointed out that the agent phrase can bind an anaphor only in indirect passives (McCawley 1972; Kuno 1973). That is, in direct passives, only the matrix subject may serve as the antecedent of an anaphor, while in indirect passives, either the matrix subject or the agent phrase can be the antecedent, thus potentially causing ambiguity.[16] See the data illustrating this point:

(10) a. Syota$_i$ -ga   Kyoko$_j$ -ni   zibun$_{i/?*j}$ -no   ie   -de
             nom   dat   self   gen   house   loc
   home-rare-ta.
   praise-PAS-PST
   'Syota was praised by Kyoko in his/?*her own house.'

   b. Syota$_i$ -ga   Kyoko$_j$ -ni   zibun$_{i/?*j}$ -no   syasin   -wo
             nom   dat   self   gen   photo   acc
   mise-rare-ta.
   shown-PAS-PST
   'Syota was shown his own pictures by Kyoko.'

(11) a. Syota$_i$ -ga   Kyoko$_j$ -ni   zibun$_{i/j}$ -no   heya   -kara
             nom   dat   self   gen   room   from
   deteik-are-ta.
   go-out-PAS-PST
   'Syota had Kyoko get out of his/her own room (to his disadvantage).'

   b. Syota$_i$ -ga   Kyoko$_j$ -ni   zibun$_{i/j}$ -no   heya   -de
             nom   dat   self   gen   room   loc
   benkyoos-are-ta.
   study-PAS-PST
   'Syota had Kyoko study in his/her own room (to his disadvantage).'

The *zibun* phrase in direct passives (10) can only be bound by the matrix subject *Syota*, while the *zibun* phrase in indirect passives (11) can be bound either by the matrix subject *Syota* or the agent phrase *Kyoko*.

The sixth difference is concerned with Subject Honorification (SH). Japanese has a very rich system of honorific expressions. One type of Subject Honorification is syntactically derived by putting the infinitival verb between *(g)o* and *ni-nar*, as illustrated in (12):[17]

(12) a. Sensei -ga hon -wo yon-da.
teacher nom book acc read-PST
'The teacher read a book. (non-honorific)'

b. Sensei -ga hon -wo *o*-yomi-*ninat*-ta.
teacher nom book acc *o*-read-HON-PST
'The teacher read a book. (honorific)'

This type of SH can be considered as a form of agreement (Kim 1989), the triggering condition presumably encoded in the CONTEXT attribute (Pollard and Sag 1994). Now, when the direct passive sentences undergo SH, only the matrix subject qualifies as the trigger of SH. When the indirect passive sentences undergo SH, on the other hand, both the matrix subject and the agent phrase can trigger SH, though the latter case is not very common (Kuno 1973, 1983; Sugioka 1984; Kubo 1990). See the following examples, where the trigger of honorification is sensei 'teacher,' italicized for clarity's sake. (Morphological order within the verbs will be discussed later):

(13) a. *Sensei* -ga Kyoko -ni *o*-tasuke-rare-*ninat*-ta.
teacherr nom dat *o*-help-PAS-HON-PST
'The teacher was helped by Kyoko.'

*b. Kyoko -ga *sensei* -ni *o*-tasuke-*ninar*-are-ta.
nom teacher dat *o*-help-HON-PAS-PST
'Kyoko was helped by the teacher.'

(14) a. *Sensei* -ga Kyok -ni ho -wo *o*-kak-are-*ninat*-ta.
teacher nom dat book acc *o*-write-PAS-HON-PST
'The teacher had Kyoko write the book (to the teacher's disadvantage).'

b. Kyoko -ga *sensei* -ni hon   -wo *o*-kaki-*ninar*-are-ta.
        nom   teacher dat book acc *o*-write-HON-PAS-PST
    'Kyoko had the teacher write the book (to Kyoko's disadvantage).'

Thus, in indirect passives (14), *sensei* 'teacher' can trigger SH either as the matrix subject or as the agent phrase. In direct passives (13), it can trigger SH only when it is the matrix subject.[18]

The seventh difference pertains to Do-Support phenomena in Japanese. Japanese has a structure corresponding to English Do-Support and that it is triggered by emphatic particles such as *sae/mo/wa* ('even/also/at least.')[19]

The distribution of these particles in part overlaps that of the topic marker *wa*. They typically occur after a noun, and replace the case marker, or are incorporated into a postposition. Their distribution goes beyond that of the topic marker *wa*, however, and they can be attached to adverbs, infinitival verbs, and even adverbial clauses. When they are attached to an infinitival verb, a light verb *s(u)* is inserted, recalling Do-Support. See the following examples:

(15) a. Syota -ga   okasi   -wo   tabe-ta.
        nom   sweets acc   eat-PST
    'Syota ate the sweets.'

   b. Syota -ga   okasi   sae/mo/wa   tabe-ta.
       nom   sweets   even/also/at least   eat-PST
    'Syota ate even/also/at least the sweets.'

   c. Syota -ga   okasi   -wo   tabe-sae/mo/wa   si-ta.
       nom   sweets acc   eat-even/also/at least do-PST
    'Syota even/also/at least ate the sweets.'

As Kubo 1990 shows, they can be attached to the passive predicate, but when this happens, an interesting difference turns up between direct and indirect passives. Namely, the emphatic particles and the supportive *s(u)* ('do') can intervene between the verb stem and the passive morpheme only in indirect passives. In the case of direct passives, the emphatic particles and the supportive *s(u)* ('do') have to be attached to the unit of the stem verb and the passive morpheme as a whole. The latter pattern is available for the indirect passives as well.

See the following examples. Only the particle *sae* ('even') is shown, for the sake of simplicity:[20]

(16) a. Syota -ga   Kyoko -ni   home-rare-*sae*   *si*-ta.
              nom   dat   praise-PAS-*even* *do*-PST

   *?b. Syota -ga   Kyoko -ni   home-*sae*   *s*-are-ta.
              nom   dat   praise-*even*   *do*-PAS-PST
       'Syota was even praised by Kyoko.'

(17) a. Syota -ga   Kyoko -ni   deteik-are-*sae* *si*-ta.
              nom   dat   leave-PAS-*even* *do*-PST

     b. Syota -ga   Kyoko -ni   deteiki-*sae*   *s*-are-ta.
              nom   dat   leave-*even*   *do*-PAS-PST
       'Syota had Kyoko even leave on him.'

So in indirect passives, the emphatic unit, consisting of the emphatic particle and the supportive verb *s(u)*, can occur either before (i.e., 17-b) or after (i.e., 17-a) the passive morpheme in the indirect passive (17-b), while it can only occur after the passive morpheme in direct passives (i.e., 16-a). The table in (18) summarizes the seven properties mentioned above:

(18)

	Direct	Indirect
1. Adversity	optional	obligatory
2. Matrix Subject	±animate	+animate
3. Agent Phrase Marker	dat/postposion	dative
4. Agent Phrase	optional	obligatory
5. Reflexive Binding	matrix subject	matrix subj/agent phrase
6. Subject Honorification	matrix subject	matrix subj/agent phrase
7. Vstem-Do-Pass order	unavailable	available

Given these data, it seems unquestionable that direct passives and indirect passives have very different syntactic properties. The next section shows that possessive passives share the same properties with direct passives.

3.2.2 Possessive Passives

Dubinsky 1989, Terada 1990, and Kubo 1990 independently recognize a third class of passive, possessive passives.[21] This construction has long been considered as a subclass of the indirect passive, since the subject argument does not correspond to any argument subcategorized for by the stem verb, but is rather added to the subcategorized arguments of the stem verb. As the name of this type suggests, there is a special semantic connection between the passive subject and the direct object of the stem verb. That is, the subject typically refers to a "possesser" and the direct object to something or someone "possessed" by it. The following are examples of the possessive passive:

(19) a. Syota   -ga   Kyoko -ni ude   -wo   or-are-ta.
             nom   dat   arm   acc   break-PAS-PST
     'Syota had his arm broken by Kyoko.'

    b. Syota   -ga   Kyoko -ni nikki -wo   yom-are-ta.
             nom   dat   diary acc   read-PAS-PST
     'Syota had his diary read by Kyoko.'

In spite of surface similarity to the indirect passive, this construction turns out to parallel the direct passive in terms of the seven properties mentioned above. First of all, the adversity interpretation is optional in this type, as shown by the following examples (Kuroda 1979; Kuno 1983; Dubinsky 1989; Kubo 1990; Terada 1990):

(20) a. Syota   -ga   Kyoko -ni atama -wo   nade-rare-ta.
             nom   dat   head   acc   rub-PAS-PST
     'Syota had his head patted by Kyoko.'

b. Syota   -ga Kyoko -ni musuko -wo   home-rare-ta.
           nom   dat son   acc   read-PAS-PST
   'Syota had his own son praised by Kyoko.'

The availability of a neutral interpretation is very interesting because once the possessive interpretation is cancelled, the adversity interpretation becomes obligatory, and the sentence is interpreted as an indirect passive. Notice that the interpretat on whereby the referent of the accusative NP belongs to the referent matrix subject is not obligatory. Another interpretation is possible where the referent of the accusative NP belongs to the referent of the dative NP or to anything else. And if the referent of the accusative phrases of the examples above is interpreted as belonging to the referent not of the matrix subject but of the dative phrase, it necessarily carries a clear adversity interpretation:

(21) a. Syota   -ga Kyoko -ni atama   -wo nade-rare-ta.
     'Syota had Kyoko pat her own head (to his disadvantage.)'

   b. Syota   -ga Kyoko -ni musuko wo home-rare-ta.
     'Syota had Kyoko praise her own son (to his disadvantage.)'

In the sentences above, where the accusative NPs *atama* 'head' and *musuko* 'son' are interpreted as belonging to Kyoko, the adversity interpretation is obligatory. The same is the case if the accusative NPs are interpreted as belonging to some unspecified person other than the referent of the matrix subject.

Second, the matrix subject can be inanimate, as the following examples show (Kubo 1990):

(22) a. Sono biru   -ga doroboo -ni doa   -wo kowas-are-ta.
        that building nom thief   dat door acc break-PAS-PST
     'The building had its door broken by the robbers.'

   b. Sono ike   -wa pompu -de mizu -wo suiage-rare-ta.
      that pond   top pump   inst water acc suck-PAS-PST
     '(lit.) The pond had its water pumped up with a pump.'

Thirdly, the agent phrase of the possessive passive can be marked with a postposition *niyotte/kara* exactly like direct passives (Kuroda 1979; Kubo 1990):[22]

(23) a. Syota -ga Kyoko -ni/-niyotte nikki -wo yom-are-ta.
           nom   dat/by   diary acc read-PAS-PST
    'Syota had his diary read by Kyoko.'

b. Syota -ga Kyoko -ni/-niyotte atama -wo nade-rare-ta.
          nom   dat/by   head acc rub-PAS-PST
   'Syota had his head patted by Kyoko.'

c. Syota -ga Kyoko -ni/-niyotte/kara musuko -wo
          nom   dat/by/from   son   acc
   home-rare-ta.
   praise-PAS-PST
   'Syota had his son praised by Kyoko.'

Fourth, the agent phrase can be omitted altogether, as with direct passives (Kubo 1990):

(24) a. Syota -ga nikki -wo yom-are-ta.
           nom diary acc read-PAS-PST
    'Syota had his diary read by someone.'

b. Syota -ga atama -wo nade-rare-ta.
          nom head acc rub-PAS-PST
   'Syota had his head patted by someone.'

c. Syota -ga musuko -wo home-rare-ta.
          nom son acc praise-PAS-PST
   'Syota had his son praised by someone.'

As a fifth point, the agent phrase in possessive passives is not able to bind a reflexive. See the following examples (Kubo 1990; Terada 1990):

(25) a. Syota$_i$ -ga Kyoko$_j$ -ni atama -wo zibun$_{i/*?j}$ -no
            nom   dat head   acc self   gen

hon   -de   tatak-are-ta.
book   inst hit-PAS-PST
'Syota had Kyoko hit his head with his/*?her own book.'

b. Syota$_i$ -ga Kyoko$_j$ -ni kodomo -wo zibun$_{i/*?j}$ -no
          nom   dat child   acc self   gen
ie   -de   home-rare-ta.
house loc   praise-PAS-PST
'Syota had Kyoko praise his child in his/*?her own house.'

The sixth point, the data on SH, also confirms the claim that possessive passives parallel direct passives. That is, it is not possible for the agent phrase of the possessive passive to trigger Subject Honorification involving *o...ni-nar* (Kubo 1990):

(26) a. *Sensei*$_i$ -ga Kyoko$_j$- -ni syasin -wo *o*-tor-are-*ninat*-ta.
        teacher   nom   dat picture acc *o*-take-PAS-HON-PST
'The teacher$_i$ had Kyoko$_j$ take his$_i$ picture.'

*b. Kyoko$_i$ -ga *sensei*$_j$- -ni syasin -wo .*o*-tori-*ninar*-are-ta.
    teacher nom   dat picture acc *o*-take-HON-PAS-PST
'Kyoko$_i$ had the teacher$_j$ take her$_i$ picture.'

The final point, Do-Support phenomena, also shows the parallelism between direct passives and possessive passives. In the case of possessive passives, the emphatic particles and the supportive *s(u)* ('do') have to be attached to the unit of the stem verb and the passive morpheme as a whole (Kubo 1990). See the following examples:

(27) a. Syota -ga Kyoko -ni atama -wo nade-rare-*sae* *si*-ta.
            nom   dat head   acc pat-PAS-*even* *do*-PST

*?b. Syota -ga Kyoko -ni atama -wo nade-*sae* *s*-are-ta.
           nom   dat head   acc pat-*even* *do*-PAS-PST
'Syota had his head even patted by Kyoko.'

Thus, there is no doubt that possessive passives share essential syntactic/semantic properties with direct passives rather than with indirect passives. The table in (28) summarizes the seven properties including the cases of possessive passives:

(28)

	Direct/Poss	Indirect
1. Adversity	optional	obligatory
2. Matrix Subject	±animate	+animate
3. Agent Phrase Marker	dat/postposion	dative
4. Agent Phrase	optional	obligatory
5. Reflexive Binding	matrix subject	matrix subj/agent phrase
6. Subject Honorification	matrix subject	matrix subj/agent phrase
7. Vstem-Do-Pass order	unavailable	available

As a preliminary we interpret the seven properties in the following way. Properties 1 and 2 are semantic, and presumably have to do with the semantic role of the arguments involved. Properties 3 through 5 seem to indicate that the agent phrase is defective as a syntactic argument in some sense. Property 6 shows that the agent phrase is not a syntactic subject in direct/possessive passives, while it is in indirect passives. Property 7 seems to show that the unity of the verb stem and the passive morpheme is tighter in direct and possessive passives than in indirect passives. These interpretations will be elaborated further in the following discussion.

This concludes the preliminary discussion of crucial data in Japanese passive constructions. We have shown that Japanese passives clearly have two syntactically distinct types: the direct passive and the indirect passive. The third type, the possessive passive has many properties in common with direct passives. Whether it is really to be incorporated into the class of the direct passives is another question, which we will address later in this chapter. The next section will review some of the influential analyses of passives that have been proposed.

3.3 Previous Analyses of Passives in Japanese

The passive construction has been a focus of attention in many linguistic studies both in English and in Japanese (and also in many other languages.) In the main trend of Generative Transformational

Grammar of the 1960's and early 1970's, English passive sentences were derived from their active counterparts through a series of transformations collectively called "passivization" (cf. Chomsky 1957, 1965). On the other hand, Relational Grammar treats passives in terms of a change in grammatical functions among NPs (cf. Perlmutter 1978; Perlmutter and Postal 1983, 1984; Johnson 1977).

Beginning around 1980 a trend toward a lexical analysis of the passive rather than a syntactic one started. Early studies in Government-Binding Theory assume a lexical operation that changes the verb form from base to the passive participle, absorbing the case-assigning property of the original verb. The rest of the derivation is taken care of by NP-movement stimulated by three major principles: the θ-criterion, Case Theory, and Binding Theory (cf. Chomsky 1981).

Later works of GB (e.g., Borer 1984; Jaeggli 1986; Roberts 1987) argue that the passive morpheme *-en* is a nominal receiving the accusative case, thus making the accusative case unavailable to any other argument. This idea eliminates the lexical operation which changes the case marking property of a verb.

Baker 1988 proposes that the passive morpheme is actually an external argument bearing the subject θ-role, which can be transmitted to the agent phrase (*by*-phrase in English) via coindexing (cf. also Baker, Johnson, and Roberts 1989). This passive morpheme, however, appears in the Infl node, a position to which the verb moves. This verb movement is considered to be the essential part of the passivization; NP movement is only a peripheral side-effect. NP movement takes place when it is allowed or forced by general principles. The often-assumed Case absorption is also inessential. Case absorption depends on the property of the passive morpheme: whether it requires the accusative case or not.

The idea of Relational Grammar which maintains the change of grammatical relations as the core operation of passivization is incorporated in earlier versions of Lexical Functional Grammar (LFG) as a lexical process. In early LFG, the passive operation is effected by a lexical rule that turns the object of the active form into the subject, and assigns the original subject either to the null function or to an Oblique Agent phrase (cf. Kaplan and Bresnan 1982; Sells 1985). Among phrase structure grammars, GPSG postulates a Passive Metarule which alters the subcategorization property of a predicate. As metarules are restricted in Gazdar et al. 1985 to apply to lexical Immediate Dominance rules, the operation is strictly lexical. As presented in the previous chapter, HPSG also takes a lexical approach, positing the passive lexical rule (Pollard and Sag 1987).

With the growing interest in thematic relations and predicate argument structure, recent studies in LFG such as Bresnan and Kanerva 1989, and Grimshaw 1990 and many others propose that the passive operation is essentially a suppression of the highest thematic role in the predicate argument strucure.

The same trends are of course found in Japanese linguistics; i.e., from transformational approaches to lexical approaches and movement approaches (for transformational approaches, see Kuroda 1965a, Kuno 1973, Inoue 1976b, 1989, etc.; for lexical approaches, see Farmer 1980, 1984, Hasegawa 1981a, 1981b; for movement approaches, see Hasegawa 1988, Miyagawa 1989a, Washio 1989-1990, Terada 1990, Kubo 1990, etc.). But the Japanese passive construction is characterized by several interesting properties that find no counterpart in the English passive. In particular the existence of the indirect passive has called for different approaches from the ones proposed for the English passive. In what follows we will present some representative analyses to see how they have tried to accommodate the two (or three) distinct types of passive. Particular attention will be paid to recent analyses such as Kubo 1990 and Terada 1990.

3.3.1 Transformational Approaches

Transformational analyses attempted to derive the passive sentence from a deep structure by transformation (cf. Kuroda 1965a; Kuno 1973; Inoue 1976b, 1989).

The non-uniform approach, represented by Kuno 1973, postulates separate structures for the direct passive and the indirect passive. The direct passive is derived from a simple active sentence through scrambling:

(29)   Naoko -ga sensei -ni sikar-are-ta.
        'Naoko was scolded by the teacher.'

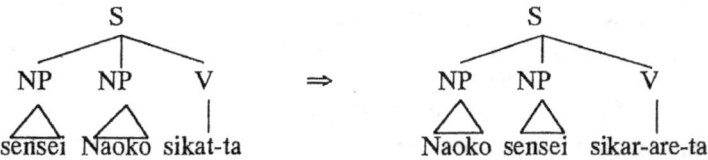

The indirect passive is, on the other hand, derived from an embedded structure through Predicate Raising and S-Pruning.

(30) Naoko -ga kodomo -ni nak-are-ta.
'Naoko was adversely affected by the child's crying.'

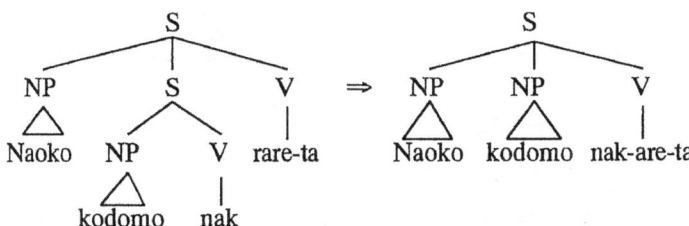

In this approach, the difference in *zibun*-binding is explained in terms of the cyclic application of reflexivization. That is, the direct passive undergoes reflexivization only once after the passivization. On the other hand, the indirect passive has a complex structure, and reflexivization applies before S-Pruning. So this structure contains two subjects, both qualified for triggering reflexivization.

The uniform approach assumes a complex (biclausal) underlying source for both the direct and indirect passives. The following shows the structure assumed by Howard and Niyekawa-Howard 1976. (31) is a direct passive, and (32) an indirect passive:

(31) Naoko -ga sensei -ni sikar-are-ta.
'Naoko was scolded by the teacher.'

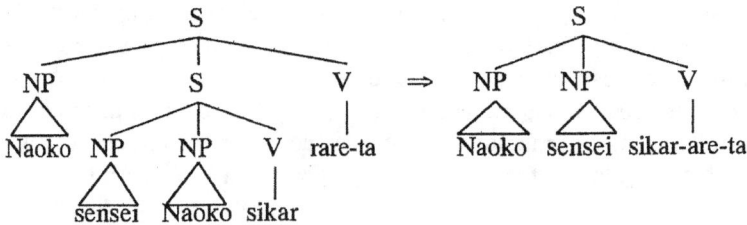

(32) Naoko -ga kodomo -ni nak-are-ta.
'Naoko was adversely affected by the child's crying.'

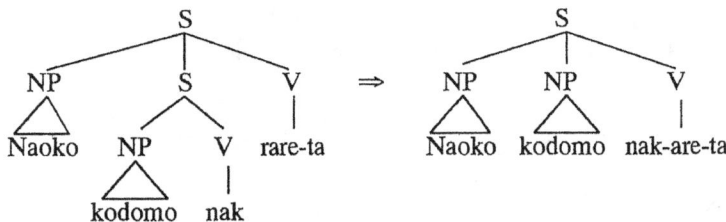

As shown in the tree diagrams above, under this approach both direct and indirect passives undergo S-pruning. Notice that the agent phrase is a subject in both direct and indirect passives in this approach. The difference in *zibun* binding has to be explained without reference to the syntactic status of the agent phrase. For instance, Howard and Niyekawa-Howard 1976 proposed a Reflexive Coreference Constraint as a device prohibiting reflexive binding by the embedded subject NP in the direct passive.[23]

In either case, transformational approaches share the strategy of deriving passive sentences by syntactic transformation. These analyses have largely been considered outdated since such construction-specific transformations are incompatible with the current model of Government Binding Theory. Besides theory-internal reasons, these transformational analyses suffer from other problems as well. For instance, they are not able to explain the case marking alternation and the optionality of the agent phrase whether in uniform approaches or in non-uniform approaches. Nor can they give any insights to the reason for the animacy requirement of the indirect passive subject. The problem of Do-Support will not find a solution, either. Non-uniform approaches are able to explain the problem of reflexive binding and SH, but uniform approaches would require another condition such as the Reflexive Coreference Constraint (cf. note 23) to accommodate SH facts. Thus, transformational approaches do not seem to fare very well in accounting for all the essential properties of Japanese passives.

3.3.2 Lexicalist Approaches

Lexicalist approaches assume that the passive morpheme *(r)are* is attached by a morphological process; that is, in the lexicon. This position, represented by Hasegawa 1981a, 1981b, and Farmer 1980, 1984, has a special appeal in Japanese because the passive morpheme is a bound morpheme in the language. Instead of a structural change, lexicalist analyses are mostly concerned with the assignment of grammatical case, thematic role, or grammatical function as a result of the morphological change.

Hasegawa 1981b proposes the following Japanese passive lexical rule for direct passives, which is basically equivalent to the English passive lexical rule of her proposal (Hasegawa 1981b, 33):[24]

(33) Change in Functional Frame   OBJ   →   ∅
                                  θ_1 →   ∅
Morphological Change V_{stem} → $[V_{stem} + rare]_{Vstem}$
Condition: OBJ must be semantically related to the V_{stem}

θ_1 is the external argument of the predicate.

This lexical redundancy rule cancels both a grammatical function OBJ and an external thematic role, accompanying the morphological change. This rule applies to the verb stem *ker* 'kick' to change the lexical entry in the following way:

(34) a. *ker*: V_{stem} : [Agent, Theme]
                                            | |
                                          SUBJ   OBJ   → (passive)

   b. *ker-are*: $[V_{stem} + rare]_{Vstem}$: [~~Agent~~, Theme]
                                            SUBJ   ~~OBJ~~

As OBJ and Agent (= θ_1) are cancelled according to the rule in (33), the Theme and SUBJ are linked together by a convention. Consequently, the passive participle has the Theme argument as the subject.

Hasegawa 1981a, 1981b treats indirect passives as derived by a very different lexical composition rule. She attempts to construct a complex predicate argument structure, which is intuitively close to an object control structure represented on a lexical level. The following is the lexical entry of *(r)are* combined with *sikar* 'scold' for an indirect passive sentence (Hasegawa 1981a, 153):[25]

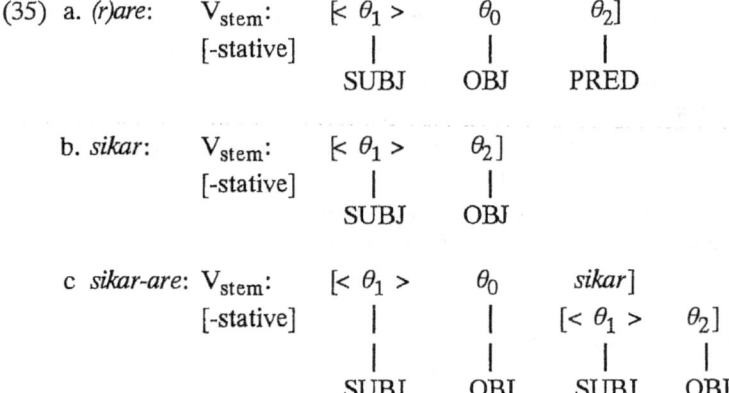

She assumes that the object argument of the passive morpheme has no thematic role; i.e., the θ_0 is void. In such cases the thematic role of the subject argument of the embedded predicate (θ_1) is percolated by convention.[26]

In sum, Hasegawa's (1981a, 1981b) approach is a non-uniform approach and does not attempt to relate the direct passive and the indirect passive. It can account for the difference in reflexive binding and SH; only indirect passive predicates are associated with two subjects. (Compare (34) and (35) above.) The problems of case marking alternation and optionality of agent phrase are easily accounted for. The agent phrase in the direct passive is cancelled; it is deprived of its argument status in some sense.

One difficulty with her approach resides in the lexical treatment of biclausality. A basic lexical rule operates on a lexical item and produces a lexical item with a different character. As mentioned in the previous chapter (section 2.1.3), a major motivation for utilizing lexical rules is that the output of the operation (e.g., passive participle) functions essentially the same as other lexical item; no special principles, or phrase structure rules are necessary in the mapping onto syntax. As the indirect passive predicates are formed by a lexical composition rule, the resultant passive predicate (*sikar-are* 'be scolded' in (35)) is supposed to function as a single lexical item, when it is mapped onto syntax. Nevertheless, its predicate argument structure is biclausal, which is totally unique, not found in other non-derivative predicates. The problem is that biclausality is fundamentally incompatible with the lexical operation. It is like constructing two phrasal projections out of one lexical head.27 Furthermore, positing a matrix object (corresponding to the lower subject) in indirect passives does not seem to be right. This point will be further discussed in section 3.3.5. Lastly, because of its non-uniformist nature, it is incapable of giving any account of the impressionistic "passive" sense common to both types of passive.28

3.3.3 Movement Approaches: Without Verb Incorporation

Miyagawa 1989a proposes a uniform movement approach based on GB-Theory. Following Borer 1984, Jaeggli 1986, and Roberts 1986, he assumes that the passive morpheme *(r)are* absorbs the Case assigning property of the verb to which it attaches, if the verb has this Case assigning feature. The attachment of the passive morpheme also suppresses the external thematic role to be assigned to the subject due to Burzio's generalization given in (36):

(36) Burzio's generalization (Burzio 1986, 178-187)

A verb assigns an external thematic role if it can assign Case.

The direct passive is generated almost exactly the same way as the English passive. Since the passive morpheme absorbs the Case assigning property of a transitive verb, the object NP must move to subject position to receive nominative case. On the other hand, however, the indirect passive does not seem to absorb Case. In order to maintain uniformity, Miyagawa stipulates that the passive predicate can optionally undo Case absorption. The indirect passive takes this option, and it regains the capacity to assign object case; hence the object can remain in its original position. Further, as the passive morpheme assigns internal case after all, it follows that it must also assign an external θ-role according to Burzio's generalization given above. To receive this external θ-role "Experiencer," a new NP is introduced in the subject position and is realized as the matrix subject NP. Concomitantly the original external role (Agent) is internalized and surfaces as a dative NP (NP-*ni*).

Thus Miyagawa's (1989a) analysis of indirect passives relies heavily on Burzio's generalization; it provides the motivation to introduce a new external argument, coupled with the stipulation that the indirect passive predicate regains the Case assigning property. However, a careful examination of his account reveals that Burzio's generalization does not really help generate the indirect passive. Burzio's generalization simply states that a transitive verb assigning an accusative case assigns an external θ-role. There is nothing that prevents the indirect passive morpheme from assigning the original external (Agentive) θ-role to the original external argument instead of introducing a new Experiencer role. That is to say, Burzio's generalization may well derive the original active sentence rather than an indirect passive.

A more serious problem with Miyagawa 1989a concerns indirect passives based on an intransitive verb. When the stem verb is an intransitive verb, it does not have Case to assign from the beginning; hence, according to Miyagawa 1989a, it is exempt from Case absorption. It follows that the stem verb does not regain the Case assigning property, either. Then Burzio's generalization has nothing to say about the derivation of indirect passives in this case. It rather seems to be a violation of Burzio's generalization, for it introduces a new external argument without getting the ability to assign Case. Miyagawa 1989a admits that Burzio's generalization does not help derive this structure. He briefly states, however, that this structure does not violate the generalization at least. For, according to Miyagawa 1989a, the external argument of the stem verb is somehow suppressed and internalized to receive dative Case. Then a new external argument must be introduced by the Extended Projection Principle which requires a subject (non-expletive in Japanese).[29] Then the indirect passives based on an intransitive verb have both an external argument and a Case (dative). A conceptual problem with this approach is that indirect passives based on intransitive verbs and those based on transitive verbs are derived in totally different ways. By trying to achieve uniformity between transitive-based direct passives and transitive-based indirect passives, Miyagawa 1989a has separated intransitive-based indirect passives from both. But the syntactic and semantic facts indicate that transitive-based passives group together with intransitive-based passives.

Furthermore, suppression and internalization of the agent phrase of intransitive-based indirect passives lacks any independent motivation. If the agent phrases of intransitive-based indirect passives were suppressed and internalized, the same analysis could hold with transitive-based indirect passives. Then transitive-based indirect passives could be derived by the Extended Projection Principle without Burzio's generalization. These problems bring into question the validity of Miyagawa's (1989a) intricate mechanism of Case absorption, which is subsequently undone to trigger the introduction of a new external argument.

Kubo 1990 presents an interesting movement analysis of passives, which very convincingly argues for the class of possessive passives. She defines direct passives as "gapped" passives, and the indirect passives as "gapless" passives. That is, the former involve NP movement from an object position, while the latter do not have the same type of NP movement.[30] The possessive passive, she argues, is a type of gapped passive, in which the subject argument in fact has been moved out of the Spec of NP position of a lower argument.

Kubo 1990 makes strong claims which go against some of the proposals made in the literature of GB; for instance, that the Japanese passive morpheme is not an argument (against Travis 1984; Jaeggli 1986; Roberts 1987), and does not absorb case (against Miyagawa 1989a; Terada 1990; but with Hasegawa 1988). Without Case absorption, Case Theory can no longer provide the motivation for NP movement. For Kubo 1990, NP movement is ultimately forced by the Extended Projection Principle (i.e., the obligatoriness of subjects), coupled with the fact that Japanese lacks expletives.

Kubo 1990 posits the following lexical entries for the two types of passive morpheme *(r)are*:[31]

(37) *(r)are*, V, $\left\{ \begin{array}{ll} +V^0 & \underline{} \\ +VP & \underline{} \ [malefactive] \end{array} \right\}$

The lexical entry in (37) conveys the following information. The passive morpheme *(r)are* is a verbal category which subcategorizes for either VP or V^0.[32] When it subcategorizes for a VP, it also has an external θ-role [malefactive] to assign. When it subcategorizes for a V^0, it has no external θ-role. The former will constitute indirect passives, and the latter direct or possessive passives.

Based on these two lexical entries, she projects syntactic structures for different types of passive. The structure in (38) represents direct passives, (39) possessive passives, and (40) indirect passives:

90   Complex Predicates in Japanese

(38)   Syota ga Kyoko ni tatak-are-ta.
        'Syota was hit by Kyoko.'

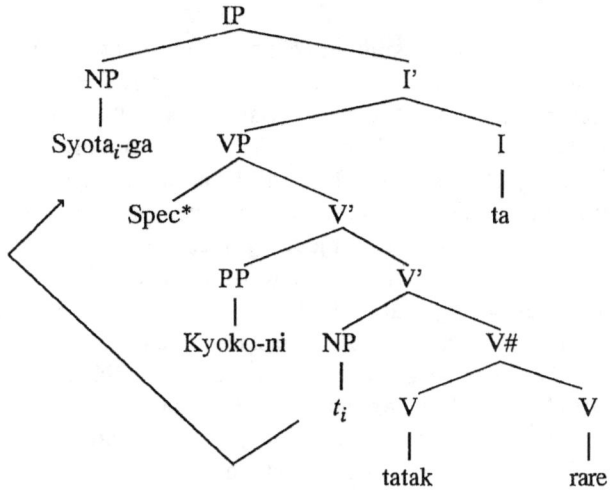

(39)   Syota-ga Kyoko-ni atama-wo tatak-are-ta.
        'Syota was hit by Kyoko on the head.'

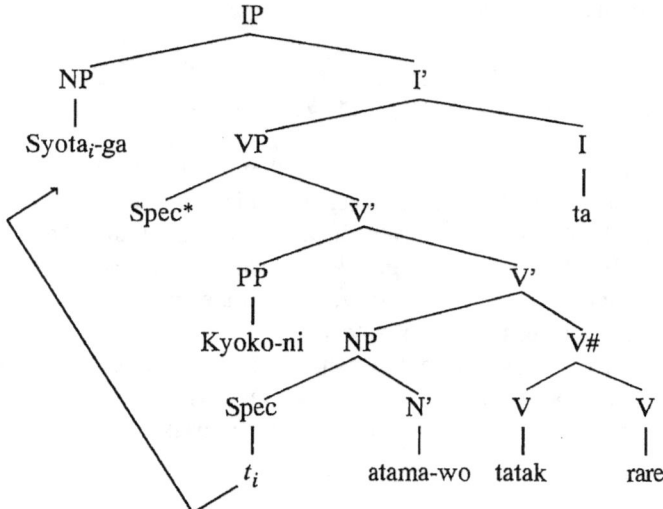

(40)   Syota-ga Kyoko-ni eiga-wo mi-rare-ta.
       'Syota was adversely affected by Kyoko's watching a movie.'

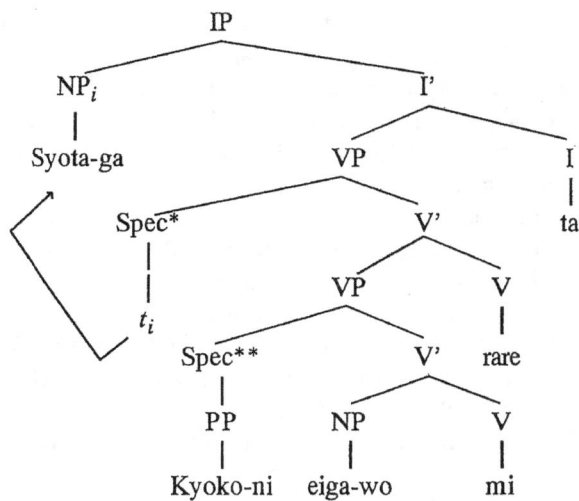

Kubo 1990 draws the syntactic differences among the three types of passive solely from the information in the lexical entry in (39) and independent general principles of grammar. Let us first take a look at gapped (direct/possessive) passives in (38) and (39). According to the lexical information, the verb stem and the passive morpheme form a verbal consituent of bar level 0, which projects a phrasal category as an amalgam; hence only one VP is involved. The head of the stem-passive constituent (marked with #) is the passive morpheme rather than the verb stem. As the head verb, i.e., the passive morpheme, does not have an external θ-role to assign, the Spec of VP positions headed by the passive verb are left empty (i.e., the position marked with * in (38) and (39)).[33] The agent phrase is an external argument not of the head (passive morpheme) but of the stem verb; hence it is not allowed to be realized at S-structure as the matrix subject.[34] Then one of the other arguments is forced to move to the subject position to satisfy the Extended Projection Principle. When it is one of the object arguments, the result is a direct passive (i.e., (38)); when it is an NP in the NP-Spec position, the result is a possessive passive (i.e., (39)).[35] Kubo

1990 stipulates that the agent phrase is realized as an adjunct as a last resort.

In the case of gapless passives (40), the stem verb and the passive morpheme each independently head verbal projections; hence there are two VPs. Further, each of the two head verbs have an external argument, so the VP-Spec positions (marked with * and **) are occupied by the matrix subject and the agent phrase. The matrix subject is then moved to the IP-Spec position to receive nominative case, and the agent subject receives dative case in the VP-Spec position. No further movement is motivated.

Kubo's (1990) approach provides an account of the distinct properties of gapped and gapless passives roughly in the following way. First of all, an adversity interpretation is available only with indirect passives, since only the passive morpheme in this structure has an external θ-role to assign. Further, the θ-role is specified as [malefactive] already in the lexicon, hence no neutral interpretation is possible. Second, as for the animacy requirement for indirect passives, she has simply to remark that only animate creatures can experience malefaction.

The case marking alternation and the optionality of the agent phrase in the direct passive are direct consequences of the fact that the phrase in question in direct passives is an adjunct. The problem of reflexive binding also falls out automatically given that the agent phrase is a subject only in the indirect passives. The difference in Do-Support finds an explanation in the assumption that the stem verb and the passive morpheme constitute a single unit V^0, which a "supportive $s(u)$" ('do') cannot break into.

Thus, Kubo's (1990) approach is very powerful in providing desirable solutions to the problems. It is also very interesting in that it is capable of deriving far-reaching syntactic consequences from the mere difference in bar level in the lexical entry. Our analyses will take some of the insights given in her approach.

There are at least two points that we disagree with in her system, besides the difference in our theoretical approaches. The first is concerned with SH. Her analysis of SH in passives draws much on the analysis of SH in general by Suzuki 1989, which is partly problematic itself. According to Kubo 1990, the subject of the indirect passive cannot be the target of SH. This, however, seems to be a wrong judgment. All the native speakers of Japanese I have consulted with (including myself) find it even better than the SH of the agent phrase of agent phrase of indirect passives. (Cf. (14-a) vs. (14-b) above). This result cannot be predicted in her system. Another point of disagreement is the postulation of a gap (and NP-movement) in possessive passives. We will argue in section 3.5 that possessive passives do not really involve NP-movement.

3.3.4 Movement Approaches: With Verb Incorporation

Terada 1990 presents analyses of passives based on the Incorporation approach of Baker 1988. As far as classification and very basic assumptions are concerned, Terada 1990 has much in common with Kubo 1990, though the actual analyses are quite different.

Terada 1990 recognizes possessive passives as an independent subtype of the class of direct passives. With Kubo 1990, she holds that direct and possessive passives contrast with indirect passives in that the former involve NP movement, while the latter do not. In particular, she argues that the subject of possessive passives has been moved out of the specifier position of the object argument of the verb stem.

She posits two kinds of passive morpheme for the two types of passives. Though both morphemes are considered to be V^0, the one associated with the the direct/possessive passive is an unaccusative verb with only one internal θ-role, Theme, which is syntactically realized as a CP. Thus it subcategorizes for a CP, and absorbs both Case and the external θ-role of the stem verb. The one associated with the indirect passive, on the other hand, is a transitive verb with the θ-grid (Experiencer, Source, Theme). It also subcategorizes for a CP with a θ-role Theme, but does not absorb either Case or a θ-role. The structure for indirect passives is a control structure; the Source argument of *(r)are* controls the subject of the CP. The following schematically shows the D-structures assumed for the direct, possessive, and indirect passives. The NP* in (41) a-b is subsequently moved to the subject position indicated by ____.

(41) a. direct   ____ [$_{CP}$ NP-ni NP* V] rare
     b. possessive   ____ [$_{CP}$ NP-ni [$_{NP}$ NP* N] V] rare
     c. indirect   NP NP$_i$-ni [PRO$_i$ VP] rare

According to Terada 1990, the contrast between the two passive types also has a bearing on the level of application of Verb Incorporation. That is the stem verb incorporates into the passive morpheme by a head-to-head movement, which can take place at two different levels: D- to S-structure for the direct and the possessive passives, and PF for indirect passives.[36] To clarify this point, let us first look at the tree structures for the three types of passive: (42) and (43) are the S-structures of direct passives and possessive passives, respectively. (44) is the PF of indirect passives:

(42) Syota -ga Kyoko -ni tatak-are-ta.
      'Syota was hit by Kyoko.'

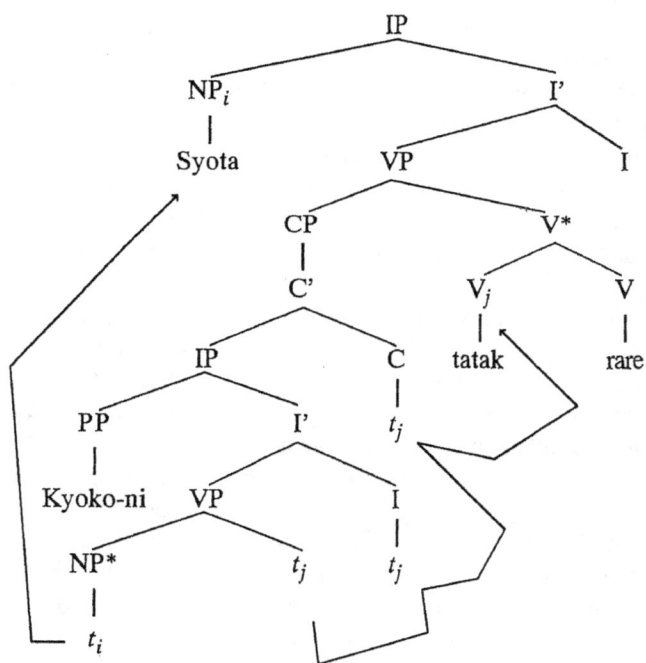

Passive Constructions

(43) Syota-ga Kyoko-ni atama-wo tatak-are-ta.
'Syota was hit by Kyoko on the head.'

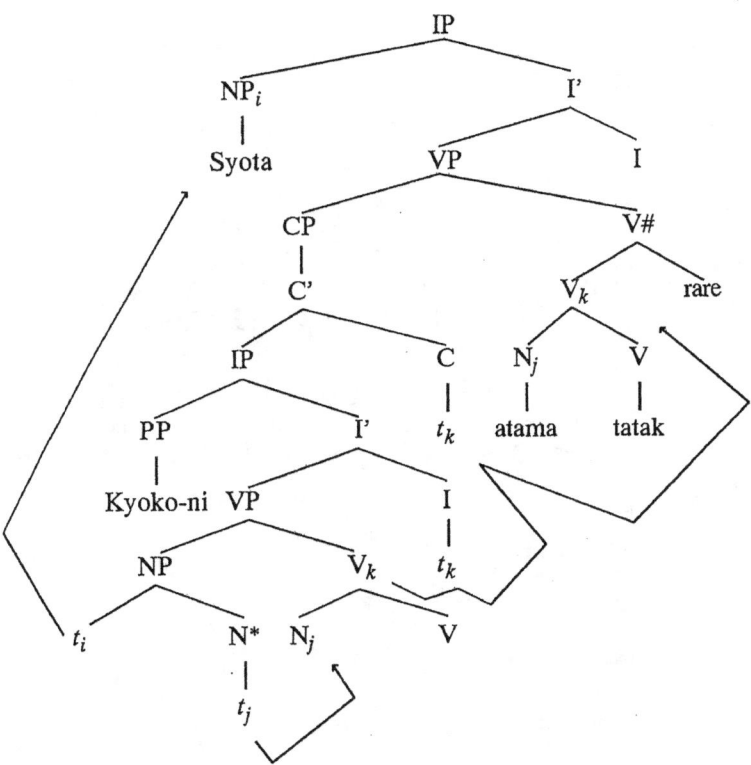

(44)   Syota-ga Kyoko-ni eiga-wo mi-rare-ta.
       'Syota was adversely affected by Kyoko's watching a movie.'

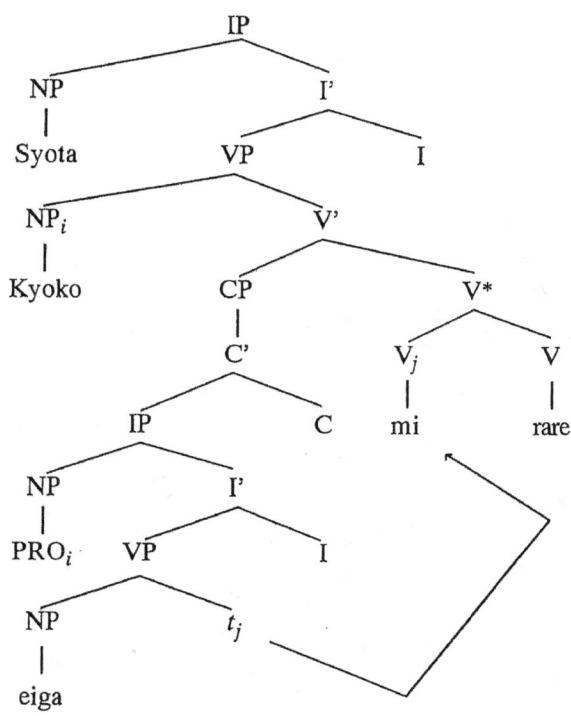

Incorporation of the verb stem into the passive morpheme of the direct/possessive passives takes place between D- and S-structure, as Terada assumes that V affixation takes place as soon as possible. V affixation of the indirect passive, however, has to wait till PF because, otherwise, PRO would be governed due to the Government Transparency Corollary (Baker 1988).[37] If the incorporation were to take place from D- to S-structures, the ECP would have to be observed. So the head verb *mi* would have to move successive cyclically, passing through the head of IP and the head of CP positions, just like the incorporation paths shown in (43) and (44). Then, by the Government Transparency Corollary, the V marked with * in (44) would govern

PRO; cyclic movement renders maximal projections IP and CP non-barriers. On the other hand, she assumes that ECP does not apply at PF, so that the trace of the head verb *mi* need not be properly governed; hence no intermediate trace is necessary, and the incoporation does not have to proceed successive cyclically. Furthermore, Terada 1990 takes the view that a PRO is invisible at PF; therefore, it does not matter whether it is governed or not.

For Terada 1990, NP movement in direct passives is motivated by Case Theory on the assumption that the passive morpheme of this type absorbs Case. NP movement in possessive passives is motivated in the same way. However, notice that in possessive passives, in fact, the possessed NP is assigned accusative case just as is true for an NP in indirect passives. (See, for instance, the example in (43).) To derive this result, Terada 1990 claims that the object argument (N* in (43)) is first incorporated into V_k in the embedded clause, and then that V_k as an amalgam moves up to affix to *(r)are*; namely, a noun incorporation preceding a verb incorporation. She further stipulates that the Case which was once absorbed by *(r)are* percolates down to the incorporated N* after all. She explains that this is possible because the N* becomes a constituent of the complex verb marked with # headed by *(r)are*.

These mechanisms allow Terada 1990 to explain the facts of the case marking alternation and the optionality of the agent phrase in direct/possessive passives in basically the same way as does Kubo 1990. The agent phrase of direct/possessive passives is an adjunctive PP, whereas that of indirect passives is an object argument subcategorized for by *(r)are*. Dative case appearing on the agent phrase of the latter type is an Inherent Case assigned by *(r)are*.

For Terada 1990, the question of reflexive binding finds a simple explanation as well. The agent phrase cannot bind a reflexive phrase in direct/possessive passives, because it is not a subject but merely an adjunct. In the case of indirect passives, Terada 1990 claims that it is not the agent phrase marked with dative case which binds a reflexive. It is actually the embedded subject PRO which binds reflexives. Though she does not discuss SH, an explanation similar to what she proposes for reflexives would be possible.

Terada's (1990) accounts of the animacy requirement and adversity interpretation of indirect passives are also similar to Kubo's (1990). An animacy requirement obtains with indirect passives because the passive predicate for indirect passives has an external θ-role Experiencer.[38]

Direct/possessive passives can take non-animate subjects and carry a neutral interpretation because they lack this external θ-role.

Thus Terada's (1990) model is able to give an account of most of the problems concerning passives. Nevertheless, we find her analysis very problematic in several respects.

First of all, as Kubo 1990 points out, the stipulation concerning noun incorporation in possessive passives is highly questionable; the noun incorporation is too abstract. Not only are the N* (*atama* in (43)) and the stem verb (*tatak*) separate words on the surface, e.g., *atama* appears with a case marker, but they do not even have to be adjacent. Any number of adverbs and PPs can intervene between the noun and the verb stem into which it has purportedly been incorporated. See the following examples. (Intervening items italicized):

(45) a. Syota -ga Kyoko -ni atama -wo tatak-are-ta.
          nom   dat   acc hit-PAS-PST
   'Syota was hit by Kyoko on the head.'

   b. Syota -ga Kyoko -ni atama -wo *tuyoku*   tatak-are-ta.
          nom   dat   acc strongly hit-PAS-PST
   'Syota was hit hard by Kyoko on the head.'

   c. Syota -ga Kyoko -ni atama -wo *boo*   *-de*
          nom   dat   acc stick   inst
   tatak-are-ta.
   hit-PAS-PST
   'Syota was hit by Kyoko on the head with a stick.'

   d. Syota -ga Kyoko -ni atama -wo *[nikusimi -wo kome-te]*
          nom   dat   acc hatred   acc put-GER
   tatak-are-ta.
   hit-PAS-PST
   'Syota was hit by Kyoko on the head with hatred.'

The intervening adverbial phrase can be even longer than that in (47-d). Therefore, there seem to be no convincing grounds for claiming that the noun head (*atama*) is incorporated into the verb head (*tatak*).

Secondly, the idea of percolating the absorbed Case in possessive passives sounds very *ad hoc*, lacking in any independent evidence. As Terada 1990 crucially relates this Case percolation to noun incorporation, it becomes even more questionable when the validity of noun incorporation is challenged.

As a third point, as we mentioned above in reviewing Hasegawa 1981a, 1981b, we disagree with the idea that the agent phrase of indirect passives is an object argument of the passive morpheme *(r)are*. Evidence for our view will be given in the next section.

A fourth and the most serious problem with Terada's (1990) approach resides in the level distinction of verb incorporation, which is a crucial mechanism in her system. As the problem shows up in the interaction with other complex predicates, we simply point out for the moment that her level distinction faces an unsurmountable problem, and come back to this issue later when it is appropriate (section 5.5.2).

3.3.5 Phrase Structure Approaches

Gunji 1987 presents a phrase structure analysis of passivization in the framework of Japanese Phrase Structure Grammar (JPSG) that he has proposed. This approach assumes that passivization is a syntactic process rather than a lexical process. Being a descendant of Categorial Grammar, JPSG has available to it the distinction between VP and TVP, and makes crucial use of this distinction in the analysis of passives (cf. Dowty 1982; Gunji 1983, 1987). Namely, the difference between the direct passive and the indirect passive is captured in terms of the syntactic category of the verbal phrase that the head (passive) verbs of each type subcategorize for. Simply put, direct passives have the structure of TVP-embedding, while indirect passives have the structure of VP-embedding. Following are the lexical structures of the two passive morphemes:[39]

(46)
  1. rare:
     {POS V: SUBCAT {PP[SUBJ], PP[OBJ;ni], TVP[+PAS]}, PAS-}

  2. rare:
     {POS V: SUBCAT {PP[SUBJ], PP[OBJ;ni], VP}, PAS-}

The following are examples of the direct and the indirect passive structures:

(47) a. Syota -ga   Naoko -ni   sikar-are-ta.
            nom   dat   scold-PAS-PST
    'Taroo was scolded by Naoko.'

b. Syota -ga   Naoko -ni   nak-are-ta.
         nom   dat   cry-PAS-PST
   'Taroo was affected by Naoko's crying.'

c. Syota -ga   Naoko -ni   kabin   -wo   war-are-ta.
         nom   dat   vase   acc   break-PAS-PST
   'Taroo was affected by Naoko's breaking the vase.'

(48) a.

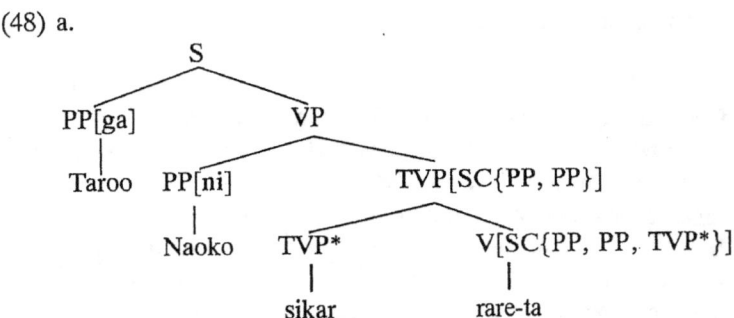

b.

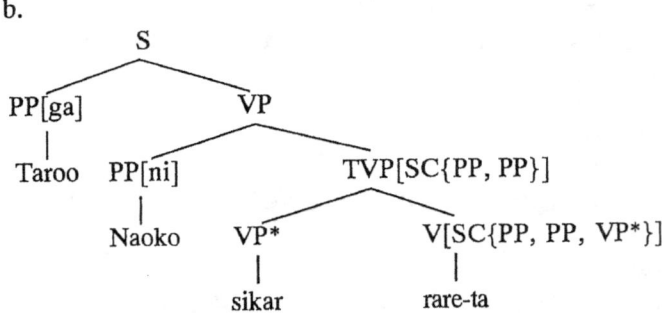

c.

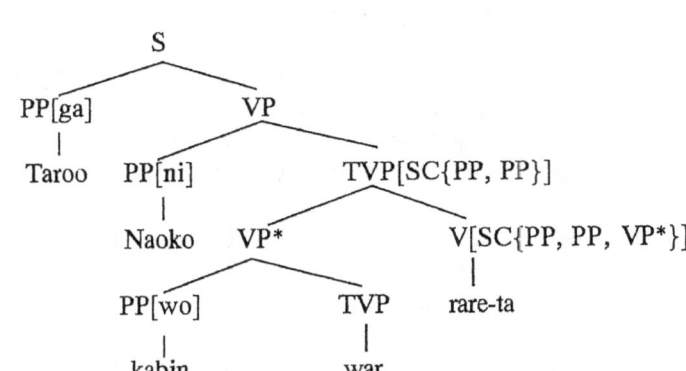

Thus, the direct passive morpheme subcategorizes for two PPs and a TVP, marked with *, while the indirect passive morpheme subcategorizes for two PPs and a VP. Therefore, Gunji's (1987) approach is uniform in the sense that the same structure is assumed for both, and is nonuniform in the sense that two different passive morphemes are postulated. This approach gives a very simple analysis unifying the two types of the passive structure, at the same time distinguishing the two types in terms of their subcategorization.

However, Gunji's (1987) system has many problems. First, the agent phrase is treated simply as a controller in both direct and indirect passives, and there seems to be no easy way to account for the differences between the agent phrases of the two types of passive. The questions of case marking alternation, optionality of agent phrase, as well as the problems of reflexive binding and SH, are all left unacccounted for.

Furthermore, note that Gunji 1987 analyzes passive constructions as an object-control structure. This position is not unique to him, when the issue is limited to indirect passives. Recall that Hasegawa 1981a, 1981 and Terada 1990 also posit an object-control structure for indirect passives. We challenge this position and claim that Japanese passives of any type do not have an object-control structure. There are two pieces of evidence for our claim. First of all, an object-control analysis seems to make wrong predictions regarding Object Honorification and passivization. An object usually can undergo syntactic Object Honorification (henceforth OH). The form of OH is slightly similar to the form of SH; the infinitival form of a verb is put between the honorific particle *o*, and a light verb *(s)u* ('do'). The following is an example of OH:

(49) a. Kyoko   -ga   sensei   -wo   tasuke-ta.
            nom   teacher   acc   help-PST
   'Kyoko helped the teacher.' (non-honorific)

   b. Kyoko   -ga   sensei   -wo   *o*-tasuke-*si*-ta.
            nom   teacher   acc   *o*-help-HON-PST
   'Kyoko helped the teacher.' (honorific)

OH is possible with the usual control structures, as shown below:

(50) a. Kyoko   -ga   sensei   -ni   soko   -e   iku-yoo
            nom   teacher   dat   there   to   go-MOD
   o-negai-*si*-ta.
   o-ask-HON-PST
   'Kyoko asked the teacher to go there (honorific).'

   b. Kyoko   -ga   *sensei*   -ni   soko   -e   iku to
            nom   teacher   dat   there   to   go-COMP
   o-yakusoku-*si*-ta.
   o-promise-HON-PST
   'Kyoko promised the teacher to go there (honorific).'

However, it is totally impossible to make an OH sentence based on any type of passive sentence, where the respect is directed toward the agent phrase, or controller. The following examples demonstrate this point:

(51) *a Kyoko   -ga   *sensei*   -ni   *o*-homer-are-*si*-ta.
             nom   teacher   dat   *o*-praise-PAS-HON-PST
   'Kyoko was praised by the teacher (honorific).

   *b. Kyoko   -ga   *sensei*   -ni   o-sake   -wo
              nom   teacher   dat   rice wine   acc
   o-nom-are-*si*-ta.
   o-drink-PAS-HON-PST
   'Kyoko was adversely affected by the teacher's drinking *sake* (honorific).'

The unavailability of OH for the passives strongly suggests that the agent phrase is not an object of the passive predicate in either the direct-type or the indirect-type.[40] Notice that this gives a strong argument against the VP-complement analysis of the passives advocated by Gunji 1987 and Fukushima 1990 and any analysis positing the agent phrase as an object argument of the passive morpheme (cf. Terada 1990).

Secondly, the agent phrase cannot undergo direct passivization, though the object phrase of a control structure can usually be passivized. Admitting that double passivization poses extra processing difficulty, even the direct passivization of the agent phrase of indirect passives is totally impossible, suggesting that it is not merely due to processing difficulties:[41]

(52) a. Kyoko -ga Syota -ni nige-rare-ta.
    nom   dat flee-PAS-PST
   'Kyoko had Syota run away on her.'

  *b. Syota -ga Kyoko -ni nige-rare-rare-ta.
      nom   dat flee-PAS-PAS-PST
   '(lit.) Syota had it that Kyoko was adversely affected by his running away from her.'

The facts of OH and passivization, therefore, indicate that the agent phrase is not an object argument of a passive predicate, and that passive constructions do not have an object-control structure. This casts doubt on Gunji's (1987) approach as well as the analyses of indirect passives by Hasegawa 1981a, 1981b and Terada 1990.

3.3.6 Summary of Previous Studies

We have surveyed some of the representative studies of Japanese passives presented in the literature. Some of them are better able to account for the data than others. In particular, Terada 1990 and Kubo 1990 seem to offer solutions to most of the data we mentioned earlier. They are not without problems, however.

Let us briefly summarize some views on the difference between direct passives and indirect passives:

1. Transformational (non-uniform)
    Kuno 1973   Direct passives are underlyingly monoclausal, whereas indirect passives are underlyingly biclausal (S-embedding).

2. Transformational approach (uniform)
    Kuroda 1965a   Both direct passives and indirect passives are underlyingly biclausal.

3. Lexicalist approach (non-uniform)
    Hasegawa 1981a,b   Direct passives are derived through a change in the argument structure of a single predicate, whereas the indirect passive predicate has a complex (composite) argument structure.

4. Movement approach (uniform)
    Miyagawa 1989a   Direct passives involve NP-movement triggered by (accusative) Case absorption; indirect passives take the option of undoing the Case abosorption. A new external argument is introduced due to Burzio's generalization. The Agent phrase is then internalized.

5. Movement approach
    Kubo 1990   Direct/possessive passives subcategorize for a lexical V^0, while indirect passives subcategorize for a phrasal projection VP. Only the latter are allowed to have an external θ-role. The former involve NP-movement due to the lack of an external θ-role, while the latter do not.

6. Movement approach
    Terada 1990   Direct/possessive passive predicates do not have an external argument, while indirect passive predicates do. Furthermore, the latter take an object-control structure involving PRO. The verb incorporation for

direct/possessive passives take place between D- and S-structures, whereas the one for indirect passives takes place as late as PF.

7. Phrase Structure approach
   Gunji 1987   Both direct and indirect passives take an object-control structure. The direct passive morpheme subcategorizes for two PPs and a VP, whereas the indirect passive morpheme subcategorizes for two PPs and a TVP.

Criticism of each appraoch has already been given above. On the other hand, some of the approaches have offered good insights in the account of data, and we will incorporate them in the following discussion. For instance, we are in rough agreement with Hasegawa 1981a, 1981b, Kubo 1990 and Terada 1990 in considering the agent phrase of direct/possessive passives as adjunct (or adjunct-like) so that it can be marked with a postposition or be deleted altogether. The adjunctive nature is also crucial in accounting for the data of reflexive binding and of SH. As for the animacy requirement, we agree with Kubo 1990 and Terada 1990 that it is because the external argument (matrix subject) of indirect passives is an Experiencer. Concerning the Do-Support phenomena, we find Kubo's (1990) structures very appealing; the verb stem and the passive morpheme constitute a single V^0 in direct and possessive passives, while the passive morpheme is an independent V^0 on its own subcategorizing for phrasal categories in indirect passives. Terada's (1990) system seems to have a similar effect, in a sense. Notice that because of her level distinction of verb incorporation, the verb stem is incorporated into the passive morpheme by the end of S-structure only in direct and possessive passives. The incorporation does not take place till PF in indirect passives, suggesting that it is simply a phonological adjustment.

Keeping these points in mind, let us now turn to our approach and see how HPSG can accommodate Japanese passive constructions.

3.4 Lexical Passives and Syntactic Passives

This section proposes an HPSG approach to Japanese passives. We will first focus on direct and indirect passives. Possessive passives will be discussed in a subsequent section.

We claim that the Japanese direct passives are lexically derived whereas indirect passives are syntactically constructed. That is, even though the morphological shape is identical, the passive morpheme *(r)are* is a derivational affix in direct passives, and is an independent verb in the indirect passives. This claim also entails that direct passives are monoclausal, and indirect passives biclausal. In what follows, we will present the lexical rule and the feature structure necessary for the passive constructions, and provide arguments to defend our position.

3.4.1 Direct Passives as Lexical Passives

We claim that direct passives are derived by a lexical rule much in line with Pollard and Sag 1987. We also accept the view that the crucial operation in the formation of direct passives is the change of grammatical relations among arguments. As mentioned in the previous chapter, if an operation triggers a change in the SUBCAT list of a predicate, i.e., grammatical relations, it has to take place at the lexical level, due to the monotonicity of the unification operation in syntax. This effect is not simply for the sake of theory, however. The data given above in fact all seem to point in this direction. The following is the lexical rule that we propose for direct passives:

(53) Direct Passive Lexical Rule

$$\begin{bmatrix} \text{SUBCAT} \langle \text{NP}[1], \ldots \text{NP}[2], \ldots \rangle \\ \text{CONT } [3] \begin{bmatrix} \text{RELATION} & R \\ \text{EXT-ARG} & [1] \\ \text{R-er} & [1] \\ \text{R-er} & [2] \\ \vdots & \vdots \end{bmatrix} \end{bmatrix} \Rightarrow$$

Passive Constructions

$$\begin{bmatrix} \text{SUBCAT} \langle \text{NP[2]}, ... \rangle \\ \text{CONT} \begin{bmatrix} \text{RELATION } \textit{affect} \\ \text{EXT-ARG} \quad [4] \\ \text{AFFECTEE } [4] \text{ [INDEX[5]]} \\ \\ \text{SOA-ARG} \quad [3] \begin{bmatrix} \text{RELATION } R \\ \text{EXT-ARG} \quad [1] \\ \textit{R-er} \qquad\quad [1] \\ \textit{R-ee} \qquad\quad [2] \text{ [INDEX[5]]} \\ \vdots \qquad\qquad \vdots \end{bmatrix} \end{bmatrix} \end{bmatrix}$$

See the example below, where the input verb is *mi* ('see'):

(54) Direct Passive *mi-rare*

$$\begin{bmatrix} \text{PHON} \mid \textit{mi} \\ \text{SYNSEM} \mid ... \begin{bmatrix} \text{SUBCAT} \langle \text{NP[1], NP[2]} \rangle \\ \text{CONT [3]} \begin{bmatrix} \text{RELATION } \textit{see} \\ \text{EXT-ARG} \quad [1] \\ \textit{seer} \qquad\quad [1] \\ \textit{seen} \qquad\quad [2] \end{bmatrix} \end{bmatrix} \end{bmatrix} \Rightarrow$$

$$\begin{bmatrix} \text{PHON} \mid \textit{mi-rare} \\ \text{SYNSEM} \mid ... \begin{bmatrix} \text{SUBCAT} \langle \text{NP[2]} \rangle \\ \text{CONT} \begin{bmatrix} \text{RELATION } \textit{affect} \\ \text{EXT-ARG} \quad [4] \\ \text{AFFECTEE } [4] \text{ [INDEX[5]]} \\ \\ \text{SOA-ARG} \quad [3] \begin{bmatrix} \text{RELATION } \textit{see} \\ \text{EXT-ARG} \quad [1] \\ \textit{seer} \qquad\quad [1] \\ \textit{seen} \qquad\quad [2] \text{[INDEX[5]]} \end{bmatrix} \end{bmatrix} \end{bmatrix} \end{bmatrix}$$

This lexical rule roughly follows the spirit underlying the passive lexical rule of English proposed by Pollard and Sag 1987 as far as the SUBCAT feature is concerned. One of the non-subject arguments is promoted to the subject, shifting to the left-most position in the SUBCAT list. The original subject is left out of the SUBCAT list, losing its argument status.[42]

The rule, on the other hand, departs from the one by Pollard and Sag 1987 in terms of the CONTENT feature. The lexical rule above indicates that direct passives specify a semantic relation tentatively referred to as Affect, with two arguments, one with the Affectee role and a soa (state-of-affairs) argument. The value of the latter is the semantic content of the stem verb, as mentioned above. Roughly put, the semantic content of the stem verb is embedded in the semantic content of the passive morpheme. (Henceforth, the former will be referred to as "lower content/relation," and the latter "higher content/relation.") In other words, we claim that the semantic content of direct passives is not identical to that of the active counterparts, as is standardly assumed across theories.[43] As this is not what is usually assumed, we believe it needs justification.

It is widely accepted that the active and the corresponding passive sentences are describing an objectively identical situation.[44] At the same time, however, it has been pointed out that the meaning of an active sentence and that of a passive sentence are not exactly the same.

One such observation is concerned with the scope of a certain class of adverbs. Jackendoff 1972 notes the existence of a set of "subject-oriented" adverbs, where the adverbs are interpreted as modifying a property of the subject:

(55) a. The doctor cleverly has examined John.
　　 b. John cleverly has been examined by the doctor.

(56) a. The police carelessly have arrested Fred.
　　 b. Fred carelessly has been arrested by the police.

(57) a. Joe intentionally has seduced Kyoko.
　　 b. Kyoko intentionally has been seduced by Joe.

When the sentences have non-perfect aspect, the passive sentences show ambiguities of orientation, though the active sentences remain unambiguous:

(58) a The doctor cleverly examined John.
   b. John was cleverly examined by the doctor.

(59) a. The police carelessly arrested Fred.
   b. Fred was carelessly arrested by the police.

(60) a. Joe intentionally seduced Kyoko.
   b. Kyoko was intentionally seduced by Joe.

The sentences (58) through (60) indicate that the adverbs are not really oriented to the subjects, not to the surface subjects at least.

Zubizarreta 1982, 1987 examines this set of adverbs and proposes that they assign a θ-role to either the structural subject or the thematic Agent of the clause.

Roberts 1987 in a sense attempts to unify the two notions of Zubizarreta 1982, 1987, the structural subject and the thematic Agent, into one by extending the class of Agent. He assumes first of all that this class of adverbs is oriented to an Agent rather than to a subject. Recall, however, that under a standard analysis the subject argument of the passive sentence is θ-marked in its original (object) position, and is never marked as Agent. To solve this dilemma, Roberts 1987 proposes that there are two independent modes of θ-role assignment: structural and inherent. Inherent θ-marking is basically the traditional notion of θ-marking based on the θ-grid of a predicate, and is assumed to hold at DS. Structural θ-marking, on the other hand, takes place at LF, and it involves only Agent and Theme. He further argues that a structurally θ-marked subject can have an agentive reading overlaid on the core inherent θ-role, and that this possibility is available for a derived subject and for predicates headed by non-θ-assigners. In other words, the adverbs in question are oriented to either the inherently-marked agent or the structurally-marked agent.

Interesting as it is, the idea of structural θ-marking seems to require more independent motivation. Besides, it is not too clear whether *Fred* modified by the adverb *carelessly* in (59-b) can really be called an Agent.

The same phenomena are observed in Japanese as well (Kitagawa 1986). In his discussion of scopal ambiguity of adverbs in causatives, Kitagawa 1986 mentions that the passives also show the same ambiguity. Thus, among the following sentences, the passives are ambiguous in exactly the same way:[45]

(61) a. Syota -ga   Kyoko -wo *umaku*   damasi-ta.
         nom   acc   cleverly   cheat-PST
     'Syota cleverly cheated Kyoko.'

   b. Kyoko -ga Syota -ni *umaku*   damas-are-ta.
         nom   dat cleverly   cheat-PAS-PST
     'Kyoko was cleverly cheated by Syota.'

(62) a. Keisatu -ga Kyoko -wo *ukkari*   tukamae-ta.
         police nom   acc   carelessly catch-PST
     'The police carelessly arrested Kyoko.'

   b. Kyoko -ga keisatu -ni *ukkari*   tukamae-rare-ta.
         nom police   dat carelessly catch-PAS-PST
     'Kyoko was carelessly arrested by the police.'

(63) a. Syota -ga Kyoko -wo *wazato*   yuuwakusi-ta.
         nom   acc   intentionally seduce-PST
     'Syota intentionally seduced Kyoko.'

   b. Kyoko -ga Syota -ni *wazato*   yuuwakus-are-ta.
         nom   dat intentionally seduce-PAS-PST
     'Kyoko was intentionally seduced by Syota.'

Similar phenomena have been observed with adverbial clauses headed by *nagara* 'while,' which is considered a clause controlled by a subject (Perlmutter 1984; Dubinsky 1989).[46] The following examples illustrate the usage of this clause:

(64) a. Sensei -ga   kodomo -wo [naki-*nagara*] sikat-ta.
         teacher nom child   acc   cry-while   scold-PST
     '(lit.) While crying, the teacher scolded the child.'
     = not 'while the child was crying...'

   b. Syota -ga Kyoko -ni [gohan -wo tabe-*nagara*] iiyot-ta.
         nom   dat meal   acc eat-while   woo-PST
     '(lit.) While eating a meal, Syota proposed to Kyoto.'
     = not 'while Kyoko was eating a meal...'

The sentences above can only mean that the teacher was crying and Syota was eating. The object phrases, *kodomo* 'child' and *Kyoko*, cannot be interpreted as the controller of *nagara* clause. In direct passives, the interpretation of controller becomes ambiguous. See the following sentence:[47]

(65) a. Kodomo -ga [naki-*nagara*] sensei -ni sikar-are-ta.
    child nom cry-while teacher dat scold-PAS-PST
    '(lit.) The child$_i$ was scolded by the teacher$_j$ while he/she$_{i/j}$ was crying.'

b. Kyoko -ga [gohan -wo tabe-*nagara*] Syota -ni
    nom meal acc eat-while dat
    iiyor-are-ta.
    woo-PAS-PST
    '(lit.) Kyoko$_i$ was proposed to by Syota$_j$ while he$_j$/she$_i$ was having a meal.'

Thus *nagara* clauses in passives are like manner adverbs in passives in that they can modify either the matrix subject or the agent phrase.

Kitagawa's (1986) focus is on causatives, and his solution is purely structural, based on the Modifier Licensing Condition at LF that he proposes. One point worth noting is that it is crucial for his account of the above-mentioned ambiguity that the passive morpheme *(r)are* (of any type) selects an Experiencer as the external argument, though he does not discuss the validity of this assumption except to cite Kuroda 1965a.[48]

We argue that passive formation creates a complex semantic content structure. The core thematic relation of the predicate, namely the part shared by the active sentence and its passive counterpart, is represented as the embedded part of the semantic structure of the pure passives. Crucially, this and only this part is maintained without alteration under passivization.

The problem of ambiguity related to manner adverbs and *nagara* adverbial clauses discussed above finds a very simple explanation in our approach. The adverbs in question, we propose, can modify only the thematically highest argument in each semantic content unit, which consists of one Relation attribute and one or more Roles participating in the Relation.[49] The semantic structure of direct passives represented above has two such semantic content units, and hence two arguments available for adverbial modification. They correspond to the subject and the agent, respectively. The fact that this kind of ambiguity is absent in the active sentence is also an automatic consequence of this proposal. Notice that we do not refer to any specific thematic roles such as Agent, nor to a grammatical notion such as subject, thus avoiding the shortcomings of the approaches mentioned above.

Now, it is also essential to ask what the relation Affect and the Affectee role really mean in our approach. We assume that these are the labels for some set of relations and roles with relevant entailments much in the same way as Dowty (1989, 1991) defines thematic roles and as Pollard and Sag (1994) classify control verbs. In particular, we propose that the relation Affect is in fact an underspecified relation; the Affectee role is also underspecified in its details. The only condition, we propose, is that the Affect relation is defined by its primary participant whose role is sufficiently removed from the Proto-Agent role.[50] Crucially, among the entailments for the Proto-Agent role suggested by Dowty 1991, the Affectee role must be neither *volitional* nor *causative*.[51] We further claim that the Affect relation and the Affectee role require more specification in order for the matrix subject to establish a specific semantic link to the lower content (henceforth, "core event").

The Affect relation and the Affectee role are thus underspecified. Now, the argument with the Affectee role is coindexed with the object argument of the lower soa; the coindexing means coreferentiality. The entailments which the non-Agent argument of the lower content has are completely compatible with the entailments it needs as the Affectee of the higher relation. Thus we assume that the underspecified Affectee role is substantiated by the semantic role it bears with respect to the core event. This point will be elaborated further in the discussion of indirect passives in the next section.

Now, we also have to make clear what the agent phrase is. As mentioned above, the present approach accepts the idea of subject demotion in passivization. That is, the original subject is left out of the syntactic SUBCAT list. This is why it can be omitted in many languages. In some languages, the agent phrase of a passive is obligatorily absent (Baker 1988; Spencer 1991). Recall also that in recent studies of Japanese passives, the agent phrase of direct passives is treated as an adjunct, while the agent phrase of indirect passives is considered an argument (Miyagawa 1989a; Kubo 1990; Terada 1990). We basically agree with these treatments.

Let us elaborate on the motivation for subject demotion. There have been a number of studies on the characterization of agent phrases. Two claims have been well-accepted. First, though the agent phrase is syntactically defective, it is thematically present (Marantz 1984; Roberts 1987; Grimshaw 1990). Second, as a plausible explanation for the first point, the agent phrase is suppressed (Bresnan and Kanerva 1989; Grimshaw 1990).

Marantz 1984, Roberts 1987, Zubizarreta 1987, and Grimshaw 1990 present many examples which support the idea that the agentive phrase is thematically present in the passive sentences of English and other languages even when the phrase is not present at the surface. This situation contrasts with the cases of the middle constructions, where the agentive phrase cannot be present. Compare the following sentences, for instance:

(66) a. The glass was broken by the child.
 *b. The glass broke by the child.

(67) a. The books were read by children.
 *b. The books read well by children.

(68) a. The books were sold to make money.
 *b. The books sold well to make money.

The agentive phrase is compatible only with passives, as (66)-(67) show. The sentences in (68) indicate that the Agent is thematically present in passives even when it is absent on the surface, so that the purpose clause can be semantically controlled. Given these data, it is clear that the agent phrase is thematically present in passives. It is clear at the same time that the agent phrase is not really a syntactically legitimate argument, either. First of all, if it were really a legitimate argument, another question would arise: Why is this argument not selected as the subject? This is a problem if one takes seriously the principle of subject selection mentioned in the previous chapter. Further, if it were really a full-fledged argument, it should not be omissible.

Recent works in LFG and GB predominantly assume that the agent θ-role is suppressed in a relevant sense. Bresnan and Kanerva

1989, for instance, explores the possibility of mapping principles which relate semantic arguments to their morphosyntactic expression by means of syntactic functions. The arguments are arranged according to the thematic hierarchy (see section 2.2.1), and the mapping principles are constructed in such a way that the highest thematic role is eventually selected as the subject. Passives are an obvious exception to the usual mapping pattern; a non-agent is selected as the subject, while the agent is not. To maintain the mapping principle and, at the same time, to make automatic the exceptional mapping of the passives, they propose that the core operation of passivization is to suppress the highest thematic role (also see Bresnan and Moshi 1990; Alsina and Mchombo 1990; Alsina 1991). Being suppressed, the highest argument is not eligible for subject selection. As a consequence, one of the other arguments will be the candidate for subjecthood.[52] A suppressed argument cannot be assigned a syntactic function, but it can be thematically bound to an adjunct, i.e., the *by*-phrase in the case of the English passive. A similar idea is defended by Grimshaw 1990, as well. The agent phrase is thus referred to by Grimshaw 1990 and others as an argument-adjunct by virtue of its connection to an argument.

We also take the view that the original subject is in a sense suppressed. We follow Bresnan and Kanerva 1989 in assuming that the Agent NP phrase holds a certain privilege, and its suppression is motivated by the need to cancel this privilege. Notice that for Bresnan and Kanerva 1989, the privilege is concerned with subject selection. As mentioned in the previous section (see section 2.2.1), it is crosslinguistically attested, with a very few exceptions, that the subject argument is the one which bears that highest thematic role in a predicate argument structure. Suppression of the highest role is a device to cancel this privilege and to allow another argument to be selected as the subject.

For us, on the other hand, the privilege is related to the coindexing relation. Sag and Pollard 1991, 87-91, posits the attribute External Argument as a feature picking out an argument which serves as the controllee in a control structure, and they assume that the Ext-Arg coincides with the subject in English.[53] In other words, the Ext-Arg is a feature whose value by definition holds priority in being coindexed with an argument of a higher soa (controller). According to our analysis of direct passives, the Affectee role is coindexed with an argument other than an Ext-Arg of the embedded soa-arg. This situation is obviously against the definition of the Ext-Arg by Sag and Pollard 1991, and we claim that it is tolerable only if the NP corresponding to the Ext-Arg is suppressed.

The following captures the coindexing condition:

(69) If SYNSEM|CONTENT| attribute has an embedding structure, an argument of a higher soa can only be coindexed with the Ext-Arg of the lower soa, when it is available, unless the Ext-Arg corresponds to a syntactically suppressed argument.

This coindexing condition thus prohibits a non-Ext-Arg of a lower relation from being coindexed with an argument in a higher relation, when there is an Ext-Arg available for coindexing.[54] In other words, the Ext-Arg, virtually equatable with the subject, has priority in the coindexing with an argument in a higher soa. We claim that the suppression of the Ext-Arg is a device to cancel this priority.

Notice that, different from Bresnan and Kanerva 1989 and Grimshaw 1990, we do not take the suppression as a primary operation that effects passivization. Our approach is quite the contrary. Conceptually speaking, suppression of an argument is a very powerful operation and should be invoked only under certain conditions; otherwise, any argument would be able to freely be suppressed and become an adjunct. In our approach, the suppression is invoked only to license the otherwise illicit coindexing relation. The passive lexical rule proposed in this chapter primarily stipulates the coindexing relation between the Affectee role and the non-Agent role of the embedded soa-arg. Then by condition (69), this structure is permissible only if the NP corresponding to the Ext-Arg is suppressed. This proposal will be defended further in the discussion of other types of passives and causatives.

In this section we have proposed that direct passives are lexically derived, and that the resultant passive predicate has a complex semantic CONTENT structure. The facts of adverbial scope ambiguity were presented as supporting evidence for our proposal. Our analysis also involves such ideas as coindexing and underspecified semantic role. These ideas will be elaborated further in the following discussion. Before discussing how the present analysis of direct passives accounts for the relevant data, let us turn to our analysis of indirect passives.

3.4.2 Indirect Passives as Syntactic Passives

In contrast with direct passives, we claim that the indirect passives involve syntactic embedding. In particular, we argue that the passive morpheme *(r)are* of the indirect passive syntactically functions as a word with its own SUBCAT attribute.

The following feature structure illustrates the relevant part of the feature structure of the indirect passive morpheme *(r)are*:

(70) Indirect Passive Morpheme *(r)are*:

$$\begin{bmatrix} \text{PHON} \mid \textit{rare} \\ \text{SYNSEM} \mid ... \begin{bmatrix} \text{SUBCAT} \langle \text{NP[4], V[SUBCAT}\langle\;\rangle]\text{:[3]}\rangle \\ \text{CONT} \begin{bmatrix} \text{RELATION} & \textit{affect} \\ \text{EXT-ARG} & [4] \\ \text{AFFECTEE} & [4] \\ \text{SOA-ARG} & [3] \end{bmatrix} \end{bmatrix} \end{bmatrix}$$

That is, we propose that the indirect passive morpheme is a verb subcategorized for one NP and an S. The embedded S intuitively corresponds to a sentence headed by the stem verb. Our reason for positing an S embedding structure instead of the VP embedding one which is common to control structures (cf. the analyses of the causatives in chapter 5) has already been given in the review of Gunji 1987. Facts about OH and passivization argue against positing an object-control (VP-embedding) structure for passives.

There is also a theory-internal problem with object-control structures. In the control theory of HPSG, controller selection is based on the semantics of the predicate. As explained in the previous chapter, object control is a characteristic of a predicate which semantically belongs to the Influence type, with the controller being the Influenced argument. In the present case, however, the passive predicate is not at all likely to be of Influence type; nor is the agent phrase likely to be an Influenced argument. Therefore there are no grounds in the context of HPSG to effect the desired control relation.[55]

One of the crucial points of our approach concerns the advantage of HPSG as a unification-based theory. Because of the way pieces of information are put together in constructing successively larger linguistic signs, when the indirect passive morpheme is combined with its S-complement, the information about the embedded soa-arg is supplied. Take the example of the sentence in (71), represented in a tree diagram in (72). The structure (73) represents the relevant part of the feature structure of the top VP marked with *:[56]

(71) Syota -ga Kyoko -ni sore -wo mi-rare-ta.
     nom   dat   that acc see-PAS-PST
  'Syota was adversely affected by Kyoko's seeing it.'

(72)

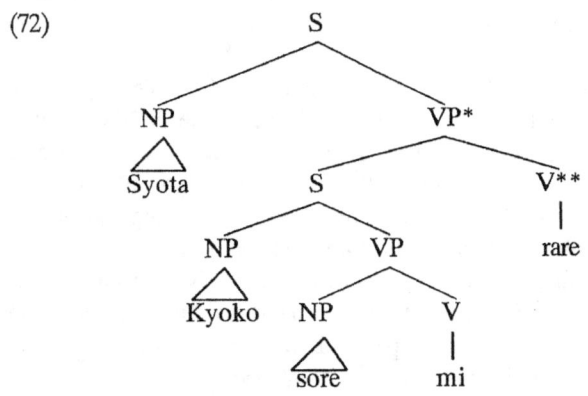

(73)
$$\begin{bmatrix} \text{SUBCAT} \langle \text{NP[4]} \rangle \\ \text{CONT} \begin{bmatrix} \text{RELATION} \quad \textit{affect} \\ \text{EXT-ARG} \quad [4] \\ \text{AFFECTEE} \quad [4] \\ \\ \text{SOA-ARG} \quad [3] \begin{bmatrix} \text{RELATION} \quad \textit{see} \\ \text{EXT-ARG} \quad [1] \\ \textit{seer} \quad [1] \\ \textit{seen} \quad [2] \end{bmatrix} \end{bmatrix} \end{bmatrix}$$

Notice that the feature structure in (73) is identical to the feature structure of the output of the passive lexical rule given in (53) in terms of the semantic content attribute. The only difference in the semantic content is the presence or absence of coindexing.

The lack of coindexing in indirect passives has several important consequences. Let us first consider the Affectee role in this case. We regard this concept in the same way as in the case of direct passives. Namely, it is an underspecified role concept whose only restriction is that it is neither volitional nor causative. This concept in indirect passives is different from the one in the direct passives, however, because, unlike the case of direct passives, this role is not directly linked to any argument in the lower relation in the case of indirect passives.

Ritter and Rosen 1990 suggests that in complex predicate formation, when an extra argument is introduced as the matrix subject, there are roughly two ways to relate it to the embedded event (= core event): either as the one who *causes* the event, or as the one who *gets some influence* from the event. We adopt their suggestion in considering the semantic roles in passive structures.

Now, let us reanalyze the situation of direct passives to incorporate Ritter and Rosen's (1990) suggestion. We have claimed that the extra argument in passives has an underspecified role, referred to as Affectee. Recall that the only crucial specification of Affectee is that it must not be Proto-Agent-like. It follows naturally, then, it cannot bear a causer-type role but must be an Influenced-type role. As mentioned in the previous section, because of the coindexing relation, the Influenced-type role is substantiated by the semantic role that the coindexed argument bears with respect to the event denoted by the verb stem. The Influenced-type role needs no further specification.

In the case of indirect passives no coindexing relation is involved. The argument is not directly connected to the core event in any way. This situation is close to the cases actually examined by Ritter and Rosen 1990; according to them, Experiencer and Causer are the two choices in such cases. As the Affectee role cannot be agentive (=causative), it is left with an Experiencer role.[57] This idea finds support in the fact that virtually all of the recent major works on the Japanese passives have defined the thematic role of the subject of at least indirect passives as Experiencer (Kitagawa 1986; Miyagawa 1989a; Terada 1990; Kubo 1990 (as malefactive); among others.) The problem of the animacy requirement of the matrix subject mentioned above is explained in the same way as Kubo 1990 and Terada 1990 suggest; simply, an argument has to be animate to experience something, except in metaphor or in fantasy.

The lack of coindexing between Affectee and an argument of the embedded soa also predicts that there is no need for the suppression of the subject argument. As the previous studies have already suggested, this seems to be a correct prediction. The agent phrase in indirect passives is an obligatory argument, and it has to carry the dative case. It cannot be omitted, nor can it alternate with a postpositional phrase.

3.4.3 Evidence for the Present Approach

So far we have shown how the present approach accommodates three of the above-mentioned properties of passives, i.e., the animacy requirement of the matrix subject, the case marking alternation of the agent phrase, and its optionality. This section will present more supporting evidence for our proposal by examining the rest of the distinctive properties of the direct and indirect passives.

3.4.3.1 Do-Support and the Syntactic Constituency of Morphemes

The first piece of evidence supporting the lexical derivation of the direct passives comes from the constituency of the verb stem and the passive morpheme. Recall that the data on Do-Support indicate that the verb stem and the passive morpheme can be separated only in indirect passives. The verb stem and the passive morpheme seem to be functioning syntactically as an inseparable unit in the case of direct passives. This is one of the reasons why Kubo 1990 proposes that the passive morpheme of the direct passives subcategorizes for V^0 instead of VP. Under the present analysis, this difference in constituency is an automatic consequence. We have proposed that the passive morpheme *(r)are* for direct passives is a derivational affix, and constitutes with the stem verb one unit syntactically functioning as a verb. The passive morpheme *(r)are* for indirect passives, on the other hand, is syntactically an independent verb by itself, subcategorizing for an NP and an S.

(R)are is a bound form; hence in either type it normally has to be adjacent to the preceding verb, and at the same time requires the morphological shape of the preceding verb to be a base (stem). No adverbs or postpositional modifiers can intervene between the verb stem

and the passive morpheme in either type, though the combination of an emphatic particle and the supportive $s(u)$ ('do') is an exception. We assume that the insertion of the emphatic particle and the supportive $s(u)$ ('do') is sensitive to the unit of a syntactic word. In particular, these items can be found only at syntactive word boundaries. In the case of direct passives, there is no syntactic boundary between the verb stem and the passive morpheme. In the case of indirect passives, on the other hand, the stem verb and the passive morpheme are each syntactic words, so the emphatic particle and the supportive $s(u)$ ('do') can occur between them as well as after them.

3.4.3.2 Reflexive Binding and the Suppression of the Agent Phrase

The crucial fact about reflexive binding is that it is only in indirect passives that the agent phrase, in addition to the matrix subject, can serve as the antecedent of a reflexive. Direct passives allow only the matrix subject to bind a reflexive (McCawley 1972; Kuno 1973, Howard and Niyekawa-Howard 1976; Miyagawa 1989a; Kubo 1990; Terada 1990). Transformational analyses argue that the NP which can be the antecedent always occupies the subject position at some level of embedding. Kubo 1990 and Terada 1990, for instance, assume that the agent phrase of indirect passives is an argument, while that of direct passives is an adjunct. Adjuncts cannot bind reflexives.

We basically accept the idea that the contrast is due to the syntactic status of the two types of agent phrases. We need to clarify the point more, however, as we have proposed in the previous chapter that reflexive binding is to be accounted for not in terms of grammatical relations but in terms of the thematic hierarchy. In particular, no account referring to the notion "subject" is available.

Recall our analysis of the problems of the case marking alternation and optionality of the agent phrase in the previous section. With Terada 1990, Kubo 1990, and many other recent studies of passives, we have argued that the agent phrase is syntactically suppressed in direct passives.

We claim that the unavailability of reflexive binding by the agent phrase of direct passives is a direct consequence of this suppression. To incorporate this claim, we redefine the condition on possible reflexive binders in Japanese. The following is the condition that we proposed in chapter 2:

(74) *Zibun* binding (preliminary)

(i) The binder of a reflexive *zibun* must be the bearer of the most thematically prominent semantic role in a semantic CONTENT structure, where the most thematically prominent role is defined as the one carrying the greatest number of Proto-Agent role entailments.

(ii) The binder can be either in the same CONTENT structure as the reflexive or in a CONTENT structure inclusive of the one involving the reflexive phrase.

To accommodate the data in passives, we modify the above condition by restricting the possible binder to "full-fledged" arguments. The following shows the revised version of our condition on reflexive binders:

(75) *Zibun* binding (revised)

(i) The binder of a reflexive *zibun* must be an unsuppressed syntactic argument which shares the PARAMETER feature with the most thematically prominent semantic role in a semantic CONTENT structure, where the most thematically prominent role is defined as the one carrying the greatest number of Proto-Agent role entailments.

(ii) The binder can be either in the same CONTENT structure as the reflexive or in a CONTENT structure inclusive of the one involving the reflexive phrase.

This revised definition eliminates the agent phrase of direct passives from the class of possible antecedents of reflexives. We believe this revision is reasonable, considering the suggestion commonly made by many studies such as Roberts 1987, Baker 1988, Zubizarreta 1987, Bresnan and Kanerva 1989, Grimshaw 1990, and many others, that a suppressed argument fails to show a full-fledged syntactic function, despite its thematic presence.[58] This syntactic deficiency makes it impossible as a reflexive binder.

In the case of indirect passives, there is no suppression of the agent phrase, as mentioned above. Consequently, the agentive phrase remains a syntactic argument, eligible as the antecedent of a reflexive.

It is very important to note that, as far as binding is concerned, the particular grammatical function of the agent phrase is irrelevant so long as it is an argument. Under our approach to the reflexive binding, the binder does not have to be the subject in any level of syntactic embedding. Though we assume an S-embedding structure for indirect passives, which entails that the agent phrase is the "subject" of the embedded S, the subjecthood has no direct bearing on the problems of reflexive binding.

3.4.3.3 Subject Honorification

The next question through which the present approach is to be assessed concerns syntactic Subject Honorification (SH). It has been shown above that the agent phrase triggers SH only in indirect passives. The matrix subject can trigger SH in either type of passive.[59] Though the contrast is very similar to the one we see with reflexive binding, there are different factors involved. We assume that SH is a type of subject agreement; the relevant information is encoded in the SUBCAT list suggested by Pollard and Sag (1994). We propose that the verb optionally takes SH morphology when the least oblique argument (subject) bears the information, here tentatively signaled by a feature [+HON]. For instance, the following SH sentence (76-b) can be schematically represented as in the accompanying diagram.

(76) a. Sensei   -ga   uta   -wo   utat-ta.
        teacher   nom   song   acc   sing-PST
        'The teacher sang a song. (non-honorific)'

   b. Sensei   -ga   uta   -wo   *o*-utawi-*ninat*-ta.
        teacher   nom   song   acc   *o*-sing-HON-PST
        'The teacher sang a song. (honorific)'

Passive Constructions

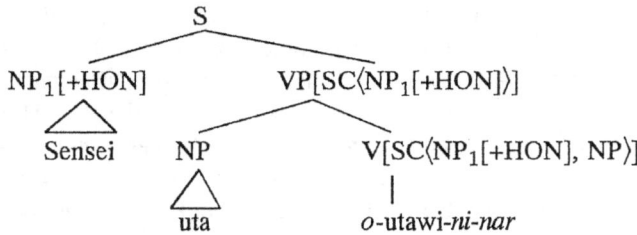

The SH in the case of passives can be accounted for in exactly the same way. To see how our analyses work, let us examine the morpheme order in each case of passive SH. As the examples presented earlier in this chapter show, the possible morpheme order is different depending on the type of passive and on the trigger of honorification. The following shows the possible and impossible patterns. In all examples, *sensei* 'teacher' is the trigger of SH:

(77) *a. *Sensei* -ga   Kyoko -ni   tasuke-*o*-rare-*ninat*-ta.
        teacher   nom   dat   help-*o*-PAS-HON-PST
    b. *Sensei* -ga   Kyoko -ni   *o*-tasuke-rare-*ninat*-ta.
        teacher   nom   dat   *o*-help-PAS-HON-PST
    *c. *Sensei* -ga   Kyoko -ni   *o*-tasuke-*ninar*-are-ta.
        teacher   nom   dat   *o*-help-HON-PAS-PST
    'The teacher was helped by Kyoko.'

(78) *a. Kyoko -ga   *sensei* -ni   tasuke-*o*-rare-*ninat*-ta.
         nom   teacher   dat   help-*o*-PAS-HON-PST
    *b. Kyoko -ga   *sensei* -ni   *o*-tasuke-rare-*ninat*-ta.
         nom   teacher   dat   *o*-help-PAS-HON-PST
    ?*c. Kyoko -ga   *sensei* -ni   *o*-tasuke-*ninar*-are-ta.
         nom teacher   dat   *o*-help-HON-PAS-PST
    'Kyoko was helped by the teacher.'

(79) *a. *Sensei* -ga Kyoko -ni hon   -wo   kaki-*o*-rare-*ninat*-ta.
        teacher nom   dat book   acc   write-*o*-PAS-HON-PST
    b. *Sensei* -ga Kyoko -ni hon   -wo   *o*-kak-are-*ninat*-ta.
        teacher nom   dat book   acc   *o*-write-PAS-HON-PST
    *c. *Sensei* -ga Kyoko -ni hon   -wo   *o*-kaki-*ninar*-are-ta.
        teacher nom   dat book   acc   *o*-write-HON-PAS-PST
    'The teacher had Kyoko write the book to the teacher' disadvantage.'

(80) *a. Kyoko -ga *sensei* -ni hon -wo kaki-*o*-rare-*ninat*-ta.
           nom teacher dat book acc write-*o*-PAS-HON-PST
    *b. Kyoko -ga *sensei* -ni hon -wo *o*-kak-are-*ninat*-ta.
           nom teacher dat book acc *o*-write-PAS-HON-PST
    c. Kyoko -ga *sensei* -ni hon -wo *o*-kaki-*ninar*-are-ta.
           nom teacher dat book acc *o*-write-HON-PAS-PST
    'Kyoko$_i$ had the teacher write the book to her$_i$ disadvantage.'

The a-sentences are all ungrammatical, suggesting either that a verb stem and the passive morpheme cannot be split, or that the honorific particle cannot be attached to the passive morpheme. The b-sentences show the grammatical pattern when the matrix subject is the trigger of honorification ((77-b) and (79-b)). The same pattern is ungrammatical for SH of the agent phrase ((78-b) and (80-b)), in either direct or indirect passives. The grammaticality of (80-c) indicates that the pattern in the c-sentences is the one available for SH of the agent phrase.[60] As mentioned above, SH of the agent phrase is unavailable for direct passives (78-c). This pattern cannot be used for SH of the matrix subject, as the asterisks of (77-c) and (78-c) indicate.

Notice that when the target is the matrix subject, the honorific morpheme *ninar* appears after the passive morpheme. When the target is the agent phrase, in contrast, the same morpheme appears between the verb stem and the passive morpheme. In other words, the honorific morpheme is directly suffixed to the predicate which subcategorizes for the target NP[+HON]. Note however, direct passives and indirect passives have different syntactic structures. The tree diagrams in (81-a) and (81-b) schematically represent the b-patterns (matrix subject SH) of the direct passive (77-b) and of the indirect passive (79-b), respectively:

(81) a.

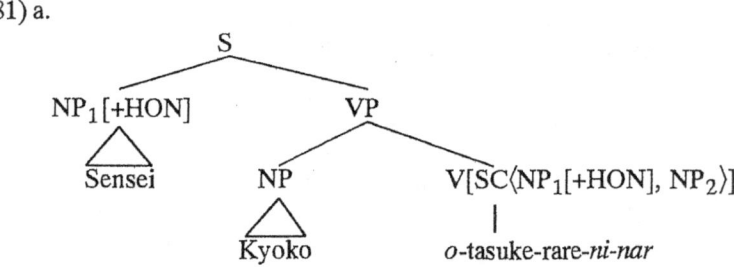

Passive Constructions 125

b.
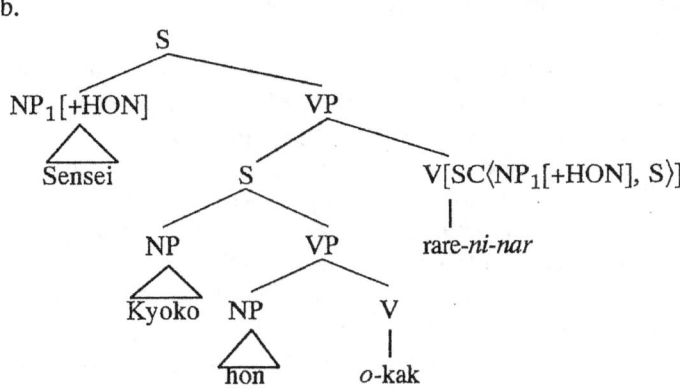

In the case of agent phrase SH, it is clear under our analysis that it is unavailable in direct passives; the agent phrase is not the least oblique argument in any SUBCAT list in the structure. The structure of agent phrase SH of indirect passives is represented in (82) below:

(82)
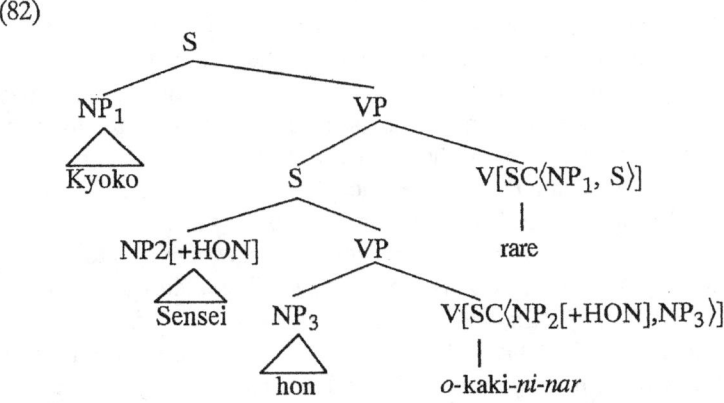

The morphological position of the honorific *ni-nar* is exactly as the present analysis predicts. The position of the other honorific particle *o* seems somewhat irregular, however. If the target verb were to be put directly between the particle *o* and the honorific predicate *ni-nar*, the correct morpheme order of the matrix subject SH in indirect passives should not be as in (79-b) but as in (79-a) instead. As the diagram in (81-b) shows, the honorific particle *o* is detached from the target verb (i.e., the passive morpheme) and has "jumped down" to the stem verb.

We propose that this is due to a morphological requirement. The honorific morpheme *ni-nar* is suffixed to the head verb which subcategorizes for the least oblique argument which is [+HON]. The honorific particle *o*, on the other hand, is prefixed to the smallest morphological unit (word) which contains the honorific morpheme.

In the case in question, the passive morpheme alone cannot be accepted as an independent morphological unit. As mentioned several times above, the indirect passive morpheme is a bound form, though syntactically a word. The attachment of the honorific particle *o* is thus sensitive to the morphological properties of the predicate.[61] In other words, the ungrammaticality of the a-sentences is due not to the splitting up of the verb stem and the passive morpheme but to the position of the honorific particle *o*. Given this proposal, the morpheme order of SH is analyzed as completely regular and predictable.

3.4.3.4 Adversity Interpretation

Thus, our approach is able to provide simple and satisfactory answers to most of the questions regarding the different behaviour of direct and indirect passives. One property distinguishing the two passives which we have not discussed is the obligatory adversity interpretation associated with the indirect passive.

The idea of thematic underspecification by Ritter and Rosen 1990 and the idea that the passives are non-volitional and non-causal have helped us propose why the matrix subject of the indirect passives is Experiencer, but nothing that we have seen so far explains why it must be a "malefactive" Experiencer. This is a rather curious issue, particularly in view of the fact that the bound morpheme *(r)are* itself is not associated with any lexical sense, and that the adversity is absent in the other types of passives. One way to guarantee the adversity interpretation is the practice taken by Kubo 1990, according to which the external θ-role of the indirect passive morpheme *(r)are* is specified as [malefactive] in the lexical entry. We assume instead that the adversity interpretation is not something inherent in the lexical entry of the passives of any type, but is something obtained from the semantic relation between the matrix subject and the event denoted by the verb stem.

Oehrle and Nishio 1981 investigates the source of adversity interpretation of passives by examining Japanese direct/indirect passives and various English constructions which carry adversity meaning. They particularly draw on the observation by Wierzbicka 1979 which correlates the adversity interprepretation with the involvement of the (matrix) subject of passives in the expressed event. They suggest that the adversity interpretation obtains when the subject is not directly involved in the event denoted by the verb stem. The indirect passive situation induces adversity because, according to them, the passive subject is not directly involved in the event denoted by the verb stem. The direct passive allows neutral interpretation because the passive subject is a participant of the expressed event. This semantic solution has been supported by Kuno 1983 and Shibatani 1990. We basically agree with this view and will elaborate it further as we proceed to the possessive passive (section 3.5.2) and to the benefactive constructions (section 4.5.3). We will ultimately argue that the semantic specification of the Affectee as a non-causal participant is essential in defining the relevant concept of involvement to the effect of bringing about the adversity interpretation.

3.4.3.5 Adverbial Scope

Another very curious fact which we believe is related to the above phenomenon concerns the ambiguity of the scope of adverbs. Recall our discussion in section 3.4.1. We have demonstrated that in the Japanese direct passives, as well as in the English passives, certain "agent-oriented" manner adverbs may modify the matrix subject which is supposed to bear the Theme role. Based on the assumption that these adverbs can only modify an Agent, Roberts 1987, for instance, stipulates that the matrix subject receives the Agent θ-role at LF. In other words, the theme argument can receive the agent role by virtue of its being the subject.

Interestingly, such adverbs cannot modify the matrix subject of indirect passives when the adverbs strongly suggest volitionality. They can modify only the agent phrases. Compare the following data with (61)-(63) above:[62]

(83) a. Kyoko -ga *umaku* Syota -ni Naoko -wo
              nom cleverly   dat   acc

damas-are-ta.
cheat-PAS-PST
'Kyoko was adversely affected by Syota's cleverly cheating Naoko.'

b. Kyoko -ga *wazato* Syota -ni Naoko -wo
   nom intentionally dat acc
yuuwakus-are-ta.
seduce-PAS-PST
'Kyoko was adversely affected by Syota's intentionally seducing Naoko.'

A more perplexing fact is that when the adverb does not force a volitional interpretation, e.g., *ukkari* ('carelessly') as opposed to *wazato* ('intentionally, deliberately'), the ambiguity of the adverb scope emerges again:

(84) Kyoko -ga *ukkari* keisatu -ni Syota -wo tukamae-rare-ta.
     nom carelessly police dat acc catch-PAS-PST
'Kyoko was adversely affected by the police's carelessly arresting Syota.'
'Kyoko carelessly had the police arrest Syota on her.'

Exactly the same effect is found with *nagara* 'while' clauses. In contrast to direct passives, indirect passives do not allow the matrix subject to be the controller of the clause. Following examples illustrate this point. Compare them with (65) above:

(85) a. 'Kyoko$_i$ -ga [warai-*nagara*] sensei$_j$ -ni
         nom smile-while teacher dat
      Syota -wo home-rare-ta.
         acc praise-PAS-PST
'(lit.) Kyoko$_i$ was adversely affected by the teacher's$_j$ praising Syota, while he/she$_{j/*?i}$ was smiling.'

b. Kyoko$_i$ -ga [terebi -wo mi-*nagara*]
      nom T.V. acc watch-while

Syota$_j$ -ni gohan -wo tabe-rare-ta.
dat meal acc eat-PAS-PST
'(lit.) Kyoko$_i$ was adversely affected by Syota's$_j$ having a meal, while he/she$_{j/*?i}$ was watching T.V.'

This contrast is surely a problem for the configuration-based solutions of both Zubizarreta 1982, 1987 and Roberts 1987. According to them, being a subject is a sufficient condition to be modified by the manner adverbs in question. If the unavailability of modification were merely due to the non-agentive character of these subjects of passives, there is no way to explain why the subject of the direct passive, which is similarly non-agentive, can be modified by the same adverbs.

These data are problems for our approach as well. However, recall that our analysis is based on the semantic structure, and does not refer to any particular thematic role or grammatical relation. To restate our proposal, the class of manner adverbs in question can modify the thematically highest argument in each semantic content unit, which consists of one Relation attribute and one or more Roles participating in the Relation. We claim that there is another independent semantic condition restricting adverb modification. The matrix subject of indirect passives cannot be modified by the adverbial phrases in question because it does not satisfy this condition.

The condition we propose is closely related to the above-mentioned reason for the obligatory adversity interpretation. Recall that the referent of the matrix subject of indirect passives only experiences some influence from the core event, and is not directly involved in the event. The point is that the core event takes place whether the referent of the matrix subject is involved or not. This contrasts with the cases of direct passives where the referent of the matrix subject is a participant of the core event, as guaranteed by the coreferentiality signaled by coindexing; the core event will not take place without his/her involvement.

We partly follow Zubizarreta 1982, 1987 and assume that the manner adverbs in question add some kind of semantic properties to the designated arguments.[63] Such adverbs as *umaku* ('cleverly') and *wazato* ('intentionally/deliberately') add volitional and possibly causative properties. We propose that for an argument to receive the volitionality and causality specifications, its referent must at least be involved in the realization of the core event. Indirect passives do not display the ambiguity of the adverbial scope when the adverbs force volitional and causative interpretation because the realization of the core event is completely independent of the contribution of the referent of the matrix subject. Direct passives allow both the passive subject and the agent phrase to be modified by the adverbs because their referents are direct participants of the core event.[64]

Now, as we mentioned above, the adverbs which do not the force volitional or causative interpretation (*ukkari* 'carelessly/unawares') induce ambiguous modification in indirect passives as well. This phenomenon can readily be explained if we assume that these non-volitional and non-causative adverbs do not require the modifiee to be directly involved in the expressed event, which is not very surprising considering the meaning of the adverbs.

Thus this line of explanation successfully gives a straightforward account not only of the lack of ambiguity with certain adverbs but also of its presence with certain others. Though the condition that the modifiee must be directly involved in the expressed event may seem *ad hoc* at this moment, we will present more evidence supporting the basic concept of this condition and at the same time try to refine it further in the discussion of possessive passives and benefactives. As is the case with obligatory adversity interpretation, it will turn out that the non-causative specification on the Affectee is essential to the lack of modification by the class of manner adverbs in question.

3.5 Possessive Passives as Lexical Passives

Possessive passives are characterized by a particular semantic link between the matrix subject and a lower object argument.[65] The semantic link is usually described as a possessive relation; i.e., the matrix subject is the possessor of the referent of the lower object. Possessive passives are superficially similar to the indirect passives in having one argument more than the arguments subcategorized for by the stem verb. We have given data in section 3.2.2, however, that show that possessive passives have crucial properties in common with direct passives. Based on the data indicating the similarities with direct passives, both Terada 1990 and Kubo 1990 propose that direct passives and possessive passives share the essential part of the derivation.[66] Particularly, they both involve an NP-movement. They agree also on positing the matrix subject of possessive passives as originating in the Spec position of the object NP (cf. sections 3.3.3 and 3.3.4).

It is unquestionable in the face of the robust syntactic/semantic similarities between direct passives and possessive passives that they are of the same type. We challenge Terada 1990 and Kubo 1990, however, in their assumption that the matrix subject of possessive passives starts out in the Spec of the object NP, or indeed positing NP-movement at all. We propose instead that the essential element of derivation shared by direct passives and possessive passives is that they are both lexically derived.[67] In what follows, we will first present a counterargument to the movement approach, and then introduce the lexical rule for the possessive passive.

3.5.1 Evidence Against NP Movement in Possessive Passives

The NP movement analyses by Kubo 1990 and Terada 1990 entail that argument addition, which is the only similarity between possessive passives and indirect passives, is simply illusory. They hold that the matrix subject is not something *added* on top of the argument structure of the stem verb, but is present in its active counterpart from the beginning, and is *moved* from the NP-Spec position. Since no argument is added, there is no real similarity between possessive passives and indirect passives. Possessive passives given in (19) above, repeated here for the sake of reference, have active counterparts given in (86):

(19) a. Syota   -ga Kyoko -ni ude   -wo or-are-ta.
            nom   dat arm acc break-PAS-PST
     'Syota had his arm broken by Kyoko.'

   b. Syota   -ga Kyoko -ni nikki -wo yom-are-ta.
            nom   dat diary acc read-PAS-PST
     'Syota had his diary read by Kyoko.'

(86) a. Kyoko -ga [[Syota -no ude] -wo] ot-ta.
            nom   gen arm   acc break-PST
     'Kyoko broke Syota's arm.'

   b. Kyoko -ga [[Syota -no nikki] -wo] yon-da.
            nom   gen diary acc read-PST
     'Kyoko read Syota's diary.'

According to Kubo 1990 and Terada 1990, the matrix subject is originally a possessive phrase modifying the object argument. For

Terada 1990, the NP consisting of the possessor and the head N cannot receive Case, as the passive morpheme has absorbed it. The possessive NP moves to the IP-Spec position to receive Case (nominative), while the head N is abstractly incorporated into a stem verb to form a noun-incorporated verb.

We will present two arguments to challenge their positions. First, we will argue that the element which by hypothesis is left in the NP-Spec is not necessarily an NP-trace. The link between the matrix subject and the NP-Spec position of the object, if there is one, does not really justify syntactic movement. Second, it is dubious whether the matrix subject has really started out in the NP-Spec position. [68] Concerning the noun incorporation of Terada, we already have given a criticism (section 3.3.4). As Kubo 1990 points out, this noun incorporation hypothesis suffers from a serious lack of evidence because the "incorporated" noun and the verb can be separated by any number of modifying phrases and even adverbial clauses.

3.5.1.1 Against NP Movement

It is observationally correct that in (19), the subject *Syota* stands in a special semantic relation with the object NPs, *ude/nikki* ('arm/diary'), and that this semantic connection is the key motivation for an analysis based on NP movement, shared by direct passives. Note that when such a semantic relation cannot be established, the construction cannot be interpreted as a possessive passive. It is interpreted as the indirect passive instead.

The argument for movement seems to suggest that when a similar semantic relation is observed between arguments, it should involve movement of the same sort. This claim does not seem to be correct, however. See the following examples:

(87) a. Syota   -ga   ude   -wo   ot-ta.
             nom   arm   acc   break-PST
     'Syota broke his arm.'

   b. Syota   -ga   Kyoko   -ni   nikki   -wo   mise-ta.
             nom   dat   diary   acc   show-PST
     'Syota showed his diary to Kyoko.'

Here exactly the same kind of semantic relation is observed between the subject and the object. That is, in the absence of any explicit specifier, it seems almost obligatory to interpret the objects *arm/diary* as belonging to *Syota*. Though the interpretation is not absolute, the preference for the possessive interpretation is exactly to the same degree as in the case of possessive passives. Intuitively, when the possessor is not specified, chances are that it is associated to the subject. The crucial thing is that it is very unlikely for the sentences in (87) to involve the same kind of NP movement as in the case of direct passives. This strongly suggests that the semantic connection and (almost) obligatory possessive interpretation do not necessarily prove the existence of NP movement.

Another piece of evidence against NP movement comes from the fact that the NP-Spec in question can be filled at surface. Recall the sentence we gave in note 8 above:

(88) Nihonsya   -ga *sono* keizaisei -wo hyookas-are-te-iru.
     Japanese car nom its   economy   acc value-PAS-GER-ASP
     '(lit.) Japanese cars have their low cost appreciated.'

The inanimate matrix subject, lack of adversity interpretation, and the omission of the agent phrase clearly indicate that this sentence is a possessive passive. And yet, notice the italicized determiner phrase *sono* 'the/its' preceding the lower object *keizaisei* 'economy.' This is the position which the movement analyses assume the passive subject *nihonsya* 'Japanese cars' to originate in. To put it differently, we would expect a trace rather than an phonologically overt element in this position. Kubo 1990 in fact argues that the trace left behind here conforms precisely to the binding condition A in the sense of Chomsky 1981.

So what is this overt category? One could argue that this is something like a resumptive pronoun.[69] However, NP-movement involved in passivization does not seem to allow a resumptive pronoun to occur in the place of NP-trace. See the following examples of direct passives. The alleged NP-trace cannot alternate with a resumptive pronoun:

(89) *a. Nihonsya   -ga   Amerikazin -ni   *sore* -wo
        Japanese car nom   Americans   dat   it   acc

hihans-are-te-iru.
criticize-PAS-GER-ASP
'(lit.) Japanese cars have been criticized (them) by the Americans.'

*b. Syota   -ga   Kyoko -ni   *kare* -wo   tatak-are-ta.
           nom   dat   him   acc   hit-PAS-PST
'(lit.) Syota was hit (him) by Kyoko.'

The case of (88) is not exceptional at all. Most of the sentences reported in the literature which ought to be recategorized as possessive passives have the overt category *sono* in them (cf. Kuno 1983, 199, etc.) The presence of the overt category *sono* establishes a semantic link between the passive subject and the lower object, but it does not argue for the involvement of NP movement in possessive passives.[70] We therefore conclude that there is not syntactic motivation for the NP movement in possessive passives.[71]

3.5.1.2 Against an NP-Spec Position

There is also evidence arguing that the semantic relation between the matrix subject and the object in question is not necessarily possessive. The two phrases have to be connected in some relevant sense, but the sense does not seem to be identifiable as possessive. See the following examples showing this point. (Note that the agent phrase is deliberately omitted to distinguish these examples from instances of the indirect passive):

(90) Kyoko -ga   (kawaigat-te-ita kinzyo -no) sono kodomo-tati-
            nom   take-care-of   neighborhood that children
     -wo   koros-are-ta.
     acc   kill-PAS-PST
'Kyoko had the children (in her neighborhood that she was taking care of) killed.'

(91) Bush -ga   Wangan Sensoo -no   koto -wo   hihans-are-ta.
               nom Gulf War   gen   thing acc criticize-PAS-PST
'(lit.) Bush had the Gulf War criticized.'
or 'Bush was criticized concerning the Gulf War.'

(92) Kootyoo -ga   yuusyuu-na   kyoosi -wo   hihans-are-ta.
     principal nom excellent   teacher acc   criticize-PAS-PST
     (lit.) The principal of the school had the excellent teachers criticized.'

The semantic connection between *Kyoko* and *children*, between *Bush* and *Gulf War*, and between *principal* and *teacher* is crucial for the above sentences to be well-formed as possessive passives. But the connection is not exactly possessive. One might still argue that it is some kind of metaphorical extension of the possessive relation. That is perhaps correct; however, the point is not whether it is semantically definable as possessive or not, but whether the matrix subject should be considered as originating from the NP-Spec position with a trace left behind. The NP-Spec analysis does not seem to be right, especially because the matrix subject of (90)-(92) cannot in fact occur in the NP-Spec position:

(93) *a. Kyoko -no sono kodomo-tati   'Kyoko's children'
     *b. Bush -no Wangan Sensoo -no koto   'Bush's Gulf War'
     *c. kootyoo -no kyoosi   'principal's teacher'

(93-a) necessarily means that Kyoko is the mother of the children, and (93-b) has a strong implication that Bush is exclusively responsible for the Gulf War. Crucially, both implications are lacking in the passives in (90)-(91).[72] Things are clearer with (93-c), which is simply impossible. Though the principal and the teacher must work in the same school, their relations do not seem to fit the semantics associated with the structural relation of NP-Spec and Head N[0].

Based on these two pieces of evidence, we conclude that the link between the matrix subject and the lower object phrase, which is essential in distinguishing possessive passives from the indirect passives, is a matter of semantics and is not to be reduced to syntax.

3.5.2 The Lexical Rule for Possessive Passives

We claim that possessive passives are derived through a lexical rule in much the same way as direct passives are. The motivation is straightforward. In the previous section, we demonstrated that the properties distinguishing the direct and the indirect passive can be sufficiently accounted for on the assumption that the former is lexically derived while the latter has a syntactic embedding. The syntactic and semantic properties of direct passives which have been explained in this fashion are exactly the set of syntactic and semantic properties displayed by possessive passives. So we assume that essentially the same account explored for the direct passives, as opposed to indirect passives, immediately extends to possessive passives.

The lexical rule for possessive passives in its essence introduces a new argument and suppresses an argument corresponding to the Agent role of the stem verb. The schematic representation of the lexical rule is given in (94):

(94) Possessive Passive Lexical Rule

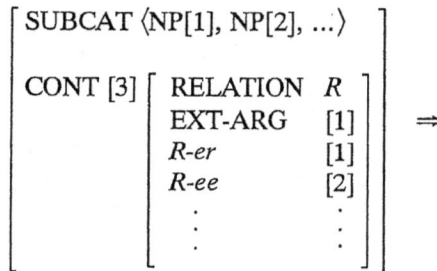

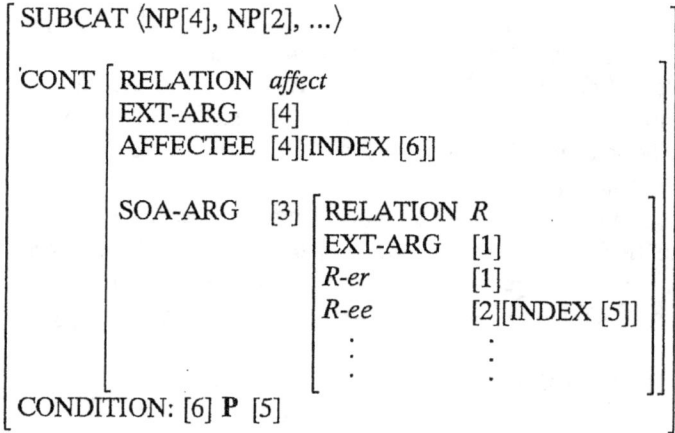

When the stem verb is *mi* ('see') the operation proceeds as shown in (95):

(95) Possessive Passive with the Stem Verb *mi* ('see')

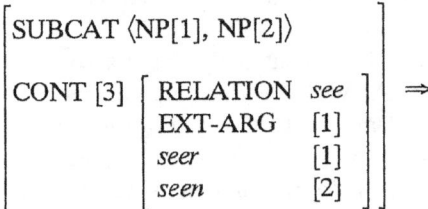

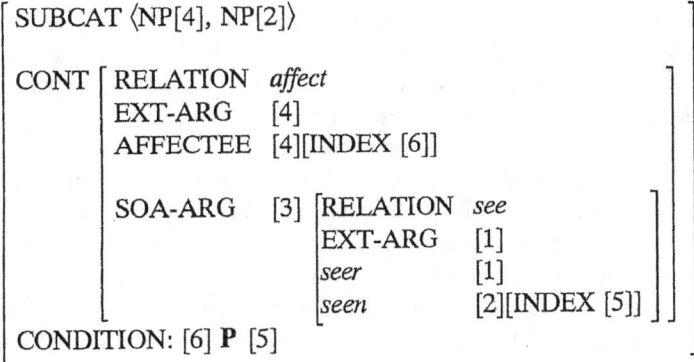

The condition phrase in (94) and (95) means that the referent indexed with [5] is related to the referent indexed with [6] in such a way that for the referent indexed with [5] to undergo the process denoted by the stem verb entails that the referent indexed with [6] gets affected in the relevant sense.[73] Inalienable possession, like body-part relations, is a typical case of this relation. In the sentence in (19) above, for instance, breaking Syota's arm necessarily entails that Syota himself is affected by the action. In the case of (91), the criticism of the Gulf War is understood as challenging President Bush.[74]

It is crucial that the index [5] and [6] are connected with each other. When the semantic condition is not met, the output of this lexical rule is unacceptable; a similar syntactic string will be interpreted instead as an indirect passive sentence, derived by syntactic embedding.

Though the semantic relation is essential, we believe that there is no hard and fast line between what is included by this condition and what is not. As mentioned above, inalienable possession is the most typical relation. However, given the data in (90)-(92), the relation must include even non-possessive ones. There is definitely an aboutness condition involved, and the only clear condition seems to be that if there is a whole-part relation, the matrix subject must be the "whole," and the lower object the "part."

Now, let us consider how the present analysis can accommodate the data of possessive passives. As we have illustrated earlier in section, 3.2.2, possessive passives demonstrate the same properties as direct passives in terms of Do-Support, the case marking alternation, the optionality of the agent phrase, reflexive binding as well as SH.

The data of Do-Support follow directly from the fact that possessive passives are lexically derived in our analysis. As in direct passives, the verb stem and the passive morpheme constitute one syntactic unit; hence the unit cannot be split. This is why the emphatic particle and the supportive $s(u)$ cannot occur between the verb stem and the passive morpheme $(r)are$.

Regarding the rest of the properties, the agent phrase can be marked either by dative case or a postposition, and it can also be deleted altogether. The agent phrase of possessive passives is not able to bind a reflexive nor to trigger SH, in contrast with the matrix subject. In direct passives, the first three properties were accounted for in terms of the suppression of the agent phrase. The last point followed from the fact that the agent phrase is not a syntactic subject in any clausal domain in our analysis. We extend the same account to the cases of possessive passives.

The point concerning SH is straightforward; in the output of the lexical rules (94) and (95), the agent phrase is not a syntactic subject. The suppression of the agent phrase, however, needs explanation. We have claimed in the cases of direct passives that the suppression is a mechanism to make permissible the otherwise illicit coindexing between the matrix subject and the lower non-subject argument, which skips over the lower subject (Ext-Arg). (see section 3.4.1, (69)). As the output of (94) and (95) shows, however, the feature structures of possessive passives do not involve coindexing exactly. To accommodate the data, we further propose that the entailment relation **P** gives rise to an effect similar to the coindexing relation. Recall that in HPSG coindexing means coreferentiality. The relationship **P** is a network of entailments in the sense mentioned above. In the case of, say, (91), referring to the Gulf War is virtually the same as referring to President Bush's political strategy, and, indirectly, to President Bush himself or at least some property belonging to him.[75] So just as the matrix subject and the lower object can be coreferential (=coindexed) only under the suppression of the lower Ext-Arg (agent phrase), only under the suppression of the lower Ext-Arg can they stand in the entailment relationship **P**.

The lack of animacy requirement is explained in the same way as for direct passives. We have interpreted the animacy requirement as a requirement on an Experiencer (Kubo 1990; Terada 1990). Based on the idea of Ritter and Rosen 1990 concerning the semantic role of an "extra argument," we have claimed that the underspecified Affectee role has to be further specified as an Experiencer in indirect passives. The Affectee role of direct passives, on the other hand, need not be specified as an Experiencer because its necessary specification is supplied by the semantic role it bears with respect to the lower soa, or the relation denoted by the verb stem.

Given the definition of the relation **P**, the lack of animacy requirement in possessive passives can be explained in exactly the same way as for direct passives. Notice that the crucial property distinguishing direct passives and indirect passives regarding the Experiencer role is that the referent of the matrix subject of the former is involved in the core event. Note that the relation **P** by definition ensures this property; the referent of the matrix subject is related to the (object) argument in such a way that affecting the latter necessarily affects the former. The referent of the matrix subject can be interpreted as a virtual participant in the core event in this sense. Consider, for instance, a situation where Kyoko hits Syota's head; it is clear that Syota is a participant directly involved in the event. In a situation like (91) above, where Bush had other people criticize the Gulf War, criticizing the Gulf War is functionally equivalent to criticizing Bush himself.[76] So it seems reasonable to assume that the entailment relation **P** leads to the lack of an animacy requirement in possessive passives just as in direct passives.

Note that our claim that the entailment relation **P** makes the referent of the matrix subject be virtually involved in the core event makes a prediction regarding the adversity interpretation. With Oehrle and Nishio 1981, Kuno 1983, and others, we have suggested that the adversity interpretation obtains when the passive subject is not involved in the event denoted by the verb stem. If we are correct in making the above claim, possessive passives will induce neutral interpretation. We have already given examples showing that this is indeed the case (cf. (21)); adversity interpretation is no more than optional in possessive passives, as in direct passives.

Another point of interest is the ambiguity of adverbial modification. We have shown above that direct passives allow the matrix subject to be modified by manner adverbs, or to be the controller of a *nagara* 'while' clause, while indirect passives only allow the agent phrase to be so modified. We have accounted for the failure of matrix subject modification in indirect passives in terms of the concept of the direct involvement in the core event. To recapitulate the point, the modifiee must be directly involved in the core event; the matrix subject of indirect passives cannot be modified by such adverbial phrases because the realization of the core event is completely independent of the contribution of the referent of the matrix subject.

We have claimed that the entailment relation **P** between the passive subject and the lower object, licensed by the semantic connection between them, ensures that the referent of the subject of the possessive passive is a virtual participant of the core event. Our analysis, therefore, predicts that the matrix subject of possessive passives can be modified by the adverbial phrases in question as is possible in direct passives. This prediction is borne out by the following data:

(96) a. Kyoko -ga *umaku* Syota -ni atama -wo
 nom cleverly dat head acc
 nader-are-ta.
 pat-PAS-PST
 'Kyoko cleverly had Syota pat her head.'
 'Kyoko had Syota cleverly pat her head.'

 b. Kyoko -ga *wazato* Syota -ni atama -wo
 nom intentionally dat head acc
 tatak-are-ta.
 hit-PAS-PST
 'Kyoko deliberately had Syota hit her head.'
 'Kyoko had Syota deliberately hit her head.'

 c. Kyoko -ga *ukkari* keisatu -ni ude -wo
 nom carelessly police dat arm acc
 tukamae-rare-ta.
 catch-PAS-PST
 'Kyoko accidentally had the policeman grab her arm.'
 'Kyoko had the policeman accidentally grab her arm.'

(97) a. Kyoko -ga [naki-*nagara*] Syota -ni atama -wo
       nom   cry-while   dat   head   acc
    tatak-are-ta.
    hit-PAS-PST
    '(lit.) Kyoko$_i$ had Syota$_j$ hit her$_i$ head while he/she$_{i/j}$ was crying.'

   b. Kyoko -ga [terebi -wo mi-*nagara*] Syota -ni
       nom   T.V.   acc watch-while   dat
    te   -wo nigir-are-ta.
    hand acc hold-PAS-PST
    '(lit.) Kyoko$_i$ had Syota$_j$ hold her$_i$ hand while he/she$_{i/j}$ was watching T.V.'

Thus, in the above examples, the matrix subject in possessive passives can be modified by manner adverbs or control *nagara* 'while' clauses, just as in direct passives. This lends further support to our claim that the entailment relation **P** renders the referent of the matrix subject of possessive passives a virtual participant of the core event.[77]

There is one more thing about the feature structure of possessive passives worth mentioning. Look at the output feature structures in (94) and (95). The output passive predicate subcategorizes for two syntactic arguments NP[4] and NP[2]. Notice that while these two are syntactically coarguments, semantically they are not. The soa in which the referent of NP[4] plays a role is distinct from the soa in which the referent of NP[2] plays a role. This is not the usual situation for coarguments.

We suggest that this situation has a further implication for the syntactic status of arguments, especially of NP[2]. Notice that although NP[4] and NP[2] are syntactically in subject and object relation, they are not semantically related by the same predicate. Given this, though NP[2] is not a suppressed argument like NP[1], it is conceivable that it will not function as an ordinary object argument.

One prediction that follows is that NP[2] will not be direct-passivized. Suppose the possessive passive predicate were to be direct-passivized, making NP[2] in (94) the subject. As can be seen in the direct passive lexical rule in (53) and the output feature structures in (94) and (95), the direct passive lexical rule (53) will not allow the Affectee role of the direct passive to be coindexed with the role tagged [2]; it is too far down, or too deeply embedded, so to speak, as it is not a semantic argument of the highest relation Affect, and the direct passive rule stipulates that it must be.

This prediction is borne out by the data shown below:

(98) *a. (Kare no) atama -ga Syota -ni Kyoko -ni
     (his) head nom dat dat
    tatak-are-rare-ta.
    hit-PAS-PAS-PST
    '(lit.) His$_i$ head had the situation happen that Syota$_i$ was hit on the head by Kyoko.'

*b. (Kare no) kodomo -ga Syota -ni Kyoko -ni
   (his) child nom dat dat
   home-rare-rare-ta.
   praise-PAS-PAS-PST
   '(lit.) [His$_i$ child]$_j$ had the situation happen that Syota$_i$ had them$_j$ praised by Kyoko.'

Note that if direct-passivization were considered as merely an operation in the SUBCAT list which changes the grammatical relation of arguments, there is no easy way to explain why NP[2] in (94) and (95) cannot be direct-passivized, since it is an object argument. We claim that the unavailability of direct-passivization of possessive passives supports our analysis that the NP in question is not an ordinary object argument in the sense that it does not share the same soa with the subject argument.[78]

Finally, before concluding our analysis of possessive passives, let us compare the feature structures of the direct passive predicates and of the indirect passive predicates proposed above. Though the SUBCAT feature is radically different in each case, the CONTENT feature is essentially identical, except in the manner of coindexing. In other words, because of the information-based architecture of the theory, the three structures share essentially an identical semantic content that appears somewhere in the "tree." They are distinguished from each other by different coindexing among arguments.

3.6 Double Passivization

This section considers what the present analysis predicts about the possibility of double passivization. Double passivization is often marginal partly due to processing difficulty. But there is a definite difference between the indirect-passivization of (any type of) passive and the direct-passivization of (any type of) passive. The former is only odd, and can be processed if elaborated contextual information is given. The latter is totally impossible.

Indirect-passivization is essentially structure-building, and no coindexing is involved. So the present approach predicts that it should be possible to have indirect passives built on a direct passive predicate, a possessive passive predicate, or an indirect passive predicate. This prediction is borne out as the following examples show:

(99) ?a. Sinzi   -ga Syota -ni Kyoko -ni (damatte)
                nom   dat   dat   silently
     tatak-are-rare-ta.
     hit-PAS-PAS-PST
     'Sinzi was adversely affected by Syota's being hit by Kyoko without protesting.'

?b. Sinzi   -ga Syota -ni Kyoko -ni (damatte)
           nom   dat   dat   silently
    atama -wo tatak-are-rare-ta.
    head   acc hit-PAS-PAS-PST
    'Sinzi was adversely affected by Syota's being hit on the head by Kyoko without protesting.'

?c. Sinzi -ga Syota -ni Kyoko -ni deteik-are-rare-ta.
           nom   dat   dat   leave-PAS-PAS-PST
    'Sinzi was adversely affected by Syota's$_i$ having Kyoko leave on him$_i$.'

(99-a) is an instance of indirect-passivization of a direct passive, (99-b) indirect-passivization of a possessive passive, and (99-c) indirect-passivization of an indirect passive. They are fairly acceptable, as predicted in our approach. This situation of indirect-passivization is in a very clear contrast with that of direct-passivization illustrated below:

(100) *a. Nimotu -ga   Syota -ni   Kyoko -ni todoke-rare-rare-ta.
       parcel   nom   dat   dat deliver-PAS-PAS-PST
    '(lit.) The parcel$_i$ had the situation happen that Syota was delivered it$_i$ by Kyoko.'

*b. (Kare no) atama -ga Syota -ni Kyoko -ni
    (his)   head   nom dat   dat
    tatak-are-rare-ta.
    hit-PAS-PAS-PST
    '(lit.) His$_i$ head had the situation happen that Syota$_i$ was hit on the head by Kyoko.'

*c. Syota -ga Kyoko -ni deteik-are-rare-ta.
            nom   dat leave-PAS-PAS-PST
    '(lit.) Syota$_i$ had the situation happen that Kyoko was adversely affected by his$_i$ leaving.'

(100-a) illustrates the case of direct-passivization of a direct passive; (100-b) direct-passivization of a possessive passive, and (100-c) direct-passivization of an indirect passive. All the examples are totally anomalous. The difference in grammaticality between the sentences in (99) and those in (100) is strikingly strong.

Now, (100-b), direct-passivization of a possessive passive is accountable in the above-mentioned way (section 3.5.2); though the NP *nimotu* is subcategorized for by the possessive passive predicate *todoke-rare*, it is not a semantic argument of the highest relation of the passive Affect; hence it is not accessible for the coindexing essential to the direct passive operation. The first case, direct-passivization of direct passives, can be explained in a similar way; the role bearer corresponding to the matrix subject is unaccessable for coindexing. The third case, direct passivization of indirect passives, is due to the subcategorization of the indirect passive morpheme, as we have already discussed in challenging VP-embedding in section 3.3.5. Recall that we have analyzed the indirect passive morpheme as an independent verb in a syntactic sense, which subcategorizes for one NP and a saturated V (=S). This verb fails to undergo the direct passive lexical rule, for it does not have an appropriate NP to become the subject.

Thus our approach readily accommodates the grammaticality contrast in double passivization between direct-passivization and indirect-passivization.[79]

3.7 On Case Distribution

Before closing this chapter, we will briefly discuss case marking in Japanese passives. Passivization has been standardly analyzed in GB

Theory as crucially involving the absorption of Case, as already mentioned earlier. In Japanese as well, the same Case absorption has been assumed to hold in direct passives. Indirect passives have presented a challenge to the "universal" characterization of the passive in that the accusative case surfaces without absorption:[80]

(3) b. Syota -ga Kyoko -ni eiga -wo mi-rare-ta.
nom dat movie acc see-PAS-PST
'Syota was adversely affected by Kyoko's watching a movie.'

In fact, indirect passives are not the only type of passives where the accusative case surfaces. Recall that possessive passives parallel indirect passives as far as the number of the surface arguments and their case marking are concerned:

(19) a. Syota -ga Kyoko -ni ude -wo or-are-ta.
nom dat arm acc break-PAS-PST
'Syota had his arm broken by Kyoko.'

In view of this, Kubo 1990 claims that Japanese passives do not involve Case absorption. Terada 1990, on the other hand, proposes that the accusative case once absorbed in possessive passives is re-assigned to the lower object argument.

If one does not assume the theoretical distinction in GB between Inherent Case and Structural Case, even the direct passives of a ditransitive verb turn out to be exceptional in relation to accusative case absorption:

(2) a. Syota -ga Kyoko -ni hon -wo watasi-ta.
nom dat book acc hand-PST
'Syota handed the book to Kyoko.'

b. Kyoko -ga Syota -ni hon -wo watas-are-ta.
nom dat book acc hand-PAS-PST
'Kyoko was handed the book by Syota.'

c. Hon -ga Syota -niyotte Kyoko -ni watas-are-ta.
book nom by dat hand-PAS-PST
'The book was handed to Kyoko by Syota.'

When the original direct object is passivized, accusative case is apparently absorbed (i.e., (2-c)). But when the original indirect object is passivized, accusative case still marks the original direct object (i.e., (2-b)). In GB style analyses of Japanese passives, such cases of ditransitive verbs are usually considered separate from the other two cases mentioned above. After Marantz 1984, it has been assumed that Japanese is a double object language, where both of the two objects receive Structural Case, one surfacing as accusative and the other as dative. So in the case of direct passives, it is only one of the Structural Cases that is absorbed. When accusative case is absorbed, dative case is still available. When dative case is absorbed, accusative case is still available. One of the main motivations for treating this particular dative case as Structural Case is that it is passivizable (= absorbable) (Miyagawa 1989a; Terada 1990).[81] In the case of possessive and indirect passives such as (3) and (19), repeated in the previous pages, on the other hand, the verbs *mi* 'see' and *or* 'break' do not have two Structural Cases to assign. So the appearance of accusative case cannot be related to the absorption of another Structural Case.

Thus, Terada 1990, for instance, distinguishes three types of dative case appearing in (3), (19), and (2): a Structural dative case on the indirect object in direct passives; an Inherent dative case on the agent phrase of indirect passives; and a dative case on adjuncts, i.e., the agent phrase of direct and possessive passives. As for accusative case, there are three types as well: an accusative case in direct passives, which appears when dative case is absorbed instead; an accusative case in possessive passives, which is once absorbed but is re-percolated; an accusative case in indirect passives, which is never absorbed.

We do not think it is adequate to make such distinctions among dative and accusative case. A very simple account is possible based on the case marking principles presented in the previous chapter. We propose that the lexical rules themselves have to carry case marking information, which is licensed by the Case Marking Schemata proposed in the previous chapter.

Consider first the cases of the ditransitive direct passives illustrated in (2), repeated here again:

(2) a. Syota   -ga   Kyoko -ni   hon   -wo   watasi-ta.
                 nom   dat   book   acc   hand-PST
    'Syota handed the book to Kyoko.'

b. Kyoko -ga   Syota -ni   hon   -wo watas-are-ta.
   nom   dat   book acc hand-PAS-PST
   'Kyoko was handed the book by Syota.'

c. Hon   -ga   Syota -niyotte Kyoko -ni watas-are-ta.
   book   nom   by   dat hand-PAS-PST
   'The book was handed to Kyoko by Syota.'

The SUBCAT list and the grammatical cases of the active verb *watas* ('hand') and those of the passives are given in (101):[82]

(101) a. < NP$_1$[nom], NP$_2$[acc], NP$_3$[dat] >   watas
                | | | 'to hand'
              Syota   hon   Kyoko

      b. < NP$_2$[nom], NP$_3$[dat] >   (NP$_1$[dat])   watas-are
                | | | 'to be handed'
               hon   Kyoko   Syota

      c. < NP$_3$[nom], NP$_2$[acc] >   (NP$_1$[dat])   watas-are
                | | | 'to be handed'
              Kyoko   hon   Syota

Note that the case marking patterns above are very regular. The second argument from the left always retains the case specified in the original active. The demoted subject always bears either the dative or the oblique postposition. The first argument (=subject) alway bears the nominative. In short, the passive lexical rules have the effect of marking the new subject with the nominative, whatever its original case is. At the same time, the demoted subject is marked with the dative. Everything else, i.e., the case marking of the other argument if there is one, is carried over from the original case.

To capture this pattern we propose to include the case marking information in the SUBCAT list of direct passive lexical rules. The relevant part to be implemented is represented below:

(102)   < NP$_1$, ... NP$_2$, ... > $\Rightarrow$

                                    < NP$_2$[nom], ... >

Recall the Case Marking Schemata proposed in the previous chapter:

(103) a. V[Vcase: +AC]:   < NP$_1$, NP$_2$[acc], ... >
 b. V[Vform: FIN]:   < NP$_1$[nom], ... >
 c. Default: Mark a non-case-marked argument with [dat]

Notice that the output of the rule in (102) is licensed by the schemata above.

On the other hand, we have to give an account of how the agent phrase, which is not in the SUBCAT list, can be marked with dative case. To this end, we propose to slightly modify (103-c) as follows: mark non-case-marked syntactic or semantic arguments with [dat].[83] In most cases, semantic and syntactic arguments coincide. The suppressed argument is the only one which lacks syntactic argument status. The basic idea is that all arguments, either syntactic or semantic, are entitled to receive case marking. The suppressed argument directly fits in this category because it is thematically present after all, and dative case, which is default, is the only case available for such an argument.

Note that this modification gives a natural explanation why the agent phrase can be marked either with dative case or with a postposition such as *niyotte* or *kara*. It is generally accepted that grammatical case normally marks syntactic arguments but postpositions mark adjuncts. The agent phrase of Japanese passives has two faces, so to speak. Our approach to case marking explains this duality in the following way: the agent phrase in question can receive dative case by virtue of being present in the semantic CONTENT structure, according to (103-c). It can also be marked with a postposition by virtue of being absent from the syntactic SUBCAT list. Thus we need no more stipulation to accommodate the case/postposition marking alternation of the agent phrase.

The case marking information which is not mentioned in the rule is left unchanged; it is carried over from the information in the input feature structure. The input of the rule does not carry the case specification of arguments, because case is not specified by this rule. It is lexically determined according to the Case Marking Schemata proposed in the previous chapter.

Case marking in the possessive passive is explained in a similar way. The active input to the lexical rule for (19-a) *or* ('break') is given in (104-a). The SUBCAT list for the passive (104-b) introduces a new argument to be the matrix subject. The examples in (19) are repeated for reference's sake:

(19) a. Syota   -ga   Kyoko -ni   ude   -wo   or-are-ta.
               nom   dat   arm   acc   break-PAS-PST
    'Syota had his arm broken by Kyoko.'

(104)
    a.   < NP_1[nom], NP_2[acc] >   or
                | | 'to break'
              Kyoko   ude

    b.   < NP_3[nom], NP_2[acc] > (NP_1[dat])   or-are
            | | | 'to be broken'
           Syota   ude   Kyoko

The case marking pattern is exactly the same as with direct passives. The new subject is marked with nominative, and the demoted subject is marked with dative. The second argument receives accusative case, as is specified in the input feature structure. This pattern is captured in the partial representation of the possessive passive lexical rule, which is to be added.

(105)   < NP_1, NP_2, ... > ⇒

           < NP_3[nom], NP_2, ... >

The case marking information which is not mentioned in the rule is carried over from the information in the input feature structure. Notice that the case marking information on the output of (105) is essentially the same as that of (102). It is licensed by the schemata (103), with another stipulation which blocks the default case assignment on NP_2. The dative case marking and postposition marking on the agent phrase follow exactly the same way as in direct passives; the agent phrase is not in the syntactic SUBCAT list, but is a semantic argument. It can be marked with a postposition because it is not a syntactic argument; it can be marked with dative case, which is default, because it is a semantic argument.

Indirect passives do not involve a lexical rule which could alter case marking. Accusative marking on a direct object of the embedded predicate, if there is any, is maintained. According to the schemata above, the embedded subject (agent phrase) fails to be marked with nominative case, as the embedded S of indirect passives is not a finite clause; hence, it carries dative case by default.

Thus, the case array associated with Japanese passives can be explained in a simple way. Accusative marking in passives, which has posed problems for analyses in GB, is analyzed as carry-over information from the lexical specification. Dative case is a default case. As our approach makes no reference to such a mechanism as Case absorption to account for the surface case pattern of Japanese passives, there is no need for such stipulations as percolating a Case or re-assigning a Case which is once absorbed (Miyagawa 1989a; Terada 1990).

3.8 Conclusion

In this chapter we have proposed a new approach to Japanese passives. We have shown that Japanese passives can be classified into two: lexical passives and syntactic passives. The former are derived through lexical rules, and comprise direct passives and the possessive passives. The latter involve S-embedding, and correspond to the indirect passives. We have shown that the properties separating direct and indirect passives, which have been recurrent problems in analyses of Japanese passives, are best accounted for in terms of the differences between lexical derivation and syntactic embedding.

There are three important implications that the present approach has. The first is concerned with the distinction between the morphological word and the syntactic word. The second concerns the coindexing constraint, which motivates the suppression of the agent phrase in the direct and the possessive passives. Thirdly, based on the information-based architecture of HPSG, we have shown the possibility of capturing the uniformity among the three types of passives, which are radically different from each other in syntactic terms.

3.8.1 Independence and Interdependence of Morphology and Syntax

The data of Do-Support and the morpheme order of SH reveal the syntactic status of the passive predicate. We have defended the idea that the morphological properties of a morpheme may be independent of its syntactic properties. The passive morpheme *(r)are* is a bound form; it cannot stand on its own. When it is used in direct and possessive passives, it functions as a derivational affix. It is attached to the stem verb, and they as a whole constitute one syntactic verb. The passive morpheme in this case triggers a change in the subcategorization of the stem verb, but does not have its own subcategorization frame. When the passive morpheme is used to form indirect passives, by contrast, it syntactically functions as a verb by itself; it has its own subcategorization frame.

The syntactic differences notwithstanding, both types of passive morpheme are equally subject to a certain morphological requirement. For instance, each has to be adjacent to the stem verb;[84] no adverbs or any modifying clauses are allowed to intervene. The honorific particle *o* of SH can be prefixed only to a free form.

At the same time, however, there are certain morphemes which are sensitive not to a morphological boundary but to a syntactic boundary. The emphatic particles *wa, sae, mo* and the supportive *s(u)* ('do'), and honorific morpheme *ni-nar* are examples of such morphemes.

Thus we have proposed to recognize the independence and interdependence of the morphological and syntactic properties of the two types of passive morpheme *(r)are*. To do so provides a very straightforward and principled way of accommodating the data of Do-Support and the morpheme order of SH.

3.8.2 Suppression of an Argument

The analytic problems of reflexive binding and Subject Honorification in passives pertain to the status of the agent phrase. The suppression of the agent phrase, a concept borrowed from Bresnan and Kanerva 1989, Grimshaw 1990, and others, deprives the agentive phrase of full-fledged argument status. Under our proposal, the domains of information crucial to reflexive binding are a predicate's semantic CONTENT and SUBCAT feature. The legitimate binder of a reflexive must be an NP which both bears the highest thematic role (closest to the Proto-Agent role), and shares the parameter value of a "full-fledged" argument.[85] The agent phrases of both direct and possessive passives are disqualified as reflexive binders, as they are suppressed. In the case of SH, the crucial information is encoded in the SUBCAT list. The argument triggering SH must be the least oblique argument in one of the SUBCAT lists. Because of their biclausal nature, only in indirect passives does the agent phrase (= the subject of the stem verb) occupy the least oblique position in the SUBCAT list of a predicate (=the stem verb). Direct passives and possessive passives are, by contrast, monoclausal, and there is no other syntactic subject than the matrix subject.

Another important aspect of our proposal concerning the suppression of the agent phrase is its restrictiveness. We have argued that the suppression interacts with an important condition on the coindexing of arguments. Namely, when the Ext-Arg of a lower predicate is available for coindexing, a non-Ext-Arg argument cannot be coindexed with an argument of a higher predicate. In other words, suppression is interpreted as a means of circumventing the violation of such a condition. Thus argument suppression in direct passives and the lack thereof in indirect passives is explained in terms of the pattern of coindexing. As for argument suppression in the possessive passives, we have proposed that the semantic entailment relation **P** has virtually the same effect as coindexing, and the **P** relation is permissible only under subject suppression. On the way to defending our position, we have explicitly denied the idea defended by some previous studies (Kubo 1990; Terada 1990) that the matrix subject of the possessive passives originates in the specifier position of the lower object.

3.8.3 Uniformity in CONTENT

We have defended throughout this chapter the idea that direct passives and indirect passives are structurally distinct. As mentioned at the outset of this chapter, the discussion of Japanese passives has always revolved around one question: how to reconcile the apparent syntactic differences in the face of apparent morphological uniformity. Not only is the identical morpheme used in both types, but there is a certain semantic commonality between the two that any native speaker would "feel," even though he/she may be unable to spell it out. This contradiction of "same" and "different" has prompted many researchers to propose either identical or distinct syntactic structures. Recent uniformists have attempted to capture the uniformity while, at the same time, deriving distinct syntactic surface structures. For instance, Miyagawa 1989a proposes that the difference is attributable only to the optional "re-assignment" of the once-absorbed accusative case: when this option is taken, indirect passives result; otherwise, direct passives result.[86] Kubo 1990 seeks uniformity in the lexical entry of the passive morpheme *(r)are*. She claims that the bar-level of the verbal category that it subcategorizes for is underspecified. When the bar-level is maximal (VP), the indirect passives result; when it is zero (V^0), direct passives result (see also Hasegawa 1988). Most other recent studies implicitly advocate a non-uniform analysis (Hasegawa 1981a, 1981b; Farmer 1984; Washio 1989-1990; Terada 1990).

Our approach suggests another domain in which to seek uniformity while maintaining syntactic distinctiveness: the semantic CONTENT structure. We have proposed three feature structure matrices for direct passives, possessive passives, and indirect passives. The SUBCAT features occurring in them are different depending on the type of passive. The semantic CONTENT features, on the other hand, are identical in the main. All of the three have a semantically complex (embedding) structure, which is not necessarily reflected in their syntactic structure. The difference in the CONTENT structure is found only in the pattern of coindexing, which leads to other consequences such as the suppression of an argument.

The common CONTENT structures are carried by different linguistic units. The direct passive (43) and the possessive passive (77) rules show the feature structure of the head verb, which is morphologically the combination of the stem verb and the passive morpheme (e.g. *tatak-are*). The feature structure (70) displays the feature structure of the indirect passive morpheme alone (i.e., *(r)are*). Nevertheless, the mechanism of feature-sharing and the Semantic Principle, ensure essentially the same CONTENT feature structure to appear as the semantic CONTENT feature of the whole sentence. Therefore, in our analysis, uniformity is guaranteed in the CONTENT structure carried by all three types of the passive sentences. Note also the uniform CONTENT structure is essential in motivating the coindexing condition mentioned above.

Notes

1. In fact, the passive morpheme is shared by another complex predicate expressing honorifics as well. Though there are some works which attempt to syntactically unify the honorific construction with the passive constructions (Hasegawa 1988; Kubo 1990), such attempts are comparatively small in number. This is presumably due to the lack of semantic/impressionistic commonality between the passives and the honorific structure.

2. Kuroda 1979 proposes a different type of non-uniform analysis of passives, contrasting *ni*-passives with *niyotte*-passives. He elaborates on the semantic difference discussed by Inoue (1976b), between passives which mark their agent phrase with dative case *ni* and those which mark the agent phrase with postposition *niyotte* and argues that the former take a biclausal structure, in which the subject argument is semantically characterized as Affectee, while the latter are monoclausal, and are semantically equivalent to their active counterparts.

3. Even Kuno and Hasegawa discarded their original position as non-uniformists in later works (Kuno 1983; Hasegawa 1988.)

4. The initial consonant /r/ appears only when the verb stem is vowel-final. It is traditionally considered as an instance of deletion, but an alternative view that it is /r/-insertion is suggested by Mester and Itô 1989.

5. Mikami 1953 already discusses this type of passive, but the class has almost been ignored until recently. See, however, Kuroda 1979 and Dubinsky 1989.

6. We examine direct and indirect passives first because (1) a great majority of existing work refer only to these two types of passive, and (2) possessive passives turn out to display the same properties as direct passives.

7. The terminology of direct and indirect passives was first introduced by Howard and Niyekawa-Howard (1976). Kuno 1973 coined the term pure vs. adversity passives. These two types of dichotomy are sometimes takes as notational variants, but precisely speaking, they are not. We follow Howard and Niyekawa-Howard in using the terms direct/indirect for expository purposes. The terms plain and adversity passives are based on the semantic import of passives. We take the view that for the most part the two dichotomies are extensionally

identical, but avoid using the latter terminology, plain vs. adversity, because we do not take adversity as the fundamental criterion of the classification. As will be shown shortly, we take the adversity associated with the indirect passive as a semantic epiphenomenon.

8. In (2-c), the agent phrase has to be marked with postposition *niyotte* instead of dative case *ni*. We take this as an instance of disambiguation. That is, the sentence would otherwise contain two dative-marked arguments in a single clause, and it would cause a processing problem. Note that *ni*-causatives, which we will analyze as biclausal in chapter 5, allow two dative-marked arguments to co-occur in a sentence (see section 5.4.2):

    (i) a. Syota -ga   Kyoko -ni Sinzi -ni aw-ase-ta.
           nom   dat   dat meet-CAS-PST
       'Syota made Kyoko meet Sinzi.'
    b. Syota -ga   Kyoko -ni Sinzi -ni hon -wo watas-ase-ta.
         nom   dat   dat book acc hand-CAS-PST
       'Syota made Kyoko give a book to Sinzi.'

9. The English translations given in examples are only approximate. We use three types of translation without discrimination: (1) ... *on him*, (2) X *had Y do* ... (*to X's disadvantage*), and (3) X *was adversely affected by Y's doing* ... Among these, (3) may be the least misleading in that it is in the passive voice; however, the "adversely affected" implication of indirect passives is often not as serious as the English translation (3) suggests. More natural translation would be: "It happened to X that ..., and X is not happy about it." It should be kept in mind that the Japanese sentence is not in the active voice when translation type (1) is used, and that the Japanese sentence has no causative meaning when translation type (2) is used.

    For a detailed examination of the adversity implication, refer to Oehrle and Nishio 1981.

10. Saito 1982 gives an apparent counterexample, in which an indirect passive sentence carries neutral interpretation:

    (i) Nihonsya   -ga   sono keizaisei -wo hyookas-are-te-iru.
       Japanese car nom its   economy acc value-PAS-GER-ASP
       '(lit.) Japanese cars have their low cost appreciated.'

However, as Dubinsky (1989, chap. 6) points out, this sentence should be considered as an instance of possessive passives, which we will discuss later in this chapter.

Sige-Yuki Kuroda has brought to my attention the following example in which the neutral interpretation cannot be ascribed to a possessive relation (p.c.):

(ii) Taroo -ga kimotiyosasoo-ni ame -ni hur-are-te tatte-ita.
nom appearing-refreshed rain dat fall-PAS-GER stand-ASP
'(lit.) Taroo was standing there refreshed, being rained on.'

The passive VP *ame-ni hur-are-ru* 'have it rain on...' is a celebrated example of an indirect passive, the base verb *hur* '(rain) to fall's being an intransitive verb. Without context, the following sentence almost unambiguously carries adversity interpretation:

(iii) Taroo -ga ame -ni hur-are-ta.
nom rain dat fall-PAS-PST
'It rained on Taroo.'

Yet, the obligatory adversity is clearly lacking in sentence (ii), as indicated by its compatibility with the adverbial phrase *kimotiyosasoo-ni* 'appearing happy, refreshed.' It is a very interesting case and it is not very clear at this moment why this is so; however, we would like at least to point out that there is a very clear and significant difference in the lexical meaning of the passive verb *hur-are* in (ii) and (iii).

Crucially, the neutral interpretation such as in (ii) is possible *only* when the rain literally poured over the referent of the passive subject *Taroo*, while the passive verb *hur-are* in its adversity interpretation has no such restriction. It is used grammatically even when the referent of the passive subject does not in fact experience the rain, so long as it rained and the referent is inconvenienced by the rain; e.g., Taroo had to cancel a picnic because it rained.

Notice that the crucial difference in the two cases is that the verb *hur* is strictly a one-place predicate in the latter, which induces adversity, while in the former, *Taroo* in this instance is a necessary participant in the event. The exact form of a proper analysis of this case is not clear yet, but it seems to give support to the claim that the adversity interpretation is correlated to a lack of involvement in the core event (see sections 3.4.3.4, 3.5.2, and 4.5.3.)

11. An apparent counterexample in the previous note is not a problem since it is understood as a possessive passive. Another possible counterexample is cited in Kuno 1973:

(i) Suutukeesu -ga basu -ni doro -wo kake-rare-ta.
  suitcase nom bus dat mud acc splash-PAS-PST
  '(lit.) (My) suitcases were splashed mud by the bus.'

Kuno 1973 explains that this is possible so long as the subject ('suitcase') has an animate possessor, who experiences the adversity. (see also Dubinsky 1989) However, the following sentence does not seem to convey any adversity toward the possessor. In fact, the interpretation is quite neutral:

(ii) Suutukeesu -ga basu -ni doro -wo kake-rare-te,
  suitcase nom bus dat mud acc splash-PAS-GER
  mitibata -ni sute-rare-te-ita.
  roadside loc leave-PAS-GER-ASP
  '(lit.) A suitcase was left on the roadside, splashed mud by the bus.'

We suggest that this example is actually a direct passive, with the following active counterpart. The inanimate passive subject is originally an indirect object marked with dative case:

(iii) Basu -ga suutukeesu -ni doro -wo kake-ta.
  bus nom suitcase dat mud acc splash-PST
  'The bus splashed mud over the suitcase.'

Furthermore, sentence (i) displays other syntactic properties of direct passives. For instance, the agent phrase *basu-ni* 'by the bus' can be omitted, and the dative case marker *ni* can be replaced by a postposition *niyotte*.

12. Here and throughout, the term "agent phrase" refers to an argument of a passive sentence which is the subject of the corresponding active sentence and/or the subject argument of the verb stem. We do not mean by this term that the phrase in question specifically carries an agentive semantic role. This term should be understood simply as a label.

13. Morphologically speaking, most Japanese "postpositions", which correspond to English prepositions, consist of case markers and a noun or gerundive form of a verb. *Niyotte*, for instance, can be decomposed into the dative case marker *ni* and the gerundive form of a verb *yor* which means 'to depend on. Other examples include *no-ue-ni* 'above,' where *no* is a genitive case marker and *ue* 'upward' is a noun, or *wo-toosite* 'through,' where *wo* is a accusative case marker and

toosite is the gerundive form of a verb *toos* 'let it through.' We treat them syntactically as postpositions.

14. As Sige-Yuki Kuroda has pointed out to me, in direct passives dative case *ni* does not always alternate freely with postposition *niyotte* (p.c.). Inoue 1976b and Kuroda 1979 discuss this issue in detail. Inoue 1976b suggests that *ni* is possible only when (1) the passive subject receives and is able to feel a direct effect of influence from the agent, or when (2) the "agent" phrase is actually instrumental. Kuroda 1979 takes this semantic difference one step further and claims that *ni* and *niyotte* are involved in syntactically different passive constructions. According to him, *ni* passives are biclausal passives and always carry an affective connotation, while *niyotte* passives are monoclausal and are direct counterparts of active sentences.

Admitting the fact that *ni* and *niyotte* are not always interchangeable even in direct passives and that there is a slight semantic difference, we still doubt if passives with *ni* and those with *niyotte* are syntactically distinct. For they do alternate in the great majority of cases (at least according to our judgment), and the semantic difference seems very delicate. So it is not clear to us whether the impossibility of alternation is really systematic or due to some type of lexical idiosyncracy. The possibility of alternation also seems to be subject to individual variation. A satisfactory settlement of this issue would require a research based on an extensive data base, so we leave this issue open.

15. Though this proposition is quite widely accepted (Miyagawa 1989a; Washio 1989-1990; Kubo 1990; Terada 1990), there are exceptional cases. Sige-Yuki Kuroda has brought the following examples to my attention:

(i) a. Hansin -no ˙fan -ga Kyozin -no-koto -wo home-rare-ta.
       gen fan nom   gen-thing acc praise-PAS-PST
   'A fan of Hanshin (a baseball team) was adversely affected by
   having (someone) praise Kyozin (another baseball team)'

 b. Ano kyattyaa -wa maikai   sekando -ni hasir-are-ru.
    that catcher top everytime second loc run-PAS-PRS
   'That pitcher always has (a batter) steal second base.'

 c. Heya -wo kasu -no-wa ii   ga   sawag-are-ru
    room acc rent gen-top good conj be noisy-PAS-PRS

        to   komaru
        COMP   be-troubled

'It's fine to rent a room but I don't want to have (the tenant) get noisy.'

These sentences are clearly indirect passives, but allow the agent phrase to be left understood. We have no explanation for these cases.

16. This point has been accepted very widely in the literature (Howard and Niyekawa-Howard 1976; Hasegawa 1981a; Miyagawa 1989a; Kubo 1990; Terada 1990), but the judgment is not always clear, and there are apparent counterexamples, where the agent phrase of direct passives seems to be able to bind a reflexive phrase. See the following examples suggested by Sige-Yuki Kuroda (p.c.):

(i) a. Syota$_i$ -ga sensei$_j$ -ni zibun$_{?*i/j}$ -no ofisu -ni
       nom   teacher   dat   self   gen   office loc
    yobituke-rare-ta.
    call-PAS-PST

    'Syota was summoned to his office by the teacher'

  b. Kono sitai$_i$ -wa hannin$_j$ -ni zibun$_{?*i/j}$ -no heya -de
     this corpse   top   culprit   dat   self   gen   room loc
     barabara-ni   s-are-ta.
     into-pieces   do-PAS-PST

     'This corpse was dissembled by the murderer in his room.'

In the sentences above, the agent phrase is the preferred binder. This may be related to the lexical meaning of the verb *yobituke* 'summon/call forth,' which has an implication of directionality, and to the fact that a *zibun* binder must be animate and have a will (Kuno 1973). That is, it might be the case that syntactic conditions on *zibun* binding can be overridden by other semantic factors. However, judgment concerning this point tends to be very delicate, and we cannot give definitive judgment ourselves regarding this issue. Here and in what follows we simply follow the traditional judgment.

But notice that our approach can accommodate the data if reflexive binding by the agent phrase of direct passive is proven to be consistently acceptable. We only have to maintain the condition on *zibun* binding given in (57) in chapter 2 as it is, and do away with the revision of the condition given in (75) later in this chapter.

17. Morphologically, the verb preceded by *(g)o* is turned into an infinitive. The particle *(g)o* is normally attached to a noun, and so is the case marker (?) *ni* preceding the verb *naru* '(lit.) to become.' So the infinitival form can probably be considered as the result of nominalization. Suzuki 1989 argues that the process of Subject Honorification is in fact that of nominalization from a syntactic point of view as well. Kubo's (1990) analysis crucially draws on his proposal. We leave this question open, however.

18. There seem to be individual differences regarding the judgment of these data. The judgment is admittedly subtle, but we agree with Kubo 1990 in recognizing the grammicality difference between the types of (13-a) and (13-b). We judge both (14-a) and (14-b) as grammatical, though Kubo 1990 judges (14-a) as ungrammatical. Several Japanese-speaking consultants of ours agreed on this.

19. The gloss of *wa* as 'at least' is borrowed from Kubo 1990. This is in fact one usage of the topic marker wa, and is often referred as as the "contrastive *wa*," a term coined by Kuno 1973.

20. The judgment of this structure is admittedly subtle. We, however, follow Kubo 1990 in recognizing a significant difference of grammaticality. The judgment here is due to Kubo 1990.

21. Dubinsky (1989) does not call them possessive passives, but analyzes them as involving Possessor Ascension preceding the passive operation.

22. Terada 1990 reports that speakers of Standard Japanese tend to find the alternation with *kara* unacceptable. We also find the same tendency among the Standard Japanese speakers.

23. The details of this constraint are not our concern here. It essentially requires two instances of *zibun* sharing the same possible antecedent to be coreferential. Notice that the matrix subject and the embedded object are the same in the direct passive (31); the embedded S in a sense contains the matrix subject NP. The possible antecedent of the reflexive is the matrix subject in the domain of the matrix S. In the domain of the embedded S, on the other hand, one of the possible antecedents is the agent phrase. Further, because of the identity of arguments, the embedded object NP is also considered as a possible antecedent. In other words, the reflexive *zibun* has two possible antecedents in the domain of the embedded S. So the Constraint states that it must be coreferential with the antecedent of *zibun* in the matrix clause; namely, the matrix subject.

In the case of indirect passives, the arguments of the matrix S and those of the embedded S have no identity; hence the Reflexive Coreference Constraint does not apply, allowing ambiguous interpretation of the reflexive.

24. This rule seems to incorporate aspects of Bresnan's lexical theory, which focusses on grammatical function, and the concept of thematic roles. Cf. Hasegawa 1981a, 1981b, Kaplan and Bresnan 1982, Sells 1985.

25. Hasegawa 1981a assumes essentially the same operation involving the lexical entries represented in (34) for *te-moraw* predicates and causative predicates, which we discuss in chapters 4 and 5, respectively.

26. Notice that Hasegawa's (1981a, 1981b) model is notionally very close to the recent analyses of causatives in LFG (Alsina 1991; Alsina and Joshi 1991) (1) in assuming a complex predicate argument structure, (2) in considering the passive (causative) morpheme as a three place predicate, and (3) in linking the upper object θ_0 with the lower subject θ_1.

27. A similar criticism may apply to the analysis of causatives in LFG (Alsina 1991; Alsina and Joshi 1991) and to the argument-structure merger approach to causatives in GB by Rosen 1989 (see section 5.3.4).

28. Interestingly, more recent work of Hasegawa 1988 gives an "extended" uniform analysis of *(r)are* constructions in the framework of GB. This analysis attempts to cover not only two types of pasive but event the honorific construction with the same morpheme *(r)are*.

29. The Extended Projection Principle is first proposed in Chomsky 1981. It requires that a clause always have a subject.

30. NP movement here refers to an NP movement which leaves a trace inside the complement of the head V. Movement from VP-Spec to IP-Spec is not included.

31. Kubo 1990 suggests that the two entries in (37) can be conflated into one with the bar level of the category V underspecified. She maintains, following the suggestions made by Baltin 1989 and Emonds 1990, that only a predicate which subcategorizes for a phrasal category can carry semantic information such as an external θ-role. Therefore, if V^0 is selected, the external θ-role [+malefactive] cannot cooccur, as she formulates other principles such as the VP-internal

subject hypothesis in such a way as to bring about a violation of the Projection Principle.

32. Subcategorization here includes only internal arguments.

33. She assumes the VP-internal subject hypothesis defended by Sportiche 1988 and many others, according to which the VP is considered as the domain where all θ-roles of the head V^0 are discharged at D-structure.

34. On this point, Kubo 1990 draws on Lieber's (1980) analysis of morphological structure. Kubo 1990 assumes that when a sentence is headed by a complex predicate composed of two verbal morphemes, only the external argument of the head morpheme of the head verb can become the matrix subject of the sentence.

35. Of course, the structure of (39) has another possibility of NP movement; namely, the object NP phrase as a whole ([*Syota-no atama(-wo)*]) can move to the matrix subject position. This movement results in a direct passive sentence.

36. The idea that verb incorporation or verb raising with indirect passives happens at PF was first proposed by Hasegawa (1988).

37. Thus, Terada 1990 takes the standard view that PRO cannot be governed (Chomsky 1981). The Government Transparency Corollary states that "a lexical category which has an item incorporated into it governs everything which the incorporated item governed in its original structural position (Baker 1988, 64)."

38. Terada 1990 does not explain why it is specifically malefactive.

39. Semantics is omitted. POS stands for parts of speech. The notation {} indicates that the SUBCAT is an unordered set rather than an ordered list. In JPSG, PP corresponds to NP in English, and they share the same semantic type. The feature [+PAS] means passivizable (i.e., certain transitive verbs cannot be passivized), while PAS- signals that the morpheme itself is not passivized.

40. Interestingly, as we will see in section 5.6.3 below, causatives do allow OH, suggesting that they are of a control structure.

41. For more discussion on double passivization, see section 3.6.

42. Recall that according to the rule by Pollard and Sag (1987) the original subject remains in the SUBCAT list, at the rightmost end, as the most oblique argument. But, as widely observed in the literature, the original subject, realized as a *by*-phrase in English, for instance, shows more properties of adjuncts than syntactic arguments except that

it is thematically related to the predicate (Roberts 1987; Grimshaw 1990). In the feature structures above, the original subject is left out of the SUBCAT list, entailing its lack of properties as a syntactic argument, but is present in the semantic CONTENT feature, entailing its thematic presence. So the original subject is not present in the syntactic SUBCAT list, but it does not mean that it is completely an adjunct. For more discussion on the status of the orginal subject (= the agent phrase), see below in this section.

43. Kuroda (1979) argues that *ni*-passives, which in part overlap with direct passives in our analysis, do not share the meaning of their active counterpart.

44. There are exceptional cases where the passive sentences do not have corresponding active sentences. See Chomsky 1981, Baker 1988, Pollard and Sag 1994, etc.

45. The position of the adverbs makes a difference. If the adverbs are put before the matrix subject, they can modify only the matrix subject. If they are either between the matrix suject and the agent phrase or after the agent phrase, ambiguity obtains (Kitagawa 1986). The proposal that we give here is to be understood as a condition on the potential modifiee. A structural condition, which we do not discuss, will filter out the impossible cases.

46. There are two types of *nagara* clauses, which roughly correspond to two usages of *while*. One is "concessive" and may be glossed as 'although'; the other type is "circumstantial" and may be glossed as 'while' in a temporal sense. These two have very distinct characters, and should not be mixed. We are referring only to the latter type.

47. Dubinsky (1989) gives a different judgment. He argues that the controller of this type of *nagara* clause must be a final 1, and observes that the agent phrase cannot be a controller, marking the sentence with two question marks. We admit slight unnaturalness in the passive sentence, but judge the control relation highly acceptable. The sentence sounds perfect particularly if the *nagara* clause is located after the agent phrase *Kyoko -ni*. The relationship between the location of *nagara* clause and ambiguity is roughly the same as the one with manner adverbs mentioned above. If the clause is placed before the matrix subject, it does not have ambiguity. If it is placed after the agent phrase, however, the agent phrase becomes the preferred modifiee.

48. As mentioned in the previous section, Kuroda (1965a) proposes a uniform transformational analysis, in which both the direct passive and the indirect passive have a biclausal underlying structure.

49. Crucial data to test our approach would be sentences in which the subject argument and the thematically highest argument do not coincide; i.e., psych predicates. In such cases, however, the argument to be modified is apparently a syntactic subject. See the following examples, due to Sige-Yuki Kuroda (p.c.):

(i) a. [Igan   -de sin-da haha -no koto -wo omoidasi
       stomach cancer with die-PST mother gen thing acc remember
       nagara] Tanaka -wa hukutuu   -ni nayamas-are-te-ita.
       while   top stomachache dat trouble-PAS-GER-ASP
   'Tanaka is suffering from a stomachache, while remembering his mother who died from stomach cancer.'

*b. [Igan   -de sin-da haha -no koto -wo omoidasi
      stomach cancer with die-PST mother gen thing acc remember
      nagara] hukutuu   -ga Tanaka -wo nayamasi-te-ita.
      while stomachache nom   acc trouble-GER-ASP
   'A stomachache was troubling Tanaka, while he was remembering his mother who died from stomach cancer.'

According to the Discrete Role Approach, illustrated in the previous chapter, *hukutuu* 'stomachache' is a Theme and *Tanaka* is an Experiencer; hence the latter is thematically higher. Then the ungrammaticality of the (ii) sentence above would be a problem because it indicates that the Experiencer, which is the highest role, cannot control the *nagara* clause, contrary to our proposal.

Notice, however, that this is not a problem in the Proto Role Approach. As we mentioned in connection with subject selection in the pair *fear* vs. *frighten*, the subject of the verb in (ii) is not merely a Theme but has a causal implication. So it is not necessarily lower than the Experiencer in terms of the thematic hierarchy, i.e., closeness to the Proto-Agent role (see section 2.2.3).

50. In this sense, the term *Affectee* is admittedly misleading. Although the term may seem to imply that the argument is affected in some sense by the event denoted by the stem verb (= lower content), the Affectee role does not really entail any physical or psychological change. It simply covers the arguments which do not share Proto-Agent

entailments. We are indebted to Kazuhiko Fukushima for reminding us of this point (p.c.)

51. The significance of this requirement will be further discussed in the next chapter in relation to the benefactive predicates.

52. It is not clear why the patient-role argument can be the subject of a passive sentence when there is still an argument of a higher thematic role, say, goal, in the passivization of a ditransitive verb.

53. It virtually coincides with the argument bearing the most prominent thematic role in Japanese.

54. The last part of the restriction is necessary in some cases of syntactic control structures discussed by Pollard and Sag (1991, 1994). In Pollard and Sag 1991, 1994, the Ext-Arg of an active predicate is the agent subject, while the Ext-Arg of a passive predicate is the derived subject, which is the original patient. They do not, however, discuss how the change of Ext-Arg through passivization can be captured by their original formulation of the passive lexical rule, which makes no change in the semantic content structure.

55. Fukushima (1990) supports Gunji's analysis of VP embedding, at least for indirect passives. He does not mention anything about this problem, however.

56. The schematic feature structure in (70) corresponds to the V marked with **.

57. In other words, in Ritter and Rosen 1990, the role which causes the event and the role which gets some influence from the event are directly spelled out as Causer and Experiencer, respectively. This is so because the extra argument is obviously independent of the arguments of the core event in their analyses. We have had to separate the notion "the one who gets some influence" and "Experiencer" to accommodate the cases where arguments involve complex coreference relations. We do not think this separation is a problem. For terms such as Causer and Experiencer are simply a convenient label covering a certain collection of significant entailments in our approach.

In fact, it is very important to take caution so as not to be misled by the thematic role label Experiencer. Though this label is used for convenience's sake, it does not mean that the matrix subject of indirect passives is thematically identical to, say, the Experiencer subject of a psych predicate. For instance, the Experiencer subject of mental state predicates in Japanese has to coincide with the holder of the point of view of the text (i.e., typically the speaker) (cf. Kuno

1973). But no such restriction is imposed on the matrix subject of indirect passives. There does not exist either the case marking alternation characteristic of Experiencer (psych) predicates.

58. This condition obviously does not hold in languages like Marathi, where the agent can bind the reflexive even in the passives (Joshi 1989).

59. As mentioned above, Kubo (1990) assumes that the matrix subject of direct passives cannot be the trigger of SH. We do not agree with her judgment.

60. Recall that in our terminology "the agent phrase" refers to the subject argument of the verb stem.

61. Recall that, as argued in a previous section, the insertion of adverbs and postpositional phrases is also sensitive to the morphological properties of the predicate, while the insertion of emphatic morphemes and *s(u)* in Do-Support is sensitive to the syntactic properties of the predicate.

62. McCawley (1972) notes this fact as a point of contrast between direct and indirect passives. She does not, however, give sufficient explanation why this is the case. Kitagawa (1986), on the other hand, argues that the ambiguity obtains both with direct passives and with indirect passives. His example of indirect passives, however, turns out to be an example of possessive passives: *Hanako-wa Taroo-ni asi-wo fum-are-ta.* 'Hanako had Taroo step on her foot.' Adverb ambiguities in possessive passives will be discussed in the next section.

63. However, we do not assume that these adverbs actually assign θ-roles to the arguments in the same way as verbs do.

64. Sige-Yuki Kuroda has brought to my attention the following example as a possible counterexample, where the subject of an indirect passive controls a *nagara* clause (p.c.):

(i) Kyoko -ga [naki-*nagara*] ame -ni hur-are-te-iru.
         nom cry-while rain dat fall-PAS-GER-ASP

'It is raining on Kyoko while she is crying.'

Interestingly, this sentence is acceptable only in a context where rain is literally pouring over Kyoko. Namely, the referent of the passive subject is a participant in the core event. This would remind readers of the exceptional behaviour of the same verb in terms of the adversity interpretation (see note 10 above). The above example seems to give strong support to our suggestion that the verb *hur* '(rain) to fall' involved in these exceptional cases is different from the other instance of the phonologically identical verb which always forms an indirect passive. The verb *hur* in the above example is actually a two-place predicate (in some sense, at least), and the passive subject is an obligatory participant.

65. Though we focus only on possessive passives where the matrix subject is linked to the direct object of the verb stem, possessive passives are equally possible involving the similar connection between the matrix subject and the indirect object. The analysis presented here readily covers those cases.

66. Kuroda 1979 also recognizes this type of passive as monoclausal passives, or *niyotte*-passives, analyzing the subject argument as starting out as a genitive phrase.

67. In fact, as we assume a lexical derivation of direct passives, there is not much conceptual point, either, in assuming a syntactic NP-movement or a gapped structure for possessive passives if we would like to capture the commonality between the two types.

68. There is a fundamental problem about assuming an NP movement out of an NP-Spec position for possessive passives, which neither Kubo 1990 nor Terada 1990 addresses. Namely, such an assumption presupposes that the genitive phrase, which is moved to become the subject of a possessive passive sentence, is initially located in an NP-Spec position. However, this presupposition involves one of the most controversial issues in Japanese syntax, and is far from being established at the moment.

It is empirically clear at least that the distribution of a determiner phrase and a genitive phrase in Japanese is distinct from that of their English counterparts (Fukui 1988). In particular, a genitive phrase can cooccur with a determiner-like phrase *sono* or another modifier phrase, and their word order is relatively free: e.g., *Syota-no hosoi sono ude* vs. *sono hosoi Syota-no ude* '(lit.) that Syota's thin arm.' It is very difficult to determine if the genitive phrase *Syota-no* in fact occupies an NP-Spec position or any position which is comparable to an NP-Spec position in languages such as English. The analyses of Kubo 1990 and Terada 1990 are open to criticism in that their assumptions ignore this issue altogether.

Admitting this problem, we tentatively accept Kubo (1990) and Terada's (1990) assumption in the rest of this section for the sake of argument. Our point is to show that their analyses do not hold under their assumption that the genitive phrase occupies an NP-Spec position in Japanese.

69. If Kubo 1990 is correct in stating that the distribution of the NP trace conforms to the binding condition A, then the overt category in question, which overlaps the alleged NP trace in distribution, could be interpreted as an anaphor. However, this would end up entailing that possessive passives do not have to involve NP movement and that their subject position is a θ-position binding the anaphor. So this is not a promising solution to take.

70. The semantic link and the possibility of a resumptive pronoun could remind one of Saito's (1985) analysis of base-generated topics in Japanese. With us, he takes the availability of a resumptive pronoun as a piece of evidence that the topic argument is not moved to the initial position but is generated there. He argues that the topic argument is licensed not by any syntactic relation but by a semantic relation that he calls an "aboutness condition," that is, the topic denotes what the rest of the sentence is about (Saito 1985, 287). The similarity between possessive passives and topic construction is intriguing, particularly because the semantic relation between the matrix subject of possessive passives and the rest of the sentence can roughly be delimited by the aboutness condition. It is obviously wrong to equate possessive passives with topic constructions, however, for the matrix subject of the former is a syntactic subject of the sentence while the base-generated topic is not. The only thing that is truly common to both constructions, therefore, is that they both involve a semantic relation which should not be accounted for in terms of syntactic movement.

71. Note that, as mentioned in a note above, the determiner-like item *sono* does not necessarily occupy a NP-Spec position. Then, the presence of *sono* in possessive passives does not preclude the possibility that the subject phrase of a possessive passive starts out as a genitive phrase in a NP-Spec position. This is certainly possible in view of the fact that *sono* is significantly different from determiners in other languages such as English: i.e., *sono* can occur with a proper noun, cooccur with a genitive phrase, quantifier phrase, and their linear order is almost free. So *sono* could be analyzed not as a determiner occupying the Spec of NP but as a noun modifier (cf. Fukui 1986). Recall, however, that the *sono* phrase can even precede a genitive phrase corresponding to the passive subject: e.g., *Syota-no sono ude* vs. *sono Syota-no ude* '(lit.) that Syota's arm.' In other words, there is not much evidence either that *Syota* in fact occupies the Spec of NP.

This involves a very controversial issue concerning phrase structure of Japanese, and we are not in a position to pursue it. We simply mention the possibility that *sono* may not be occupying an NP-Spec position, and hasten to add that this alternative conception does not lend support to the NP movement analyses, either. For it suggests that a genitive phrase does not occupy the Spec of NP, either, which is inconsistent with the assumptions of Kubo 1990 and Terada 1990.

72. Sige-Yuki Kuroda points out (p.c.) that a genitive phrase in Japanese can have quite a vague relationship with the noun heading the larger NP. Admitting that fact, we still find all the examples in (93) anomalous, while all the sentences in (90)-(92) are perfect. The clear difference in acceptability is left unaccounted for if the passive subjects in (90)-(92) start out in the forms given in (93).

73. To be precise, "the referent indexed with ..." should read "the referent of the expression indexed with ...."

74. Different from coindexing, the entailment relation **P** is context-dependent. So the possessive passive of (92) is licensed in a social context where criticizing a teacher can mean criticizing the quality of a school of which the principal is a representative. For another thing, let us emphasize that the entailment relation depends not on the particular event/action but on the notion of Affect. For instance, in (19-b), reading Syota's diary never entails reading Syota. The entailment relation **P** means that the diary's undergoing the action (reading) entails *affecting* Syota.

75. Note again that the crucial semantic relation is not possessive.

76. Kuno (1983) examines what are now categorized as possessive passives, and gives a similar explanation for the availability of neutral interpretations with them. However, he neither sets up an independent category for them nor takes them as a subtype of direct passives. He classifies them as indirect passives, instead, and simply gives a semantic account of the neutral interpretation.

77. For more discussion on this issue, see section 4.5.3.

78. For more discussion of double passivization, see section 3.6 below.

79. As Sige-Yuki Kuroda has suggested (p.c.), a semantic explanation is also possible to account for the impossibility of direct-passivization of passives. Namely, the passive agent, or the referent of the agent phrase marked with *ni/niyotte*, has to have some degree of instigatorship. The "agent" phrases in (100) are in fact a Goal (100-a), a

Theme (100-b), and an Experiencer (100-c), and do not hold any instigatorship.

80. Miyagawa (1989a) claims that with indirect passives the accusative case is once absorbed and is reassigned.

81. Passivizability is often the only syntactic test distinguishing between Structural Case and Inherent Case in Japanese. As we will argue in the chapters to come as well, however, passivizability does not seem to be an adequate test to define or classify dative case. For instance, Japanese has a small set of transitive verbs which idiosyncratically mark the object not with accusative case but with dative. The dative case, we believe, may well be considered as Inherent Case in this context. However, some such verbs are perfectly passivizable, the subject thus derived appearing in nominative case; this contrasts with the behaviour of quirky case in Dutch, Icelandic, etc., where Inherent case is maintained through passivization (Zaenen and Maling 1984; Belletti and Rizzi 1988; Kempchinsky 1988; Van Valin 1991):

(i) a. Syota -ga   Kyoko -ni   sawat-ta.
        nom   dat   touch-PST
    'Syota touched Kyoko.'
    b. Kyoko -ga   Syota -ni   sawar-are-ta.
        nom   dat   touch-PAS-PST
    'Kyoko was touched by Syota.'
(ii) a. Syota -ga   Kyoko -ni   soodansi-ta.
        nom   dat   consult-PST
    'Syota consulted with Kyoko.'
    b. Kyoko -ga   Syota -ni   soodans-are-ta.
        nom   dat   consult-PAS-PST
    'Kyoko was consulted with by Syota.'

Though many such idiosyncratic dative-marking verbs can be passivized, some of them cannot. Dubinsky (1989, 1990), in Relational Grammar, proposes to classify them into two distinct syntactic classes: one with an initial 2 surfacing as 3, and the other remaining as 3 throughout. Interestingly, such unpassivizable dative-marking verbs include *ni* 'resemble' which cannot be passived in English, either. Dubinsky's (1989, 1990) analysis is very interesting, but we are not sure what really determines the passivizability of individual verbs.

82. NP_1 in parentheses is a syntactic adjunct. It is aligned with syntactic arguments (NP_2, NP_3) in a SUBCAT list in (101) simply for the sake of exposition. More formally, adjuncts are sorted separately from syntactic arguments. The general issue concerning the treatment of adjuncts is beyond the scope of this study, however. Readers are referred to Pollard and Sag (1987, section 5.6; 1994, section 1.9).

83. Here, we define syntactic arguments as those listed in the SUBCAT feature, and semantic arguments as those mentioned in the semantic CONTENT structure. In this case, an overt semantic argument which is not a syntactic one will be an adjunct.

84. In particular, both types of passive morpheme seem to participate in the same phonological process. How the phonological processes involving the passives and the causatives are to be accounted for, however, is not in the scope of the present study.

85. As mentioned several times, particular grammatical functions such as "subject" are irrelevant. See more argument in chapter 5.

86. We have argued above that his device in fact fails to derive indirect passives.

IV
Benefactive Constructions

4.1 Introduction

In the previous chapter we have given analyses of passive constructions. We have argued that (1) direct/possessive passives are monoclausal passives, whereas indirect passives are biclausal passives; and that (2) the passive morpheme *rare* is a bound form and functions as a derivational affix in the direct/possessive passives, but it syntactically functions as an independent verb in the indirect passives. This chapter discusses the structures of the benefactive construction, with the main focus on *te-moraw* benefactives. We will argue that *te-moraw* benefactives syntactically parallel the passives. They fall into three types; among them, the direct/possessive-types are monoclausal, whereas the indirect-type is biclausal. In the monoclausal structure *moraw* is syntactically a derivational affix, and in the biclausal structure it is syntactically a word, just as in the case of passives. Unlike the passive morpheme *(r)are*, however, the benefactive morpheme *moraw* isa free form, though, being an auxiliary, it basically has to be adjacent to the gerundive verb. We will also propose that the benefactive relation defines a MODAL relation, which is independent of the semantic CONTENT relation. A closer examination of other types of benefactive constructions in Japanese supports this claim.

This chapter is organized in the following way. We will start with a sketch of *te-moraw* benefactive constructions. A brief review of previous studies on this construction will then be given. After pointing out differences from the passives, we will present our analysis of the *te-moraw* benefactives. Finally two other types of benefactive construction will be examined to support our approach.

4.2 Syntactic Parallels between Passives and Benefactives

The *te-moraw* benefactive constructions have attracted much less attention than passives and causative constructions in Japanese linguistics (but see Kuroda 1965a, 1965b; Inoue 1976b; Nakau 1973;

McCawley and Momoi 1985; Gunji 1987; Terada 1990). Morphologically speaking, the passives and the causatives appear to constitute a group, to which the benefactives do not belong. That is, passive and causative predicates are formed by a stem verb followed by a bound morpheme *(r)are* and *(s)ase*, respectively. The *te-moraw* benefactive predicates, on the other hand, are composed of a gerundive verb followed by *te* and *moraw*. The first morpheme *te* is arguably a gerundive marker, while the second morpheme is an auxiliary verb corresponding to a lexical verb of the same phonological shape with a meaning 'to receive.'[1]

There are several auxiliary verbs that seem to belong to the same morphological class as *moraw*, i.e., they have a lexical verb counterpart in exactly the same shape, and when they function as an auxiliary verb, they are attached to a gerundive verb. This class will include *age* 'give,' *kure* 'give,' *yar* 'give,' *sasi-age* 'give,' *kudasar* 'give,' *moraw* 'receive,' *itadak* 'receive,' *mi* 'see,' *hosii* 'want' (adjective), *simaw* 'put back,' *ok* 'put down,' *ku* 'come,' *ik* 'go,' etc. The 'give' and 'receive' verbs participate in the benefactive construction, which we discuss later in this chapter. *Mi* is concerned with mood, meaning 'try V-ing,' while *hosii* 'want' forms a desiderative construction which denotes a situation where the matrix subject wants somebody else to do something. The others seem to convey aspectual meaning.

4.2.1 Three Types of *Te-Moraw* Benefactives

Morphological issues aside, syntactic similarities between the passives and the benefactives have been much recognized in the literature (Gunji 1987; Terada 1990). The passives and the benefactives seem to constitute a mirror image of each other; the passives in Japanese frequently convey implication of disadvantageous affectedness on the part of the matrix subject, whereas the *te-moraw* benefactives always carry the opposite implication, i.e., the subject receives benefit. Otherwise, they are almost identical, for example, in terms of the thematic relations among the arguments.

In particular, the *te-moraw* benefactives seem to fit into the three types posited for the passive: direct, possessive, and indirect. The following sentences exemplify the three types of *te-moraw* benefactives. Compare them with the corresponding passive sentences:

(1) a. Syota -ga   Kyoko -ni   homete-morat-ta.
           nom   dat   praise-BEN-PST
   'Syota was praised by Kyoko (for his benefit).'

   b. Syota -ga   Kyoko -ni   home-rare-ta.
           nom   dat   praise-PAS-PST
   'Syota was praised by Kyoko.'

(2) a. Syota -ga   Kyoko -ni   kodomo -wo   homete-morat-ta.
           nom   dat   child   acc   praise-BEN-PST
   'Syota had Kyoko praise his child (for Syota's benefit).'

   b. Syota -ga   Kyoko -ni   kodomo -wo   home-rare-ta.
           nom   dat   child   acc   praise-PAS-PST
   'Syota had Kyoko praise his child.'

(3) a. Syota -ga   Kyoko -ni   deteitte-morat-ta.
           nom   dat   go-out-BEN-PST
   'Syota had Kyoko get out (for his benefit).'

   b. Syota -ga   Kyoko -ni   deteik-are-ta.
           nom   dat   go-out-PAS-PST
   'Syota had Kyoko get out (to his disadvantage).'

The sentences in (1) share an active counterpart with roughly the same meaning (except for the benefactive implication): *Kyoko ga Syota wo home-ta* 'Kyoko praised Syota.' The sentences in (2) both imply that the subject *Syota* has a close relation to the direct object *kodomo* 'child' (e.g. possessive). (2) and (3) show that the valency of the stem/gerundive verb is increased by one both in the passive and in the benefactive. As shown in the glosses, all of these sentence pairs share roughly the same meaning except for the benefactive/adversative implication.

The parallelism between the passives and the benefactives is found not only in terms of the surface arrangement of their arguments. The parallelism is further confirmed by their behavior with respect to reflexive binding, the optionality of the *ni*-phrase, and Subject Honorification.

4.2.1.1 Reflexive Binding

It has been observed that the matrix subject of a passive is always able to bind a non-local reflexive *zibun*, whereas the agent phrase can bind it only in the indirect passive. Exactly the same behavior is observed with benefactives (Gunji 1987; Terada 1990).[2] Thus in (4), the agent phrase *Kyoko-ni* can bind the reflexive only in the indirect benefactive (4-c):

(4) a. Syota$_i$ -ga Kyoko$_j$ -ni zibun$_{i/?*}$ -no ie de
      nom   dat   self   gen house   loc
homete-morat-ta.
praise-BEN-PST
'Syota was praised by Kyoko in his/?*her house (for his benefit).'

  b. Syota$_i$ -ga Kyoko$_j$ -ni kodomo -wo zibun$_{i/*}$ -no ie
      nom   dat   child   acc   self   gen house
de homete-morat-ta.
loc praise-BEN-PST
'Syota had Kyoko praise his child in his/*her own house (for his benefit).'

  c. Syota$_i$ -ga Kyoko$_j$ -ni zibun$_{i/j}$ -no heya kara
      nom   dat   self   gen room   from
deteitte-morat-ta.
go-out-BEN-PST
'Syota had Kyoko get out of his/her own room (for his benefit).'

Thus, in (4-a) and (4-b), the reflexive phrase can only be bound by the matrix subject. In (4-c), on the other hand, the reflexive can be bound either by the matrix subject or by the agent phrase.

4.2.1.2 Suppression of the Agent Phrase

We have seen in the previous chapter that direct passives and possessive passives allow dative case on the agent phrase to be replaced by an agentive postposition *niyotte*. The agent phrase can even be deleted altogether, suggesting that the agent phrase is not a full-fledged argument in the direct/possessive passives. With the indirect passives, neither of these options exists. The *te-moraw* benefactives show exactly the same property. The alternation of *ni* and *niyotte*, and the potential for deletion of the agent phrase exist with the direct/possessive type of benefactives (5) and (6), but are not possible with the indirect benefactive (7):

(5) a. Syota -ga Kyoko -niyotte home-te-morat-ta.
           nom   by   praise-BEN-PST
      'Syota was praised by Kyoko (for his benefit).'

    b. Syota -ga home-te-morat-ta.
           nom praise-BEN-PST
      'Syota was praised (for his benefit).'

(6) a. Syota -ga Kyoko -niyotte kodomo -wo homete-morat-ta.
           nom   by   child   acc praise-BEN-PST
      'Syota had his child praised by Kyoko (for Syota's benefit).'

    b. Syota -ga kodomo -wo home-te-morat-ta.
           nom child   acc   praise-BEN-PST
      'Syota had his child praised (for Syota's benefit).'

(7) *a. Syota -ga Kyoko -niyotte deteitte-morat-ta.
           nom   by   go-out-BEN-PST
      'Syota had Kyoko get out (for his benefit).'

   *b. Syota -ga deteitte-morat-ta.
           nom go-out-BEN-PST
      'Syota had someone go out (for his benefit).'

4.2.1.3 Subject Honorification

Another similarity between passives and benefactives is found regarding Subject Honorification. As illustrated in the previous chapter, one type of Subject Honorification (henceforth, SH) is syntactically derived by putting an infinitival verb between *(g)o* and *ni-naru*. As we have seen in the previous chapter, when passive sentences undergo the SH, not only the matrix subject but also the agent phrase qualifies as trigger of honorification in the indirect passives, though the latter case is not very common (Kuno 1973; Sugioka 1984; Kubo 1990). The direct passives and the possessive passives, however, allow only the matrix subject to trigger SH. The same holds true with the *te-moraw* benefactives. See the following examples where respect is supposed to be directed toward *sensei* 'teacher.' (The morpheme order will be discussed later):

(8) a. *Sensei* -ga Kyoko -ni tasukete-*o*-morai-*ninat*-ta.
teacher nom dat help-*o*-BEN-HON-PST
'The teacher was helped by Kyoko (for the teacher's benefit).'

?*b. Kyoko -ga *sensei* -ni *o*-tasuke-*ninatte*-morat-ta.
nom teacher dat *o*-help-HON-BEN-PST
'Kyoko was helped by the teacher (for Kyoko's benefit).'

(9) a. *Sensei* -ga Kyoko -ni syasin -wo totte-*o*-morai-*ninat*-ta.
teacher nom dat picture acc take-*o*-BEN-HON-PST
'The teacher$_i$ had Kyoko$_j$ take his/her$_i$ picture (for the teacher's benefit).'

?*b. Kyoko -ga *sensei* -ni syasin -wo *o*-tori-*ninatte*-morat-ta.
nom teacher dat picture acc *o*-take-HON-BEN-PST
'Kyoko had the teacher take her (=Kyoko's) picture (for Kyoko's benefit).'

(10) a. *Sensei* -ga Kyoko -ni hon -wo kaite-*o*-morai-*ninat*-ta.
teacher nom dat book acc write-*o*-BEN-HON-PST
'The teacher had Kyoko write the book (for the teacher's benefit).'

b. Kyoko -ga *sensei* -ni hon -wo *o*-kaki-*ninatte*-morat-ta.
nom teacher dat book acc *o*-write-HON-BEN-PST
'Kyoko had the teacher write the book (for Kyoko's benefit).'

To make a legitimate honorific sentence corresponding to the b-sentences of (8)-(9), a lexical substitution has to take place: the honorific verb *itadak* mentioned in the previous section will be used in the place of *moraw* (e.g., *tasukete-itadak*). No syntactic derivation involving *(o) ... ni-nar* is possible.[3] The data concerning SH thus gives another piece of evidence that the benefactive syntactically patterns with the passive and that the agent phrase of the direct-type and possessive-type of passives and benefactives does not really qualify as a subject argument.

4.2.2 Do-Support Phenomena

In the previous chapter, under the title of Do-Support, we have shown that emphatic particles *wa/sae/mo* 'only/even/also' and the supportive light verb *s(u)* 'do' can intervene between the verb stem and the passive morpheme *(r)are* only in the indirect passives. We have explained the data by referring to the syntactic property of the passive morpheme *(r)are*. Under our analysis, the passive morpheme *(r)are* is a derivational affix in direct and possessive passives, whereas it functions as an independent syntactic verb in indirect passives.

We claimed that the insertion of the emphatic particle and the supportive *s(u)* ('do') is sensitive to the unit of a syntactic word. In particular, these items can be inserted only at a syntactic word boundary. In the case of direct passives, there is no syntactic boundary between the verb stem and the passive morpheme. In the case of indirect passives, on the other hand, the stem verb and the passive morpheme are each syntactic words, so the emphatic particle and the supportive *s(u)* ('do') can occur between them as well as after them.

Now, benefactives show a parallel fact regarding Do-Support as well. The insertion of the emphatic particle and the light verb *s(u)* is possible between the gerundive verb and the benefactive morpheme only in indirect benefactives. See the following examples. (11) illustrates the case of direct benefactives, (12) possessive benefactives, and (13) indirect benefactives:[4]

(11) a. Syota -ga   Kyoko -ni   homete-morai-*sae*   *si*-ta.
          nom   dat   praise-BEN-*even*   *do*-PST
   *b. Syota -ga   Kyoko -ni   home-*sae*   *site*-morat-ta.
          nom   dat   praise-*even*   *do*-BEN-PST
   'Syota was even praised by Kyoko (for Syota's benefit.)'

(12) a. Syota -ga   Kyoko -ni   atama   -wo   nadete-morai-*sae*
          nom   dat   head   acc   pat-BEN-*even*
   si-ta.
   do-PST

?*b. Syota -ga Kyoko -ni atama -wo nade-*sae*
nom dat head acc pat-*even*
site-morat-ta.
do-BEN-PST
'Syota had his head even patted by Kyoko (for Syota's benefit.)'

(13) a. Syota -ga Kyoko -ni deteitte-morai-*sae* *si*-ta.
nom dat leave-BEN-*even* *do*-PST
b. Syota -ga Kyoko -ni deteiki-*sae* *site*-morat-ta.
nom dat leave-*even* *do*-BEN-PST
'Syota had Kyoko even leave (for Syota's benefit.)'

Thus, as in the case of passives, an emphatic particle and the light verb *s(u)* can break up the unit of gerundive verb and the benefactive morpheme *moraw* only in the indirect type.

Thus these data clearly show that the benefactive constructions syntactically parallel the passive constructions. In the next section we review Gunji 1987 and Terada 1990 to see how the benefactive constructions have been treated in comparison with the passive constructions.

4.3 Previous Analyses of *Te-Moraw* Benefactives

Gunji 1987 proposes a phrase structure analysis of the *te-moraw* benefactives. His analysis of the *te-moraw* benefactives exactly parallels that of the passives. Thus, he posits two types of *te-moraw* morphemes;[5] the *te-moraw* for the direct benefactives is subcategorized for a TVP, while the one for the indirect benefactives is subcategorized for a VP, parallel to the passive morphemes:

(14)
1. temoraw: {POS V: SIBCAT {PP[SUBJ], PP[OBJ;ni], TVP}, PAS -}
2. temoraw: {POS V: SIBCAT {PP[SUBJ], PP[OBJ;ni], VP}, PAS -}

In Gunji's (1987) model, both the passives and the benefactives have an object control structure. The distinction between the direct-type and the indirect-type is made in terms of the distinction between the TVP embedding and the VP embedding.6

The same criticism we have raised in relation to Gunji's (1987) analysis of passives directly applies to his analysis of benefactives. Namely, it is impossible, without stipulation, to account for the syntactic differences between the direct type and the indirect type. Particularly, there seems to be no way to explain why the agent phrase (dative PP) of direct passives/benefactives lacks some properties shown by the agent phrase of indirect passives/benefactives, as mentioned in section 4.2.1.

Furthermore, the data of Object Honorification (OH) again challenge the idea of positing the agent phrase as an object argument of the matrix benefactive verb. The situation is the same in passives and in *te-moraw* benefactives. The agent phrase of *te-moraw* of either type cannot trigger OH. See the data in (15) and compare them with (51) in the previous chapter:7

(15) *a. Kyoko -ga   *sensei* -ni   homete-*o*-morai-*si*-ta.
              nom   teacher dat   praise-*o*-BEN-HON-PST
      'Kyoko$_i$ was praised by the teacher for her$_i$ benefit (honorific).'

   *b. Kyoko -ga   *sensei* -ni   o-sake   -wo
              nom   teacher dat   rice wine acc
       nonde-*o*-morai-*si*-ta.
       drink-*o*-BEN-HON-PST
       'Kyoko$_i$ had the teacher drink *sake* for her$_i$ benefit (honorific).'

Thus it does not seem to be correct to assume the dative-marked agent phrase as an argument of the matrix clause.

Terada 1990, on the other hand, presents a verb incorporation analysis of the *te-moraw* benefactives. She recognizes the parallelism between the passives and benefactives, but she does not really provide parallel structures for the passives and the benefactives. Crucially, she does not postulate the same type of NP movement for the direct benefactives as for the direct passives.

The main reason for her not assuming a passive-type NP movement in the benefactives comes from an observation concerning θ-roles. In a standard analysis of GB, NP movement to the subject position in passivization is supported by an assumption that the subject position is a θ'-position. The subject argument of the passives bears the θ-role assigned in its original object position. The direct passive in Japanese has been assumed to accord with these assumptions. The matrix subject of the indirect passives, on the other hand, is assumed to have an independent θ-role, termed variously as Experiencer, Malefactive, etc. The subject position of the indirect passives has, therefore, been assumed to be a θ-position, and no independently θ-marked argument is allowed to move into that position.[8]

Now, Terada 1990 observes that the matrix subject of the *te-moraw* benefactives always carries a Beneficiary θ-role, whether in the direct benefactives or in the indirect benefactives. This suggests that the subject of the *te-moraw* benefactives is a θ-position in either type. This situation contrasts with the direct passives, where the subject position is allegedly a θ'-position.

Another aspect of Terada's (1990) analysis which contrasts with her treatment of passives concerns the morphological constituency of the benefactive predicates. She argues that the *te* in the benefactive predicates is not the conjunction 'and,' but is an inflectional morpheme occupying Infl (or C).[9] According to her, the verb incorporation in either type of benefactive takes place in two steps: first, the verb stem is raised and incorporated into the Infl (*te*) between D- and S-structure; then, the verb stem and *te* as a unit moves to incorporate into the benefactive verb *moraw* at PF.

The *te-moraw* benefactive predicate of the direct type, therefore, selects a Beneficiary and subcategorizes for a Theme (sentential complement). This sentential complement, at D-structure, has an empty subject position, adjunct PP, and the direct object position occupied by PRO. See the D-structure of the direct benefactives illustrated below:

(16) Syota ga Kyoko ni homete-morat-ta.
'Syota was praised by Kyoko (for his benefit).'

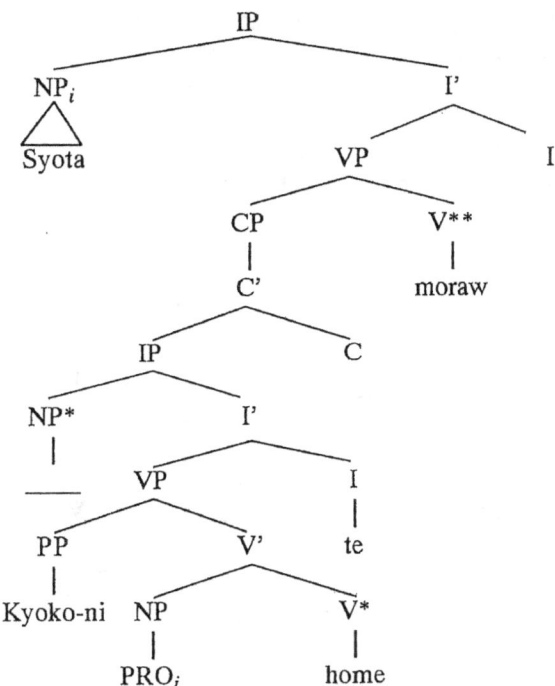

The subject position of the complement (NP*) is empty because the *te* that appears in this sentential complement is assumed to select a non-thematic subject. The adjunctive PP corresponds to the agent phrase. The PRO in the direct object position is controlled by the matrix subject.

The Infl *te* absorbs the Case of the stem verb under V affixation. Case absorption is optional, but is necessary in the direct type of *te-moraw* benefactives, because, otherwise, Case would be assigned to the object position. The PRO in the object position must move to the NP* position so as not to be governed by the V marked with *. As the final step of the verb incorporation does not take place until PF, under Terada's (1990) assumption, PRO in the NP* position manages to avoid government by the V marked with **.

The *te-moraw* benefactive of the indirect type, on the other hand, has essentially the same structure as the indirect passive. The benefactive predicate of this type selects Beneficiary, Source and Theme (sentential complement). The subject of the sentential complement is a PRO, which is controlled by the matrix object NP. The following diagram shows the D-structure for this type:

(17) Syota-ga Kyoko-ni ringo-wo muite-morat-ta.
      'Syota had Kyoko peel an apple.'

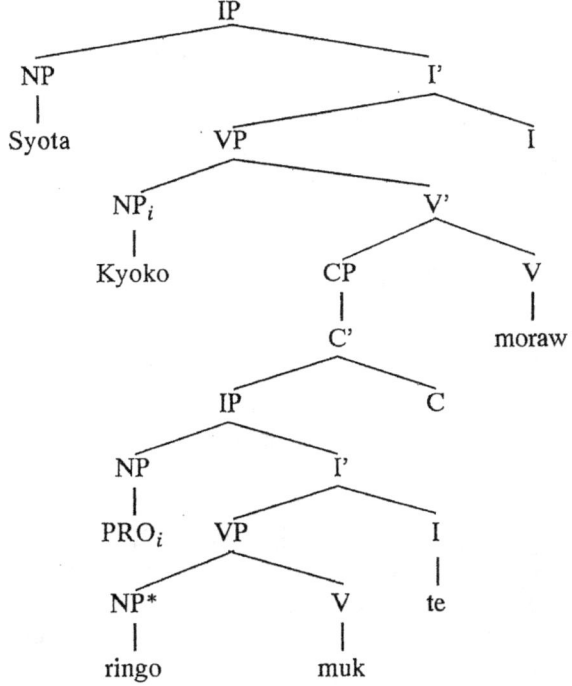

The Infl *te* of this type selects a thematic subject, which is realized as PRO. It is also stipulated that the Infl *te* does not absorb Case in this case, because, otherwise, the NP marked with * in (16) would fail to receive any Case. The final step of the verb incorporation which does not take place until PF guarantees that the PRO is ungoverned at S-structure.

Thus, in spite of the data showing syntactic parallelism between the passives and the *te-moraw* benefactives, Terada 1990 posits an identical structure only for the indirect type of passives and benefactives. The direct benefactives do not involve the NP movement characteristic of the direct passives, though Case absorption is crucial in both. One of the problems we see in her approach is the postulation of Infl *te* as a θ-role selector. As we mentioned above, we believe that *te* is an inflectional morpheme forming a gerund and nothing more. Another problem with her approach is the postulation of PRO in the direct object position of the lower verb. To avoid government, the movement of the PRO and the movement of the verb require an intricate ordering relation, together with a specification of the levels at which each principle applies. As we will show in the chapter on causatives, the intricate level ordering of Terada's (1990) analysis simply fails in the interaction with causatives.

This section has presented two of the previous analyses of *te-moraw* benefactives. Gunji's (1987) phrase structure analysis fails to account for why the agent phrase of direct benefactives does not share syntactic properties with that of indirect benefactives, and why OH is unavailable in benefactives. Terada 1990, excepting the involvement of Case absorption in each, posits different structures for direct passives and direct benefactives though they demonstrate robust syntactic similarities according to the relevant tests. Terada 1990 proposes an intricate level ordering of the verb incorporation operations, which is to be shown untenable in the next chapter.

Besides these empirical problems in the mechanism of accounting for the data, we find a more fundamental problem in both of the analyses. Namely, they do not offer any insight in capturing the overall system of benefactive complex predicates in Japanese. Japanese is known to have three types of benefactive complex predicate, *te-yar*, *te-kure*, and *te-moraw*, based on the set of verbs of giving and receiving. It is fairly clear that *te-moraw* constructions alone are similar to passive constructions, while *te-kure* and *te-yar* constructions are not. Thus it is a very curious question how such differences are brought about and how *te-moraw* benefactives can be related to the other two types, *te-yar*/*te-kure* benefactives. Neither Gunji's (1987) nor Terada's (1990) system sheds any light on this issue.

In the next section we will present our analyses of *te-moraw* benefactives. They are basically the same as the analyses of passives. After presenting the preliminary version, we will examine the differences between passives and benefactives to revise the preliminary feature structures. At the end of the chapter the overall system of benefactive constructions in Japanese will be brought to light.

4.4 Analysis of *Te-Moraw* Benefactives Paralleling Passives

Based on the data suggesting the syntactic parallelism between the passives and the *te-moraw* benefactives, we propose that they in fact share essentially the same derivation and the same syntactic structures. We propose, in particular, that the direct/possessive types of the *te-moraw* benefactives are lexically derived, while the indirect benefactives are syntactically constructed with an S-complement. The problem of the beneficiary role of the matrix subject in benefactives, which has motivated Terada 1990 to assume distinct structures for the direct passives and benefactives, will be accounted for from a different perspective. The lexical rule (18) derives a direct benefactive predicate:

(18) Direct *Te-Moraw* Benefactive Lexical Rule (preliminary)

$$\begin{bmatrix} \text{SUBCAT} \langle \text{NP}[1], \ldots \text{NP}[2], \ldots \rangle \\ \text{CONT [3]} \begin{bmatrix} \text{RELATION} & R \\ \text{EXT-ARG} & [1] \\ \textit{R-er} & [1] \\ \textit{R-ee} & [2] \\ \vdots & \vdots \end{bmatrix} \end{bmatrix} \Rightarrow$$

$$\begin{bmatrix} \text{SUBCAT} \langle \text{NP}[2], \ldots \rangle \\ \text{CONT} \begin{bmatrix} \text{RELATION} & \textit{benefit} \\ \text{EXT-ARG} & [4] \\ \text{BENEFICIARY} & [4] \text{ [INDEX[5]]} \\ \\ \text{SOA-ARG} & [3] \begin{bmatrix} \text{RELATION} & R \\ \text{EXT-ARG} & [1] \\ \textit{R-er} & [1] \\ \textit{R-ee} & [2] \text{[INDEX[5]]} \\ \vdots & \vdots \end{bmatrix} \end{bmatrix} \end{bmatrix}$$

The following shows the application of the rule in the case of (1-a) above, where the input verb is *home* ('praise'):

(19) Direct Benefactive *homete-moraw*

$$\begin{bmatrix} \text{PHON} \mid home \\ \text{SYNSEM} \mid \ldots \begin{bmatrix} \text{SUBCAT} \langle \text{NP}[1], \text{NP}[2] \rangle \\ \text{CONT} [3] \begin{bmatrix} \text{RELATION} & praise \\ \text{EXT-ARG} & [1] \\ praiser & [1] \\ praisee & [2] \end{bmatrix} \end{bmatrix} \end{bmatrix} \Rightarrow$$

$$\begin{bmatrix} \text{PHON} \mid homete\text{-}moraw \\ \text{SYNSEM} \mid \ldots \begin{bmatrix} \text{SUBCAT} \langle \text{NP}[2] \rangle \\ \text{CONT} \begin{bmatrix} \text{RELATION} & benefit \\ \text{EXT-ARG} & [4] \\ \text{BENEFICIARY} & [4][\text{INDEX}[5]] \\ \text{SOA-ARG}[3] \begin{bmatrix} \text{RELATION} \; praise \\ \text{EXT-ARG} & [1] \\ praiser & [1] \\ praisee & [2][\text{INDEX}[5]] \end{bmatrix} \end{bmatrix} \end{bmatrix} \end{bmatrix}$$

Note that through the operation of this rule, the original subject is dropped from the SUBCAT list. This demotion reflects the suppression of the Ext-Arg of the lower soa, following the coindexing condition laid out in the previous chapter. The benefactive morpheme *moraw* of this type functions as a derivational affix, forming one syntactic word with the gerundive verb. Thus, the *te-moraw* benefactives of this type are monoclausal.

The *te-moraw* benefactives of the possessive type undergo a lexical rule as given in (20):

(20) Possessive *Te-Moraw* Benefactive Lexical Rule (preliminary)

$$\begin{bmatrix} \text{SUBCAT} \langle \text{NP}[1],... \text{NP}[2],...\rangle \\ \text{CONT [3]} \begin{bmatrix} \text{RELATION} & R \\ \text{EXT-ARG} & [1] \\ R\text{-er} & [1] \\ R\text{-ee} & [2] \\ \vdots & \vdots \end{bmatrix} \end{bmatrix} \Rightarrow$$

$$\begin{bmatrix} \text{SUBCAT} \langle \text{NP}[4], \text{NP}[2],...\rangle \\ \text{CONT} \begin{bmatrix} \text{RELATION} & \textit{benefit} \\ \text{EXT-ARG} & [4] \\ \text{BENEFICIARY} & [4][\text{INDEX}[6]] \\ \text{SOA-ARG} & [3] \begin{bmatrix} \text{RELATION} & R \\ \text{EXT-ARG} & [1] \\ R\text{-er} & [1] \\ R\text{-ee} & [2][\text{INDEX}[5]] \\ \vdots & \vdots \end{bmatrix} \end{bmatrix} \\ \text{CONDITION: [6] } \mathbf{P} \text{ [5]} \end{bmatrix}$$

When the input verb is *home* ('praise') as in (1-b) above, the operation proceeds as shown in (21):

(21) Possessive benefactive *homete-moraw*

$$\begin{bmatrix} \text{PHON} | \textit{home} \\ \text{SYNSEM} | ... \begin{bmatrix} \text{SUBCAT} \langle \text{NP}[1], \text{NP}[2]\rangle \\ \text{CONT [3]} \begin{bmatrix} \text{RELATION } \textit{praise} \\ \text{EXT-ARG} & [1] \\ \textit{praiser} & [1] \\ \textit{praisee} & [2] \end{bmatrix} \end{bmatrix} \end{bmatrix} \Rightarrow$$

Benefactive Constructions

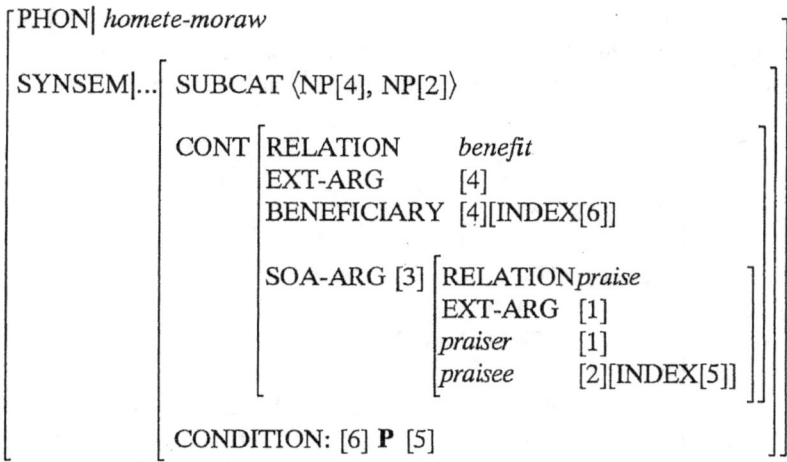

The suppression of the lower Ext Arg and the demotion of the original subject is guaranteed by the semantic relation between the output matrix subject and the lower object (see section 3.5.2). As this is also a lexical rule, the benefactive morpheme *moraw* in this type is a derivational affix

The *te-moraw* benefactives of the indirect type, on the other hand, do not undergo any lexical rule. The indirect benefactive morpheme *moraw* functions as a syntactic verb on its own, subcategorizing for one NP and an S-complement. The feature structure in (22) illustrates the feature structure of the indirect benefactive morpheme *moraw*:

(22) Indirect Benefactive Morpheme *Moraw* (preliminary)

$$\begin{bmatrix} \text{PHON} | \ moraw \\ \text{SYNSEM}|... \begin{bmatrix} \text{SUBCAT} \ \langle \text{NP[4]}, \text{V[SC} \ \langle \ \rangle, \text{Vform:ger]:[3]} \rangle \\ \text{CONT} \begin{bmatrix} \text{RELATION} & benefit \\ \text{EXT-ARG} & [4] \\ \text{BENEFICIARY} & [4] \\ \text{SOA-ARG} & [3] \end{bmatrix} \end{bmatrix} \end{bmatrix}$$

As in the case of passives, the information about the embedded S ([3]) is supplied from the gerundive verb. For instance, the sentence in (2-a) as a whole has the feature structure given in (23)

(23)

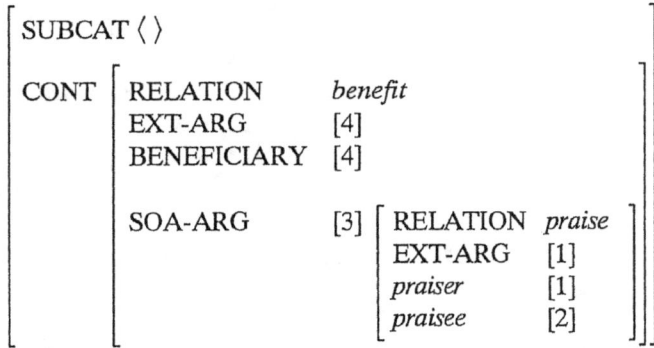

This type of *te-moraw* benefactive does not involve the coindexing relation between arguments of the higher soa and those of the lower soa. No argument suppression is motivated, and no argument suppression actually takes place.

The observed contrast between the direct/possessive benefactives and the indirect benefactives is accounted for in exactly the same way as the corresponding contrast in the passives. The case marker alternation and the omissibility of the agent phrase of the direct/possessive benefactives reflect the syntactic suppression of the agent phrase. The SH facts show directly that the indirect benefactives are biclausal, with two syntactic subjects. The direct/possessive benefactives do not allow the agentive phrase to trigger SH because the agent phrase is not a syntactic subject in these types. The contrast in reflexive binding also follows from the fact that the agent phrase in the direct/possessive benefactives is syntactically suppressed, hence does not qualify as a reflexive binder.

The difference between the passives and the benefactives is encoded only in the semantic specification of the higher relation and the semantic role of the matrix subject. Benefactives involve a relation Benefit, and the matrix subject bears a role Beneficiary, while passives involve a relation Affect, and the matrix subject bears a role Affectee.

These lexical rules and feature structures adequately explain the syntactic similarities between the passives and the *te-moraw* benefactives which have been observed in the literature. However, there are several points of contrast between the passives and the *te-moraw* benefactives which our analyses fail to express. The next section illustrates such contrastive properties. We will demonstrate that, with slight revision in the feature structures of the benefactives, the essential syntactic parallelism between the passives and the *te-moraw* benefactives can be maintained.

4.5 Evidence against the Parallelism

In spite of the similarities illustrated above, the passives and the benefactives are not in fact exact parallels. Differences are found in morphological structure and in the semantic properties of the matrix subject. The two constructions show different morpheme orders when the honorific morphology *o ... ninar* is inserted. Semantic properties of the matrix subject also present a curious difference between the passives and the benefactives. As mentioned above, the matrix subject of the benefactives always carries the beneficiary interpretation and therefore has to be animate in all types of benefactives. This contrasts with the case of passives, where the obligatory malefactive interpretation and the animacy requirement obtain only in the indirect passives. Further, the benefactives optionally take a causative interpretation, which is totally unavailable with the passives. This section will first illustrate the problem of morpheme order, and then discuss the question of the semantic properties of the matrix subject.

4.5.1 Morpheme Order in Subject Honorification

The SH structures for the passives were discussed in the previous chapter. We found that the morphological order varies depending on the trigger of the SH and on the morphological/syntactic status of the passive morpheme. To recapitulate the point, when the matrix subject is the trigger, the stem verb and the passive morpheme in infinitive form occur between the honorific particle *o* and the honorific morpheme *ni-nar*, in either type of passive. Indirect passives in addition allow the agentive phrase to trigger SH, and in this case only the lower verb occurs between the honorific particle *o* and *ni-nar*, and the passive morpheme follows.

As shown in (8)-(10) above, the morpheme order of SH in the case of the benefactives is different from that of the passives when the trigger is the matrix subject (Sugioka 1984). In both the direct/possessive and the indirect benefactives, only the benefactive morpheme occurs between the honorific particle *o* and the honorific morpheme *ni-nar*. The stem/gerundive verb occurs preceding the honorific particle *o*.

See the examples given below. For the sake of simplicity, only the direct-type and the indirect-type are compared; The possessive-type shows the same pattern as the direct-type. (24)-(25) illustrate the direct passives, and (26)-(27) the direct benefactives. (28)-(29) are the indirect passives, and (30)-(31) the indirect benefactives. The trigger of the SH is italicized. Observe, in particular, that the passives and the benefactives show different morpheme order in the case of the SH of the matrix subject. To be more precise, V-*o*-BEN-HON is the order for both the direct and the indirect benefactives, and *o*-V-PAS-HON is the order for both the direct and the indirect passives.

(24) *a. *Sensei* -ga   Kyoko -ni tasuke-*o*-rare-*ninat*-ta.
         teacher nom   dat help-*o*-PAS-HON-PST
     b. *Sensei* -ga   Kyoko -ni *o*-tasuke-rare-*ninat*-ta.
         teacher nom   dat *o*-help-PAS-HON-PST
    *c. *Sensei* -ga   Kyoko -ni *o*-tasuke-*ninar*-are-ta.
         teacher nom   dat *o*-help-HON-PAS-PST
        'The teacher was helped by Kyoko.'

(25) *a. Kyoko -ga   *sensei* -ni tasuke-*o*-rare-*ninat*-ta.
              nom   teacher   dat help-*o*-PAS-HON-PST
    *b. Kyoko -ga   *sensei* -ni *o*-tasuke-rare-*ninat*-ta.
              nom   teacher   dat *o*-help-PAS-HON-PST
   ?*c. Kyoko -ga   *sensei* -ni *o*-tasuke-*ninar*-are-ta.
              nom   teacher   dat *o*-help-HON-PAS-PST
        'Kyoko was helped by the teacher.'

(26) a. *Sensei* -ga   Kyoko -ni tasukete-*o*-morai-*ninat*-ta.
          teacher nom   dat help-*o*-BEN-HON-PST
    *b. *Sensei* -ga   Kyoko -ni *o*-tasukete-morai-*ninat*-ta.
          teacher nom   dat *o*-help-BEN-HON-PST

*c. *Sensei* -ga Kyoko -ni o-tasuke-*ninatte*-morat-ta.
   teacher nom   dat o-help-HON-BEN-PST
   'The teacher was helped by Kyoko (for the teacher's benefit.)'

(27) *a. Kyoko -ga *sensei* -ni tasukete-o-morai-*ninat*-ta.
             nom teacher   dat help-o-BEN-HON-PST
   *b. Kyoko -ga *sensei* -ni o-tasukete-morai-*ninat*-ta.
             nom teacher   dat o-help-BEN-HON-PST
   ?*c. Kyoko -ga *sensei* -ni o-tasuke-*ninatte*-morat-ta.
             nom teacher   dat o-help-HON-BEN-PST
   'Kyoko was helped by the teacher (for Kyoko's benefit.)'

(28) *a. *Sensei* -ga Kyoko -ni hon -wo kaki-o-rare-*ninat*-ta.
        teacher nom   dat book acc write-o-PAS-HON-PST
   b. *Sensei* -ga Kyoko -ni hon -wo o-kak-are-*ninat*-ta.
        teacher nom   dat book acc o-write-PAS-HON-PST
   *c. *Sensei* -ga Kyoko -ni hon -wo o-kaki-*ninar*-are-ta.
        teacher nom   dat book acc o-write-HON-PAS-PST
   'The teacher had Kyoko write the book (to the teacher's
   disadvantage.)'

(29) *a. Kyoko -ga *sensei* -ni hon -wo kaki-o-rare-*ninat*-ta.
             nom teacher   dat book acc write-o-PAS-HON-PST
   *b. Kyoko -ga *sensei* -ni hon -wo o-kak-are-*ninat*-ta.
             nom teacher   dat book acc o-write-PAS-HON-PST
   c. Kyoko -ga *sensei* -ni hon -wo o-kaki-*ninar*-are-ta.
             nom teacher   dat book acc o-write-HON-PAS-PST
   'Kyoko had the teacher write the book (to Kyoko's
   disadvantage.)'

(30) a. *Sensei* -ga Kyoko -ni hon -wo kaite-o-morai-*ninat*-ta.
        teacher nom   dat book acc write-o-BEN-HON-PST
   *b. *Sensei* -ga Kyoko -ni hon -wo o-kaite-morai-*ninat*-ta.
        teacher nom   dat book acc o-write-BEN-HON-PST
   *c. *Sensei* -ga Kyoko -ni hon -wo o-kaki-*ninatte*-morat-ta.
        teacher nom   dat book acc o-write-HON-BEN-PST
   'The teacher had Kyoko write the book (for the teacher's
   benefit.)'

(31) *a. Kyoko -ga *sensei* -ni hon -wo kaite-*o*-morai-*ninat*-ta.
　　　　　 nom teacher dat book acc write-*o*-BEN-HON-PST
　　*b. Kyoko -ga *sensei* -ni hon -wo *o*-kaite-morai-*ninat*-ta.
　　　　　 nom teacher dat book acc *o*-write-BEN-HON-PST
　　c. Kyoko -ga *sensei* -ni hon -wo *o*-kaki-*ninatte*-morat-ta.
　　　　　 nom teacher dat book acc *o*-write-HON-BEN-PST
　　'Kyoko had the teacher write the book (for Kyoko's benefit.)'

The following table summarizes the pattern of the morpheme order of the SH in the passives and the benefactives. (HN stands for the honorifical morpheme *ninar*. The position of *te*, the gerundive morpheme, is ignored):

(32)

	Verbal Forms with Subject Honorification			
	matrix subject		lower subject/agent phrase	
	Passive	Benefactive	Passive	Benefactive
Direct	*o*-V-*rare*-HN	V-*o*-*moraw*-HN	not applicable	not applicable
Indirect	*o*-V-*rare*-HN	V-*o*-*moraw*-HN	*o*-V-HN-*rare*	*o*-V-HN-*moraw*

Notice that when the honorification is triggered by the agent phrase, passives and benefactives parallel each other in terms of morpheme order. The stem/gerundive verb occurs between the honorific particle *o* and *ninar*. When the trigger is the matrix subject, however, they do not show parallelism. In both direct and indirect passives, not only the stem verb but also the passive morpheme *(r)are* occurs between *o* and *ninar*, while in both direct and indirect benefactives, only the benefactive morpheme *moraw* can occur between *o* and *ninar*. The direct-type and the indirect-type show no difference in this regard. At first sight, these patterns of morpheme order may seem to undermine the syntactic difference between the direct-type and the indirect-type that we have proposed. Recall that according to our approach, the passive/benefactive morpheme of the direct-type is a derivational affix, whereas the passive/benefactive morpheme of the indirect-type is a syntactic word on its own. The morpheme order patterns seem to suggest, however, that the indirect passive morpheme is no more independent than the direct passive morpheme, and the direct benefactive morpheme is no less independent than the indirect benefactive morpheme.

We claim that the above phenomenon does follow from our analysis. The morphological unity of the stem verb and the passive morpheme, in contrast with the looseness of the unity in the benefactive predicate, is illusory. What causes the apparent contrast is actually a morphological condition on the prefixing of the honorific particle *o*. The crucial difference between the passives and the benefactives responsible for the contrast in morpheme order is the morphological status of the passive morpheme and the benefactive morpheme. To be more exact, the passive *(r)are* is a bound form, while the benefactive *moraw* is a free form.[10]

Recall that we have proposed in the previous chapter that the honorific morpheme *ni-nar* is sensitive to the syntactic character of the preceding verb, while the honorific particle *o* is sensitive to the morphological property of the following word. The former is suffixed to a syntactic word, while the latter is prefixed to a morphologically free form. The honorific morpheme *ni-nar* is suffixed to the syntactic target verb of the SH; the honorific particle *o* is prefixed to the minimal unit of a free form which contains the target verb. As a result, the stem verb and the passive morpheme together occur between the honorific particle *o* and the honorific morpheme *ni-nar* in both the direct and the indirect passives when the trigger is the matrix subject. When the trigger is the lower subject, as may occur in the indirect passives, only the stem verb occurs between the honorific morphemes (see section 3.4.3.3).

In other words, the honorific particle *o* cannot in any case be directly prefixed to a morpheme *(r)are* because it is not a morphological word. To accommodate the data of the benefactives, we only have to set up another condition: More than one free form cannot occur between the honorific particle *o* and the honorific morpheme *ni-nar*. That is, the honorific particle *o* must be prefixed to the smallest unit of a free form which contains the target verb of the SH.

The following tree diagrams show schematic structures for SH. (33-a) illustrates SH of the matrix subject of the direct benefactives, and (33-b) of the indirect benefactives:

(33)
a.

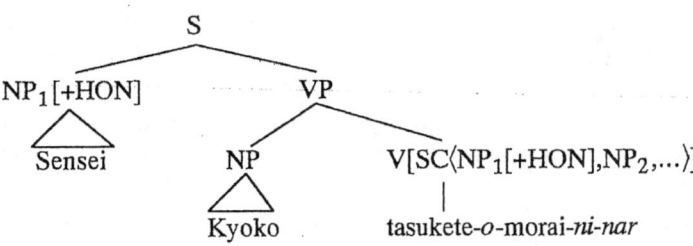

b.

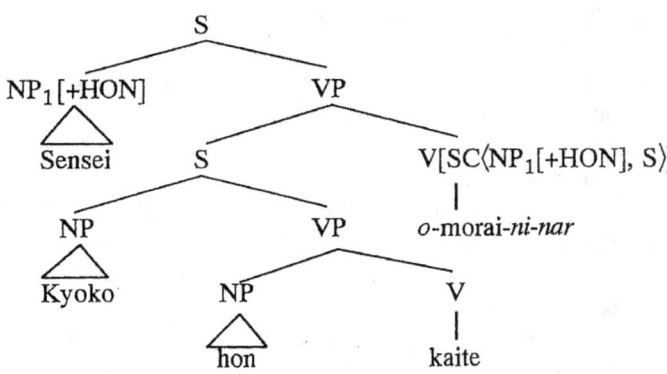

Agent phrase SH is unavailable for the direct benefactives, exactly as in the case of the direct passives. The structure of agent phrase SH of the indirect benefactives is illustrated in (34) below:

(34)

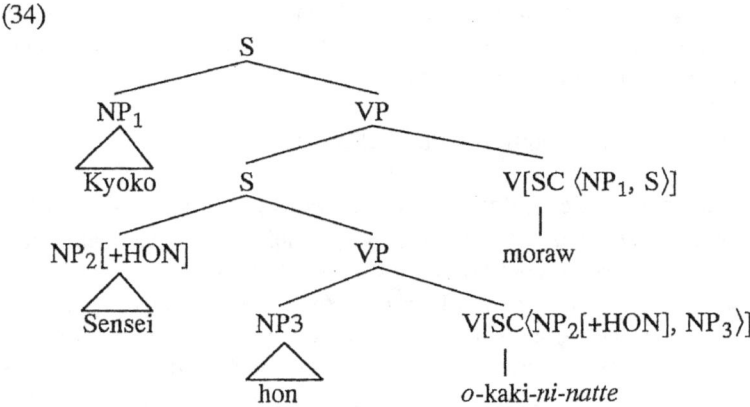

Thus, the morpheme order for each case is completely predictable in our approach. By recognizing the independence and interdependence of morphological and syntactic properties, our analysis of SH in *te-moraw* benefactives is rendered perfectly consistent with our analysis of SH in passives.

Our position of ascribing the unexpected order to the prefixal condition of *o* and the morphological properties of the passive/benefactive morphemes is further justified by the following observations. First, as SH triggered by the agent phrase demonstrates, the verb stem and the indirect passive morpheme can be split, casting doubt on their unity. The pattern of the c-row can be captured only if we assume that the indirect passive morpheme is syntactically an independent verb. Second, the morphological conditions given above seem quite general. Just as in the case of passives, in causatives V-*o*-sase-*ni-nar* is an impossible sequence as discussed in chapter 5. Further, the sequence *o*-V-te-AUX-*ni-nar* is totally impossible in any complex predicates involving a gerundive verb and an auxiliary:[11]

(35)   -te-simaw   *o-kat-te-simai-*ni-nar*
       (aspectual)   kat-te-*o*-simai-*ni-nar*

       -te-ok   *o-kat-te-oki-*ni-nar*
       (aspectual)   kat-te-*o*-oki-*ni-nar*

       -te-yar   *o-kat-te-yar-*ni-nar*
       (benefactive)   kat-te-*o*-yar-*ni-nar*

Therefore, we conclude that the difference in morpheme order does not provide any counterargument to our claim that the passives and the benefactives are syntactically parallel.

4.5.2 Semantic Properties of the Matrix Subject

The lexical rules and the feature structures given above suggest that the matrix subjects of passives and benefactives share the same semantic properties, contrastive only in the benefactive vs. adversative (=positive vs. negative) implication. However, as suggested several times above, the parallelism is not really complete. There are two more points of contrast. First of all, the benefactive interpretation is obligatory in all types of benefactive, while the malefactive interpretation is obligatory in only indirect passives. This has the further consequence that the matrix subject must be animate in all types of benefactive, but only in indirect passives.

Secondly, *te-moraw* benefactives allow both the matrix subject or the agent phrase to be modified by manner adverbs in either type, while, as we have discussed in the previous chapter (sections 3.4.1, 3.4.3.5, and 3.5.2), the matrix subject cannot be so modified in indirect passives. (36) shows the case of the indirect passives, and (37) the case of the indirect benefactives:

(36) a. Kyoko -ga *umaku*   Syota -ni Naoko -wo
            nom cleverly   dat   acc
     damas-are-ta.
     cheat-PAS-PST
     'Kyoko was adversely affected by Syota's cleverly cheating Naoko.'

     b. Kyoko -ga *wazato*   Syota -ni Naoko -wo
            nom intentionally   dat   acc
     yuuwakus-are-ta.
     seduce-PAS-PST
     'Kyoko was adversely affected by Syota's intentionally seducing Naoko.'

(37) a. Kyoko -ga *umaku*   Syota -ni Naoko -wo
            nom cleverly   dat   acc

damasite-morat-ta.
cheat-BEN-PST
'Kyoko cleverly had Syota cheat Naoko for Kyoko's benefit.'
'Kyoko had Syota cleverly cheat Naoko for Kyoko's benefit.'

b. Kyoko -ga *wazato* Syota -ni Naoko -wo
       nom intentionally   dat   acc
yuuwakusite-morat-ta.
seduce-BEN-PST
'Kyoko deliberately had Syota seduce Naoko for Kyoko's benefit.'
'Kyoko had Syota deliberately seduce Naoko for Kyoko's benefit.'

The manner adverbs in (36) unambiguously take a narrow scope; they specify the manner with which the agent phrase carried out the action denoted by the gerundive verb. The manner adverbs in (37) are ambiguous; they can modify either the agent phrase or the matrix subject.

The third point of contrast between passives and *te-moraw* benefactives is that the matrix subject of the *te-moraw* benefactive is not only the one who experiences the consequence of the event denoted by the original predicate, but also could be the initiator of the event. Gunji 1987 gives a translation of the benefactives as "ask and receive the favor of." Nakau 1973 refers to the *te-moraw* benefactives as "polite causative."[12] It is "polite" in the sense that it implies that the causation is executed by request and not by force, as the translation by Gunji (1987) also suggests. The causative interpretation is unavailable with the passives.[13] But it is not very accurate to regard the *te-moraw* benefactives as a form of causatives, because the causative interpretation is actually only optional.

The following examples show the semantic contrast among the passives, benefactives, and causatives. The matrix subject of the indirect passives is always an Experiencer, and is never a Causer. Exactly the opposite is the case with the causatives. The matrix subject of the causatives is always the Causer and is never Experiencer; there is no significant implication that the subject is affected in any way by the event that he/she caused. By contrast, the matrix subject of the benefactives is always an Experiencer and is optionally a Causer:

(38) a. Syota -ga Kyoko -ni yane -ni nobor-are-ta.
         nom   dat   roof loc climb-PAS-PST
  'Syota was adversely affected by Kyoko's climbing on the roof.'

  b. Syota -ga Kyoko -ni yane -ni nobor-ase-ta.
        nom   dat   roof loc climb-CAS-PST
  'Syota made Kyoko climb up on the roof.'

  c. Syota -ga Kyoko -ni yane -ni nobotte-morat-ta.
        nom   dat   roof loc climb-BEN-PST
  'Syota received a benefit from Kyoko's climbing on the roof; Syota may have asked Kyoko to do so.'

Note in this connection that the English causative *have* shows a very similar Experiencer/Causer ambiguity:

(39) a. Tom had Mary climb on the roof.
  b. John had his hair cut.

In the examples above, the subjects *Tom* and *John* can be interpreted either as a Causer or as an Experiencer (or both) just like the matrix subject of the *te-moraw* benefactives.[14] This suggests that the Japanese *te-moraw* benefactives and the English *have* causative construction may have certain properties in common, which give rise to the semantic role ambiguity observed here.[15]

Cowper 1989 presents a "thematic underspecification" analysis to give a unified treatment of the verb *have* both in its auxiliary and main verb uses. In a similar vein, Ritter and Rosen 1990 analyzes the Experiencer-Causer ambiguity observable in the English causative *have*, and claims that the ambiguity is due to the underlying lack of specification. As quoted in the previous chapter as well, Ritter and Rosen 1990 suggests that in complex predicate formation, when an extra argument is introduced as the matrix subject, there are roughly two ways to relate it to the embedded event: either as the one who causes the event or as the one who gets some influence from the event; that is, either as a Causer or as an Experiencer.

According to Ritter and Rosen 1990, the causative *have* does not specify the choice between the two, hence ambiguity results.[16] Disambiguation between the experiencer and causer reading is largely a task of the semantics of the embedded verb, and the ambiguity is sometimes even left unsolved. The main verb *make*, on the other hand, always expresses a causal meaning, whether "creation" or "change of state" and the causative *make* is strictly causative, and no ambiguity is observed. Therefore, ambiguity is a direct reflection of the lack of thematic role specification of the verb *have*.

As we discussed in the previous chapter, the matrix subject of the indirect passives is specified to be non-causal and non-volitional, so the Experiencer interpretation is obligatory.

Now, the question is how Ritter and Rosen's approach should be extended to the Japanese benefactives. Notice that Ritter and Rosen's approach cannot be directly carried over to the analysis of the *te-moraw* benefactives.[17] The ambiguity between the experiencer reading and the causative reading is "symmetrical" with *have*, though the readings can overlap. On the other hand, the ambiguity is "asymmetrical," so to speak, with *te-moraw*; the beneficiary reading is obligatory while the causative reading is an optional addition. In other words, the subject is always associated with a Beneficiary (Experiencer) role, whether it is additionally a Causer or not. The idea of underspecification of thematic role will not capture this asymmetry.

To incorporate Ritter and Rosen's (1990) approach in the Japanese benefactive construction, we claim that beneficiary is not a thematic role *per se*; the benefactive relation does not participate in a thematic relation itself. A benefactive relation is part of the predication, but its meaning is independent of thematic relations much like modality, being on a different level. We will argue that the benefactive morpheme *moraw* does not specify the thematic roles of its arguments.

We propose that the benefactive predicates have a complex semantic structure like the passives and the causatives. The causatives specify the matrix subject as [+causative], hence Causer; the indirect passives specify the matrix subject as [-causative], hence Experiencer. The benefactives, on the other hand, are unspecified regarding causality; hence the additional matrix subject can be either Causer or Experiencer.

We revise the lexical rules and the feature structures of the benefactives as in (40)-(42). The lexical rules in (40) and (41) derive the direct and the possessive *te-moraw* benefactives, respectively. The feature structure in (42) represents the indirect benefactive predicate *moraw*. Compare them with the earlier versions given in (18)-(23):

202 Complex Predicates in Japanese

(40) Direct *Te-Moraw* Benefactive Lexical Rule

$$\begin{bmatrix} \text{SUBCAT} \langle \text{NP}[1], \ldots \text{NP}[2], \ldots \rangle \\ \text{CONT}\ [3] \begin{bmatrix} \text{RELATION} & Q \\ \text{EXT-ARG} & [1] \\ Q\text{-}er & [1] \\ Q\text{-}ee & [2] \\ \vdots & \vdots \end{bmatrix} \end{bmatrix} \Rightarrow$$

$$\begin{bmatrix} \text{SUBCAT} \langle \text{NP}[2], \ldots \rangle \\ \text{CONT} \begin{bmatrix} \text{RELATION}\ R \\ \text{EXT-ARG}\quad [4] \\ R\text{-}er \qquad\ [4][\text{INDEX}[5]] \\ \\ \text{SOA-ARG}\ [3] \begin{bmatrix} \text{RELATION} & Q \\ \text{EXT-ARG} & [1] \\ Q\text{-}er & [1] \\ Q\text{-}ee & [2]\ [\text{INDEX}[5]] \\ \vdots & \vdots \end{bmatrix} \end{bmatrix} \\ \text{MODAL} \begin{bmatrix} \text{RELATION} & benefit \\ \text{BENEFICIARY} & [4] \\ \text{SOA-ARG} & [3] \end{bmatrix} \end{bmatrix}$$

(41) Possessive *Te-Moraw* Benefactive Lexical Rule

$$\begin{bmatrix} \text{SUBCAT} \langle \text{NP}[1], \ldots \text{NP}[2], \ldots \rangle \\ \text{CONT}\ [3] \begin{bmatrix} \text{RELATION} & Q \\ \text{EXT-ARG} & [1] \\ Q\text{-}er & [1] \\ Q\text{-}ee & [2] \\ \vdots & \vdots \end{bmatrix} \end{bmatrix} \Rightarrow$$

$$\begin{bmatrix} \text{SUBCAT} \langle \text{NP}[4], \text{NP}[2], \ldots \rangle \\ \text{CONT} \begin{bmatrix} \text{RELATION } R \\ \text{EXT-ARG} \quad [4] \\ \text{R-er} \quad\quad [4][\text{INDEX}[6]] \\ \\ \text{SOA-ARG} \quad [3] \begin{bmatrix} \text{RELATION } Q \\ \text{EXT-ARG} \quad [1] \\ \text{Q-er} \quad\quad [1] \\ \text{Q-ee} \quad\quad [2][\text{INDEX}[5]] \\ \vdots \quad\quad\quad \vdots \end{bmatrix} \\ \\ \text{MODAL} \begin{bmatrix} \text{RELATION} \quad benefit \\ \text{BENEFICIARY} \quad [4] \\ \text{SOA-ARG} \quad [3] \end{bmatrix} \end{bmatrix} \\ \text{CONDITION: } [6] \textbf{ P } [5] \end{bmatrix}$$

(42) Indirect Benefactive Morpheme *moraw*

$$\begin{bmatrix} \text{PHON} | \; moraw \\ \text{SYNSEM}|\ldots \begin{bmatrix} \text{SUBCAT} \langle \text{NP}[4], \text{V}[\text{SUBCAT} \langle \, \rangle \; \text{Vform: ger}]{:}[3] \rangle \\ \text{CONT} \begin{bmatrix} \text{RELATION } R \\ \text{EXT-ARG} \quad [4] \\ \text{R-er} \quad\quad [4] \\ \\ \text{SOA-ARG} \quad [3] \begin{bmatrix} \text{RELATION } Q \\ \text{EXT-ARG} \quad [1] \\ \text{Q-er} \quad\quad [1] \\ \text{Q-ee} \quad\quad [2] \end{bmatrix} \end{bmatrix} \\ \text{MODAL} \begin{bmatrix} \text{RELATION} \quad benefit \\ \text{BENEFICIARY} \quad [4] \\ \text{SOA-ARG} \quad [3] \end{bmatrix} \end{bmatrix} \end{bmatrix}$$

There are two crucial points in the above feature structures. First, the higher relation is underspecified, represented by R; it is unspecified even with respect to causality. Compare this with the passives and causatives, which we propose are [-causative] and [+causative], respectively. The semantic role of the argument corresponding to the matrix subject is also underspecified. Given Ritter and Rosen's (1990) assumption, the matrix subject of the *te-moraw* benefactives can be either Experiencer, Causer or both.

Second, the benefactive relation is specified as a separate relation, coexisting with the core semantic content relation. The feature name MODAL is only tentative. The benefactive relation is obligatory, and the matrix subject is obligatorily the Beneficiary, whatever role it bears as a CONTENT attribute. Notice that the Benefactor argument is not specified in the rule. The Benefactor coincides with the agent role of the embedded relation Q, but we claim that this information is not necessary in the feature specification. The selection of the Benefactor is done by a general principle, as we will show later.

Now, as mentioned above, the matrix subject of the benefactive can be either Experiencer or Causer. When Experiencer is selected, Experiencer and Beneficiary are notionally so close to each other that they are virtually conflated into one. To be more exact, the set of entailments for an Experiencer constitutes a proper subset of the set of entailments for Beneficiary. When Causer is the choice, on the other hand, the matrix subject will be conceived as functioning as both Causer and Beneficiary. This is why, we claim, it has been observed that the benefactive interpretation is obligatory and the causative interpretation is optional, in contrast with the English *have* causatives. In other words, conceptual closeness between Beneficiary and Experiencer has obscured a more complete parallelism between the *te-moraw* benefactive and the *have*-causatives.

Thus in our approach the obligatoriness of the Beneficiary role does not seem to be enough to motivate distinct syntactic structures for the direct passives and for the direct benefactives, as in Terada 1990. The benefactive relation is encoded independently of the semantic CONTENT relation. The passive relation is non-causative, while the benefactive is unspecified in terms of causality. Once these properties are factored out, syntactic parallelism between the passives and the *te-moraw* benefactives is clearly manifested.

4.5.3 Implications of the Semantic Underspecification

In this section we will consider the implications of underspecification in the semantic roles of benefactives in comparison with the cases of passives. The point that we focus on is the non-causative specification in the passives and the lack thereof in the benefactives. We will propose that the negative specification of causality of the Affectee role is the clue to understanding the peculiar semantic properties of indirect passives; namely, the obligatory adversity interpretation and the lack of matrix subject modification by certain manner adverbs.

As mentioned above, the indirect passives are always associated with the interpretation that the matrix subject is adversely affected by the event described in the rest of the sentence, while this interpretation is not obligatory in the direct and the possessive passives.

We have suggested that the matrix subject of indirect passives is an Experiencer, based (1) on the idea that the Affectee role corresponding to the passive subject has to be less like a Proto-Agent in Dowty's (1991) sense, i.e., crucially non-volitional and non-causal, and (2) on the idea of thematic underspecification proposed by Ritter and Rosen 1990 (section 3.4.2). But the specification of an Experiencer role does not explain why it is obligatorily a malefactive Experiencer.

As for the adversity interpretation *per se*, we have suggested, with Oehrle and Nishio 1981, and Kuno 1983 that the adversity interpretation obtains when the passive subject is not directly involved in the core event (cf. section 3.4.3.4). We have assumed that an argument is directly involved in an event if it is one of the participating roles which define the semantics of the event or it is coreferential with a directly participating role or related to it by the entailment relation **P**. This explanation directly accommodates the neutral interpretation of possessive passives (cf. section 3.5.2). We have also demonstrated that direct involvement in the core event and the lack thereof have interesting repercussions in the possibility of adverbal modification of a certain type (cf. sections 3.4.3.5 and 3.5.2). Namely, modification of the passive subject by certain manner adverbs is possible only when the referent of the subject is directly involved in the core event. This condition correctly excludes the subject of indirect passives from being modified, and at the same time allows modification of the subject of either direct passives or possessive passives.

Thus the concept "directly involved in the event" is able to account for the otherwise quite puzzling contrast between direct/possessive passives and indirect passives. So the concept seems every effective as far as the passive constructions go. However, when the data of *te-moraw* benefactives are considered, it turns out that the definition of direct involvement requires refinement.

Recall that the matrix subject of indirect benefactives can become the modifiee, as shown in the examples in (37) above. Notice, however, that we assume a parallel structure for passives and benefactives, and there is neither coindexing nor entailment relation that could link the matrix subject of indirect benefactives to any role in the embedded soa (= core event). To solve the problem, we will claim that the concept of direct involvement should more properly be extended to include a causal involvement. Put differently, the matrix subject of indirect passives demonstrates peculiar properties not only because it is not directly involved in the core event but because it is not even causally related to the core event.

Our discussion on this issue is based on the observation that the adversity interpretation is crucially associated with the non-causative reading. Ritter and Rosen 1990 lists several examples involving the causative *have* and argue that the disambiguation is largely a task of the embedded verb. See some of the examples they give:

(43) a. David had Sam wash behind his ears. (causative)
   b. Brenda has Katie put on her helmet whenever she bikes. (causative)
   c. Jason had Monica practice the piano before she went out to play. (causative)
   d. John had Mary die on him. (experiencer)
   e. Have you ever had someone pick your pocket? (experiencer)
   f. The teacher had three students walk out on him. (experiencer)
   g. I had a total stanger kiss my hand this morning. (experiencer)
   h. John had Mary work. (causative/experiencer)
   i. John had Mary eat an apple. (causative/experiencer)

Observe that Experiencer reading and Causative reading can overlap; however, for the verb *have* to carry unambiguous Experiencer meaning, it almost always has to have an adversity meaning at the same time (See 43-d to 43-g). The pragmatic reason is rather obvious: it is unlikely that somebody intentionally causes an event that affects him/herself in an adversative way. The sentences in (43) strongly suggest that the adversity interpretation closely interacts with the lack of causal relation to the event. Importantly, the semantic factor crucial here is not direct involvement but causal involvement in the event.

Recall in this connection that under the present analysis, what distinguishes the matrix subject of indirect passives from that of indirect benefactives is their semantic specification; the former is strictly non-causal, while the latter lacks the negative specification of causality. In other words, the matrix subject of the indirect benefactives has a potential to be causally related to the core event. As mentioned above, the matrix subject of indirect passives, which cannot be causally related to the core event, cannot be modified by the manner adverbs, while the matrix subject of indirect benefactives, which can be causally related to the core event, can be modified by the manner adverbs.

Given these data contrasting indirect passives with *have*-causatives and indirect benefactives, it seems reasonable to suggest that the adversity interpretation and the lack of subject modification are related to the negative specification of causality on the Affectee role.

Now, what is curious about this situation is that a causally related argument shares properties with directly involved arguments, to the exclusion of causally unrelated arguments, even though the former is not directly involved in the core event. The association between a causally related argument and directly involved arguments is not hard to make, however. Very informally put, a causal argument by definition is responsible for the realization of the core event. It is virtually the initiator of the core event. In this sense, a causally related argument can be considered as directly involved in the event in an extended sense. This property sharply contrasts with a causally unrelated argument; it plays no role in the realization of a core event.[18]

Therefore, we maintain that it is the negative specification of causality that is crucial in bringing about the peculiar character of indirect passives. Because of its non-causality, the matrix subject has no way to get involved in the realization of the core event. We suggest, following Oehrle and Nishio 1981, that this is why the indirect passives are obligatorily associated with the adversity interpretation.

We also extend our condition on adverbial modification to accommodate the cases where the relevant argument is causally related to the event. The revised condition goes: a modifiee must be either directly involved in the core event or causally related to the event. A causally unrelated argument fails to share the relevant properties with causally related arguments or directly involved arguments because it makes no contribution toward the realization of the core event.

This concludes our analysis of *te-moraw* benefactives. We have claimed that *te-moraw* benefactives parallel passives syntactically. Both of them consist of three types: direct, possessive, and indirect passives/benefactives. The first two are lexically derived, whereas the last one has an S-complement structure. Data from reflexive binding, the suppression of the agent phrase, Subject Honorification, and Do-Support all support the parallelism.

We have also pointed out several differences manifested between passives and benefactives. It has been shown that such differences do not challenge our parallel analysis of the two. In our system, morphological and semantic information is encoded separately, and the morphological and semantic peculiarities of benefactives are accounted for without reference to their syntactic parallelism encoded in SUBCAT information.

One of the crucial points bringing about the differences between passives and *te-moraw* benefactives is the morphological independence of the auxiliary *moraw* as opposed to the bound morpheme *(r)are*. The optional causative interpretation peculiar to *te-moraw* benefactives is accounted for in terms of the notion of thematic underspecification of the benefactive relation. In particular, thematic relations in *te-moraw* benefactives are neutral with respect to causality, whereas passives are specifically non-causative. This semantic difference has a further repercussion in adverbial modification.

To explain the obligatoriness of a benefactive interpretation, it has been suggested that the benefactive relation is independent of thematic relation, and is encoded separately as MODAL information. The next section demonstrates that the last proposal sheds light necessary for providing a unified account of benefactive constructions in Japanese.

4.6 Three Types of Japanese Benefactives

In the rest of this chapter we will examine other types of benefactive constructions and try to capture the general system of the Japanese benefactive construction. Our discussion will defend the proposal that the benefactive relation is specified independently of the semantic CONTENT relation.

As briefly mentioned at the onset of this chapter, *te-moraw* is not the only form of benefactive construction in Japanese. Two more types of benefactive constructions can be identified.[19] They all are formed using auxiliary verbs corresponding to lexical verbs meaning 'to give' or 'to receive.' The seven verbs involved can be classified into three types, cutting across different politeness levels, as shown in the table (44):

(44)

	I: 'give'	II: 'give'	III: 'get'
basic	YAR	KURE	MORAW
polite	AGE		
honorific	SASIAGE	KUDASAR	ITADAK

The three sets of items as lexical verbs are used in the following way:

(45) a. Watasi -ga Kyoko -ni hon -wo yat-ta.
       I   nom   dat book acc give-PST
    'I gave Kyoko a book.'

   b. Kyoko -ga watasi -ni hon -wo kure-ta.
            nom I   dat book acc give-PST
    'Kyoko gave me a book.'

   c. Watasi -ga Kyoko -ni hon -wo morat-ta.
      I   nom   dat book acc receive-PST
    'I received a book from Kyoko.'

'Give' of type I and that of type II are not interchangeable; in fact, they are mutually exclusive in distribution. *Yar* (type I) is used when the situation is described from the subject (giver)'s point of view, whereas *kure* (type II) is used when the situation is described from the indirect object (receiver)'s point of view. So type I is anomalous if the goal phrase is in the first person as in (45-b), and type II is anomalous if the subject (giver) phrase is in the first person as in (45-a). See the following data showing this point:

(46) *a. Kyoko -ga watasi -ni hon -wo yat-ta.
             nom I   dat book acc give-PST
     'Kyoko gave me a book.'

*b. Watasi -ga Kyoko -ni hon -wo kure-ta.
    I   nom   dat   book acc give-PST
    'I gave Kyoko a book.'

When the speaker him/herself is not involved, something/someone related to him/her necessarily holds the point of view. So, for example, *kure* (type II) cannot be used to describe a situation where the speaker's brother gave a book to a stranger. The "point of view" phrase can be in the second person or in the third person as well, but there is still a strong sense that the phrase holds the viewpoint of the text. In the same way, *moraw* (type III) describes the situation from the subject (receiver)'s point of view. In sum, the following pattern emerges from this comparison. ("p.o.v." stands for the holder of the point of view):

(47)

	I: YAR	II: KURE	III: MORAW
SUBJECT	giver	giver	receiver
P.O.V	giver	receiver	receiver

When these three types of verbs function as auxiliaries and form benefactive sentences, the specification of point of view is carried over. First see the examples given below. (Henceforth the beneficiary is italicized):

(48) a. Watasi -ga *Kyoko* -ni hon -wo katte-yat-ta.
        I   nom   dat book acc buy-BEN-PST
        'I bought Kyoko a book (for her benefit.)'

   b. Kyoko -ga *watasi* -ni hon -wo katte-kure-ta.
         nom I   dat book acc buy-BEN-PST
        'Kyoko bought me a book (for my benefit.)'

   c. *Watasi* -ga Kyoko -ni hon -wo katte-morat-ta.
       I   nom   dat book acc buy-BEN-PST
        'I had Kyoko buy me a book (for my benefit.)'

Aside from the question of point of view, the benefactive *te-yar* and the benefactive *te-kure* both mean that the argument with goal role gets benefit from the action/state described by the sentence. The benefactive with *te-moraw*, on the other hand, means that the subject (goal role) is the beneficiary. In other words, the beneficiary (the one who receives benefit) seems to correspond to the goal role of the giving/receiving verb. The following chart captures this pattern:

(49) Three Types of Benefactives: (to be revised)

	I: YAR	II: KURE	III: MORAW
SUBJECT	agent	agent	goal
P.O.V.	agent	goal	goal
BENEFICIARY	goal	goal	goal

So far it seems that the three benefactive predicates are exactly parallel in terms of the number of arguments. However, such is not really the case. Crucially, *te-yar* and *te-kure* are not in fact able to increase the (syntactic) valency of the embedded (gerundive) verb, while *te-moraw* is. It may seem from (48) that type I & II also increase the valency, adding a beneficiary argument, but the stem verb *kaw* 'buy' may as well be considered as ditransitive right from the beginning. See the following examples in which a- and b-sentences carry the same argument as the corresponding sentences in (48); notice that the sentences in (50) do not involve benefactive morphemes. Clearly, it is not the benefactive morphemes *yar* and *kure* which has introduced the dative-marked argument in (48). Those arguments are present without the benefactive morphemes:

(50) a. Watasi -ga   Kyoko -ni   hon   -wo   kat-ta.
        I   nom   dat   book   acc   buy-PST
     'I bought Kyoko a book.'

   b. Kyoko -ga   *watasi* -ni   hon   -wo   kat-ta.
             nom   I   dat   book   acc   buy-PST
     'Kyoko bought me a book.'

If the verbs are unambiguously intransitive or transitive, i.e., if no goal role is available, the beneficiary role cannot be realized as a dative-marked NP. It can occur only as a postpositional phrase (*notameni* 'for the sake of'):

(51) a. Watasi -ga Kyoko *-ni/-notameni hayaku okite-yat-ta.
       I   nom   dat/for   early   wake-BEN-PST
       'I woke up early for Kyoko.'

   b. Kyoko -ga watasi *-ni/-notameni hayaku okite-kure-ta.
              nom I   dat/for   early   wake-BEN-PST
      'Kyoko woke up early for me.'

   c. *Watasi* -ga Kyoko -ni hayaku okite-morat-ta.
       I   nom   dat early   wake-BEN-PST
      'I had Kyoko wake up early for me.'

(52) a. Watasi -ga Kyoko *-ni/notameni Syota -wo butte-yat-ta.
       I   nom   dat/for   acc beat-BEN-PST
      'I hit Syota for Kyoko.'

   b. Kyoko -ga watasi *-ni/notameni Syota -wo butte-kure-ta.
             nom I   dat/for   acc beat-BEN-PST
      'Kyoko hit Syota for me.'

   c. *Watasi* -ga Kyoko -ni Syota -wo butte-morat-ta.
       I   nom   dat   acc beat-BEN-PST
      'I had Kyoko hit Syota (for my benefit.)'

The sentences in (51) involve an intransitive verb *oki* ('wake up'), while those in (52) have a transitive verb *but* ('beat'). In either case, the a- and b-sentences, i.e., type I & II, do not allow the beneficiary phrase to be marked with the dative case. It has to be followed by a postposition *notameni* 'for the sake of.'[20] As mentioned in the discussion of the agent phrase of the passives, a postposition typically marks an adjunct, while a case marker typically marks a syntactic argument.

The unavailability of a case marker for the beneficiary in the a- and b-sentences above, therefore, indicates that the beneficiary is not really a syntactic argument in the type I & II benefactives. In other words, the beneficiary morphemes of type I & II are not able to introduce a syntactic argument. This is contrastive with the type III benefactives, which clearly increases the valency of the gerundive verb by one.[21]

There is another piece of evidence further supporting our claim that type I & II benefactives do not increase the valency of the gerundive verb and that the beneficiary phrase marked with postposition *notameni* is not licensed by the type I & II benefactive morphemes. See the data in (53)-(54) below, in which (53-a) is a type I benefactive sentence and (54-a) type II. Notice that the beneficiary phrase with postposition *notameni* can occur even without the benefactive morphemes *yar* and *kure*. This situation sharply contrasts with (55), the type III benefactive, where the beneficiary phase is the matrix subject and cannot occur without the benefactive morpheme *moraw*:22

(53) a. Watasi -ga *Naoko* -notameni honya -e itte-yat-ta.
         I   nom   for   bookstore to go-BEN-PST
     b. Watasi -ga *Naoko* -notameni honya -e it-ta.
         I   nom   for   bookstore to go-PST
     'I went to a bookstore for Naoko.'

(54) a. Naoko -ga *watasi* -notameni honya -e itte-kure-ta.
         nom   I   for   bookstore to go-BEN-PST
     b. Naoko -ga *watasi* -notameni honya -e it-ta.
         nom   I   for   bookstore to go-PST
     'Naoko went to the bookstore for me.'

(55) a. *Naoko* -ga Syota -ni honya   -e itte-morat-ta.
         nom   dat   bookstore to go-BEN-PST
    *b. *Naoko* -ga Syota -ni honya   -e it-ta.
         nom   dat   bookstore to go-PST
     'Naoko had Syota go to the bookstore for her.'

Let us clarify the implication of the data (51)-(55). (51)-(52) indicate that the beneficiary phase in type I & II cannot be marked with a case marker (dative), suggesting that it is an adjunct. The exception is a beneficiary phrase which is originally a goal phrase with dative case as shown in (50). (53)-(54) further support the claim and show that the beneficiary phrase marked with a postposition *notameni* is an adjunct which can occur freely without being introduced by a specific complex predicate. In type III, in contrast, the benefactive morpheme *moraw* is required in the presence of a beneficiary phase, as shown in (55). All these imply that the occurrence of the beneficiary postpositional phrase N-*notameni* is totally independent of the benefactive morphemes *yar* and *kure*, and that type I & II benefactives do not increase the valency of the gerundive verb.

Not only can type III, *te-moraw* benefactives, increase the valency of the gerundive verb by one, it can in fact even decrease valency. This section has so far focused only on indirect benefactives. Recall that the direct/possessive benefactive suppresses the agent argument of the gerundive verb, demoting it to an adjunct status; the agent argument can even be omitted. If this suppression is interpreted as a decrease of valency (Shibatani 1985, 1990), then type III benefactives can either increase (= indirect benefactives) or decrease (= direct/possessive) the valency of the gerundive verb. Based on this characterization, let us refer to type I & II benefactives as valency-preserving benefactives, and type III as a valency-changing benefactive.

Now, the questions we address are: (1) what is the consistent system of Japanese benefactives in which the three types of benefactives are distributed? (2) Why are types I & II valency-preserving, whereas type III is valency-changing? We propose that the key factor behind the distinction between the valency-preserving and the valency-changing benefactives is the selection of the beneficiary.

To elaborate on the above claim, let us further investigate more about the beneficiary of type I & II benefactives. In the examples we have given so far, the beneficiary of type I & II has always been represented as the dative-marked goal phrase or as a *notameni* postpositional phrase. Examination of more data reveals that the beneficiary of type I & II can in fact be anything so long as it does not coincide with the matrix subject. See the following data. (56)-(57) involve a transitive verb *home* 'praise,' and (58)-(59) a ditransitive verb *syookais* 'introduce':[23]

(56) a. Watasi -ga *Kyoko* -wo homete-yat-ta.
       I   nom   acc   praise-BEN-PST.
    'I praised Kyoko (for her benefit.)'

    b. Watasi -ga Kyoko -wo (*Syota* notameni) homete-yat-ta.
        I   nom   acc   for   praise-BEN-PST.
      'I praised Kyoko for Syota.'

(57) a. Kyoko -ga *watasi* -wo homete-kure-ta.
             nom   I   acc   praise-BEN-PST.
    'Kyoko praised me (for my benefit.)'

b. Kyoko -ga   Syota -wo (*watasi* notameni) homete-kure-ta.
   nom   acc   I   for   praise-BEN-PST.
   'Kyoko praised Syota for me.'

(58) a. Watasi   -ga *Syota*   -wo Kyoko   -ni syookaisite-yat-ta.
        I   nom   acc   dat introduce-BEN-PST
        'I introduced Kyoko to Syota (for his benefit.)'

   b. Watasi   -ga Syota   -wo *Kyoko*   -ni syookaisite-yat-ta.
      I   nom   acc   dat introduce-BEN-PST
      'I introduced Kyoko to Syota (for her benefit.)'

   c. Watasi -ga (*Naoko* -notameni) Syota   -wo   Kyoko -ni
      I   nom   for   acc   dat
      syookaisite-yat-ta.
      introduce-BEN-PST
      'I introduced Kyoko to Syota for the benefit of Naoko.'

(59) a. Syota   -ga   *watasi*   -wo Kyoko   -ni syookaisite-kure-ta.
        nom   I   acc   dat introduce-BEN-PST
        'Syota introduced me to Kyoko (for my benefit.)'

   b. Syota   -ga   Kyoko   -wo *watasi*   -ni syookaisite-kure-ta.
      nom   acc   I   dat introduce-BEN-PST
      'Syota introduced Kyoko to me (for my benefit.)'

   c. Naoko   -ga   (*watasi*   -notameni)   Syota   -wo   Kyoko -ni
      nom   I   for   acc   dat
      syookaisite-kure-ta.
      introduce-BEN-PST
      'Naoko introduced Kyoko to Syota (for my benefit.)'

Thus, in (56)-(57), the beneficiary can be either the direct object (*theme*) or a benefactive adjunct. In (58)-(59), it can be either the direct object (*theme*), the indirect object (*goal*), or an adjunct. The adjunct phrase can be omitted, in which case, the beneficiary is left unspecified. This shows that the argument carrying the beneficiary role is quite unrestricted. The real restriction on the beneficiary role of type I & II benefactives is only that it cannot be the matrix subject. Notice that this sharply contrasts with type III, where the beneficiary is invariably the matrix subject.[24]

The revised table given below captures the system of the three benefactives:[25]

(60) Three Types of Benefactives: (revised)

	I: YAR	II: KURE	III: MORAW
	'give'	'give'	'receive'
BENEFACTOR	stem.subj	stem.subj	stem.subj
BENEFICIARY	¬mat.subj	¬mat.subj	mat.subj
P.O.V	benefactor	beneficiary	beneficiary
MAT.SUBJ	benefactor	benefactor	beneficiary

This table shows, first of all, that the benefactor in any type should coincide with the agent (subject) of the process denoted by the verb stem. A benefit is accrued by some action, the action denoted by the gerundive verb, so it is natural that the individual responsible for this action coincides with the benefactor. Further, with the benefactive auxiliaries *yar* and *kure* corresponding to lexical verbs meaning 'give,' the subject of the benefactive construction is the benefactor, paralleling its role as a 'giver' in lexical uses of these forms. Therefore, in types I & II, the matrix subject and the subject of the gerundive verb both designated as benefactor, will be non-distinct. The Beneficiary in these cases, on the other hand, can be anything but the subject. With the receiving verb *moraw*, the subject is a 'receiver,' and in the benefactive construction, it is the beneficiary. As noted above, the subject of the stem verb in gerundive form is the benefactor. As one argument cannot be both a benefactor and a beneficiary at the same time,[26] the subject of the stem verb (benefactor) must be distinct from the matrix subject (beneficiary). There are obviously two ways by which these requirements can be met: an argument other than the subject of the stem verb in gerundive form serves as the matrix subject, or a new argument is introduced. The former case corresponds to the direct benefactive, and latter to the indirect benefactive.

The type I & II benefactive constructions have no need to change their argument structure, as the agent of the stem verb can be the subject without causing contradiction. So they will be derived simply by adding the modal content "benefactive relation" into the feature structure. Thus we analyze the type I & II benefactives as derived through a lexical rule given in (61).[27] Compare them with the feature structures for type III benefactives given in (38)-(40). (The specification of point of view is omitted for the sake of simplicity):

(61) Benefactive Lexical Rule for *yar, kure*

$$
\begin{bmatrix}
\text{PHON} \mid X \\
\text{SYNSEM} \mid \ldots \begin{bmatrix} \text{SUBCAT} \langle \text{NP}[1] \ldots \rangle \\ \text{CONT} [2] \end{bmatrix}
\end{bmatrix} \Rightarrow
$$

$$
\begin{bmatrix}
\text{PHON} \mid X\text{-}yar/kure \\
\text{SYNSEM} \mid \ldots \begin{bmatrix} \text{SUBCAT} \langle \text{NP}[1] \ldots \rangle \\ \text{CONT} [2] \\ \text{MODAL} \begin{bmatrix} \text{RELATION} & benefit \\ \text{BENEFICIARY} & \neg [1] \\ \text{SOA-ARG} & [2] \end{bmatrix} \end{bmatrix}
\end{bmatrix}
$$

The above lexical rules do not change the SUBCAT attributes or the semantic CONTENT attributes, but simply add information about the benefactive relation. The Type I and II benefactives have a non-subject restriction on the beneficiary. No more specification is made on the choice of the beneficiary, because it is in fact open, as discussed above. The specification of the subject of the stem verb as benefactor obtains as a general rule stated elsewhere in the grammar.

Thus, the present approach identifies the core operation of Japanese benefactives as the introduction of the MODAL relation, benefactive. The MODAL relation in *te-moraw* benefactives is different from the one in *te-kure* and *te-yar* benefactives in terms of the specification of beneficiary.

Syntactic differences between *te-moraw* benefactives and *te-kure/te-yar* benefactives are very obvious. It is only the former which parallel passives. The SUBCAT features and the CONTENT features are accordingly different between *te-moraw* benefactives and *te-kure/te-yar* benefactives.

Our proposal to encode the benefactive relation as an independent MODAL information, therefore, makes it possible to capture the common denominator of benefactive constructions, at the same time as describing the syntactic differences among different types of benefactives.

4.7 Conclusion

In this chapter we have examined benefactive constructions, particularly *te-moraw* benefactives. Our central claims are (1) that the *te-moraw* benefactives syntactically parallel the passives, and (2) that the benefactive relation constitutes MODAL information, which is independent of a thematic relation.

In the first half of the chapter, we compared *te-moraw* benefactives and passives. Based on the data from reflexive binding, the suppression of the agent phrase, Subject Honorification, and Do-Support, we argued that the direct and possessive *te-moraw* benefactives have monoclausal structure and the benefactive morpheme *moraw* functions as a derivational affix, whereas the indirect *te-moraw* benefactive has biclausal structure and the benefactive morpheme is syntactically a word, heading a VP.

We have presented data which appear to argue against the parallelism between passives and *te-moraw* benefactives, but demonstrated that they do not challenge our approach. The incongruities between them are not in fact syntactic, and our approach can provide an account in terms of morphology and semantics.

The difference in morpheme order between the SH of the passives and the *te-moraw* benefactives was explained in terms of the morphological status of the benefactive/passive morpheme. Semantic role ambiguity observed with the benefactive was accounted for by proposing that "beneficiary" is not really a thematic role *per se* and that the benefactive relation is independent of thematic relations. Being unspecified in terms of thematic role, the benefactive subject can be interpreted either as Experiencer or as Causer. This contrasts with the situation in passives, where the relation is also underspecified but is specifically non-causal and non-volitional. The concept of causality also provides an account of the difference in adverbial scope between *te-moraw* benefactives and passives.

In the last section we examined the other two types of benefactive constructions in comparison with the *te-moraw* benefactives to support our proposal of a separate MODAL feature for the benefactive relation. The syntactic differences between the *te-moraw* and *te-kure/te-yar* benefactives are very obvious, and only the former show significant similarities with passives. Informally, the former change the valency of the verb stem in gerundive form, while the latter do not. Despite the syntactic disparity, our assumption that the benefactive relation MODAL is independent of the SUBCAT feature or the semantic CONTENT structure has made it possible to unify different types of Japanese benefactives into a comprehensive system.

Note that the discussion in this chapter has also supported our general approach that each linguistic sign consists of several independent levels of information. This approach provides a new dimension in representing the syntactic and semantic properties of a given sign. In particular, it makes it possible to capture the uniformities among benefactive constructions, among *te-moraw* benefactives, and between passives and *te-moraw* benefactives, at the same time as referring to their syntactic differences.

That is to say, we have examined the three *te-moraw* benefactives in terms of three comparisons: (1) with passives, (2) with each other, and (3) with other types of benefactives. We have demonstrated that, in terms of the first comparison, similarities with passives are encoded in SUBCAT features and in the general structure of semantic CONTENT; differences follow from the thematic underspecification of the thematic relation involved in the *te-moraw* benefactive relation, the postulation of a MODAL feature, and the morphological status of auxiliary verbs as opposed to affixes. As for the second comparison, all of the *te-moraw* benefactive constructions share the semantic CONTENT structure, while syntactic differences between them are reflected in SUBCAT features. The third comparison identifies MODAL information as the common denominator of the three types of Japanese benefactive constructions. The SUBCAT feature and the semantic CONTENT structure, on the other hand, represent the differences between *te-moraw* benefactives and *te-kure/te-yar* benefactives.

Thus the approach which we defended in the analysis of passives finds support in the analysis of benefactives as well. In the next chapter we will examine causative constructions in Japanese, and demonstrate that our approach brings a number of desirable consequences in the analysis of causatives as well.

Notes

1. Bloch (1946), for example, lays out ten classes of verb inflection, where V-*te* is defined as Gerund. Bloch's treatment has been accepted by a number of linguists, including Martin (1974), Jacobsen (1982), among others. The definition of the morpheme *te* is not uncontroversial, however. It has often been glossed as 'and,' as well, because that is the form one would find at the end of a verb or an adjective in conjunction (Gunji 1987). So the benefactive predicate involving a stem verb *yom* 'read' is *yom-de-moraw* after assimilatory voicing of /t/, which is phonologically identical to the conjoined verb meaning 'read and receive.'

Although the complex predicate involving this class of auxiliary verbs is thus basically indistinguishable on the surface from a conjoined verb of the form Verb-*te*-Verb, it is beyond doubt that they are syntactically different. Evidence includes the following facts: (1) the auxiliary form allows only a V^0-*te*-V^0(*moraw*) sequence, whereas in conjunction not only V^0 but also VP and S (where NPs are preceding V^0) can follow *te*; (2) no adverb or Adjunct NPs can be inserted between *te* and *moraw* in the case of the auxiliary; (3) the semantic content of auxiliary verbs is altered; the lexical meaning is more or less lost.

We claim two points. First, we follow Bloch (1946) and call V-*te* a gerundive form. Second, we do not recognize a separate conjunction morpheme *te*. In other words, the morpheme *te* is alway a gerundive marker, and nothing else.

The point is not the particular term "gerund," but that the morpheme *te* is an inflectional suffix. This claim draws on data from morphophonology in Japanese. Namely, suffixation of *te* involves assimilatory voicing of /t/: when the stem ends in a voiced consonant, /t/ surfaces as /d/. The same process can be found in the suffixation of the past tense morpheme *ta*, and nowhere else. Detailed examination of phonological processes in verb morphology in Japanese demonstrates that the past tense morpheme *ta* shows a number of other phonological properties found exclusively in affixes (Ishihara 1991; Uda 1992), and they are all shared by the morpheme *te* and by nothing else. Therefore it seems reasonable to assume that the past tense morpheme *ta* and the gerundive morpheme *te* belong to the same category: inflectional morpheme.

Positing the conjunctive morpheme *te* as an independent class obscures the morphophonological system of Japanese. The "conjunctive" morpheme *te* behaves exactly the same as the morpheme *te* in the complex predicate. As the environment of the phonological processes is very strictly limited, one would naturally expect that the environments would form a natural class; i.e., inflectional affix.

We assume that in Japanese, VPs (including Ss) can be conjoined without any conjunctive morpheme. A verb can be followed by another sentence, a VP, or a lexical verb if it is in either infinitive or gerundive form. See the examples given below:

(i) a. Syota -ga   yama   -e iki   ringo -wo tot-ta.
       nom   mountain to go (INF) apple acc pick-PST
    b. Syota -ga   yama   -e it-te   ringo -wo tot-ta.
       nom   mountain to go (GER) apple acc pick-PST
    'Syota went to the mountain and picked some apples.'

The idea that there is no conjunction word *te* in Japanese can be further supported by the fact that *te* can optionally be followed by conjunction word *sosite* 'and' or *sorede* 'then' etc. without sounding redundant.

Thus we assume that the *te-moraw* benefactive predicate is actually a lexical verb in gerundive form followed by a benefactive morpheme *moraw*. We will use the term "*te-moraw* benefactive," including *te*, simply as a convention. We do not recognize a major boundary between verb stem and *te*.

There is an alternative analysis that the *te* form coordination is actually a gerundive construction which corresponds to the English participial construction such as the first clause in *Eating an apple, Tom drew a picture* rather than *Tom ate an apple and drew a picture* (Shuichi Yatabe, p.c.). It is a possibility, but we leave the issue open here to avoid digression.

2. As with the data of reflexive binding in passives, there seems to be individual variation regarding the judgment of data. We do not discuss this issue, however.

3. The verb *itadak* is a member of the set of "humble" verbs where the subject (=speaker) expresses respect toward someone else *by degrading him/herself*.

4. There is another pattern of emphatic particle insertion in benefactives. In this pattern, the emphatic particle comes between the

verb in gerundive form and the benefactive morpheme, and no light verb is necessary. This is presumably because, as mentioned above in relation to Subject Honorification, *moraw* is a morphologically independent word. Interestingly, in this pattern, the emphatic particle seems to be able to intervene between the gerundive verb and the benefactive morpheme irrespective of type:

(i) a. Syota -ga Kyoko -ni homete-*sae* morat-ta.
 nom dat praise-*even* BEN-PST
 'Syota was even praised by Kyoko (for Syota's benefit.)'
 b. Syota -ga Kyoko -ni atama -wo nadete-*sae* morat-ta.
 nom dat head acc pat-*even* BEN-PST
 'Syota had his head even patted by Kyoko (for Syota's benefit.)'
 c. Syota -ga Kyoko -ni deteitte-*sae* morat-ta.
 nom dat leave-*even* BEN-PST
 'Syota had Kyoko even leave (for Syota's benefit.)'

We suggest that Do-Support and emphatic particle insertion (without the light verb $s(u)$) are completely separate phenonema. We assume that insertion of the emphatic particle itself is sensitive only to the morphological boundary. It is perhaps the insertion of the light verb $s(u)$ which requires the syntactic boundary. We do not pursue this suggestion any further.

5. While Gunji 1987 recognizes that the "suffix" *temoraw* consists of two morphemes, he treats them as a single unit. For, he claims, this sequence behaves as a unit and does not differ syntactically from such monomorphemic suffixes as *(r)are* or *(s)ase*. We argue against this point in the following section. For another thing, he regards the morpheme *te* as a conjunctive "and," a position which we rejected in note 1 above. He gives as an English translation of the *te-moraw* benefactive sentences expressions such as "ask (and receive) the favor of." This point will also be discussed later.

6. The feature specification [PAS -] indicates that the verb phrase (TVP) formed by the benefactive cannot undergo passivization (see section 3.3.5).

7. There are other possibilities of morpheme order, but (15) shows the expected one for the OH in question. No other morpheme order works, either.

8. This description does not assume a VP-internal subject hypothesis. Under a VP-internal subject hypothesis, the surface position of the matrix subject, Spec of IP, is not a θ-position in any case. The subject position mentioned in the above description corresponds to the Spec of VP. The Spec of VP is a θ'-position in direct passives, while it is a θ-position in indirect passives. So, in direct passives, the Spec of IP is occupied at S-structure by an argument θ-marked in the object position, while in indirect passives it is occupied by an argument θ-marked in the Spec of VP position.

9. Terada 1990 observes that phrases can intervene between *te* and a verb in a conjunctive clause, while they cannot between *te* and *moraw* in *te-moraw* benefactives. She uses this fact to support her claim that *te* occupies Infl. Though her observation is correct and we agree that *te* is an inflectional morpheme, we do not agree with her interpretation; we believe that inseparability is a property not of *te* but of *moraw* as auxiliary. We do not think it is because *te* is a conjuctive word instead of an inflectional morpheme that phrases can come between *te* and a verb in conjunction. The problem that we see in Terada 1990 is that for her it is essential to posit two separate categories of *te*, conjunction and Infl, the view we argue against. See note 1 above.

10. A qualification is in order. The benefactive *moraw* is not a lexical verb like the homophonous verb meaning 'to receive.' With the verbs of the same category, e.g., aspectual auxiliary verbs such as *simaw*, *ok*, etc., it must occur adjacent to a gerundive verb, i.e., no phrasal category can be inserted between them, and it has only grammaticized meanings. We characterize this class of verbs as the class of auxiliaries, and recognize its morphological independence. The passive and the causative morphemes *(r)are*, and *(s)ase*, contrast with those auxiliaries in not being related to a homophonous lexical verb.

11. *Te-simaw* roughly corresponds to perfect aspect, with a slight connotation of regret for doing it. *Te-ok* is also aspectual, referring to a situation where one does something for future use. The last one, *te-yar*, is a benefactive predicate which we will discuss in section 4.6.

12. Kuroda 1965b also suggests a semantic association between *ni*-causatives and *te-moraw* benefactives, though he analyzes them as distinct constructions.

13. As demonstrated in the previous chapter, some manner adverbs can impose a causative interpretation on the direct/possessive passives. But this causative interpretation is usually unavailable without the

adverbials. The indirect passives never allow the manner adverbs to induce a causative interpretation.

14. Japanese indirect passive sentences have sometimes been translated into English with causative *have* for its potential Experiencer meaning. As we show, however, this type of translation is not very accurate because causative *have* potentially induce Causer interpretation, which indirect passives do not share.

15. Note that the optional causative interpretation is not enough to claim that *te-moraw* benefactives are syntactically closer to causatives rather than to passives. Besides the syntactic similarities with passives reported above, benefactives are the same as passives in not being able to trigger Object Honorification (cf. sections 3.3.5 and 4.3). On the other hand, as will be shown in the next chapter (section 5.6.3), causatives allow Object Honorification. This we take as clear indication that benefactives do not share the same syntactic structure as causatives.

16. According to them, the fact that *have* has several meanings where the subject can be either Theme, Experiencer, Goal, Location, Source, etc. gives support for the claim that the causative *have* has no event thematic role specification.

17. Lexical meaning provides no help. The meaning of the main verb *moraw* is quite specific: 'to receive,' the subject argument being invariably a goal. The meaning of *(r)are* and *(s)ase* is, of course, untestable because they never constitute independent lexical verbs.

Ritter and Rosen's (1990) analysis involves the idea of argument merger elaborated in Rosen 1989. Most of the syntactic argument concerning IP- vs. VP-embeddeding is untestable due to the syntactic difference between English and Japanese: e.g., Japanese does not have expletive words corresponding *it*, etc. A brief summary of the idea of argument merger by Rosen 1989 is given in chapter 5.

18. Croft (1991) refers to such roles as Causer as antecedent roles, and Experiencer as a subsequent role, to capture their difference in function with respect to the causal chain of an event. He further claims that the grammatical relations (obliqueness) hierarchy corresponds to the order of participants in the causal chain (184). When the matrix subject is the Causer, it is the initiator of the event and the highest in the causal chain. Very intuitively, we could suggest that the causal chain of the core event is extendable to include the Causer, as it is after all the initiator of the core event. Such an extension is impossible with

a causally unrelated argument, as it is by definition independent of the causal chain of the core event. But this is sheer speculation and we do not pursue it any further.

19. Though the three types of benefactive construction are usually grouped together and described together in comparison with each other in traditional Japanese grammar and in grammars for language learning, hardly any comprehensive analysis has been made of them in the Western linguistic frameworks. *Te-moraw* has sometimes been discussed in comparison with the passive (Inoue 1976b; Nakau 1973; Gunji 1987; Terada 1990), but, to my knowledge, it has never been analysed relative to the overall picture of benefactive constructions. This is presumably because the *te-moraw* benefactives show an interesting argument structure alternation parallel to the passives, while the other two do not.

20. To be precise, *notameni* glossed as 'for' is not a postposition but a postpositional phrase headed by *ni*. It consists of the genitive marker *no*, a noun *tame* meaning 'sake,' and a postposition *ni*. These morphemes do not necessarily form a constituent. A conjunctive phrase can intervene between *no* and *tame* or between *tame* and *ni*. Thus *for Kyoko and Syota* is translated either as *Kyoko to Syota* no-tame-ni, *Kyoko* no- *sosite Syota* no-tame-ni, or *Kyoko* no-tame *sosite Syota* no-tame-ni. We are indebted to Kazuhiko Fukushima for this remark.

21. This is a very informal description of the situation. By valency increase, we do not mean that the operation is lexical. Here we simply mean that the matrix subject of indirect benefactives does not correspond to any argument subcategorized for by the gerundive verb, so it must be the one introduced due to the presence of the benefactive morpheme *moraw*.

22. The a- and b-sentences in (53)-(54) have roughly the same meaning, though the ones with the benefactive morpheme perhaps carry a slightly stronger sense of benefactive relation.

23. Notice that the a- and b-sentences of (56)-(57) roughly correspond to the direct benefactive and the indirect benefactive, respectively, of *te-moraw* (type III) benefactives. That is, the beneficiary is the original *theme* argument in the direct *te-moraw* benefactive, and an argument which is not subcategorized for by the gerundive verb in the indirect *te-moraw* benefactive:

(i) a. *Watasi* -ga   Kyoko -ni(yotte) homete-morat-ta.
       I   nom   dat   praise-BEN-PST
   'I was praised by Kyoko (for my benefit.)'
   b. *Watasi* -ga   Kyoko -ni   Syota -wo homete-morat-ta.
       I   nom   dat   acc   praise-BEN-PST
   'I had Kyoko praise Syota (for my benefit.)'

24. It is in fact possible to make a benefactive sentence of type III with a *notameni* phrase, which explicitly introduces a beneficiary. Even in such cases, however, the matrix subject retains its status as a (secondary) beneficiary:

(i) Watasi -ga   Kyoko -notameni Syota -ni   kite-moratta.
    I   nom   for   dat   come-BEN-PST
   'I had Syota come over for Kyoko.'

Thus in the sentence above, the subject *watasi* 'I' necessarily remains as a (secondary) beneficiary in addition to *Kyko*, which is the primary beneficiary; hence it is different from 'Syota came over for Kyoko.' No argument in Type I & II benefacitives functions as an invariable beneficiary. We are indebted to Kazuhiko Fukushima for this remark.

25. The term "stem.subj" stands for the subject of the verb stem in gerundive form, whereas "mat.subj" stands for the matrix subject. This terminology is simply for the sake of convenience. We actually do not assume a syntactic embedding for the type I & II benefactive.

26. This does not mean that a person in the real world cannot do something for oneself. Consider an English sentence, *Mary knit a sweater for herself*, which denotes a situation where Mary is both a benefactor and a beneficiary. Note, however, that the linguistic expression *Mary* can only convey the information that its referent is an Agent and a benefactor. The beneficiary must be expressed by a different noun phrase, *herself*, though it is coreferential with *Mary*.

It is very important to distinguish between the identity of the Agent and the benefactor, on the one hand, and the coreferentiality of the benefactor and the beneficiary, on the other. This distinction is captured in HPSG in terms of parameter identity and parameter coindexing. Parameter identity refers to the former identity, while parameter coindexing refers to the corefentiality.

Therefore, the restriction that a linguistic argument cannot be both benefactor and beneficiary means that a benefactor and a beneficiary cannot share the same parameter; the fact that they still can be coreferential means that their parameters can be coindexed.

27. Fukushima 1990 analyzes these constructions as syntactic subject control structures of the commitment type (see section 2.1.4), for the matrix subject of Type I & II benefactives *offers* benefit. Admitting the plausibility of the approach, we leave the issue open.

V
Causative Constructions

5.1 Introduction

Japanese causative constructions have attracted much attention in studies of causatives. They are formed with a bound morpheme *(s)ase* attached to the stem verb.[1] Typologically speaking, therefore, the Japanese causatives have been classified as morphological causatives (Marantz 1984; Spencer 1990) in contrast to syntactic (periphrastic) causatives.

In a crosslinguistic survey of the grammatical relations involved in causative constructions, Comrie 1976 argues that morphological causativization increases the valency of a predicate by one. Intransitive verbs with a single argument end up with two arguments, subject and direct object. When the original verb is transitive, the causative verb apparently has three arguments, subject, direct object, and indirect object. The direct object often corresponds to the direct object of the lower predicate, and the indirect object to the subject of the lower predicate. This characterization seems to apply to Japanese. When the original verb is intransitive, the causativized verb has two arguments, marked with the nominative and the accusative. When the original verb is transitive, the causativized verb has three arguments, one each marked with the nominative, the accusative, and the dative.

However, this characterization of causatives have not gone unchallenged. Zubizarreta 1985, Rosen 1989, Falk 1991 and others show that the subject of the lower predicate actually does not share many of the properties of ordinary direct/indirect object with the exception of case marking. In terms of their syntactic properties, such arguments are reported to behave similar to a subject. This is exactly the case with Japanese causatives in terms, for instance, of reflexive binding and the scope of adverbial modification (Kuno 1973; Shibatani 1973). This has provided motivation, therefore, for the claim that Japanese causatives display biclausal properties.

In fact, patterns of case marking in Japanese causatives can lead to questions about their monoclausality in view of the above-mentioned crosslinguistic characterization of morphological causatives. The intransitive-based causatives can mark the lower subject (=the subject argument of the stem verb) with the dative case instead of with the expected accusative case. The different patterns of case marking are noted as carrying slightly different semantic interpretations, but it is not clear whether the semantic difference reflects also a syntactic difference.

So it has been a long-standing issue (1) whether Japanese causatives are monoclausal or biclausal and (2) whether there are two syntactically distinct classes of causatives in Japanese. We will answer yes and no to the first question, and yes to the second. That is, we propose that Japanese has both monoclausal and biclausal causatives. We will identify in this chapter two types of monoclausal causative and one type of biclausal causative in Japanese.

This chapter is organized in the following way. First, a theory-neutral description of the two types of causatives will be given. After a review of some of the representative previous studies of causatives, we will propose two different syntactic types of causatives: one lexically derived, and the other syntactically constructed. At the end of this chapter, we will suggest that a third type of causative exists in Japanese, which corresponds to the *faire par* causatives in Romance causatives.

5.2 Two Types of Causatives in Japanese

Japanese is well-known for having two types of causatives: *wo*-causatives and *ni*-causatives. These two types are readily identifiable when the lower predicate is an intransitive verb. The former marks the Causee[2] with the accusative case *wo*, and the latter with the dative case *ni*. The distinction is obscured when the lower predicate is a transitive verb; the lower subject is uniformly marked with the dative case.

The distinction between the two types of causatives is also captured in terms of a difference in meaning. *wo*-causatives are very often characterized as coercive causatives, while the *ni*-causatives are called non-coercive causatives.[3]

Just as a recurrent issue in the study of Japanese passives has been whether or not to recognize different syntactic structures for different types of passives, the recurrent issue with Japanese causatives has been whether or not *wo*-causatives and *ni*-causatives are to be associated with different syntactic structures. Non-uniformists recognize syntactic differences between *wo*-causatives and *ni*-causatives, while uniformists do not. We will first illustrate the two types of causatives based on intransitive verbs, and then those based on transitive verbs. The similarities and the differences between *wo*-causatives and *ni*-causatives will subsequently be examined.

5.2.1 Intransitive-Based Causatives

The Japanese causatives are formed by a stem verb and the suffixal causative morpheme *(s)ase*. The matrix subject, Causer, is always marked with the nominative case. When the stem verb is intransitive, the Causee is marked with either the accusative or the dative:

(1) a. Syota -ga   Kyoko -wo soko -e   ik-ase-ta.
            nom   acc there loc go-CAS-PST

    b. Syota -ga   Kyoko -ni soko -e   ik-ase-ta.
            nom   dat there loc go-CAS-PST
       'Syota made/let Kyoko go there.'

These two types of causatives are often noted as carrying slightly different meanings. The one with accusative marking (*wo*-causative) has been characterized as coercive causative, whereas the the one with the dative marking (*ni*-causative) has been referred to as non-coercive causative. The former has often been glossed as *make*, and the latter as *let* (Kuroda 1965b).

5.2.2 Transitive-Based Causatives

Different from the intransitive-based causatives, the transitive-based causatives usually do not show evidence of two distinct types, not on the surface at least. In most cases, the transitive-based causatives uniformly mark the Causer with nominative case, the Causee with dative, and the direct object of the original transitive verb with accusative. As the Causee is invariably marked with dative case, the transitive-based causatives are inherently ambiguous between the coercive and non-coercive readings. The examples of transitive-based causatives are given below:

(2) a. Syota -ga Kyoko -ni hon -wo yom-ase-ta.
       nom   dat   book acc read-CAS-PST
  *b. Syota -ga Kyoko -wo hon -wo yom-ase-ta.
       nom   acc   book acc read-CAS-PST
  'Syota made/let Kyoko read the book.'

(3) a. Syota -ga Kyoko -ni Sinzi -wo tatak-ase-ta.
       nom   dat   acc hit-CAS-PST
  *b. Syota -ga Kyoko -wo Sinzi -wo tatak-ase-ta.
       nom   acc   acc hit-CAS-PST
  'Syota made/let Kyoko hit Sinzi.'

The unavailability of accusative-case marking on the Causee has been ascribed to the ban on double-*wo* marking independently established in Japanese (Shibatani 1973; Inoue 1976b). That is, a simple clause cannot contain more than one accusative case in Japanese. Two accusative cases can appear in separate finite clauses:

(4) *a. Syota -ga eigo -wo benkyoo -wo si-ta.
        nom   English acc study   acc do-PST
   b. Syota -ga eigo -wo benkyoo-si-ta.
        nom   acc study-do-PST
   c. Syota -ga eigo -no benkyoo -wo si-ta.
        nom   English gen study acc do-PST
   'Syota studied English.'

(5) a. Syota -wa [Kyoko ga Sinzi -wo tatai-ta] to-iu
        top   nom   acc hit-PST COMP
       uwasa -wo kii-ta.
       rumor acc hear-PST
   'Syota heard the rumor that Kyoko hit Sinzi.'

  b. Syota -wa [Sinzi -wo tatak-u yoo] Kyoko -wo
       top   acc hit-PRS MOD   acc
     settokusi-ta.
     persuade-PST
   'Syota persuaded Kyoko so that she would hit Sinzi.'

  c. Syota -wa [Sinzi -wo tataki nagara] Kyoko -wo
       top   acc hit-PRS while   acc

sikat-ta.
scold-PST
'Syota scolded Kyoko, while hitting Sinzi.'

If the apparent lack of contrast between *wo*-causatives and *ni*-causatives based on transitive verbs is really due to the double-*wo* constraint, we will expect the contrast to show up when the constraint is not violated. This is indeed the case with the transitive verbs which idiosyncratically mark the direct object with the dative case. The causatives based on these verbs allow the Causee to be marked with either the accusative case or the dative case, just as with the intransitive-based causatives:[4]

(6) a. Kyoko -ga Naoko -ni sawat-ta.
 nom dat touch-PST
 'Kyoko touched Naoko.'

 b. Syota -ga Kyoko -wo Naoko -ni sawar-ase-ta.
 nom acc dat touch-CAS-PST
 c. Syota -ga Kyoko -ni Naoko -ni sawar-ase-ta.
 nom acc dat touch-CAS-PST
 'Syota made/let Kyoko touch Naoko.'

(7) a. Kyoko -ga Naoko -ni at-ta.
 nom dat tough-PST
 'Kyoko met Naoko.'

 b. Syota -ga Kyoko -wo Naoko -ni aw-ase-ta.
 nom acc dat touch-CAS-PST
 c. Syota -ga Kyoko -ni Naoko -ni aw-ase-ta.
 nom acc dat touch-CAS-PST
 'Syota made/let Kyoko meet Naoko.'

The data in (6)-(7) have been taken by the non-uniformists as evidence for two syntactically distinct classes of causatives based on transitive verbs, even when the difference is not apparent on the surface. They assume that the transitive-based *wo*-causatives mark the Causee with the accusative, which surfaces as dative case due to the double-*wo* constraint. The dative case is an accusative case in disguise, so to speak. *Ni*-causatives mark the Causee with the dative case whether the lower predicate is an intransitive verb or a transitive verb (Shibatani 1973; Kuno 1973; Terada 1990).

5.2.3 *Wo*-Causatives and *Ni*-Causatives

Thus the difference between the *wo*-causatives and the *ni*-causatives has been observed mainly in terms of case marking and semantic interpretation. The received view is that *wo*-causatives mark the Causee with accusative case, and carry a coercive interpretation. *Ni*-causatives, on the other hand, mark the Causee with dative case, and have a non-coercive interpretation. Non-uniformists have attempted to relate the contrast in meaning and case marking difference to a structural difference. Uniformists, on the other hand, claim that the case difference has no structural basis.

Non-uniformists typically assume the two classes of causatives equally for the intransitive-based and transitive-based causatives. Thus they attribute two structures to transitive-based causatives: one for the coercive interpretation, and the other for the non-coercive interpretation. Motivation for assuming two distinct syntactic structures even in the absense of a surface difference comes from the data of the passivization of causatives.

It has been widely known since Kuno 1973 and Harada 1973 that direct passives of the causatives only carry the coercive interpretation. The surface distinction between *wo*-causatives and *ni*-causatives of intransitives is obliterated under passivization, because the crucial argument is realized as the matrix subject, uniformly marked with the nominative case. See the following examples of direct passives based on intransitive-based causatives:

(8) a. Syota -ga Kyoko -ni soko -e ik-as(e)-(r)are-ta.
nom dat there to go-CAS-PAS-PST
'Syota was forced/*allowed by Kyoko to go there.'

b. Syota -ga Kyoko -ni soto -de asob-as(e)-(r)are-ta.
nom dat outside loc play-CAS-PAS-PST
'Syota was forced/*allowed by Kyoko to play outside.'

The same holds true with transitive-based causatives. As mentioned above, transitive-based causatives have been noted as inherently ambiguous between coercive and non-coercive reading; however, the ambiguity disappears when the causatives are passivized. They uniformly bear the coercive interpretation, just as do the direct passives of the intransitive-based causatives:

(9) a. Syota -ga Kyoko -ni hon -wo yom-as(e)-(r)are-ta.
　　　　　　nom　　　　dat　book　acc　read-CAS-PAS-PST
　　'Syota was forced/*allowed by Kyoko to read a book.'

　　b. Syota -ga Kyoko -ni pan -wo tabe-sas(e)-(r)are-ta.
　　　　　　nom　　　　dat　bread　acc　eat-CAS-PAS-PST
　　'Syota was forced/*allowed by Kyoko to eat bread.'

The unavailability of the non-coercive interpretation and the obligatoriness of the coercive interpretation have provided motivation for some non-uniformists to propose two syntactic structures for the transitive-based causatives, one which is passivizable, and the other which is not (Harada 1973; Kuno 1976b, 1983; Rosen 1989; Terada 1990), though semantic solutions have also been suggested (Inoue 1976b; Marantz 1981).

Besides case marking and passivizability, the syntactic difference between *wo*-causatives and *ni*-causatives is not as robust as the difference between the direct passives and the indirect passives. Recall that direct passives and indirect passives contrast in terms of reflexive binding, the optionality of the agent phrase and Subject Honorification, as discussed in chapter 3. *Wo*-causatives and *ni*-causatives, on the other hand, fail to display many of the distinctive properties we have seen in the case of the passives. There are data that have motivated a biclausal structure for both types of causatives: reflexive binding and adverb scope.

Shibatani 1973 observes that the Causee can bind a reflexive phrase, whether it is marked with the accusative or with the dative:

(10) a. Syota -ga Kyoko -wo zibun$_{i/j}$ -no heya -ni
　　　　　　nom　　　　acc　self　gen　room　to
　　hair-ase-ta.
　　enter-CAS-PST

　　b. Syota -ga Kyoko -ni zibun$_{i/j}$ -no heya -ni
　　　　　　nom　　　　dat　self　gen　room　to

hair-ase-ta.
enter-CAS-PST
'Syota made Kyoko enter his/her own room.'

(11) a. Syota -ga Kyoko -wo zibun$_{i/j}$ -no kuruma kara
      nom   acc self   gen car   from
   ori-sase-ta.
   get out-CAS-PST
   b. Syota -ga Kyoko -ni zibun$_{i/j}$ -no kuruma kara
      nom   dat self   gen car   from
   ori-sase-ta.
   get out-CAS-PST
   'Syota made/let Kyoko get out of his/her own car.'

As it has been traditionally assumed that the reflexive *zibun* can only be bound by the subject, these data have provided strong evidence that the causatives contain two syntactic subjects; hence, that they are biclausal.

Shibatani 1973 also provides data on adverb scope to argue for the biclausality of the two types of causatives. He observes that subject-oriented adverbs can modify either the matrix subject or the Causee in both the *wo*-causatives and *ni*-causatives:

(12) a. Syota -ga Kyoko -wo damatte heya -ni hair-ase-ta.
        nom   acc silently room to enter-CAS-PST
   b. Syota -ga Kyoko -ni damatte heya -ni hair-ase-ta.
        nom   dat silently room to enter-CAS-PST
   'Syota silently made Kyoko enter the room.'
   'Syota made Kyoko silently enter the room.'

(13) a. Syota -ga seito   -wo hata -wo hutte,   basu
        nom student acc flag acc wave-GER bus
      kara ori-sase-ta.
      from go-down-CAS-PST
   b. Syota -ga seito   -ni hata -wo hutte,   basu
        nom student dat flag acc wave-GER bus
      kara ori-sase-ta.
      from go-down-CAS-PST
   'Waving a flag, Syota made/let the students get off the bus.'
   'Syota made/let the students, waving a flag, get off the bus.'

On the assumption that these adverbial phrases are subject-oriented, Shibatani 1973 explains these data by appealing to the biclausality of the causatives of both types.[5]

Another argument for biclausality comes from the passivizability of the lower object of causatives. In either the coercive or non-coercive interpretation, the lower object cannot be passivized (Farmer 1980; Marantz 1981):[6]

(14) a. Syota -ga Kyoko -ni   hon   -wo   yom-ase-ta.
              nom   dat   book   acc   read-CAS-PST
   'Syota made/let Kyoko read the book.'
  *b. Hon   -ga Syota -niyotte Kyoko -ni/-wo
      book   nom   by   dat/acc
      yom-as(e)-(r)are-ta.
      read-CAS-PAS-PST
   'The book was made by Syota to be read by Kyoko.'

(15) a. Syota -ga Kyoko -ni   Sinzi -wo   tatak-ase-ta.
              nom   dat   acc   hit-CAS-PST
   'Syota made/let Kyoko hit Sinzi.'
  *b. Sinzi -ga Syota -niyotte Kyoko -ni/-wo
             nom   by   dat/acc
      tatak-as(e)-(r)are-ta.
      hit-CAS-PAS-PST
   'Sinzi was made by Syota to be hit by Kyoko.'

If causatives were indeed monoclausal, either the accusative-marked NP or the dative-marked NP should be able to undergo direct passivization, given that Japanese simple clauses allow both direct and indirect objects to be passivized (cf. section 3.2.1). So this provides another strong piece of evidence for the biclausality of causatives.

Shibatani's (1973) argument for the biclausality of the causatives has been widely accepted in the literature except by the lexicalists. Even non-uniformists have assumed a biclausal structure for both *wo*-causatives and *ni*-causatives. Syntactic differences between them have been postulated in such a way as to explain the passivizability of *wo*-causatives, or the obligatory coercive interpretation of the passivized causatives. We will see in the next section how Japanese causatives have been analyzed in the literature.

5.3 Previous Analyses of Japanese Causatives

Causatives have been analyzed from a number of points of view. In early transformational approaches, Japanese causatives are analyzed in a way similar to the periphrastic causatives of English. The causative morphemes are considered as independent verbs, and the causative is derived through a syntactic operation such as Equi-NP deletion. In the early 1980's, lexical approaches are proposed by Miyagawa 1980, Farmer 1984. The core operation of the causativization is carried out on the lexical level and it increases the valency of the original verb by one.

Marantz 1984 has opened a new perspective on the analysis of morphological causatives by proposing that the causative verb (morpheme) and the stem verb can merge at different levels of derivation. He argues that at the l(ogico)-s(emantic) level, causatives have exactly the same universal structure.

Marantz's (1984) idea has been developed in two directions (Spencer 1990). Baker 1988, on the one hand, has explored the universality of underlying structures. In his system, morphological causatives are no different from periphrastic causatives at D-structure. The differences are derived by the incorporation of the stem verb into the causative morpheme, controlled by general principles of grammar, such as the ECP, Case theory, and so on.

Rosen 1989, on the other hand, explores the idea of argument merger with Romance and Japanese causatives. She argues that the causative predicate and the embedded verb are merged at the level of a(rgument)-structure preceding D-structure. Recent studies in LFG also analyze morphological causatives as deriving from an operation at the level of a-structure, where the patient role of the causative predicate is fused with a role in the embedded predicate (Alsina 1991; Alsina and Joshi 1991).7

5.3.1 Transformational Approaches

Most of the transformational approaches to causatives advocate a non-uniform analysis. In particular, Kuroda 1965b, Kuno 1973, Shibatani 1973, and Inoue 1976b argue that *wo*-causatives and *ni*-causatives are syntactically distinct, while Shibatani 1976a argues that they are the same.

All of the transformational approaches analyze both types of causatives as involving sentential complements. In Kuno 1973, *wo*-

Causative Constructions

causatives have a control structure in which the direct object of the matrix clause triggers Equi NP Deletion of the subject of the embedded sentence. In *ni*-causatives, on the other hand, the higher predicate is intransitive, the lower subject having no role in the matrix clause. The following tree diagrams, taken from Kuno 1973, represent the D-structures of the *wo*-causatives and of *ni*-causatives, respectively:

(16) Syota -ga Kyoko -wo ik-ase-ta.
     nom   acc   go-CAS-PST
  'Syota made/let Kyoko go.'

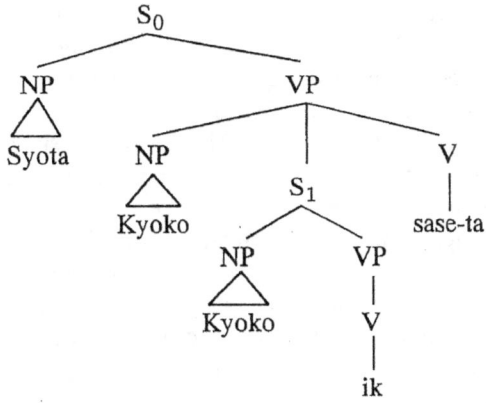

(17) Syota -ga Kyoko -ni ik-ase-ta.
     nom   dat   go-CAS-PST
  'Syota made/let Kyoko go.'

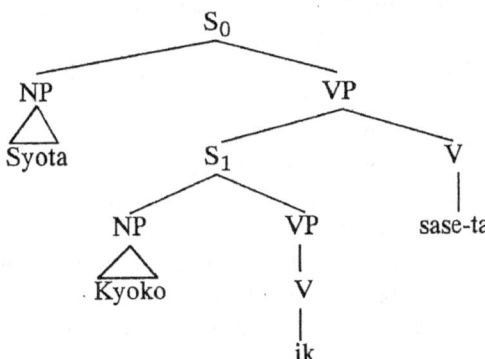

Note that both *wo*-causatives and the *ni*-causatives take a sentential complement. This accommodates Shibatani's (1973) observations on the biclausality of the causatives.

The distinct structures for the two types of causatives are motivated partly by semantic considerations and partly by the passivizablity of each type of causative. *Wo*-causatives have a direct object in the matrix clause which corresponds to the lower subject. Being the direct object of the causative morpheme, it is likely to receive accusative case and carry a patient-like, i.e., coerced, interpretation, which is characteristic of the *wo*-causatives. When the embedded verb is transitive and its object is marked with accusative, the direct object in the matrix clause ends up with dative case due to the double-*wo* constraint. Harada 1973 and Kuno 1976b, 1983 account for the obligatory coercive interpretation of direct-passivized causatives in terms of the structure of *wo*-causatives. According to Kuno 1976b, 1983, the Causee of *wo*-causatives can be raised to the subject position (i.e., passivized) because it is a direct object argument of the causative morpheme (=matrix verb). *Ni*-causatives, on the other hand, carry a more agentive interpretation (non-coercive, volitional, i.e., more actively involved in bringing about the caused event), because the Causee is not an argument of the causative morpheme. Furthermore, according to Kuno 1976b, 1983, the Causee of *ni*-causatives cannot be passivized because it is located inside an embedded S and has no corresponding NP in the higher S at the underlying structure.

5.3.2 Lexicalist Approaches

Miyagawa 1980 and Farmer 1980, 1984 challenge the idea of positing sentential complements for causatives. Both of them assume that the causative predicates are derived in the lexicon by means of a morphological rule of affixation. The operation of causativization increases the valency of the original verb by one, and the added argument becomes the matrix subject playing the Causer role. In contrast with the transformational approaches, most of the lexical approaches argue for a uniform analysis of causatives.

The unavailability of the accusative case marking has a very important implication for the syntactic structure of the transitive-based causatives. That is, so long as the double-*wo* constraint or the double-direct-object constraint applies in a single clausal domain as shown in (5) and (6) above, the unavailability of accusative case marking on the

Causee implies that the causative sentence is monoclausal (Miyagawa 1980).

Farmer 1984 argues that the causative morpheme has a predicate argument structure of the form in (18-a). The position indicated by the inner brackets is filled by the predicate argument structure of the stem verb. The composite predicate argument structure of the causative predicate is exemplified in (18-b), where the stem verb is *tabe* ('eat').

(18) a. (_____ (_____) sase)
     b. (_____ (_____ _____ tabe) sase)

The leftmost slot in (18-b) is for the matrix subject (Causer). The case marking on each slot is carried out by a set of case-linking rules. The regular case linking rules link nominative case to the leftmost argument slot, and accusative case to the rightmost argument slot. The dative case is linked to all other slots. According to the regular case linking rules of Farmer 1984, the intransitive-based causatives mark the Causee with accusative case. To derive the intransitive-based *ni*-causatives, she stipulates a special, semantic-based, dative case marking rule which precedes the regular case linking rules.

Thus, the lexical approaches do not recognize any syntactic differences between *wo*-causatives and *ni*-causatives aside from case marking. The differences are solely semantic, and the difference in case marking does not point to any syntactic difference.

5.3.3 Movement Approaches

Kitagawa 1986 proposes an affix raising approach, in which biclausality and monoclausality are maintained on different levels of derivation. The stem verb and the causative morpheme are derived in the lexicon as a complex predicate. They start out as a constituent, forming a V^0, and maintain their constituency until S-structure. By LF, however, the causative morpheme (affix) is raised out of the terminal V^0 as schematically illustrated below. Kitagawa 1986 assumes that *wo*-causatives and *ni*-causatives are not syntactically distinct:

(19) Syota -ga   Kyoko -ni   ringo   -wo   tabe-sase-ta.
            nom   dat   apple   acc   eat-CAS-PST
     'Syota let Kyoko eat the apples.'

a. S-structure

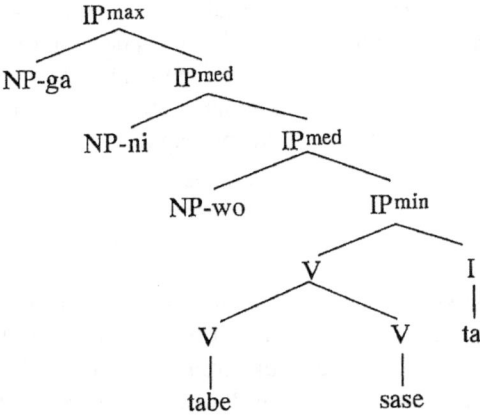

b. Pre-LF

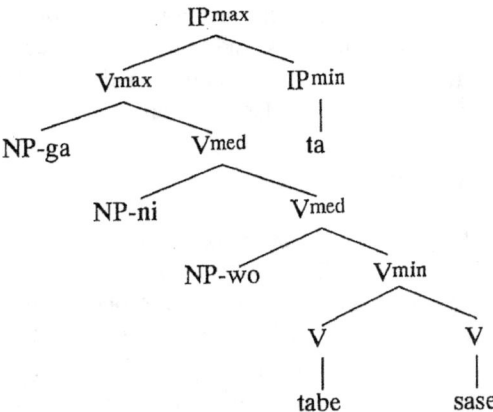

c. LF

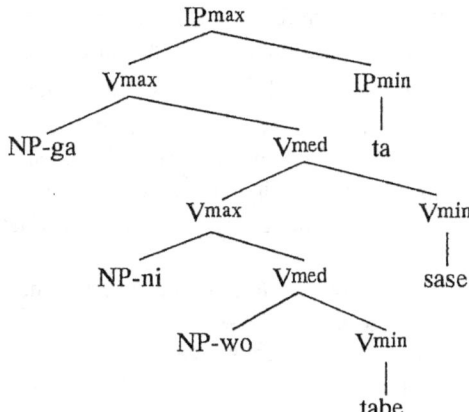

This way, lexical approaches and syntactic approaches are reconciled; both monoclausality and biclausality are attained at different phases of derivation. The data arguing for biclausality assumed since Shibatani 1973 are accounted for on the basis of the LF structure, which involves two maximal projections of V. The data arguing for the lexical derivation are readily accommodated as well, since the causative predicates are lexically derived in his approach.

Terada 1990, on the other hand, proposes a verb incorporation analysis following the line of Baker 1988. She recognizes a syntactic difference between the two types of causatives. She argues that the stem verb and the causative morpheme come to form a constituent through movement. Terada's (1990) approach contrasts with Kitagawa's (1986) in this sense, as the latter recognizes the constituency of the stem verb and the causative morpheme at the outset of the derivation.

Terada 1990 postulates the following structures for the two types of causatives:

(20) *wo*-Causatives
    a. intransitive-based
       NP-ga [NP-wo V] sase
    b. transitive-based
       NP-ga [NP-ni NP-wo V] sase

(21) *ni*-Causatives
       NP-ga NP_1-ni [PRO_1 VP] sase

Note that, for Terada, *ni*-causatives have a control structure much like the one she proposed for the indirect passives (see section 3.3.4). The VP in (21) can be either an intransitive verb phrase [$_{VP}$ V], or a transitive verb phrase [$_{VP}$ NP-wo V]. This accommodates the common observation that *ni*-causatives are formed based either on intransitive or on transitive verbs. The structure of the *wo*-causatives, on the other hand, varies according to the transitivity of the embedded verb.[8] The first NP inside the square brackets in (20-b) is marked with dative case due to the double-*wo* constraint.

As for the level of verb incorporation, Terada 1990 argues that the verb incorporation operates from D- to S-structure in the case of *wo*-causatives, and at PF in the case of *ni*-causatives.

The following trees illustrate the derivation of the two types of causatives. (22) shows the S-structure of the *wo*-causative, while (23) represents the PF of the *ni*-causative:[9]

(22) Syota -ga   Kyoko -ni   sara   -wo   araw-ase-ta.
           nom   dat   dish   acc   wash-CAS-PST
     'Syota made Kyoko wash the dishes.

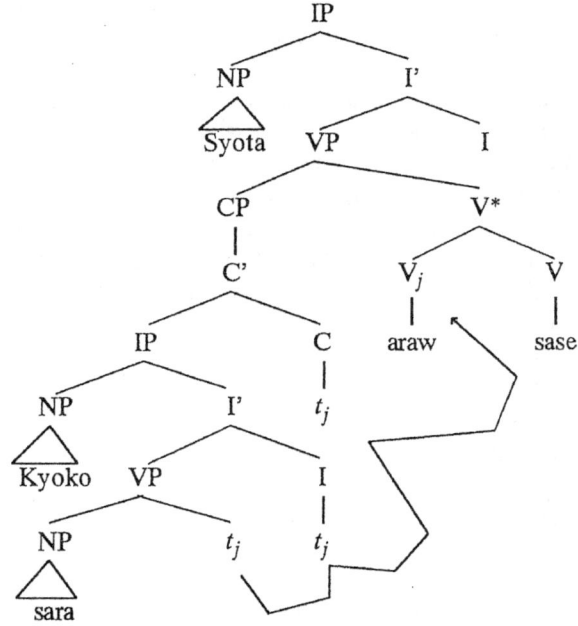

(23) Syota -ga Kyoko -ni ringo -wo tabe-sase-ta.
　　　 nom　　　　 dat　 apple　acc　eat-CAS-PST
'Syota let Kyoko eat an apple.'

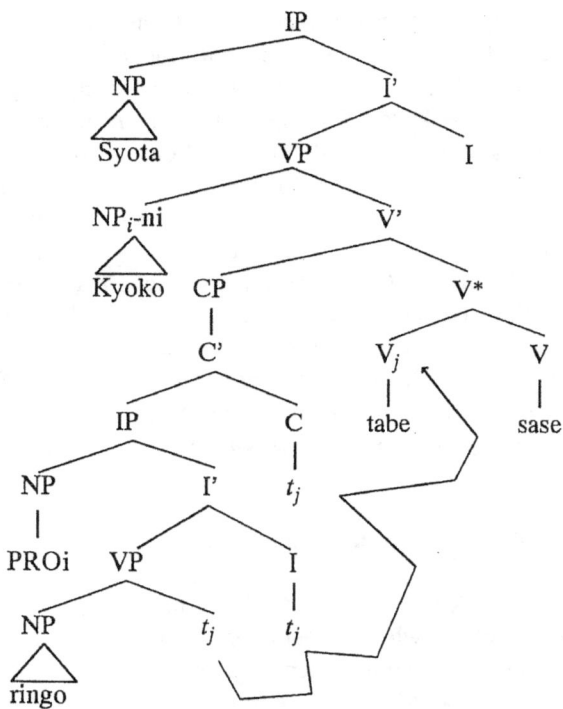

Let us first examine the *wo*-causative represented in (22). After verb incorporation, the stem verb and the causative predicate form a V^0 marked with *. As the causative morpheme is a transitive verb under her analysis and the stem verb is a transitive verb in this case, V* ends up with two Structural Cases, one showing up as accusative on the lower object and the other as dative on the higher object (Causee).[10] Crucially, as this instance of the dative case is a Structural Case, it can be absorbed under direct passivization.

Ni-causatives, on the other hand, have a control structure, where the embedded subject PRO is controlled by the direct object of the causative morpheme which carries the dative case. Analogous to the analysis of the indirect passives, the verb incorporation has to wait till

PF because, otherwise, the PRO would be governed by the causative predicate due to the Government Transparency Corollary (see section 3.3.4 above). The dative case on the argument controlling the PRO is claimed to be an Inherent Case, and hence cannot be absorbed. This explains, she says, why *ni*-causatives cannot be passivized.

The specification of the levels of verb incorporation makes an interesting prediction on the interaction of different complex predicates. Terada 1990 follows Baker's (1988) restriction on incorporation that V affixation (incorporation) proceeds in a bottom-up fashion. The V affixation of a higher clause cannot precede the V affixation of a lower clause.

The operation at PF cannot precede the operation at D- to S-structure. Thus Terada's (1990) system predicts that *ni*-causatives cannot be direct passivized, while *wo* causatives can be direct passivized because both of the incorporation operations take place at D-S structures (section 3.3.4). However, her system of level ordering of verb incorporation makes wrong predictions in some cases, seriously undermining her approach. We will discuss this issue later in section 5.5.2.

5.3.4 Argument Structure Merger Approaches

Rosen 1989 explores the concept of argument merger at the level of a(rgument)-structure, which constitutes the basis for the syntactic mapping from the predicate argument structure of each predicate to d-structure. Merger is defined as a process whereby a complete argument structure replaces the event argument in a causative verb's argument structure. With Marantz 1984, Rosen 1989 assumes that merger is optional. When it does not apply, periphrastic causatives result. The merger can also be either partial or total, resulting in the differences which are observed in the syntactic properties of the lower object.[11] When the merger is total, the argument structures of the two predicates are completely merged together, and the output simply has the structure of a two/three-place predicate. In the cases of partial merger, on the other hand, although the argument structures collapse and the argument structure of the lower verb becomes part of that of the causative verb, the lower verb still retains its own internal structure.[12]

Rosen 1989 proposes that Japanese causatives are instances of partial argument merger, just like the Spanish/French causatives.[13] They have a VP-complement structure. The following representation illustrates the process of partial merger that takes place in Japanese causatives:

(24) Partial Merger

$$\begin{matrix} sase \text{ 'make'} & [\text{ w (x) }] \\ yom \text{ 'read'} & [\text{ y (z) }] \end{matrix} \Big\} \rightarrow sase\text{-}yom \quad [\text{ w } [\text{ y (z) }]] <\!\underline{e\!>\ <\!e}\!>$$

Following Grimshaw and Mester 1988, and Grimshaw 1990, Rosen 1989 assumes a hierarchically-structured argument structure. An external argument is defined as the most prominent argument which is represented as the outermost argument in the structure. In the notation above, the causative morpheme *sase* 'make' takes two arguments, *w* and *x*, among which *w* is the external argument, or Causer, and *x* is an argument representing an event, or caused event. When the causative complex predicate is formed, this a-structure is merged with the a-structure of the verb stem, in the above example, *yom* 'read.' The latter is also a two-place predicate, *y* standing for the external argument, and *z* for the internal argument. To be more precise, the argument *x* (=caused event), is replaced by the a-structure of the verb stem, [y (z)]. Being an instance of partial merger, the argument structure of the embedded predicate is retained, which is indicated by the presence of the inner square brackets. The two <e> merged together at the right end of this formula means that the complex predicate has only one event role, in the sense of Higginbotham 1985, after the merger, entailing that the whole structure needs only one I^0.

According to Rosen's (1989) analysis, the complex verb in a partial merger construction is predicted not to undergo passivization because of the opacity of the embedded argument structure. But it is theoretically possible that either of the constituent verbs may undergo passivization before merger. Rosen 1989 shows this is indeed the case in Japanese as well as in Spanish/French. The passivization of the lower subject in a partial-merger language is explained as the passivization of the causative predicate before the merger process. The following representation illustrates the passivization of the Causee in *wo*-causatives:[14]

(25) Passive of the Lower Subject in *wo*-Causatives (Japanese)

    Syota   -ga   Kyoko   -ni   hon   -wo   yom-as(e)-(r)are-ta.
    nom   dat book acc   read-CAS-PAS-PST
    'Syota was forced/*allowed by Kyoko to read a book.'

    sase-rare 'be made'   [w-∅ (x)] <e> ⎫
    yom 'read'   [y (z)] <e>   ⎭

    →   sase-rare yom [w-∅ [y (z)]]   <e> <e>

As shown in (25), the a-structure of the causative morpheme *sase* is passivized, as indicated by the affixation of *rare* and the suppression (-∅) of its external argument, before it merges with the a-structure of verb stem *yom* 'read.'

The difference in passivizability between *wo*-causatives and *ni*-causatives is accounted for in terms of the case assigning property. Rosen 1989 proposes that the causative morpheme of *ni*-causatives is not a case assigner, while that of *wo*-causatives assigns an accusative case.[15] She assumes that dative case is assigned by default. So the Causee which has failed to receive any case from the causative verb will eventually get dative case by default.[16] Rosen 1989 suggests that there is some connection between the case-assigning property of the verb, its transitivity, and its ability to passivize. So, though she does not work out the details, she claims that as *ni*-causatives have no case to assign before merger, they cannot undergo passivization. That is why, according to Rosen 1989, the *ni*-causatives do not allow passivization while *wo*-causatives do.

5.3.5 Phrase Structure Approaches

Gunji 1987 proposes a phrase structure analysis of causatives, whereby the causatives are analyzed essentially as control structures. The causative morpheme is just another kind of control verb except that it is a bound morpheme; it subcategorizes for a subject, an object and a complement VP.

The distinction between *wo*-causatives and *ni*-causatives is not made in terms of phrase structure. The different case marking on the controller, which corresponds to the Causee, is accommodated by adding the relevant information to the lexical structure of the causative morphemes in the following two ways:

(26) a. Causative Suffix for *wo*-marked Object
sase: {POS V; SUBCAT {PP[SBJ], PP[OBJ; wo], VP[-AO]};
SEM CAUS'
b. Causative Suffix for *ni*-marked Object
sase: {POS V; SUBCAT {PP[SBJ], PP[OBJ; ni], VP[+SC]};
SEM CAUS'}

The feature AO (for accusative object) in (26-a) is assumed to be a HEAD feature. The specification [-AO], therefore, means that the embedded VP cannot have an object marked with the accusative case. The effect of this feature is the same as the double-*wo* constraint; when the lower object is marked with accusative case, the controller (Causee) cannot be marked with the accusative. The feature SC (for self-control) in (26-b) specifies that the embedded predicate in *ni*-causatives has to be a self-controllable action. Except for these features on the embedded VP, the causative structure in Gunji's (1987) system is essentially the same as the structures of the indirect passive and benefactive.17

For Gunji 1987, *wo*-causatives and *ni*-causatives are distinguished, not based on passivizability and the semantic property of coerciveness but on case marking and the semantic property of self-controllability. We essentially agree with Gunji's (1987) position on this point, and we will give more discussion on this matter in sections 5.5.1 and 5.5.2.

5.4 Lexical Causatives and Syntactic Causatives

In this section we will propose a new analysis of the Japanese causative construction. We recognize the distinction between *wo*-causatives and *ni*-causatives, but we do not relate it to the semantic distinction between coercion vs. non-coercion. We propose that *wo*-causatives are derived through a lexical rule while the *ni*-causatives have a syntactic control structure, with a VP-complement. This distinction also entails that *wo*-causatives are monoclausal while *ni*-causatives are biclausal, and that the causative morpheme *(s)ase* of *wo*-causatives is morphologically a bound form and functions as a derivational affix, while that of *ni*-causatives syntactically functions as a verb.

As we mentioned above, *wo*-causatives and *ni*-causatives fail to display many of the distinguishing properties that we have seen in the contrasts between types of passives or benefactives. In particular, as already illustrated above, both types of causative show the same properties in terms of reflexive binding and adverb scope. The Causee can bind a reflexive phrase, whether it is marked with the accusative or with the dative. Adverb scope is ambiguous in causative sentences, whether the Causee is marked with the accusative case or with the dative case. We will present our analysis in this section, and provide supporting evidence for it in the next. It will be shown that the lack of contrast in the above mentioned properties is also predicted in our approach.

5.4.1 *Wo*-Causatives as Lexical Causatives

We claim that *wo*-causatives are derived by a lexical rule. The rule crucially introduces a new argument to be the least oblique argument (=subject) in the SUBCAT list of the predicate. At the same time, the semantic CONTENT value of the original verb will be embedded in a larger psoa. The following is the lexical rule that we propose for *wo*-causatives:

(27) *Wo*-Causative Lexical Rule

$$\begin{bmatrix} \text{SUBCAT} \ \langle NP[1], ... \rangle \\ \text{CONT [3]} \begin{bmatrix} \text{RELATION} & R \\ \text{EXT-ARG} & [1] \\ R\text{-}er & [1] \\ \vdots & \vdots \end{bmatrix} \end{bmatrix} \Rightarrow$$

Causative Constructions

$$\begin{bmatrix} \text{SUBCAT} \langle \text{NP[2], NP[1], ...} \rangle \\ \text{CONT} \begin{bmatrix} \text{RELATION } cause \\ \text{EXT-ARG} \quad [2] \\ \text{CAUSER} \quad [2] \\ \text{PATIENT} \quad [4][\text{INDEX}[5]] \\ \\ \text{SOA-ARG} \quad [3] \begin{bmatrix} \text{RELATION } R \\ \text{EXT-ARG} \quad [1][\text{INDEX}[5]] \\ R\text{-}er \quad [1] \\ \vdots \quad \vdots \end{bmatrix} \end{bmatrix} \end{bmatrix}$$

Take an example of a stem verb *ik* ('go') that is mapped to the causative predicate *ik-ase* ('make go'):

(28) *Wo*-Causative of *ik-ase*

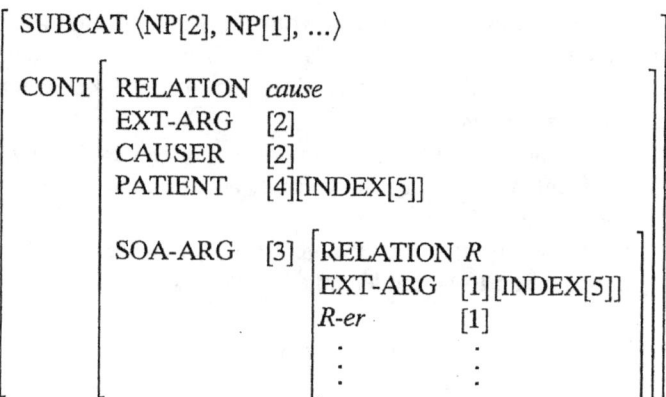

$$\begin{bmatrix} \text{PHON} \mid ik \\ \text{SYNSEM} \mid ... \begin{bmatrix} \text{SUBCAT} \langle \text{NP[1]} \rangle \\ \text{CONT[3]} \begin{bmatrix} \text{RELATION } go \\ \text{EXT-ARG} \quad [1] \\ goer \quad [1] \end{bmatrix} \end{bmatrix} \end{bmatrix} \Rightarrow$$

$$\begin{bmatrix} \text{PHON} \mid ik\text{-}ase \\ \text{SYNSEM} \mid ... \begin{bmatrix} \text{SUBCAT} \langle \text{NP[2], NP[1]} \rangle \\ \text{CONT} \begin{bmatrix} \text{RELATION } cause \\ \text{EXT-ARG} \quad [2] \\ \text{CAUSER} \quad [2] \\ \text{PATIENT} \quad [4][\text{INDEX}[5]] \\ \\ \text{SOA-ARG} [3] \begin{bmatrix} \text{RELATION } go \\ \text{EXT-ARG} \quad [1][\text{INDEX}[5]] \\ goer \quad [1] \end{bmatrix} \end{bmatrix} \end{bmatrix} \end{bmatrix}$$

Thus the causative relation is defined by three arguments: Causer, Patient,[18] and caused event. Partly following Gunji 1987 and Alsina 1991, we assume that the causative relation involves a Patient argument. The Patient is coindexed with the agentive argument (Ext-Arg) of the embedded soa; thus the Causee intuitively plays a dual role: a patient with respect to the causative relation, and an agent with respect to the caused event.[19]

We assume that this rule marks the argument corresponding to the Patient argument with the accusative case, and the matrix subject with the nominative case.

The following portion of feature structure represents the case marking information to be implemented in the lexical rule (27):

(29) $\langle NP_1, ... \rangle \rightarrow \langle NP_2[\text{nom}], NP_1[\text{acc}], ... \rangle$

Notice that this case marking is consistent with the Case Marking Schemata proposed in chapter 2 repeated below:

(30) a. V[Vcase: +AC]: $\langle NP_1, NP_2[\text{acc}], ... \rangle$
     b. V[Vform: FIN]: $\langle NP_1[\text{nom}], ... \rangle$
     c. Default: Mark non-case-marked argument with [dat]

As we discussed regarding the case marking of passives (section 3.7), an argument which is not mentioned in the rule will have the case marking carried over from its lexical specification prior to the operation of the lexical rule. It follows, therefore, that transitive verbs with an accusative case marking on their direct object cannot undergo this rule. If they did, they would end up with two arguments with accusative case, violating the double-*wo* constraint.

Transitive verbs can undergo this rule, however, so long as they do not violate the double-*wo* constraint. As we saw earlier, transitive verbs which (idiosyncratically) mark their direct object with dative case exemplify such a possibility. The following sentences illustrate the dative marking transitive verbs undergoing the lexical rule.

(31) a. Kyoko -ga   Naoko -ni   sawat-ta.
            nom   dat   touch-PST
        'Kyoko touched Naoko.'

     b. Syota -ga   Kyoko -wo   Naoko -ni   sawar-ase-ta.
            nom   acc   dat   touch-CAS-PST
        'Syota made/let Kyoko touch Naoko.'

Causative Constructions

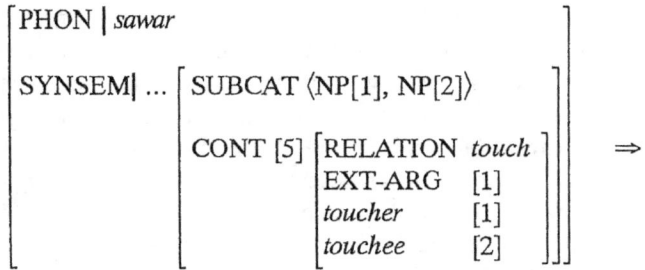

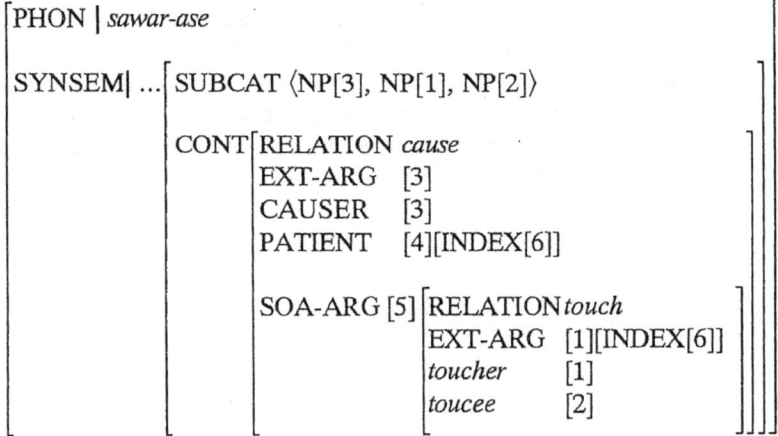

Notice that we are claiming that the double-*wo* constraint blocks the operation in case of a possible violation. We do not assume, as has been generally assumed in the literature (except Gunji 1987, for instance), that the double-*wo* constraint has the effect of deriving a dative case instead of the expected accusative case. In our conception of case marking, sketched in section 2.4, the dative case is always a default case, and is not likely to appear as a replacement of the accusative case.[20]

Thus, the lexical causatives are derived through a lexical rule (27) which changes the SUBCAT list of the original verb by adding one NP argument to the least oblique position. As a result, the original subject argument is deprived of its subject status. At the same time, the semantic CONTENT also constitutes a complex structure. The causative relation embeds the original relation denoted by the verb stem. The causative relation is defined by three things: a Causer participant, a Patient participant, and a caused event. The caused event is carried out by the Patient argument. We claim that the argument in the SUBCAT list which corresponds to the Patient role receives accusative case in the lexical (*wo-*) causatives, and the matrix subject nominative case. All the rest of the arguments are assumed to have a case carried over from the original (input) specification. It thus follows that the transitive verbs with an accusative case cannot undergo this rule. The operation is blocked because otherwise the double-*wo* constraint would be violated.[21]

Now, let us consider what our analysis of *wo*-causatives predicts concerning the passivization of causatives. First, look at NP[1] in the output feature structures in (27), (28), and (31). NP[1] is the one marked with accusative case, and corresponds to the Causee role. To be more precise, it is the subject argument of the verb stem, and coindexed with the Causee role. Recall our rule of direct passives given in section 3.4.1, repeated here for the sake of reference:

(32) Direct Passive Lexical Rule

$$\begin{bmatrix} \text{SUBCAT} \langle \text{NP}[1], \ldots \text{NP}[2], \ldots \rangle \\ \text{CONT [3]} \begin{bmatrix} \text{RELATION} & R \\ \text{EXT-ARG} & [1] \\ R\text{-}er & [1] \\ R\text{-}ee & [2] \\ \vdots & \vdots \end{bmatrix} \end{bmatrix} \Rightarrow$$

$$\begin{bmatrix} \text{SUBCAT} \langle \text{NP}[2], \ldots, (\text{NP}[2]) \rangle \\ \text{CONT} \begin{bmatrix} \text{RELATION } \textit{affect} \\ \text{EXT-ARG} \quad [4] \\ \text{AFFECTEE } [4][\text{INDEX}[5]] \\ \text{SOA-ARG} \quad [3] \begin{bmatrix} \text{RELATION} & R \\ \text{EXT-ARG} & [1] \\ R\text{-}er & [1] \\ R\text{-}ee & [2] [\text{INDEX}[5]] \\ \vdots & \vdots \end{bmatrix} \end{bmatrix} \end{bmatrix}$$

When the *wo*-causative undergoes the direct passive rule, turning NP[1] in (27), (29), and (31) into the subject, the Affectee role will be coindexed with the Causee role, tagged [4] in (27), (29), and (31), and consequently with the Ext-Arg of the most deeply embedded soa-arg, which shares the parameter with the new subject NP[1]. Thus, our analysis predicts that the Causee of *wo*-causatives can be passivized.

Note that there is another NP potentially available for direct-passivization, namely NP[2] in (31), or the dative-marked direct object of the verb stem. Notice that under our analysis the *wo*-causative in question is syntactically monoclausal. Considering the fact that either accusative- or dative-marked objects are direct-passivizable in Japanese, one would expect that the NP[2] could well be passivized just like the Causee NP[1]. Contrary to expectation, the direct passive of the NP[2] is totally impossible, as shown in (33):22

(33) a. Syota -ga Kyoko -wo Naoko -ni sawar-ase-ta.
          nom   acc   dat   touch-CAS-PST
    'Syota made Kyoko touch Naoko.'

*b. Naoko -ga Syota -ni Kyoko -wo sawar-as(e)-(r)are-ta.
      nom   dat   acc   touch-CAS-PST
    '(lit.) Naoko was made Kyoko to touch by Syota.'
    = 'Naoko had Syota make Kyoko touch her.'

The ungrammaticality of (33-b) would be a puzzle if direct passivization involved simply a change in the grammatical relation held by arguments and if the *wo*-causativization were a lexical operation simply introducing a new subject argument. The ungrammaticality of (33-b) directly follows from our analysis, however.

See the output feature structure in (31) again. This feature structure is supposed to undergo the rule (32) above to derive a direct passive sentence. Notice that the role corresponding to NP[2] is embedded in the lowest soa-arg and has no corresponding role in a higher soa-arg. So the operation fails to go through because the Affectee role cannot access the role tagged [2]; for it is embedded too deeply, so to speak, and there is no mediating role coindexed with it available.23

In this section we have proposed that *wo*-causatives are lexically derived. We have claimed that this type of causatives can be constructed based on intransitive and transitive verbs which do not assign accusative case. The operation is blocked when the verb stem has an accusative case to assign, due to the double-*wo* constraint. We have also shown that the Causee can be passivized in this type, while the object argument of the verb stem cannot. Before presenting evidence supporting our approach, let us now turn to the case of *ni*-causatives.

5.4.2 *Ni*-Causatives as Syntactic Control Structures

We propose that *ni*-causatives have a syntactic control structure. In particular, they have an object control structure much like the English *persuade*. The causative morpheme *(s)ase* is a bound form, but it syntactically functions as a verb.

We claim that the causative morpheme *(s)ase* of the *ni*-causatives has the following feature structure:

(34) *Ni*-Causative Morpheme *(s)ase*:

$$\begin{bmatrix} \text{PHON} \mid sase \\ \text{SYNSEM}\mid ... \begin{bmatrix} \text{SUBCAT}\langle \text{NP}[1],[2]\text{NP}_{[5]}, \text{V}[\text{SUBCAT}\langle[4]\text{NP}_{[5]}\rangle]{:}[3]\rangle \\ \text{CONT} \begin{bmatrix} \text{RELATION} & cause \\ \text{EXT-ARG} & [1] \\ \text{CAUSER} & [1] \\ \text{PATIENT} & [2] \\ \text{SOA-ARG} & [3] \end{bmatrix} \end{bmatrix} \end{bmatrix}$$

Thus the causative morpheme *(s)ase* is essentially a control verb, subcategorized for two NP arguments and a VP. The VP is controlled by the object NP. Control entails that the unexpressed subject of the VP is coreferential with the object NP. Controller selection is based on the semantics of the causative morpheme. As explained in section 2.1.4, control theory in HPSG refers to the semantic class of the control predicate. Object control is a property characteristic of verbs belonging to the Influence class. The Influence-type verbs specify a relation in which an agentive participant exerts influence on another participant so that a particular action will be brought about. The influenced participant is the performer of the action. Clearly, the causative relation fits into this semantic class, qualifying for the object control structure. The coindexing relation, signaled by the tag [5]

Causative Constructions

above, therefore, is guaranteed by the semantics of the causative relation.

Note, as discussed by Fukushima 1990, Alsina 1991, and Pollard and Sag 1994, the VP-complement analysis contrasts with the S-complement analysis, which is standardly assumed in GB.[24] That is, we assume that the Causee is directly subcategorized for by the matrix causative verb, and is not syntactically encoded as the subject argument.

Now, take an example of a *ni*-causative in (35), whose structure is represented in the tree diagram (36). Due to the feature sharing mechanism, the VP marked with * in the structure of (36) will have the feature structure given in (37):

(35) Syota   -ga   Kyoko -ni   hon   -wo   yom-ase-ta.
             nom   dat   book   acc   read-CAS-PST
     'Syota made/let Kyoko read the book.'

(36)

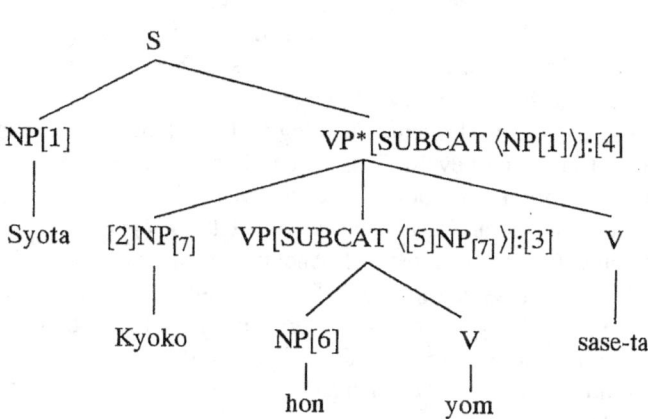

(37) *Ni*-Causative with the Stem Verb *yom*:

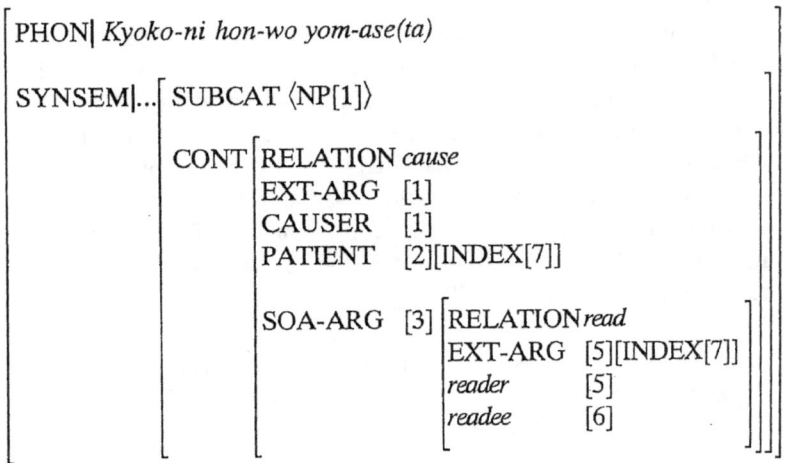

Compare the feature structure in (37) with that of the *wo*-causatives in (27), (28), and (31). Here we see essentially the same semantic CONTENT structure shared by *wo*-causatives and *ni*-causatives. That is, a causative relation is defined by a Causer role, a Patient role, and a caused event. The Patient role is coindexed with the Ext-Arg of the caused event, meaning that the Patient is the one who carries out the caused event. This semantic structure and the coindexing relation are common to both *wo*-causatives and *ni*-causatives. We take this situation as an advantage of an HPSG approach over other approaches. Just as passives and benefactives of any type are identified as such by their semantic CONTENT structure, with their respective type being identified by their syntactic category feature which includes a SUBCAT feature, so are causatives. Uniformity among different types of causatives is readily captured in the domain of a semantic CONTENT structure.

One might object to positing a common semantic CONTENT structure for all types of causatives, by pointing out the well-noted semantic difference between *wo*-causatives and *ni*-causatives, i.e., coerciveness vs. non-coerciveness. We will argue shortly that coerciveness is not the correct concept for distinguishing the two types of causative, and claim that the real semantic difference between the *wo*-causatives and *ni*-causatives can be derived from their structural difference.

There is one more point worth mentioning in the feature structure of causatives. Notice that a causative relation consists of two soas, one embedded in the other. Under the mechanism of HPSG, the information about the embedded soa, corresponding to the caused event, is correctly supplied by the semantic CONTENT of the verb stem. The embedding structure of the semantic CONTENT feature will prove to be crucial in accounting for the data of reflexive binding and adverbial modification (see section 5.5.3).

The dative case on the Causee argument is inherently associated with the causative predicate; it is independent of the embedded verb. Recall that *ni*-causatives can be formed irrespective of the transitivity of the stem verb, as the following examples show (Rosen 1989; Terada 1990). The verb stem involved in (38-a) is intransitive, (38-b) transitive with accusative marking, and (38-c) transitive with dative marking.

(38) a. Kyoko -ga   Naoko -*ni* hasir-ase-ta.
         nom   dat   run-CAS-PST
      'Kyoko made Naoko run.'

   b. Syota -ga   Kyoko -*ni* hon   -wo yom-ase-ta.
         nom   dat   book   acc read-CAS-PST
      'Syota made Kyoko read a book.'

   c. Syota -ga   Kyoko -*ni* Naoko -ni sawar-ase-ta.
         nom   dat   dat touch-CAS-PST
      'Syota made Kyoko touch Naoko.'

Further, the object argument of a control predicate is standardly marked with the dative case in Japanese, as illustrated below:

(39) a. Syota -ga Kyoko -*ni* hon   -wo yom-u   to
         nom   dat   book   acc read-PRS COMP
      yakusokusi-ta.
      promise-PST
      'Syota promised Kyoko to read a book.'

   b. Syota -ga Kyoko -*ni* hon   -wo yom-u   yoo
         nom   dat   book   acc read-PRS MOD

susume-ta.
advise-PST
'Syota advised Kyoko to read a book.'

c. Syota -ga Kyoko -ni hon -wo yom-u yoo
        nom   dat   book   acc   read-PRS   MOD
   meizi-ta.
   order-PST
   'Syota ordered Kyoko to read a book.'

Thus, given the semantics of the causative relation as a type of Influence relation in the sense of Sag and Pollard 1991 and dative case marking on the Causee, it is not unreasonable to identify *ni*-causatives as having a control structure. Case marking is not the only evidence, of course. Other evidence comes from the semantic restriction on the class of *ni*-causatives, Do-Support, and the interaction between Subject Honorification and Object Honorification, which we discuss fully in the next section.

Before moving on to the discussion of evidence, let us call attention to one important aspect of our claim; i.e., the passivizability of the Causee of *ni*-causatives. Notice that there is nothing in the feature structure (34) that blocks it from undergoing direct passivization. The Affectee role will be successfully coindexed with the Causee role, which is coindexed with the Ext-Arg of the embedded soa, as guaranteed by the HPSG Control Theory. Note that the dative-marked argument of object-control structures is generally allowed to be passivized, as shown in (40):

(40) a. Kyoko -ga Syota -ni hon -wo yom-u yoo
             nom   dat   book   acc   read-PRS   MOD
   susume-rare-ta.
   advise-PAS-PST
   'Kyoko was advised by Syota to read a book.'

b. Kyoko -ga Syota -ni hon -wo yom-u yoo
         nom   dat   book   acc   read-PRS   MOD
   meizi-rare-ta.
   order-PAS-PST
   'Kyoko was ordered by Syota to read a book.'

Therefore, it is theoretically possible to make a direct passive from *ni*-causatives, and we indeed assume, contrary to the view on passivization of causatives assumed by many (Harada 1973; Kuno 1976b, 1983; Rosen 1989; Dubinsky 1989; Terada 1990; among others), that the causee of *ni*-causatives can be direct-passivized. This position will be defended in the next section.

Direct-passivization of a lower object, on the other hand, is predicted to be impossible, and this is borne out by data. The causative predicate, represented in (34), subcategorizes for only two NPs, corresponding to a Causer and a Causee (Patient). The object of the embedded predicate (verb stem), therefore, is not accessible for passivization.

In this section we have proposed that *ni*-causatives are syntactic causatives and have a syntactic control structure. Because of the semantics of the causative relation, as a subtype of the Influence relation, it is predicted to be object-control. The causative predicate *(s)ase* of the syntactic (*ni*-) causatives syntactically functions as an independent verb, subcategorized for two NP arguments and a VP argument. The VP argument is controlled by the object, or the Causee argument. The object argument is marked with the dative case, as is standard in a control structure. The transitivity or case marking properties of the head verb of the VP-complement have no bearing on the case marking or any other syntactic property of the syntactic causatives. The semantic CONTENT of the syntactic causatives shares exactly the same structure with the semantic CONTENT of the lexical causatives.

5.5 In Defense of the Present Approach

As we have shown in the previous sections, the present approach posits two types of causatives: lexical and syntactic. The former, *wo*-causatives, are derived through a lexical rule, while the latter, *ni*-causatives, have a syntactic control structure. Though *ni*-causatives can be formed based on either intransitive, transitive, or ditransitive verbs regardless of their case marking properties, *wo*-causatives can be formed only from verbs without accusative case. That is, the *wo*-causative formation is blocked in the case of a possible violation of the double-*wo* constraint. In other words, we do not recognize two distinct types of transitive-based causative which are nondistinctive at surface.

Notice that our approach goes counter to the oft-assumed view of causatives in three points. Namely, it has been often claimed that (1) *wo*-causatives express coercive causation, while *ni*-causatives express non-coercive causation (cf. Shibatani 1973;[25] Kuno 1973); (2) based on the above assumption, the Causee can be passivized only in *wo*-causatives and not in *ni*-causatives, as passives of causatives obligatorily carry the coercive interpretation (cf. Kuno 1976b, 1983; Dubinsky 1989; Rosen 1989; Terada 1990); (3) either type of causative is biclausal, as indicated by reflexive binding and adverb scope (cf. Shibatani 1973; Kitagawa 1986). We challenge these points by claiming that (1) the difference between *wo*-causatives and *ni*-causatives is not related to coerciveness, (2) the Causee can be passivized in either type of causative, and (3) only *ni*-causatives are biclausal, and *wo*-causatives monoclausal.

This section gives arguments to defend our position. We will start with the discussion of the coerciveness interpretation. With Tonoike 1978, Gunji 1987, Dubinsky 1989, and Terada 1990, we claim that coerciveness is not an adequate notion for characterizing the two types of causatives. The second point, passivizability, will be discussed next. It will be shown that the obligatory coercive interpretation of passivized causatives not only fails to support positing syntactically distinct causatives but also makes wrong predictions concerning the benefactivization of causatives. We will argue that the data pertaining to the third point, biclausality of causatives, do not really prove syntactic biclausality.

5.5.1 Coerciveness and Self-Controllability

As mentioned above, accusative case marking on the Causee has traditionally been associated with a coercive interpretation, and dative case marking with a non-coercive interpretation. Even when the Causee is marked with dative case in the transitive-based causatives, it has been considered as the accusative case in disguise, so to speak, if the sentence has a coercive interpretation.

However, the concept of coerciveness is not really adequate to distinguish between *wo*-causatives and *ni*-causatives. Tonoike 1978 argues that the difference is no more than a preferred interpretation, which is largely pragmatic at best, and can be cancelled. The *wo*-causatives can have a non-coercive interpretation, and *ni*-causatives are compatible with a coercive interpretation. See the following examples showing this point:

(41) a. Syota -ga   Kyoko -wo hutyuui-de   kegas-asete-simat-ta.
         nom   acc   carelessly   be injured-CAS-PER-PST
    'Syota carelessly caused Kyoko to be injured.'

   b. Syota   -ga   Kyoko -ni muriyari   gakko -e   ik-ase-ta.
         nom   dat forcefully school to go-CAS-PST
    'Syota forced Kyoko to go to school.'

   c. Keisatu -ga   Kyoko -ni saibansyo -ni   syuttoos-ase-ta.
      police nom   dat court   loc   appear-CAS-PST
    'The police made Kyoko make an appearance at the court.'

Thus, (41-a) is a *wo*-causative sentence, but it does not involve a coercive causation. That is, the referent of the matrix subject *Syota* did not force the Causee *Kyoko* to get injured. In (41-b) and (41-c), on the other hand, the causation is coercive, though the sentences are *ni*-causatives. These examples clearly show that the semantic contrast between coercion vs. non-coercion does not adequately characterize the distinction between *wo*-causatives and *ni*-causatives. Tonoike's (1978) claim has been supported by Gunji 1987, Dubinsky 1989, Terada 1990, and others.

Tonoike (1978) and his followers claim that the difference between *wo*-causatives and *ni*-causatives is more appropriately captured by the concept of self-controllability or protagonist control. That is, as Harada (1973) first notes, *ni*-causatives are possible only when the Causee holds control over the action he/she performs.[26] The following examples clearly demonstrate that only the self-controllable actions can form *ni*-causatives:

(42) a. Hana   -ga   sai-ta.
       flower nom bloom-PST
    'The flower has bloomed'

   b. Syota   -ga   hana   -wo sak-ase-ta.
         nom   flower acc bloom-CAS-PST
    'Syota made the flower bloom.'

*c. Syota -ga hana -ni sak-ase-ta.
   nom flower dat bloom-CAS-PST
   'Syota made the flower bloom.'

(43) a. Yasai -ga kusat-ta.
     vegetable nom rot-PST
     'The vegetables rotted.'

   b. Syota -ga yasai -wo kusar-ase-ta.
      nom vegetable acc rot-CAS-PST
      'Syota made the vegetables rot.'

   *c. Syota -ga yasai -ni kusar-ase-ta.
       nom vegetable dat rot-CAS-PST
       'Syota made the vegetables rot.'

(44) a. Kyoko -ga yorokon-da.
     nom happy-PST
     'Kyoko was delighted'

   b. Syota -ga Kyoko -wo yorokob-ase-ta.
      nom acc happy-CAS-PST
      'Syota made Kyoko happy.'

   *?c. Syota -ga Kyoko -ni yorokob-ase-ta.
        nom dat happy-CAS-PST
        'Syota made Kyoko happy.'

(45) a. Kyoko -ga kizetusi-ta.
     nom faint-PST
     'Kyoko fainted.'

   b. Syota -ga Kyoko -wo kizetus-ase-ta.
      nom acc faint-CAS-PST
      'Syota made Kyoko faint.'

   *c. Syota -ga Kyoko -ni kizetus-ase-ta.
       nom dat faint-CAS-PST
       'Syota made Kyoko faint.'

In the above examples, to bloom, to rot, to be delighted, and to faint are usually not considered as self-controllable actions. The causatives using the verb stems denoting such uncontrollable events cannot be *ni*-causatives. *Ni*-causatives of (44) and (45) are possible only in such a context that Syota is a movie director and he makes the actress Kyoko act as he directs. In other words, *ni*-causatives require a context where the action "be delighted" and "faint" can felicitously be construed as self-controllable.

With Tonoike 1978 and others, we take the view that both the lexical and syntactic causatives are inherently ambiguous in terms of coerciveness. The actual distinction between the two types of causatives should be made in terms of self-controllability. Semantic ambiguity between the coercive reading and the non-coercive reading provides no good evidence for positing two distinct structures for one surface structure of the transitive-based causatives.27

Now the question is whether the difference in self-controllability between *wo*-causatives and *ni*-causatives has any syntactic, structural basis. We suggest that the requirement of self-controllability derives from syntactic control structure. Predicates which denote non-self-controllable action, *kusar* ('rot'), *kizetus* ('faint'), etc., cannot have a *ni*-causative sentence because they cannot enter into a syntactic control structure. The controller must have control over the action denoted by the controlled VP. The reason for this semantic constraint on the syntactic control structure is not clear to us, but this constraint seems to be valid in Japanese as the following sentences show:28

(46) ??a. Syota -ga Kyoko -*ni* kizetusu-ru to yakusokusi-ta.
nom dat faint-PRS COMP promise-PST
'Syota promised Kyoko to faint.'

??b. Kyoko -ga Syota -*ni* kizetusu-ru yoo susume-ta.
nom dat faint-PRS MOD advise-PST
'Kyoko advised Syota to faint.'

??c. Kyoko -ga Syota -*ni* kizetusu-ru yoo meizi-ta.
nom dat faint-PRS MOD order-PST
'Kyoko ordered Syota to faint.'

All the sentences in (46) are anomalous. They are judged grammatical only when *Syota* can intentionally faint, i.e., pretending or acting in a play. Note that this is exactly the same semantic restriction as we have seen in discussing the semantic restriction on *ni*-causatives. Therefore, we claim that the semantic difference between *wo*-causatives and *ni*-causatives derives from the structural differences between them. The restriction on the latter that the caused event must be controllable by the Causee is inherent in the syntactic control structure.

5.5.2 Passivized Causatives and the Coercive Interpretation

The statement made above, that all causative sentences are inherently ambiguous in terms of coerciveness, may seem to need justification in view of the fact that the passives of the causatives unambiguously carry a coercive interpretation. Recall the data of passives of causatives, repeated here for the sake of reference. The data in (8) illustrate the direct-passivization of an intransitive-based causative sentence, and those in (9) that of a transitive-based causative:

(8)   a. Syota -ga   Kyoko -ni soko -e   ik-as(e)-(r)are-ta.
            nom   dat   there to   go-CAS-PAS-PST
        'Syota was forced/*allowed by Kyoko to go there.'

    b. Syota -ga   Kyoko -ni soto -de asob-as(e)-(r)are-ta.
            nom   dat   outside loc play-CAS-PAS-PST
        'Syota was forced/*allowed by Kyoko to play outside.'

(9)   a. Syota -ga   Kyoko -ni hon   -wo yom-as(e)-(r)are-ta.
            nom   dat   book acc read-CAS-PAS-PST
        'Syota was forced/*allowed by Kyoko to read a book.'

    b. Syota -ga   Kyoko -ni pan   -wo tabe-sas(e)-(r)are-ta.
            nom   dat   bread acc eat-CAS-PAS-PST
        'Syota was forced/*allowed by Kyoko to eat bread.'

The direct-passives of causatives in the above examples carry only a coercive interpretation. It is not a cancellable preference. The obligatoriness of the coercive interpretation has found a syntactic explanation, whereby only *wo*-causatives have a passivizable structure (Kuno 1976b). A transitive-based causative sentence has been associated with two distinct structures; one for coercive interpretation, which is passivizable, and the other for non-coercive interpreation, which is not passivizable. Though semantic accounts have also been offered to the obligatory coercive interpretation (Inoue 1976b), followed particularly by uniformists (Marantz 1981; Kitagawa 1986), syntactic explanations have been attempted in recent works such as Dubinsky 1989, Rosen 1989 and Terada 1990.

According to Rosen 1989, for instance, the causative predicate of *ni*-causatives cannot undergo passivization because it lacks Case (cf. section 5.3.4). Terada's (1990) system doubly guarantees the unpassivizability of *ni*-causatives. Simply put, first, the dative case on the Causee in *ni*-causatives is an Inherent Case, so it cannot be absorbed under direct-passivization. Secondly, the verb incorporation for *ni*-causatives does not take place till PF, so it cannot precede direct passivization whose verb incorporation takes place between D- and S-structure (section 5.3.3).

We claim, in contrast, that the obligatory coercive interpretation is purely semantic or pragmatic, and not syntactic. We maintain that a semantic explanation is not only a viable alternative, but is the only possible account. Crucial data come from direct-benefactivization of causatives. In the previous chapter we established that benefactives syntactically parallel passives, providing a semantic account for apparent incongruities between them. If the obligatory coercive interpretation of the direct passives of causatives has a syntactic origin, direct-benefactivization ought to show exactly the same obligatory interpretation. But this is not the case. See the following examples of direct-benefactivization of causatives:29

(47) a. Syota -ga   Kyoko -ni   soko -e   ik-asete-morat-ta.
         nom   dat   there to   go-CAS-BEN-PST
    'Syota was *forced/allowed by Kyoko to go there.'

   b. Syota -ga   Kyoko -ni   soto   -de   asob-asete-morat-ta.
          nom   dat   outside loc   play-CAS-BEN-PST
    'Syota was *forced/allowed by Kyoko to play outside.'

(48) a. Syota -ga   Kyoko -ni   hon   -wo   yom-asete-morat-ta.
         nom   dat   book   acc   read-CAS-BEN-PST
    'Syota was *forced/allowed by Kyoko to read a book.'

b. Syota   -ga   Kyoko -ni   pan   -wo   tabe-sasete-morat-ta.
          nom   dat   bread   acc   eat-CAS-BEN-PST
'Syota was *forced/allowed by Kyoko to eat bread.'

As the glosses show, direct-benefactives of causatives obligatorily carry non-coercive interpretation, in sharp contrast to direct passives of causatives. The non-coercive interpretation in these cases is obligatory to the same degree as the coercive interpretation of the passives of causatives. If the obligatory coercive interpretation of passives of causative were to show the passivizability of *wo*-causatives, the obligatory non-coercive interpretation of benefactives of causatives could be understood as an indication of the exclusive benefactivizability of *ni*-causatives. However, as we mentioned above, benefactives syntactically parallel passives in Japanese.

Syntactic explanations, therefore, necessarily run into a serious problem. Kuno 1976b would have to block the Causee embedded in the lower S of *ni*-causatives from being raised to the matrix subject position under passivization, and at the same time, allow the very same argument to be raised to the matrix subject position under benefactivization. No syntactic explanation seems possible as to why this should be the case.

In Rosen's (1989) system, a predicate without Case (=*ni*-causatives) would have to undergo benefactivization, while benefactivization of a predicate with Case (=*wo*-causatives) would have to be blocked. Again, there seems no way to avoid the paradox, given the parallel syntactic properties of passives and benefactives.

For Terada's (1990) approach, the problems seem to be more serious.[30] To maintain her analysis of causatives and passives, Terada 1990 would have to claim that Inherent Case is absorbed while Structural Case is blocked from absorption under benefactivization (cf. section 5.3.3). Furthermore, given her proposal concerning the level of operation of verb incorporation, the verb incorporation of *ni*-causatives at PF would have to precede verb incorporation of the direct benefactivization which relates D- to S-structure.[31] Notice that in her approach there is nothing to prevent the direct-benefactivization of *wo*-causatives, either. This is a problem for the view that the lack of coercive interpretation in benefactives of causatives reflects the structural failure of *wo*-causatives to undergo benefactivization.

This paradoxical problem is not exclusive to those approaches mentioned above. It is a problem common to any approach that attempts to construct distinct syntactic structures based on the coerciveness interpretation, and explain the obligatory coercive interpretation of passivized causatives in structural terms.

Semantic and pragmatic considerations, on the other hand, readily provide a straightforward and natural account of the obligatory non-coercive interpretation of the benefactivized causatives and of the obligatory coercive interpretation of passivized causatives. Considering the passivized causatives first, as has been discussed, passives in Japanese tend to carry an adversity interpretation, intuitively speaking, even though the adversity interpretation is cancellable in the direct and the possessive passives (see section 3.2.1). The subject of the direct passive of a causative sentence corresponds to the Causee. If the Causee is interpreted as adversely affected by the causative event, the causative event is unlikely to be performed by the Causee on his/her own will. It is pragmatically more likely that the Causee is coerced into performing the action. In direct-benefactives of causatives, on the other hand, the Causee receives benefit from the caused event. As mentioned in the previous chapter, the benefactive often carries the implication that the subject actually initiates an action (by asking, for instance) to bring about the event. So, chances are that the Causee voluntarily performed the action for the benefit of him/herself. This is exactly the situation of non-coercive causation.

Therefore, we conclude that both the coercive interpretation of passivized causatives and the non-coercive interpretation of benefactivized causatives are a matter of semantics or pragmatics, and are not syntactic. The obligatory coercive interpretation of direct passives of causatives does not challenge the present analysis according to which the Causee is direct-passivizable in either *wo*-causatives or *ni*-causatives.

5.5.3 Biclausality of Causatives

Since Kuroda 1965a, 1965b and Shibatani 1973, it has been argued that both *ni*-causatives and *wo*-causatives are biclausal (see also Shibatani 1976a; Kitagawa 1986; Terada 1990). The evidence comes from the data concerning reflexive binding and adverbial scope. Shibatani 1973 demonstrated that productive causatives, i.e., *ni*-causatives and *wo*-causatives, allow both the Causer and the Causee to bind a reflexive phrase and to define the scope of adverbial phrases, in contrast to causative transitives (i.e., transitive verbs with causal meaning), which allow only the Causer to display those properties. We have proposed that *wo*-causatives are lexically derived and monoclausal, while *ni*-causatives are syntactically constructed and biclausal. This section attempts to defend our position regarding the biclausality of causatives.

5.5.3.1 Reflexive Binding

Unlike reflexive binding in the two types of passives and benefactives, reflexive binding in causatives does not display any contrast between *wo*-causatives and *ni*-causatives; both the matrix subject and the Causee can bind a reflexive phrase in either type of the productive causatives.

See the data repeated below:

(10) a. Syota -ga   Kyoko -wo   zibun$_{i/j}$ -no   heya   -ni
            nom   acc   self   gen   room   to
      hair-ase-ta.
      enter-CAS-PST
   b. Syota -ga   Kyoko -ni   zibun$_{i/j}$ -no   heya   -ni
            nom   dat   self   gen   room   to
      hair-ase-ta.
      enter-CAS-PST
      'Syota made Kyoko enter his/her own room.'

(11) a. Syota -ga   Kyoko -wo   zibun$_{i/j}$ -no   kuruma -kara
            nom   acc   self   gen   car   from
      ori-sase-ta.
      get out-CAS-PST
   b. Syota -ga   Kyoko -ni   zibun$_{i/j}$ -no   kuruma -kara
            nom   dat   self   gen   car   from
      ori-sase-ta.
      get out-CAS-PST
      'Syota made Kyoko get out of his/her own car.'

These data have provided strong motivation for positing a biclausal structure for both types of causatives, as reflexive binding has traditionally been attributed exclusively to the subject of a clause (Shibatani 1973, 1976a; Kitagawa 1986; Terada 1990; among others).

These data of reflexive binding pose no problem to our approach, however. We have defended the idea that reflexive binding in Japanese is based on thematic prominence (sections 2.5.4 and 3.4.3.2).[32] Recall that we proposed in chapter 3 that the antecedent of a reflexive phrase is the bearer of the highest thematic role (= the largest number of the Proto-Agent role entailments) in one soa attribute, and that it has to function as a full-fledged syntactic argument. The agent phrases of the direct/possessive passives and benefactives are excluded because they are syntactically suppressed. The agent phrases of the indirect passives and benefactives qualify as reflexive antecedents, because they are both syntactic arguments and the bearer of the highest thematic role in an embedded soa.

In the present cases, the same principle correctly predicts that the Causee can bind a reflexive phrase in either type of causative. Let us first consider *wo*-causatives (10-a) and (11-a). Compare the feature structure in (27)-(28). The NP *Kyoko* in the examples above is not a syntactic subject at any level of embedding in our approach; it is only a syntactic object of the matrix clause. However, it is the most prominent argument in terms of thematic role in the embedded soa of the causative predicate. Further, the NP syntactically functions as an argument; i.e., it is the object in the SUBCAT of *wo*-causatives. Notice that our principle only requires that the antecedent be a syntactic argument. It does not matter what grammatical function it bears.

Now, look at the feature structures of *ni*-causatives in (34) and (37). Notice that NP[2], which corresponds to the dative-marked *Kyoko* is not a syntactic subject; it is a syntactic object of the matrix clause.[33] We claim that the actual syntactic antecedent of the reflexive is not the NP *Kyoko* marked with dative case; it is the subject argument left in the SUBCAT list of the embedded VP, i.e., NP[5] in (37), which is coreferential with the dative NP *Kyoko*. Notice that our condition for reflexive binding requires that the antecedent be a full-fledged argument (i.e., not suppressed), but nothing rules out the case of an antecedent which is the argument remaining in the SUBCAT list of an unsaturated predicate.

Thus, the reflexive binding facts do not force a biclausal analysis of either type of causatives, or indeed an analysis involving an S-complement at all. The present approach posits a monoclausal structure for *wo*-causatives and a VP-complement structure for *ni*-causatives. Given the account of reflexive binding based on thematic prominence, which we have defended in chapters 2 through 4, our approach readily accommodates the reflexive binding data without any modification or stipulation.

5.5.3.2 Adverb Scope

Another phenomenon which has motivated the biclausal approach is adverb scope. It has been observed since Shibatani 1973 that a certain class of manner adverbs and adverbial phrases can modify either the matrix subject or the Causee in either *wo*-causatives or *ni*-causatives. Recall the relevant data, repeated below:

(12) a. Syota -ga   Kyoko -wo damatte heya -ni hair-ase-ta.
              nom   acc silently room to enter-CAS-PST
    'Syota silently made Kyoko enter the room.'
    'Syota made Kyoko silently enter the room.'

   b. Syota -ga   Kyoko -ni damatte heya -ni hair-ase-ta.
              nom   dat silently room to enter-CAS-PST
    'Syota silently made Kyoko enter the room.'
    'Syota made Kyoko silently enter the room.'

(13) a. Syota -ga seito   -wo [hata -wo   hutte],   basu
              nom student acc flag   acc wave-GER   bus
    ori-sase-ta.
    go-down-CAS-PST
    'Waving a flag, Syota made the students get off the bus.'
    'Syota made the students, waving a flag, get off the bus.'

   b. Syota -ga seito   -ni [hata -wo   hutte],   basu
              nom student dat flag   acc wave-GER   bus
    kara ori-sase-ta.
    from go-down-CAS-PST
    'Waving a flag, Syota made the students get off the bus.'
    'Syota made the students, waving a flag, get off the bus.'

On the assumption that these adverbs and adverbial phrases are subject-oriented, this fact has been used as evidence for positing a biclausal structure for both *wo*-causatives and *ni*-causatives (Shibatani 1973; Kitagawa 1986).

We argue, however, that the observed facts do not motivate biclausal structures; the adverbs and the adverbial phrases are not in fact subject-oriented. Recall our discussion of similar adverb scope phenomena in passives and benefactives. We have seen that direct and possessive passives display a similar adverb scope ambiguity, which is also shared by the English passives. The sentences in (49) illustrate these facts for direct passives, and (50) for possessive passives:

(49) a. Kyoko -ga   Syota -ni *umaku*   damas-are-ta.
         nom   dat   cleverly   cheat-PAS-PST
    'Kyoko was cleverly cheated by Syota.'

   b. Kyoko -ga   Syota -ni *wazato*   yuuwakus-are-ta.
         nom   dat   intentionally seduce-PAS-PST
    'Kyoko was intentionally seduced by Syota.'

(50) a. Kyoko -ga   Syota -ni *umaku*   atama -wo nader-are-ta.
         nom   dat   cleverly   head   acc pat-PAS-PST
    'Kyoko cleverly had her head patted by Syota.'
    'Kyoko had her head cleverly patted by Syota.'

   b. Kyoko -ga   Syota -ni *wazato*   saihu -wo nusum-are-ta.
         nom   dat   intentionally wallet acc steal-PAS-PST
    'Kyoko intentionally had her purse stolen by Syota.'
    'Kyoko had her purse intentionally stolen by Syota.'

If these adverbs are really subject-oriented, both direct and possessive passive sentences should be analyzed as involving a biclausal structure. The agent phrases of these two types of passives will have to be analyzed as the subjects of embedded clauses. We have provided ample evidence, however, that they are monoclausal structures. The agent phrases are syntactically suppressed arguments, and are not syntactic subjects of any clause. The analysis of passives makes it clear that these adverbs are not in fact subject-oriented. In addition, indirect passives in Japanese, which almost uncontroversially have a biclausal structure, curiously lack the scope ambiguity with some adverbs. In particular, against the alleged subject-orientation of these adverbs, it is the matrix subject which cannot be modified. Recall the data, repeated below:

(51) a. Kyoko -ga *umaku*   Syota -ni Naoko -wo
         nom   cleverly   dat   acc
    damas-are-ta.
    cheat-PAS-PST
    'Kyoko was adversely affected by Syota's cleverly cheating Naoko.'

   b. Kyoko -ga *wazato*   Syota -ni Naoko -wo
         nom   intentionally   dat   acc
    yuuwakus-are-ta.
    seduce-PAS-PST
    'Kyoko was adversely affected by Syota's intentionally seducing Naoko.'

Interestingly, in contrast to passives, benefactives display the adverb scope ambiguity in all three types.

We have explained these curious facts first by introducing the notion of "direct involvement in the core event," which is also responsible for accounting for the obligatory adversity interpretation of indirect passives. The notion has been extended to include "causal involvement" to accommodate the data of benefactives. To recapitulate the point, we have claimed that the manner adverbs in question can modify an argument with the thematically highest role in the domain of each soa, analogous to the reflexive binder. To be felicitously modified by a manner adverb which imposes volitionality and causality, the argument has to satisfy another semantic requirement; that is, the referent of the argument has to be either directly involved in the core event or causally related to the event. This requirement can be reduced to one referring to arguments whose involvement is essential in realizing the core event. The matrix subject of the indirect passive is excluded from being modified because its referent makes no contribution toward the realization of the event.

Now, it is clear how the causative constructions in either the *wo*-causatives or in *ni*-causatives come to display the adverb scope ambiguity. In our approach, both types of causative have a complex soa structure, with each of the two soa having a most prominent thematic role. Further, by definition, the matrix subject is causally related to the core event. It thus follows that both the matrix subject and the Causee can potentially be modified by the manner adverbs in question.[34]

Therefore, our claim that *wo*-causatives are monoclausal, while *ni*-causatives are biclausal, is not challenged by the data involving reflexive binding and adverbial scope. The present approach is able to accommodate the relevant facts not only in causatives, but in passives and in benefactives in a very consistent way.

This section has provided evidence to defend our claim which goes counter to some of the well-accepted views. By way of defending our position, we have demonstrated that it is wrong to account for the obligatory coercive reading of direct passives of causatives in terms of the structure of *wo*-causatives. Such an account inevitably runs into a conflicting situation with the data of direct-benefactivization of causatives. We have also argued with Tonoike 1978, Gunji 1987, Dubinsky 1989, and Terada 1990 that the semantic difference between *wo*-causatives and *ni*-causatives is best accounted for in terms of self-controllability of the Causee over the caused event. We have proposed that the semantic restriction on self-controllability is associated with the syntactic object control structure in Japanese. In the last subsection, we have shown that the well-known data supporting the biclausality of both types of causative do not really prove biclausality, based on our analysis of the relevant issue that we have defended in preceding chapters. Having defended our approach against the opposing received analyses, let us provide in the next section more data that support our analysis.

5.6 More Supporting Evidence for the Present Approach

In the previous section we have defended our approach against the conflicting received analyses of causatives. The present analysis is able to do more than merely circumvent possible objections. This section will provide more evidence for our analysis. The syntactic constituency of the stem verb and the causative morpheme will be examined in terms of the Do-Support phenomena. Another piece of evidence for the distinction between lexical causatives and syntactic causatives is found in the Subject Honorification phenomena. The data of Object Honorification will be used to defend the VP-complement analysis of the causatives, contrasting with the S-complement analysis of the indirect passives/benefactives.[35]

5.6.1 Evidence from Do-Support

Deriving *wo*-causatives through a lexical rule and positing a syntactic control structure for the *ni*-causatives entails a monoclausal structure for the former and a biclausal structure for the latter. It also entails that the causative morpheme *(s)ase* is a derivational affix in the former, but is syntactically an independent word in the latter. Being a bound form in both cases, the causative morpheme *(s)ase* has to occur adjacent to the stem verb on the surface, and no adverbial phrases can intervene.

In the discussion of the passives above, we saw that there is a phenomenon which is sensitive to the syntactic status of the morphemes, i.e., Do-Support. We have shown that the emphatic particles *wa, mo, sae* and the supportive *(s)u* ('do') can occur only between two syntactic words; they can never break into one syntactic word. Thus, the emphatic particles and the supportive *(s)u* ('do') can appear between the verb stem and the passive morpheme *(r)are* in the indirect passives, but they cannot appear in the same position in the direct/possessive passives.

The same contrast obtains in the causatives. As the following data show, the emphatic particles and the supportive *(s)u* ('do') can appear either between the verb stem and the causative morpheme *(s)ase* or after the causative morpheme in the *ni*-causatives, but they can appear only after the causative morpheme in *wo*-causatives:[36]

(52) a. Syota -ga hana -wo sak-ase-*mo* *si*-ta.
　　　　　　nom　　　　acc bloom-CAS-*also*　*do*-PST
　　*b. Syota -ga hana -wo saki-*mo* *s*-ase-ta.
　　　　　　nom　　　　acc bloom-*also*　*do*-CAS-PST
　　'Syota also made the flowers bloom.'

(53) a. Syota -ga Kyoko -wo yorokob-ase-*mo* *si*-ta.
　　　　　　nom　　　acc rejoice-CAS-*also*　*do*-PST
　　*b. Syota -ga Kyoko -wo yorokobi-*mo* *s*-ase-ta.
　　　　　　nom　　　acc rejoice-*also*　*do*-CAS-PST
　　'Syota also made Kyoko happy.'

(54) a. Syota -ga Kyoko -ni deteik-ase-*mo* *si*-ta.
　　　　　　nom　　　dat leave-CAS-*also*　*do*-PST

b. Syota -ga Kyoko -ni deteiki-*mo*   *s*-ase-ta.
   nom   dat   leave-*also*   *do*-CAS-PST
   'Syota also made Kyoko leave.'

(55) a. Syota -ga Kyoko -ni ringo -wo tabe-sase-*mo* *si*-ta.
        nom   dat   apple acc eat-CAS-*also* *do*-PST
     b. Syota -ga Kyoko -ni ringo -wo tabe-*mo* *s*-ase-ta.
        nom   dat   apple acc eat-*also* *do*-CAS-PST
     'Syota also made Kyoko eat an apple.'

In (52)-(53), *wo*-causatives, the emphatic particle and the supportive *(s)u* cannot occur between the verb stem and the causative morpheme. This is because the verb stem and the causative morpheme constitute one syntactic word with no internal boundary at which the emphatic morphemes may occur. *Ni*-causatives, on the other hand, let the emphatic morphemes appear between the verb stem and the causative morpheme as shown in (54)-(55). This is because the verb stem and the causative morpheme are both independent words in syntax, and are separated by a boundary at which the emphatic morphemes can occur. Thus the data of Do-Support lend support to the present analysis that *wo*-causatives are lexically derived, while the *ni*-causatives have a syntactic control structure.

5.6.2 Subject Honorification with Causatives

As illustrated in chapter 3, the Subject Honorification (SH) phenomena display contrast between the direct passives and the indirect passives. SH, which puts the verb between the honorific particle *o* and the honorific morpheme *nar*, is possible in either type of passive when SH is directed toward the matrix subject. SH triggered by the agent phrase, however, is possible only in indirect passives. We have explained the contrast by showing that the agent phrase is a syntactic subject only in the indirect passives, as the indirect passives are analyzed as involving an S-complement.

The matrix subject triggers SH in either type of causatives (Kuno 1983):

(56) a. *Sensei* -ga   Kyoko -wo *o*-hasir-ase-*ninat*-ta.
        teacher nom   acc *o*-run-CAS-HON-PST

b. *Sensei* -ga Kyoko -ni *o*-hasir-ase-*ninat*-ta.
   teacher nom   dat   *o*-run-CAS-HON-PST
   'The teacher made Kyoko run.'

(57) *Sensei* -ga Kyoko -ni hon   -wo *o*-yom-ase-*ninat*-ta.
      teacher nom   dat   book acc *o*-read-CAS-HON-PST
      'The teacher made Kyoko read a book.'

The SH of the Causee, however, has been observed to be marginal in either type (Kuno 1983; Dubinsky 1989):

(58) *a. Kyoko -ga *sensei* -wo soko -e   *o*-iki-*ninar*-ase-ta.
              nom   teacher acc there to   *o*-go-HON-CAS-PST
     *?b. Kyoko -ga *sensei* -ni soko -e   *o*-iki-*ninar*-ase-ta.
              nom   teacher dat there to   *o*-go-HON-CAS-PST
     'Kyoko made the teacher go there.'

Causatives often carry coercive interpretation, so it is pragmatically contradictory to impose a coercion on somebody and express respect toward him/her at the same time. These honorifics of the causatives are often rephrased in the honorific form of a benefactive sentence. As discussed in the previous chapter, the benefactives can carry the meaning that the matrix subject "asks" the Causee to perform the action to receive benefit. The indirectness of the implication of causation in benefactives makes them suitable for the situation where the matrix subject is expected to pay respect to the Causee. In the following example, *te-itadak* is an honorific form of the *te-moraw* benefactive:

(59) Kyoko -ga *sensei* -ni soko -e   itte-*itadai*-ta.
           nom   teacher dat there to   go-BEN-PST
      'Kyoko had the teacher go there.'

It is even possible to form syntactic SH out of sentence (59), which involves an honorific benefactive morpheme, in exactly the same way as syntactic SH of a non-honorific benefactive, discussed in the previous chapter.

(60) Kyoko -ga *sensei* -ni   soko -e *o*-iki-*ninatte*-*itadai*-ta.
      nom   teacher dat there to *o*-go-HON-BEN-PST
   'Kyoko had the teacher go there.'

Now, a question arises whether the impossibility of syntactic SH by the Causee is a matter of syntax or pragmatics. Kuno 1983 gives evidence that it is indeed a matter of pragmatics (see also Kitagawa 1986; Dubinsky 1989). Though SH of the Causee is usually judged anomalous, contextualization can significantly enhance grammaticality, suggesting SH of the Causee is syntactically possible. See the following examples:

(61) ? Kyoko -wa *sensei* -ni [o-mati-ninari-tai   dake]
       top   teacher dat *o*-wait-HON-DES   just
   o-mati-*ninar*-asete-sasiage-ta.
   o-wait-HON-CAS-BEN-PST
   'Kyoko let the teacher wait as long as he/she wanted.'

(62) ? Kyoko -wa *sensei* -ni [o-nemuri-ninari-tai   dake]
       top   teacher dat *o*-sleep-HON-DES   just
   o-nemuri-*ninar*-asete-sasiage-ta.
   o-sleep-HON-CAS-BEN-PST
   'Kyoko let the teacher sleep as long as he/she wanted.'

The morpheme *sasiage* following the causative morpheme above is an honorific form of *age*, which is one of the valency-preserving benefactive morphemes (see section 4.6). The benefactive morpheme serves to underscore the honorific import of the sentence, but it does not alter the subcategorization of the verb.[37]

On the other hand, contextualization does not help with the *wo*-causatives. SH of the Causee is ungrammatical with *wo*-causatives in the same context as (61)-(62):

(63) ?* Kyoko -wa *sensei* -wo [o-mati-ninari-tai   dake]
        top   teacher acc *o*-wait-HON-DES   just
   o-mati-*ninar*-asete-sasiage-ta.
   o-wait-HON-CAS-BEN-PST
   'Kyoko let the teacher wait as long as he/she wanted.'

(64) ?* Kyoko -wa *sensei* -wo [o-nemuri-ninari-tai dake]
     top   teacher acc   o-sleep-HON-DES   just
     o-nemuri-*ninar*-asete-sasiage-ta.
     o-sleep-HON-CAS-BEN-PST
     'Kyoko let the teacher sleep as long as he/she wanted.'

One might wish to claim that this contrast is also semantic; this is because *wo*-causatives often carry a coercive interpretation which is incompatible with the respect paid toward the Causee.38 Admitting this possibility, we still claim that the contrast is syntactic. For, as argued above, the coercive interpretation is not really inherent in *wo*-causatives, and should be cancellable by contextualization. The above examples involving *wo*-causatives would in fact be acceptable non-coercive causative sentences without the honorific morphemes.

Recall that we have proposed in chapter 3 that the information concerning SH is encoded in the SUBCAT list of the target verb. SH is triggered by the [+HON] feature on the least oblique argument in the SUBCAT list, and the target verb is suffixed with the honorific morpheme *ninar*. The honorific particle *o*, on the other hand, can be prefixed only to the minimal free form.

Now let us consider how our approach explains the SH facts of the causatives. We first list the observed morphological patterns:39

(65) a. *Sensei* -ga   Kyoko -wo *o*-mat-ase-*ninat*-ta.
        teacher nom   acc   *o*-wait-CAS-HON-PST
    *b. *Sensei* -ga   Kyoko -wo *o*-mati-*ninar*-ase-ta.
        teacher nom   acc   *o*-wait-HON-CAS-PST
        'The teacher made Kyoko wait.'

(66) *a. Kyoko -ga   *sensei* -wo *o*-mat-ase-*ninat*-ta.
         nom   teacher acc   *o*-wait-CAS-HON-PST
    *b. Kyoko -ga   *sensei* -wo *o*-mati-*ninar*-ase-ta.
         no   teacher acc   *o*-wait-HON-CAS-PST
        'Kyoko made the teacher wait.'

(67) a. *Sensei* -ga   Kyoko -ni *o*-mat-ase-*ninat*-ta.
        teacher nom   dat   *o*-wait-CAS-HON-PST
    *b. *Sensei* -ga   Kyoko -ni *o*-mati-*ninar*-ase-ta.
        teacher nom   dat   *o*-wait-HON-CAS-PST
        'The teacher made Kyoko wait.'

(68) *a. Kyoko -ga sensei -ni o-mat-ase-*ninat*-ta.
              nom teacher dat o-wait-CAS-HON-PST
     b. Kyoko -ga sensei -ni o-mati-*ninar*-ase-ta.
              nom teacher dat o-wait-HON-CAS-PST
     'Kyoko had the teacher wait.'

The examples in (65)-(66) are SH of *wo*-causatives, and those in (67)-(68) are SH of *ni*-causatives. The morpheme order is essentially the same in both types of causatives. When the matrix subject is the trigger, the combination of stem verb and causative morpheme occurs between the honorific particle *o* and the honorific morpheme *ninar*. When the Causee is the trigger -- this is possible only in *ni*-causatives -- only the stem verb occurs between the honorific morphemes, and the causative morpheme follows them.[40]

SH of the matrix subject is explained exactly as in the passives. The operation is represented in diagrams below. (69-a) illustrates (65-a), SH in *wo*-causatives, and (69-b) illustrates (67-a), SH in *ni*-causatives:

(69)
a.

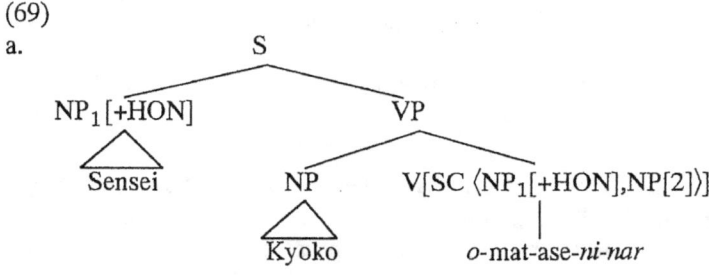

b.

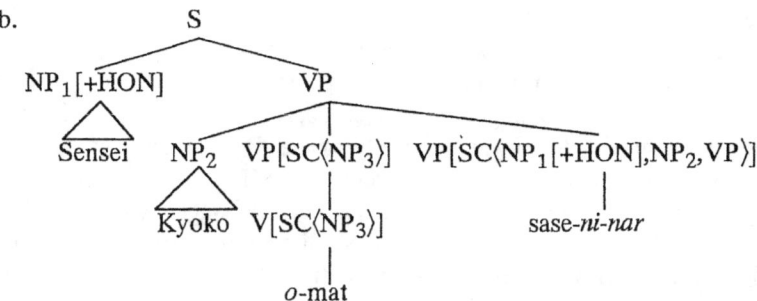

As mentioned above, the honorific particle *o* is prefixed to the smallest *morphologically independent* unit. The causative morpheme *(s)ase* is a bound morpheme, even when it stands as a syntactic word. So, the honorific particle *o* is prefixed to the stem verb in either type of causatives.

As for SH of the Causee, it is clear under our analysis that it is not available for the *wo*-causatives; the Causee is not a syntactic subject in *wo*-causatives. It is the direct object instead. SH of the Causee of *ni*-causatives, (68-b), is formed as illustrated in (70) below:

(70)

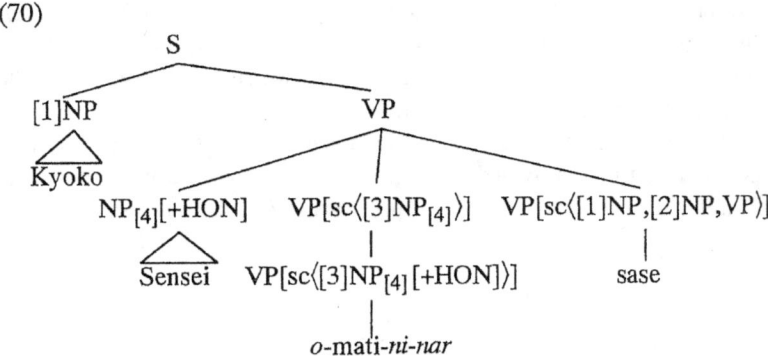

Note that *ni*-causatives have been analyzed as having VP-complement structure, following our account above, in contrast to the S-complement structure of the indirect passives. In this structure, the embedded VP has one NP yet to be satisfied; intuitively speaking, it is a subjectless complement. At first sight, this may seem to be a problem in explaining SH in *ni*-causatives, as the trigger argument *sensei* is the direct object of the matrix clause and is not the subject of the complement.

Given our approach to SH, however, this is not a problem at all. Recall that the information necessary for SH is encoded in the SUBCAT list of the target verb. Our approach does not require the trigger argument to be syntactically realized as a subject. In the example above the real linguistic trigger of SH is not the NP *sensei* tagged with [2], but the unrealized subject NP tagged with [3]. The subject NP[3] remains in the SUBCAT list of the stem verb, but it triggers SH on the stem verb by virtue of being located in that position. NP[2] and NP[3] are linguistically distinct arguments: the former is the direct object of the causative morpheme; the latter the subject of the stem verb. However, they are coindexed, and hence coreferential. If NP[2] is a legitimate trigger of honorification, so should the coreferential NP[3] be.

5.6.3 Object Honorification with Causatives

There is another interesting phenomenon concerning honorification in causatives. Marantz 1984 very briefly mentions that causatives can undergo syntactic Object Honorification (henceforth OH). As mentioned in section 3.3.5, the form of OH is reminiscent of the form of SH; the infinitival form of a verb occurs between the honorific particle *o*, and the light verb *(s)u* ('do'). The following is an example of OH:

(71) a. Kyoko -ga   *sensei*   -wo   tasuke-ta.
             nom   teacher   acc   help-PST
    'Kyoko helped the teacher.' (non-honorific)

  b. Kyoko -ga   *sensei*   -wo   *o*-tasuke-*si*-ta.
             nom   teacher   acc   *o*-help-HON-PST
    'Kyoko helped the teacher.' (honorific)

Wo-causatives and *ni*-causatives can undergo the process of OH, with respect directed to the Causee as shown in (72)-(74) below: In the transitive-based causatives, OH can also be triggered by the lower object as in (75).[41] See the following data:

(72)   Kyoko -ga   *sensei*   -wo   *o*-yorokob-ase-*si*-ta.
               nom   teacher   acc   *o*-happy-CAS-HON-PST
    'Kyoko made the teacher happy.'

(73) ? Kyoko -ga   *sensei*   -wo/-ni soko -de   *o*-mat-ase-*si*-ta.
               nom   teacher   acc/dat there loc   *o*-wait-CAS-HON-PST
    'Kyoko made the teacher wait there.'

(74)   Kyoko -ga   *sensei*   -ni o-sake   -wo *o*-nom-ase-*si*-ta.
               nom   teacher   dat rice wine acc *o*-drink-CAS-HON-PST
    'Kyoko let the teacher drink *sake*.'

(75) a. Kyoko -ga Syota -ni *sensei* -wo *o*-okuri-*s*-ase-ta.
         nom   dat teacher acc *o*-send-HON-CAS-PST
    'Kyoko made Syota see the teacher off.'

   b. Kyoko -ga Syota -ni *sensei* -wo *o*-motenasi-*s*-ase-ta.
         nom   dat teacher acc *o*-treat-HON-CAS-PST
    'Kyoko made Syota take care of the teacher.'

Note also that the morpheme order is different depending on the trigger of OH; compare (72)-(74) with (75). We propose that the operation of OH also crucially refers to the SUBCAT list of the target verb. More specifically, we claim that OH is triggered by the [+HON] feature borne by a non-subject argument.[42] Similar to the cases of SH, the operation of OH results in the honorific morpheme (=light verb) *s(u)* occurring suffixed to the infinitival verb. The operation of OH of the *wo*-causative (72) and of *ni*-causative (74) is represented in the diagrams (76-a) and (76-b), respectively:

(76) a.

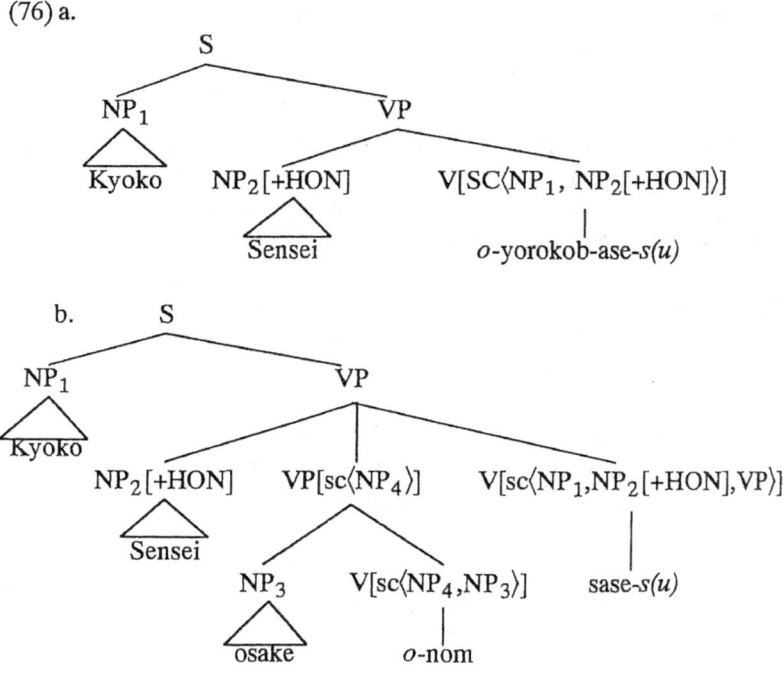

As in the case of SH, the honorific particle *o* in OH is prefixed to the smallest morphologically independent unit; that is, to the stem verb in either type of causative. The morpheme order in OH of the Causee is thus exactly as our approach predicts.

The following diagram illustrates OH of the lower object in (75-a):

(77)

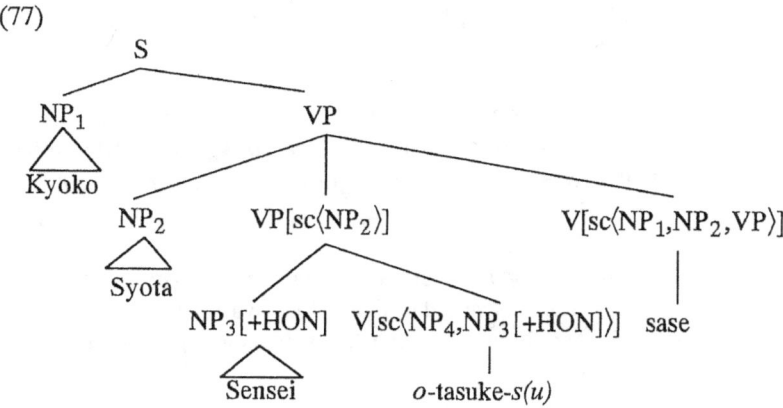

The trigger of OH is an argument subcategorized for by the stem verb, and the stem verb is the smallest morphologically independent unit, because this is a *ni*-causative. Hence the honorific particle *o* in OH is prefixed to the stem verb, and the light verb *s(u)* immediately is attached to the stem verb. Observe that the difference in morpheme order between OH of the Causee and that of the lower object directly follows from our approach. No stipulation is necessary to obtain the expected morpheme order.

These facts about OH show an interesting contrast with passives and benefactives. Although the SH phenomena are shared by all three constructions, passives, benefactive, and causatives, OH, on the other hand, is possible only with the causatives. As mentioned in sections 3.3.5 and 4.3, it is totally impossible to make an OH sentence from passives and benefactives with the respect directed toward the agent phrase. See the following examples demonstrating this point. (78) illustrates direct passives/benefactives, and (79)-(80) indirect passives/benefactives. Observe in particular the very sharp contrast in acceptability between (73)-(74) and (79)-(80), respectively, both denoting a similar objective situation:

(78) *a. Kyoko -ga *sensei* -ni *o*-home-rare-*si*-ta.
         nom teacher dat *o*-praise-PAS-HON-PST
    'Kyoko was praised by the teacher (honorific).'

   *b. Kyoko -ga *sensei* -ni home-*o*-morai-*si*-ta.
         nom teacher dat praise-*o*-BEN-HON-PST
    'Kyoko was praised by the teacher (for Kyoko's benefit) (honorific).'

(79) *a. Kyoko -ga *sensei* -ni soko -de *o*-mat-are-*si*-ta.
         nom teacher dat there loc *o*-wait-PAS-HON-PST
    'Kyoko was adversely affected by the teacher's waiting there (honorific).'

   *b. Kyoko -ga *sensei* -ni soko -de matte-*o*-morai-*si*-ta.
         nom teacher dat there loc wait-*o*-BEN-HON-PST
    'Kyoko had the teacher wait there (for Kyoko's benefit) (honorific).'

(80) *a. Kyoko -ga *sensei* -ni o-sake   -wo
         nom teacher dat rice wine acc
    o-nom-are-*si*-ta.
    o-drink-PAS-HON-PST
    'Kyoko was adversely affected by the teacher's drinking *sake* (honorific).'

   *b. Kyoko -ga *sensei* -ni o-sake   -wo
         nom teacher dat rice wine acc
    nonde-*o*-morai-*si*-ta.
    drink-*o*-BEN-HON-PST
    'Kyoko had the teacher drink *sake* (for Kyoko's benefit) (honorific).'

As mentioned in chapter 3, the unavailability of OH for the passives/benefactives shown in (78)-(80) finds a straightforward account in the present analysis: the agent phrase is not an object of the passive/benefactive predicate in either the direct-type or the indirect-type. The agent arguments are syntactically suppressed, and consequently have syntactic behaviour which is reminiscent of that of adjuncts.

Recall that we used these data to argue against the VP-complement analysis of the passives and benefactives advocated, for instance, by Gunji 1987, or any analysis positing the agent phrase as an object argument of the passive/benefactive morpheme (Terada 1990). The availability of OH for *wo/ni*-causatives, on the other hand, strongly suggests that the Causee is actually a syntactic object. The data of SH which we saw above show that the Causee of *ni*-causatives is a syntactic subject as well. The possibilities of SH and OH jointly indicate that the Causee of *ni*-causatives is syntactically playing dual roles, which can be readily accommodated in the object control structure analysis. The unavailability of SH of *wo*-causatives suggests that the Causee in this type is only a syntactic object, and is not a controller.

This concludes our analysis of *wo*-causatives and *ni*-causatives. We have argued that *wo*-causatives are lexically derived, whereas *ni*-causatives have a syntactic control structure. This claim entails that the former is a monoclausal causative, whereas the latter is a biclausal causative.

As mentioned above, differences between *wo*-causatives and *ni*-causatives are not as robust as those between lexical and syntactic passives/benefactives. The lack of contrast does not pose a problem to our approach at all. Our general approach of factoring out the phenomena into levels of information, e.g., syntactic and semantic, readily accommodates the apparent lack of contrast.

It has been widely assumed, particularly since Shibatani's (1973) observation on reflexive binding and adverbial scope, that both *wo*-causatives and *ni*-causatives are biclausal (cf. Kuroda 1965a, 1965b; Kitagawa 1986; Terada 1990). We have demonstrated, consistent with our claim in passives and benefactives, that neither of the crucial supporting phenomena are subject-oriented, contrary to Shibatani's (1973) claim, and therefore, do not constitute valid tests for biclausality. We have claimed that these phenomena are sensitive to the complexity of semantic CONTENT structure instead. In our approach, both causatives are analyzed as involving embedded semantic CONTENT structures.

The data of OH provides support for the claim that (*ni-*) causatives have object control structures, whereas indirect passives/benefactives have S-embedding structures.

The data of Do-Support show that an emphatic morpheme and the supportive light verb *s(u)* can intervene between the verb stem and the causative morpheme *(s)ase* only in *ni*-causatives, suggesting a syntactic boundary between them.

We have also given counterargument to dividing *wo*-causatives and *ni*-causatives in terms of coercive vs. non-coercive causation. We have made clear with strong evidence that it is wrong to account for the obligatory coercive interpretation of the direct passives of causatives by positing a passivizable structure for *wo*-causatives and an unpassivizable structure for *ni*-causatives. Given the syntactic parallelism between passives and *te-moraw* benefactives that we have established in the previous chapter, there is no syntactic way to simultaneously account for the obligatory coercive interpretation of direct passives of causatives, on the one hand, and the obligatory non-coercive interpretation of direct benefactives of causatives, on the other.

Under our analysis, *wo*-causatives and *ni*-causatives share the same semantic CONTENT structure. In this sense alone, our analysis belongs to the uniformist approaches. The semantic differences observed between the two types, particularly the restriction on the Causee of *ni*-causatives that it must potentially exert control over the caused event, is reduced to a general semantic restriction on the controller in syntactic control structures.

In the next section, we will propose another type of lexical causatives in Japanese. It also shares the semantic CONTENT structure with the two types studied above. But it involves a different type of coindexing relation, which induces a passive-like character.

5.7 A Third Type of Causative

In the rest of this chapter, we describe another class of Japanese causatives, which has not been recognized in the literature. We will show that it is possible to identify a class of transitive-based lexical causatives in which the Patient role of the causative relation is coindexed not with the lower subject but with the lower object.

So far we have claimed that the Japanese causatives constructions fall into two classes: lexical and syntactic. The former is derived through a lexical rule, and marks the direct object with the accusative case. Because of this case marking property, the operation is usually limited to intransitive bases. Ordinary transitive verbs fail to undergo the lexical rule, because the output would violate the double-*wo* constraint. The syntactic causative, on the other hand, has a syntactic control structure. The causative morpheme in this construction is subcategorized for two NPs and a VP. The object NP is marked with the dative case, as is standard in control structures. The control theory of HPSG guarantees that the object NP controls the VP.

5.7.1 Passive Causatives

In a typological study of causatives, Comrie 1976 mentions that transitive-based causatives often mark the lower subject with dative case. He further observes that many languages also show an instance of "extended demotion," whereby the lower subject is further "demoted" to an oblique position. As a result, the lower subject often (but not always) carries the same case marker as the agent phrase of passives.

Interestingly, this phenomenon occurs in Japanese. The lower subject of the transitive-based causatives is marked alternatively with dative case *ni* or the agentive postposition *niyotte*.[43] This alternation is not possible with the intransitive-based causatives. See the data below:

(81) a. Syota -ga   Kyoko -ni   otya -wo hakob-ase-ta.
            nom   dat   tea   acc carry-CAS-PST
     b. Syota -ga   Kyoko -niyotte otya -wo hakob-ase-ta.
            nom   by   tea   acc carry-CAS-PST
     'Syota had Kyoko bring some tea.'

(82) a. Syota -ga   hisyo   -ni   tegami -wo taipus-ase-ta.
            nom   secretary dat   letter acc type-CAS-PST
     b. Syota -ga   hisyo   -niyotte tegami -wo taipus-ase-ta.
            nom   secretary by   letter acc type-CAS-PST
     'Syota had the secretary type the letter.'

(83) a. Syota -ga   Kyoko -ni   oyog-ase-ta.
             nom   dat   swim-CAS-PST
     *b. Syota -ga   Kyoko -niyotte oyog-ase-ta.
             nom   by   swim-CAS-PST
     'Syota made Kyoko swim.'

(84) a. Syota -ga   Kyoko -ni   benkyoos-ase-ta.
             nom   dat   study-CAS-PST
     *b. Syota -ga   Kyoko -niyotte benkyoos-ase-ta.
             nom   by   study-CAS-PST
     'Syota made Kyoko study.'

The two versions of (81) and (82) are slightly different in meaning. Intuitively speaking, the *niyotte* version implies that the Causer's main point is to cause some effect on the referent of the lower object, and that it matters little who performs the action to bring about the effect.

In fact, the lower subject can even be omitted altogether. See the following examples showing this point:

(85) a. Syota -ga otya -wo hakob-ase-ta.
            nom   tea   acc   carry-CAS-PST
    'Syota had someone bring some tea.'

   b. Syota -ga tegami -wo taipus-ase-ta.
            nom   letter acc   type-CAS-PST
    'Syota had the letter typed.'

Though the omissibility of an NP does not always constitute a very strong syntactic argument in languages such as Japanese, it is still significant that the sentences in (85) do not sound elliptical at all. It is also important to note that the controller phrase in a control structure is very unlikely to be omitted. As the following examples of control structures show, the dative case on the controller is not interchangeable with the agentive postposition, and the omission of the controller usually results in anomaly or has a strong sense of ellipsis:

(86) a. Syota -ga   Kyoko -ni   otya -wo   nomu-yoo
              nom   dat   tea   acc   drink-MOD
        susume-ta.
        advise-PST

   *b. Syota -ga   Kyoko -niyotte otya -wo   nomu-yoo
              nom   by   tea   acc   drink-MOD
        susume-ta.
        advise-PST
    'Syota asked Kyoko to drink some tea.'

  ??c. Syota -ga otya   -wo   nomu-yoo   susume-ta.
              nom tea   acc   drink-MOD   advise-PST
    'Syota asked someone to drink some tea.'

The alternation between the dative case and the agentive postposition *niyotte* and the omissibility of a NP in fact would remind one of the direct passives in Japanese.

5.7.2 *Faire Par* Construction

A very similar phenomenon is observed in the discussion of the *faire par* constructions of the Romance causatives, illustrated below:

(87) a. Jean a fait manger ce gateau à Nathalie.
  b. Jean a fait manger ce gateau par Nathalie.
   'Jean made Natalie eat this cake.'

  c. Jean a fait manger ce gateau.
   'Jean made someone eat this cake.'

(88) a. Jean a fait travailler Marie.
  *b. Jean a fait travailler par Marie.
   'Jean made Marie work.'

Zubizarreta 1985 and Rosen 1989 convincingly show that, in contrast with the dative *à*-phrase, the *par*-phrase is not a syntactically full-fledged argument but behaves just like the suppressed *par*-phrase in passives. The syntactic differences identified by them include pronominal binding. Zubizarreta 1985 demonstrates that only the agentive phrase marked with the dative case can be the antecedent of *sa* ('his/her'), as in the following sentences:

(89) a. Elles ont fait peindre sa_i maison à $Jean_i$.
  *b. Elles ont fait peindre sa_i maison par $Jean_i$.
   'They made Jean paint his house.'

According to her, this is because *sa maison* can be referentially dependent on *Jean* only if *Jean* is a syntactic argument. The same binding fact obtains in passive sentences:

(90) a. $Jean_i$ a peint sa_i maison.
    'Jean painted his maison.'
  *b. Sa_i maison a été peinte par $Jean_i$.
    'His house was painted by Jean.'

Another piece of evidence comes from the data on inalienable possession. Kayne 1975 points out that in transitive-based causative sentences the inalienable object can only be bound by the agentive phrase with dative case, and not by the *par*-phrase. See the following data:

(91) a. *Jean* lèvra *la main*.
'Jean$_i$ will raise his$_i$ hand.'

b. Pierre fera lever *la main* à *Jean*.
*c. Pierre fera lever *la main* par *Jean*.
'Pierre will make Jean$_i$ raise his$_i$ hand.'

*d. *La main* sera levée par *Jean*.
'His hand was raised by Jean.'

Zubizarreta 1985 suggests that this type of verb with an inalienable object (and not others) requires the body-part noun to be referentially bound to an external argument which is syntactically present (= not suppressed).

Very interestingly, these binding facts are observed in Japanese causatives as well.

(92) a. Syota -ga Kyoko$_i$ -ni   kanozyo$_i$ -no heya -wo
             nom   dat   she   gen room acc
     soozis-ase-ta.
     clean-CAS-PST

*?b. Syota -ga Kyoko$_i$ -niyotte kanozyo$_i$ -no heya -wo
             nom   by   she   gen room acc
     soozis-ase-ta.
     clean-CAS-PST
     'Syota had Kyoko clean her room.'

(93) a. Syota -ga *Kyoko* -ni   te   -wo araw-ase-ta.
             nom   dat   hand acc wash-CAS-PST

*b. Syota -ga *Kyoko* -niyotte te   -wo araw-ase-ta.
             nom   by   hand acc wash-CAS-PST
     'Syota had Kyoko wash her hands.'

Causative Constructions

A precise theory of pronominal binding in Japanese is yet to be worked out, but the similarity between these Japanese cases and those of the Romance causatives is significant. In particular, in both languages, the *niyotte*-phrase and the *par*-phrase seem to be indicative of the affinity of the causative with the direct passive.

5.7.3 Causatives with the Function of Passives

Comrie 1976 in fact suggests that cases of "extended demotion" in his terms could be analyzed as the causatives of passives. Comrie 1976, however, withholds a definite statement on this problem. For one thing, some languages use distinct postpositions for the passives and for the causatives in question (e.g., Finnish).[44] Further, these causatives do not in general involve passive morphemes (Alsina 1991).

Rosen 1989 claims that the *faire par* constructions are derived by passivization applying to the embedded verb before the causative merger process has applied. The lack of passive morphology is accidental. In her analysis of Japanese causatives, the passivization of the predicate embedded under causative *(s)ase* surfaces with the passive morpheme overt, as shown below. (Example from Rosen 1989):

(94) ? Kantoku -ga John -wo/-ni (Bill -ni) nagur-are-sase-ta.
     director nom   acc/dat   dat   hit-PAS-CAS-PST
     'The director made/let John be hit by Bill.'

Zubizarreta 1985 claims that the *faire par* construction syntactically deletes the external argument (though it is lexically retained), much like the passive construction does. In this sense, the causative verbs in the *faire par* construction functionally substitute for passive morphology. She calls attention to the fact that the passive morphology is not only unnecessary but is totally prohibited in the *faire par* construction of the Romance causatives, as the following examples illustrate:

(95) a. Pierre a fait lire ces passages par Jean.
    *b. Pierre a fait (être) lu(s) ces passages par Jean.
       'Pierre made this passage read by Jean.'

To explain this fact, Zubizarreta 1985 appeals to the Principle of Morphological Nonredundancy. Given this principle, a verb with passive morphology cannot appear embedded under the causatives of the *faire par* construction, because the latter already have the function of passivization.

We suggest that the causative can have the same effect as passivization in Japanese as well, even without passive morphology. Though the presence of passive morphology is not as strictly prohibited in Japanese as in the Romance causative, as (94) shows, the passive morpheme is not absolutely necessary. See the following example, which does not involve the passive morpheme:

(96) Kantoku -ga John -wo (Bill -niyotte) nagur-ase-ta.
      director nom   acc   by   hit-CAS-PST
      'The director made/let John be hit by Bill.'

Further, the structure, i.e., a passive embedded in a causative, seems to impose semantic conditions. As may be recalled, *ni*-causatives require the lower subject to hold control over the caused event. The lower subject must be Agentive, i.e., animate, causative, and volitional, in particular. This condition is carried over when the embedded VP is passive; that is, when the lower subject is derived through direct passivization, the passive subject is required to be Agentive. However, this obviously goes counter to the characterization of the subject of passives, which is specified as non-causative Affectee. Interestingly, the lower subject must be animate even in *wo*-causatives of passive verbs, See the examples showing this point:

(97) *a. Syota -ga sono hon -wo/-ni syuppans-are-sase-ta.
           nom that book   acc/dat   publish-PAS-CAS-PST
         'Syota had the book published.'

    *b. Syota -ga ryokoo -wo/-ni keikakus-are-sase-ta.
           nom travel   acc/dat   plan-PAS-CAS-PST
         'Syota had the trip planned.'

    *c. Syota -ga tegami -wo/-ni todoke-rare-sase-ta.
           nom letter   acc/dat   deliver-PAS-CAS-PST
         'Syota had the letter delivered.'

All these examples are totally ungrammatical, even though, as we discussed earlier, *wo*-causatives normally allow a non-agentive lower subject. Given (94), which is marginal but acceptable, we believe that the factor prohibiting these cases of embedding passives is semantic. Interestingly, the most natural paraphrase denoting the same situation would be a simple causative structure, with the Causee omitted:

(98) a. Syota   -ga   sono hon   -wo   syuppans-ase-ta.
          nom   that book acc   publish-CAS-PST
      'Syota had the book published.'

   b. Syota   -ga   ryokoo   -wo   keikakus-ase-ta.
          nom   travel   acc   plan-CAS-PST
      'Syota had the trip planned.'

   c. Syota   -ga   tegami   -wo   todoke-sase-ta.
          nom   letter   acc   deliver-CAS-PST
      'Syota had the letter delivered.'

Notice that these sentences in (98) almost exactly parallel the *faire par* construction of the Romance causatives. No passive morpheme is used, but the Causee is suppressed as if the lower predicate had undergone passivization.

We therefore propose that Japanese also has a causative structure which is reminiscent of the *faire par* construction of the Romance causatives. In particular it has the lower subject suppressed in the same sense as in the passives, in the absence of passive morphology.

5.7.4 Passive-Type Causatives Based on a Transitive Verb

To accommodate the third type of causatives identified in the previous section, we propose to extend our approach to the lexical causatives. Recall that the operation of lexical causatives has so far been restricted to intransitive verbs or to transitive verbs with idiosyncratic dative case marking. In both the lexical causatives and the syntactic causatives, the Patient role of the causative relation is coindexed with the lower subject. The new class of causatives described in the preceding sections, we propose, is different from either of them in that the Patient role of the causative relation is coindexed with the lower object.

In a typological study of morphological causatives in the framework of LFG, Alsina 1991 and Alsina and Joshi 1991 claim that languages can vary according to which argument of the lower predicate is to be "fused" with the patient argument of the higher (causative) predicate. The fused argument typically surfaces as the direct object of the causative predicate. In languages where the lower object can be fused with the higher patient argument, the lower subject typically shows up as an oblique (e.g., in Marathi, and in a dialect of Chichewa).

We adopt the insight of Alsina 1991 and Alsina and Joshi 1991, and propose the following lexical rule for the third class of causatives.[45]

(99) Passive-Type Causative Lexical Rule

$$\begin{bmatrix} \text{SUBCAT} \langle \text{NP}[1], \text{NP}[2], ... \rangle \\ \text{CONT }[4]\begin{bmatrix} \text{RELATION} & R \\ \text{EXT-ARG} & [1] \\ R\text{-}er & [1] \\ R\text{-}ee & [2] \\ \vdots & \vdots \end{bmatrix} \end{bmatrix} \Rightarrow$$

$$\begin{bmatrix} \text{SUBCAT} \langle \text{NP}[3], \text{NP}[2], ... \rangle \\ \text{CONT} \begin{bmatrix} \text{RELATION} & cause \\ \text{EXT-ARG} & [3] \\ \text{CAUSER} & [3] \\ \text{PATIENT} & [5][\text{INDEX}[6]] \\ \\ \text{SOA-ARG} & [4] \begin{bmatrix} \text{RELATION } R \\ \text{EXT-ARG} & [1] \\ R\text{-}er & [1] \\ R\text{-}ee & [2][\text{INDEX}[6]] \\ \vdots & \vdots \end{bmatrix} \end{bmatrix} \end{bmatrix}$$

The verb *hakob* 'carry' in example (81) above undergoes the rule in the following way:

Causative Constructions

(100) Passive-Type Causative of *hakob-ase* in (77)

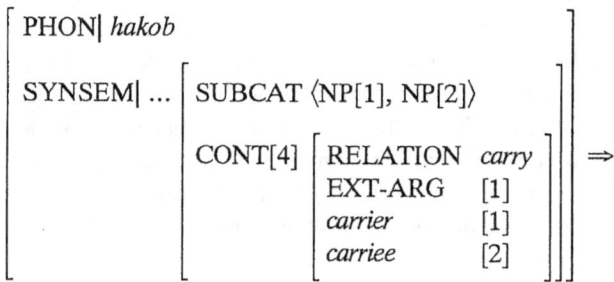

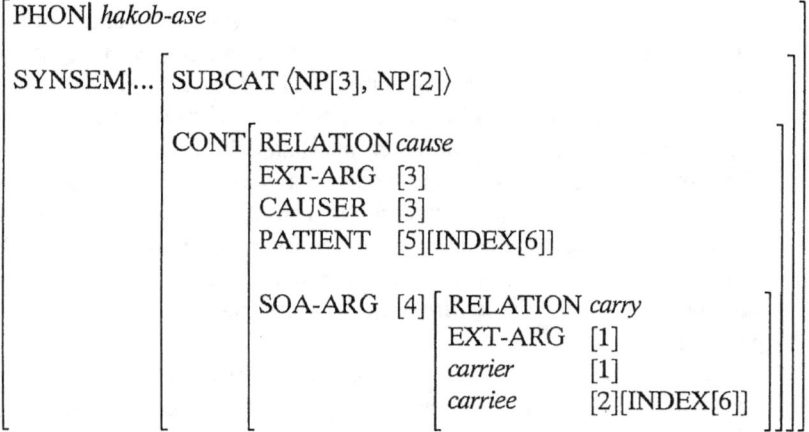

Notice that in the above lexical rule the Patient role of the causative relation is coindexed with the object of the lower soa. This coindexing pattern is exactly the same as the one observed in the direct passives. Crucially, in our approach, this coindexing pattern is permissible only if the lower subject is suppressed. We have proposed in the discussion of the direct passives that the coindexing normally cannot skip over the Ext-Arg of the lower predicate; to make it possible, the Ext-Arg has to be suppressed. The same thing happens in the causative lexical rule in question. The lower object is coindexed with the Patient role of the causative relation, and, concomitantly, the lower subject is left out from the syntactic SUBCAT list, just as in the direct passives. The case marker alternation and the omissibility of the lower subject lend support to the claim that the lower subject is suppressed.

Thus the present approach explains not only why the lower subject can behave like the agent phrase of the direct passives, but also, more importantly, why the passive morpheme is not necessary to bring about this effect. Our approach only refers to the coindexing relation; the suppression of the lower subject is a consequence of a particular coindexing pattern. This pattern is not exclusive to a particular morphological construction; it is common to the direct passive. It also automatically follows that this type of causative only applies to transitive or ditransitive causatives, as the stem must have at least two arguments associated with it.[46]

One thing needs to be mentioned before we close our discussion of this type of causative. The class of passive-type lexical causatives proposed in this section are often difficult to single out in syntactic tests. We suggest this is because the passive-type lexical causative is very similar on the surface to the ordinary *ni*-causatives. Further, whenever the former is available, the latter is also available. The situation is similar to the Romance causatives, where the distinction between the ordinary transitive-based causatives and the *faire par* causatives is often evident only in the preposition *à* vs. *par*. The situation is even worse, in fact, because the dative case *ni* and the agentive phrase marker *niyotte* are often interchangeable even in direct passives.[47]

The Japanese passive-type lexical causatives are different from the *faire par* causatives in another respect as well. That is, unlike the Romance Causatives, passive morphology within the causative is not strictly prohibited, though it is considerably restricted in terms of semantic condition. We assume that the third type of causative is available in Japanese for any type of transitive verbs, but not to the exclusion of the syntactic causatives embedding passives. However, because there are strict semantic restrictions on syntactic causatives with embedded passives, these restrictions often make the passive-type lexical causatives the only possibility.

5.8 Conclusion

In this chapter we have proposed a new approach to Japanese causatives. Japanese causatives are classified into three types. They all share essentially the same semantic CONTENT structure, with the differences encoded in terms of the manner of coindexing.

The first type, the *wo*-causative, is analyzed as a lexical causative, the causative morpheme *(s)ase* functioning as a derivational affix. Through the operation of the lexical rule, the Patient role of the causative relation is coindexed with the Ext-Arg of the relation denoted by the verb stem. The lexical rule deriving this type of causative applies only to intransitive verbs and to those transitive verbs which mark their direct object with dative case; otherwise, the output would violate the double-*wo* constraint.

The second type, *ni*-causatives, is analyzed as entering into a syntactic control structure, with the causative morpheme *(s)ase* functioning as a syntactic word. In contrast with *wo*-causatives, *ni*-causatives are not sensitive to transitivity and the case marking properties of the lower predicate. Similar to the case of *wo*-causatives, the Patient role of the causative relation is coindexed with the Ext-Arg of the relation denoted by the verb stem, but the coindexing relation is guaranteed by the control theory of HPSG. The causative relation is considered as a member of the class of Influence-type relations, and hence the object argument of the causative verb becomes the controller (= the one coindexed with the Ext-Arg) of the VP-complement.

The data of Do-Support are consistent with our claim that the causative morpheme in syntactic causatives functions as a verb, while that in lexical causatives is a derivational affix.

The data of SH have demonstrated that the Causee of the *wo*-causatives is not a syntactic subject, while that of the *ni*-causatives is. The data of OH indicate that the Causee of both the *wo*-causatives and the *ni*-causatives is a syntactic object in a causative sentence. So the data of SH and OH jointly support our claim that *ni*-causatives have an object control structure, in which the Causee plays both the role of a syntactic object and the role of a syntactic subject.

The above claim based on the data of OH, that the Causee is a syntactic object in either type of causatives, is relevant to the passivizability of causatives. We have argued that the Causee of either type is passivizable, and that the lack of a non-coercive interpretation for the direct passives of causatives does not indicate the unpassivizability of *ni*-causatives. The data from the direct benefactivization of causatives constitute very strong evidence that the obligatory coercive interpretation is a matter of semantics. We have also refuted the association of coerciveness and non-coerciveness with *wo*-causatives and *ni*-causatives, and have claimed that the core semantic difference pertains to the potential of the Causee to exert control over the caused event.

In the present analysis, *wo*-causatives and *ni*-causatives share essentially the same semantic CONTENT structure. The semantic difference between them, particularly the semantic restriction that the Causee of *ni*-causatives must be able to have control over the caused event, is attributed to the semantic restriction on Japanese syntactic control structures in general.

The noticeable lack of contrast between the *wo*-causatives and the *ni*-causatives in some of the major syntactic tests obtains under our approach as natural consequences. We have claimed that reflexive binding and adverbial scope, which have conventionally been taken as syntactic tests of biclausality, are the indication of the complexity of semantic CONTENT structures. So the data do not challenge our claim that *wo*-causatives are monoclausal, whereas *ni*-causatives are biclausal.

The third type of causative we have identified is a passive-type causative, which is derived through a lexical rule. It involves coindexing between the Patient role of the causative relation and the non-Agent role of the relation of the stem verb. This type of causative shares certain properties with direct passivization: it cannot be formed based on an intransitive verb, and the lower subject is syntactically suppressed. Our approach readily accommodates the fact that passive-type causatives have the agent phrase suppressed even though it does not involve passive morphology. Our mechanism of argument suppression in passives established in chapter 2 refers only to the pattern of coindexing, and not to a specific morphology, and the coindexing relation involved in this type of causative is exactly the same as the one involved in direct passives. Thus, the analysis of passive-type causatives has provided strong support for our analysis of agent phrase suppression and coindexing relation that we proposed in chapter 3.

Advantages of the general approach of HPSG are evident in several points. It helps us achieve a reconciliation between uniform and non-uniform analyses. The recognition of several independent levels of information which are simultaneously available allows one to capture the uniformity which exists across different types of causatives, and their syntactic differences at the same time.

Just as in the cases of passives and benefactives, the causative morphemes in lexical and syntactic causatives are very different from each other in terms of syntactic status: the former is a derivational affix while the latter functions as a syntactic verb. In the former, it does not have a subcategorization frame itself, but affects the subcategorization of the verb stem it attaches to. In the latter, on the other hand, the causative verb has its own SUBCAT feature, and the stem verb is treated as a part of its complement. Despite this great disparity between lexical causative morphemes and syntactic causatives morphemes, the information-based nature of HPSG makes it possible for each type of causative to share the same semantic CONTENT structure as the information of the whole sentence.

Thus, our approach has opened a new dimension to the study of causatives. The properties displayed by each construction are factored out into semantic information and syntactic information, and are analyzed independently in a proper domain. It has been shown that the present approach makes it possible to provide a consistent account of passives, benefactives, and causatives.

Notes

1. Just like the passive morpheme *(r)are*, the initial consonant is deleted when the preceding verb stem is consonant-final. The passive morpheme and the causative morpheme seem to belong to the same class of affixes regarding phonological rules.

2. The Causee is the one who is forced/allowed by the Causer to perform an action to bring about an event. Throughout this chapter, the term *Causee* is used to refer to the argument which, informally, bears both an patient-like role with respect to the causative verb and an agent-like role with respect to the caused event. When the distinction is crucial, the terms *the Patient of the causative verb* and *the lower subject* are used instead.

3. We are going to refer to this semantic distinction, coercive vs. non-coercive, in reviewing the literature. However, in our own account in sections 5.5.1 and 5.5.2, this concept will be challenged.

4. Though the double-*wo* constraint is observationally true in most cases, there are data which suggest that the issue is not the surface number of accusative cases but the number of direct object arguments within one clause (Dubinsky 1989; Shibatani 1990). For instance, accusative case marking on the Causee is ungrammatical in (i-a) and (ii-b) even if the lower object is topicalized and is marked with the topic marker *wa* instead. Note that in the following starred b-sentences, there is no more than one accusative case:

(i) a. Hon -wa Syota -ga Kyoko -ni yom-ase-ta.
     book top   nom   dat read-CAS-PST
  *b. Hon -wa Syota -ga Kyoko -wo yom-ase-ta.
      book top   nom   acc read-CAS-PST
     'As for the book, Syota made/let Kyoko read it.'

(ii) a. Sinzi -wa Syota -ga Kyoko -ni tatak-ase-ta.
              top   nom   dat hit-CAS-PST
  *b. Sinzi -wa Syota -ga Kyoko -wo tatak-ase-ta.
             top   nom   acc hit-CAS-PST
      'As for Sinzi, Syota made/let Kyoko hit him.'

The same phenomenon is observed when the accusative marked NP undergoes relativization. Although there is no more than one accusative case in (iii-b) and (iv-b) below, they are ungrammatical:

(iii) a. Syota -ga   Kyoko -ni yom-ase-ta   hon
         nom   dat   read-CAS-PST book
   *b. Syota -ga   Kyoko -wo yom-ase-ta   hon
         nom   acc   read-CAS-PST book
       'the book which Syota made Kyoko read.'
(iv) a. Syota -ga   Kyoko -ni tatak-ase-ta kodomo
         nom   dat   hit-CAS-PST   child
   *b. Syota -ga   Kyoko -wo tatak-ase-ta kodomo
         nom   acc   hit-CAS-PST   child
       'the child whom Syota made Kyoko hit.'

Thus the double-*wo* constraint may be reformulated as the double-direct-object constraint (cf. Dubinsky 1989). However, it is also possible to analyze the NPs topicalized or relativized as receiving a case specification of accusative anyway, though it does not surface because, say, the structures of topicalization and relativization do not require the percolation of case. This is quite a reasonable analysis, given that in our approach, case is specified lexically in the SUBCAT list. For, otherwise, any argument bearing the topic marker *wa* would have to be analyzed as having no other lexical case specified in the SUBCAT list.

Kazuhiko Fukushima has pointed out that all the ungrammatical b-sentences become fine if the accusative marker *wo* is changed to *wo-motte/-site*, postpositional phrase involving the accusative case marker (p.c.) The sentences would sound a little archaic, but are fine, as he remarks, and the *wo-motte/-site* phrase surely is not a dative phrase. This is a very interesting observation, but let us notice that the *wo-motte/-site* phrase is not an accusative phrase, either; it is presumably a postpositional phrase corresponding to the English instrumental phrase headed by *with*. Though it involves the accusative marker and marks an argument corresponding to the (embedded) Causee as in the *wo*-causative, *wo-motte/-site* never marks a direct object in other contexts: *hon -wo/*wo-motte yomu* 'read a book.' We tentatively regard it as somewhat similar to the *niyotte*-phrase (N.B. they both consist of a case marker plus a gerundive verb), and distinguish the structure from *wo*-causatives. Further support for this approach will be given later (see note 6 and section 5.7.4).

For more discussion on double-*wo* constraint, see Poser 1981.

5. Shibatani's (1973) point is to show the syntactic biclausality of the productive causatives (*wo*-causatives and *ni*-causative) in contrast

with the monoclausality of the causative transitives (lexical causative, in his terminology).

6. It has been reported that some speakers find such sentences as these marginal but acceptable. Martin (1988), however, speculates that this is due to some type of performance error. We regard these as ungrammatical. See also Marantz 1984, Kitagawa 1986, Rosen 1989, and others.

One point to note. Though the b-sentences are ungrammatical whether the Causee (*Kyoko*) is marked with dative or accusative, the one with accusative marking is far worse than the one with dative marking, even thought there is no other accusative-marked phrase in the sentence. This suggests that the absence of accusative marking on the Causee of transitive-based causatives (i.e., a-sentences in (14)-(15)) is not merely a surface matter.

Kazuhiko Fukushima (p.c.) also finds the above-mentioned difference in grammaticality between *wo*-causative and *ni*-causative of (14)-(15), the former being far better than the latter, but further points out that b-sentences in (14)-(15) are improved extensively if the dative/accusative case marker on *Kyoko* is replaced by *mo-motte/-site*. To put it another way, he observes that the passivization of the lower object is indeed possible with *ni*-causatives and particularly when the Causee is marked with *wo-motte/-site*, which we regard as a postposition analogous to *niyotte* (see note 4 above). We do not pursue the difference between *wo*-causatives and *ni*-causatives in this matter, but the point concerning *wo-motte/site* will be discussed further in section 5.7.4.

7. Alsina and Joshi 1991 argues that the typological difference among the morphological causatives can be reduced to essentially whether the agent or the patient argument gets fused with the higher patient role, if there is one.

8. Note first that her structures contrast with the ones proposed by Kuroda 1965a, 1965b and Kuno 1973. In Kuroda 1965a, 1965b and Kuno 1973, *wo*-causatives have the Causee in the matrix clause, while in *ni*-causatives, the Causee occurs only in the embedded clause. According to Terada 1990, in contrast, the Causee is located in the matrix clause only in *ni*-causatives. This underlying structure follows the tradition of what Tonoike (1978) termed the *ni*-extra analysis.

9. As mentioned several times, the transitive-based *wo*-causatives and the transitive-based *ni*-causatives are indistinguishable on the

surface. Terada 1990 agrees with Tonoike 1978 and others that coerciveness is not a valid criterion distinguishing the two types of causatives, and opts for the notion "volitionality." However, throughout her discussion, the distinction is extremely subtle and is often made virtually on the basis of coerciveness.

10. Terada 1990 follows Marantz 1984 and Baker 1988 and assumes that Japanese is a double object language.

11. The main focus of Rosen's (1989) study is placed on the Romance causatives. It has been observed that the Romance causatives are periphrastic on the surface, the causative morpheme being an independent verb, but that they show a number of syntactic properties common to morphological causatives. The lower verb and the causative verb seem to constitute one syntactic unit in many respects, and the lower object instead of the lower subject can get accusative case.

As Zubizarreta (1985) has pointed out, there are important differences between causatives in Italian, on the one hand, and Spanish and French, on the other. To explain the differences among the Romance causatives, she has also proposed that the argument structures are totally merged in Italian, while they are only partially merged in Spanish and French.

12. The merger of the argument structures, be it partial or total, also means that two event roles in the sense of Higginbotham 1985 are identified. Following Higginbotham 1985, Rosen 1989 assumes that each event role (<e>) must be discharged to some I. When two <e>'s are identified under the argument merger process, there results only one open <e>. Thus it follow that only one I is required to satisfy the open <e> role. According to Rosen 1989, this crucially allows the Romance causatives to have a VP-complement instead of IP- or CP-complement as Baker 1988 postulates. Rosen 1989 adopts the VP-internal subject hypothesis so that the complement VP includes the subject argument of the complement clause.

13. The only difference between the Romance and Japanese causatives is that the causative morpheme is a bound morpheme in Japanese. Because of this morphological requirement, the stem verb must be raised out of the complement VP to incorporate into the causative morpheme. Rosen 1989 assumes that the affixal nature of the causative morpheme of Japanese must be satisfied at S-structure. So the operation of verb incorporation must take place between D- and S-structure. Compare this assumption with Terada's (1990) approach

whereby the verb incorporation can (and must) take place as late as at PF in some cases.

14. Rosen 1989 basically follows the proposal of Grimshaw 1990 that passivization is essentially the suppression of the external argument in the argument structure.

15. Rosen 1989 assumes the tier-based case linking theory proposed by Yip, Maling, and Jackendoff 1987.

16. With Farmer 1980, 1984 and Miyagawa 1980, she also suggests that the case difference follows from the difference in meaning; the causative verb marks the Causee with the accusative only when it is an affected patient in the sense of Jackendoff 1990 (i.e., in coercive causatives).

17. Fukushima 1990 follows both Gunji 1987 and Pollard and Sag 1991, 1994, and proposes that Japanese causatives, as well as indirect passives, are control structures with a VP-complement. For Fukushima 1990, however, controller selection is based on the semantic property of the matrix (causative) verb, as suggested by Pollard and Sag 1991, 1994.

18. The term Causee as a patient role of a causal relation is deliberately avoided here to avoid confusion. The term Causee here informally refers to an entity which plays a dual function: i.e., the patient of the causal relation and the one carrying out the caused event.

19. The coindexing relation in this case is, as we will see shortly, basically the same as in the syntactic causatives which draw on the syntactic control theory in HPSG. We do not, however, propose to extend Pollard and Sag's syntactic control theory to a lexical operation. This extension is not necessary in this case, as it does not involve any unsaturated VP. This issue is beyond the scope of this study but warrants further research.

20. Rosen 1989 also takes the view that dative case is a default, and explains the dative case marking in "non-coercive" (*ni-*) causatives as an instance of a default case. At the same time, however, she assumes that the dative case can be a Structural Case much like the accusative case, and assumes that it substitutes for the accusative case in the "coercive" (*wo-*) causatives. We find her approach to Japanese case marking, particularly to dative case, inconsistent. Dative case marking has always been a problem in Japanese. Concerning the various approaches to this issue, particularly to dative case marking in the causatives, see Inoue 1982.

21. As mentioned in the previous paragraph, we do not assume that *ni* appears in the place of *wo* to save the situation from the double-*wo* constraint. One of the motivations is that there seems to be no case in Japanese where *ni* replaces *wo* to circumvent the violation of double-*wo* constraint. See, for instance, the following examples of the light verb construction in Japanese. Two instances of accusative case are not allowed to surface at once (cf. (i)). Crucially, as (ii) shows, replacement of accusative case by dative case does not help the situation at all but simply results in ungrammaticality:

(i) *a. Syota -ga   eigo   -wo benkyoo -wo si-ta.
            nom   English acc study   acc do-PST
    b. Syota -ga   eigo   -wo benkyoo-si-ta.
            nom   English acc study-do-PST
    c. Syota -ga   eigo   -no benkyoo -wo si-ta.
            nom   English gen study   acc do-PST
        'Syota studied English.'

(ii)*a. Syota -ga   eigo   -ni benkyoo -wo si-ta.
            nom   English dat study   acc do-PST
   *b. Syota -ga   eigo   -wo benkyoo -ni si-ta.
            nom   English dat study   acc do-PST
        'Syota studied English.'

So we do not think it is a well-grounded operation to have dative case appear in the place of accusative case.

22. As the verb *sawar* 'touch' marks the direct object with either dative or accusative, the sentence in (33-b) is grammatical in the reading that *Naoko was made to touch Kyoko by Syota*, i.e., *Naoko* is the Causee.

23. Note that the above explanation is essentially the same as the one we presented in accounting for the unpassivizability of passives (cf. section 3.5.2). Compare also the account of the unpassivizability of the lower object by Marantz (1984) and Rosen (1989). According to Rosen's (1989) argument merger, for example, a Japanese causative of either type is an instance of partial merger, so the internal structure of the lower predicate is opaque.

24. Note that the *ni*-causative structure proposed by Terada 1990 is very close to the one proposed here. She also assumes that the *ni*-causative morpheme takes two NP arguments and a sentential complement, whose subject, PRO, is controlled by the matrix object

NP (see (19) above). Rosen 1989 claims a VP-complement, but her VP includes the subject and is notionally a sentential complement.

25. Shibatani 1976a no longer claims that the concept of coercion can clearly separate *wo*-causatives and *ni*-causatives. As mentioned above, Shibatani 1976a takes the view that there is no syntactic difference between *wo*-causatives and *ni*-causatives. Shibatani 1976a still maintains that *wo*-causatives express "coercive directive" causation and *ni*-causatives "non-coercive directive" causation; however, he argues that the semantic domains of two types of causation are in fact intersecting. In particular, according to Shibatani 1976a, the nonintersecting part is so small that the distinction is often unclear. This shift of Shibatani's view is sometimes unjustly neglected in the literature (cf. Tonoike 1978).

26. Terada 1990, on the other hand, uses the term "volitionality" to contrast with "coerciveness." But her term is still confusing with "coerciveness." In (41-b) and (41-c), above, for instance, going to school and going to the court are both self-controllable actions, but do not seem to be volitional action in those contexts.

27. Note that the concept of self-controllability is notionally close to volitionality and, hence, non-coerciveness. The lack of self-controllability is easily confused with the lack of volition, and hence, coerciveness. We therefore conclude that coerciveness vs. non-coerciveness is wrongly associated with the lexical vs. syntactic causatives due to their notional closeness.

28. As Leslie Saxon pointed out to me (p.c.), the English translations of the sentences in (46) are odd in the same way. But causative verbs such as *make* and *cause* make a perfect sentence. Other languages including Romance languages seem to display the same contrast between causative verbs and control verbs. We do not have an explanation for this contrast at this moment. It may be interpreted as suggesting that genuine causative verbs and control verbs form separate sets, and that the Japanese *wo*-causatives are close to the causative verbs while *ni*-causatives are close to the control verbs.

29. Inoue (1976b, 71) notes this type of data and questions the validity of syntactic explanations of the obligatory coercive interpretation. But she does not establish the parallelism between passives and benefactives.

30. Terada 1990 does not exactly claim that the direct passives and the direct benefactives share the same syntactic structure (cf. section

4.3). No NP movement is assumed in the direct benefactives. The direct benefactives have a kind of subject-control structure, in which the matrix subject is coindexed with a PRO in the object position of an embedded clause. It is still crucial that Case absorption takes place for the direct benefactives so that the PRO will not receive Case.

31. Recall that in Terada's system, the incoporation of verb stem to Infl (=*te*) takes place between D- and S-structure, while the verb stem plus *te*, as an amalgam, is incorporated into the benefactive morpheme *moraw* at PF. Terada 1990 fairly extensively discusses the interaction among passives, causatives, and benefactives. She in fact discusses the benefactivization of causatives (Terada 1990, section 5.7). For some reason, however, she takes her examples only from the indirect benefactives, and concludes that *ni*-causatives cannot undergo benefactivization across the board. No mention is made of direct benefactives, which pose a serious problem to her approach.

32. Rosen 1989 also defends the idea of prominence binding in analyzing Japanese causatives.

33. Its syntactic status as a matrix object will be defended in section 5.6.3, with the data from Object Honorification.

34. A word of clarification will be in order. Readers may wonder whether causative transitives (i.e., verbs which have causal meaning such as *oros* 'put down,' *age* 'raise,' and *okos* 'wake (someone) up') also have a complex semantic CONTENT structure. If that were the case, our analysis would not be able to account for the fact that the causative transitive verbs do not show adverbial scope ambiguity, as observed in Shibatani 1973.

Recall, however, that the semantic CONTENT attribute in HPSG is a value of SYNSEM (syntax-semantic) attribute (section 2.1.1.3). That is, this feature encodes semantic information which is relevant to syntax. It is not semantic information independent of syntactic structure. So causative transitives, i.e., non-derivational causatives, will not have the same type of semantic CONTENT structure as *wo*-causatives or *ni*-causatives. The exact form of analysis of causative transitives is beyond the scope of this book, and awaits further research.

35. Miyagawa (1980, 1989a) proposes a lexical derivation of causatives based on an examination of the lexical organization of verbs. According to his observation, a predicate with the causative morpheme *(s)ase* fails to appear when there is an existing transitive verb with the

same meaning. Based on the data, Miyagawa (1980, 1989a) claims that this kind of sensitivity to the organization of the lexicon, or blocking effect, is a strong piece of evidence for lexicalist approaches to the causatives. Miyagawa's (1980, 1989a) claim has not gone unchallenged (cf. Kuroda 1981), however, although it has been relatively well-accepted (cf. Kitagawa 1986).

The blocking effect is a very controversial issue, particularly because, we believe, a model which successfully accommodates all the interactions between lexicon and syntax is not available yet. Due to these circumstances, we do not discuss the blocking effect in the text but refer the reader to the appendix of Uda 1992.

36. We have chosen examples of *wo*-causatives from those which do not have corresponding *ni*-causatives. The judgment becomes considerably subtle with *wo*-causatives which also make *ni*-causatives. We take the subtlety of judgment as a consequence of potential analogy with *ni*-causatives. With the cases which have no corresponding *ni*-causatives available, the judgment is quite clear.

37. As Kitagawa 1986 notes, the sentences above sound odd without the benefactive morpheme *sasiage*. However, as we have discussed in the previous chapter, this morpheme is not likely to change the syntactic properties of the predicates which appear inside. Besides, the benefactive morpheme is not the only possibility. Kuno 1983 and Dubinsky 1989 use another expression, *o-oki-moosiage* '(lit.) leave-speak (HON),' which is mostly honorific and partly aspectual. It is even more unlikely to alter the subcategorization of the predicate. Therefore, we conclude that the contribution of the morpheme *sasiage* is simply honorific and that it is not this morpheme that makes SH possible.

38. The judgment with (63) and (64) is admittedly subtle. But we believe that there is a difference between (61)-(62) and (63)-(64), beyond the semantic reason mentioned above. Kuno 1982, however, accepts SH of the Causee in *wo*-causatives. Sige-Yuki Kuroda also accepts SH of the Causee in both *wo*-causatives and *ni*-causatives (p.c.). Incidentally, he does not recognize their difference in terms of Do-Support, either (p.c.).

This may imply the following: for those who share Kuno (1973) and Sige-Yuki Kuroda's grammatical judgment, there is no syntactic distinction between *wo*-causatives and *ni*-causatives, and both are syntactic causatives. Note that this situation, if it is proven to be the case, does not challenge our basic system, as the two types of causative already share almost all other properties, e.g. reflexive binding, OH, adverbial scope, etc. Both types of causative would be analyzed almost exactly like *ni*-causative, except case marking. Their difference in semantic requirement would have to find an explanation in a different way.

39. For the sake of simplicity, we have omitted the benefactive morpheme and contextualizing phrases.

40. Kitagawa 1986 does not discuss the importance of morpheme order, but gives an example corresponding to the (68-a) pattern (= honorific directed toward the Causee) as acceptable, which we rule out. In a footnote, however, he mentions that Kuno has pointed out to him that the examples in question sound as if the speaker is showing respect toward the matrix subject rather than toward the Causee. Though Kitagawa 1986 rejects Kuno's comment for no good syntactic reason, we claim that Kuno is correct. The pattern (68-a) is really the morpheme order for the SH of the matrix subject.

41. Due to the pragmatic reasons discussed above in connection with SH of the lower subject, not all lexical verbs are able to form OH based on the causatives. However, it seems that OH is slightly more easily available than SH.

As Sige-Yuki Kuroda has pointed out (p.c.), there seems to be a difference in acceptability between dative case marking and accusative case marking in (73). That is, OH of dative-marked Causee sounds worse than that of accusative-marked Causee. But (74), where the Causee is marked with dative case, is accepted by him. We agree with him that the dative case marking lowers acceptability of (73) to some degree, but we believe that the dative-marked version of (73) is distinctly better than the sentences in (78)-(80), i.e., OH of passives and benefactives, which are simply hopeless.

42. It seems that only the most oblique object can be the trigger of OH. Harada 1976 observes that when a verb has both direct and indirect objects, only the latter can trigger OH. So in a sentence based on a transitive verb, the accusative-marked direct object triggers OH; in a sentence based on a ditransitive verb, the dative-marked indirect object, but not the accusative marked direct object, triggers OH:

(i) Kyoko -ga *sensei* -wo *o*-tasuke-*si*-ta.
      nom teacher acc *o*-help-HON-PST
'Kyoko helped the teacher.' (honorific)

(ii) a. Kyoko -ga Syota -no koto -wo *sensei* -ni *o*-hanasi-*si*-ta.
       nom Syota's thing acc teacher dat *o*-speak-HON-PST
    'Kyoko talked to the teacher about Syota.' (honorific)
   *b. Kyoko -ga *sensei* -no koto -wo haha -ni *o*-hanasi-*si*-ta.
       nom teacher's thing acc mother dat *o*-speak-HON-PST
    'Kyoko talked to her mother about the teacher.' (honorific)

So we could make a stronger restriction that OH is triggered by the [+HON] feature borne by the most oblique NP argument in the SUBCAT list. This seems plausible, but we leave this issue open because we have not examined all possible forms of OH.

43. In most of the cases listed here the agentive postposition *niyotte* can be replaced by the postposition *wo-motte/-site*, though the latter sounds somewhat more archaic. As mentioned in note 4 above, both consist of a case marker *ni/wo* (dat/acc) and a gerundive verb *yotte* 'depend' or *motte/site* 'use/do.' Different from *niyotte*, however, *wo-motte/-site* is exclusive to causatives, and not used in passives.

44. For more on the problem of postposition on the Causee, see note 45 below.

45. Without providing much evidence, we assume that this class of causatives is a lexical causative, primarily because it involves a change in the SUBCAT list. As mentioned earlier, HPSG does not allow this kind of change to take place in syntax.

46. As mentioned above, some languages use distinct postpositions/case markers for the Causee of this type of causative and for the agent phrase of passives, casting doubt on the analogy between causatives and passives. For instance, Hungarian marks the Causee with instrumental case, while the language lacks a passive construction. The case marker on the Causee in Gilyak is also limited to the causative construction. In Malayalam, which has both instrumental case (*-aal*) and instrumental postposition (*koṇṭə*), the Causee can only be marked with the instrumental postposition and the agent phrase of the passives can only be marked with the instrumental case (Falk 1991).

This situation is certainly a problem if one analyzes these causatives as derived through passivization. Note that it is hardly a problem for us because our analysis does not involve an actual operation of passivization. The formation of passive-type causatives does not evoke the operation of the direct passive lexical rule. Though the identity of the adposition for the Causee and the agent phrase of passives in Japanese and in Romance *faire-par* causative has motivated us to set up a class of passive-type causatives, the adpositional identity is not a necessary condition for the rule to apply. (Direct) passives and passive-type causatives simply have one thing in common; i.e., suppression of the Ext-Arg of the lower predicate. But the morphological realization of the suppressed argument may well vary depending on the particular rule, i.e., either passivization or causativization.

47. One thing merits attention. Notice from the lexical rule for passive-type causatives (99) that there is theoretically nothing that blocks the Patient argument tagged with [5], coindexed with the lower object [2], from being direct-passivized, which is found illegitimate (5.4.1 and 5.4.2). Recall, however, Kazuhiko Fukushima's observation that the passivization of the lower object seems fine particularly when the Causee (=coindexed with the lower subject) is marked with *wo-motte/-site* (note 4 above). As this phrase is now characterized as an instrumental phrase which can mark the suppressed lower subject in passive-type causatives (cf. note 4), the sentences that Fukushima observes fine are interpreted as instances of passive-type causatives. This amounts to say that the availability of the strucutre of the passive-type causative significantly improves the passivization of the lower object. Thus Fukushima's observation provides support for our analysis of the *wo-motte/-site* phrase and the passive-type causative.

VI
Conclusion

This book has presented an analysis of passive, benefactive, and causative complex predicates in Japanese in the framework of HPSG. Our general purpose has been to argue for the multi-level model, in which syntactic, semantic, and other kinds of information are co-present and are represented separately from each other.

We have started out with an assumption that a morphological unit and a syntactic unit are two different concepts. A morphologically bound form can syntactically play the role of an independent word, while the reverse is also possible.[1]

We have taken this assumption one step further and assumed that phonologically identical morphemes which form analogous constructions are not necessarily identical in terms of their syntactic status; that is, one of them can be a syntactic word when others are derivational affixes.

One of the central issues we have concerned ourselves with is the monoclausality and biclausality of complex predicates. Complex predicates are by definition composed of two predicates combined into one, and it is not very surprising, intuitively at least, that they display monoclausal properties and biclausal properties at the same time. But accommodating the duality in a coherent system is not a straightforward matter.

Many previous studies have attempted to reconcile the dualities. It is particularly not easy for lexicalist approaches to represent biclausality. Farmer 1984 draws on the mechanism of bracketing in predicate argument structure to indicate the biclausality. This mechanism is notionally very close to the partial argument merger in Rosen's (1989) system. One of the significant differences between them is that the operation refers to a syntactic category (slot) in the former, while it refers to a logical variable, or thematic argument in the latter. In this sense, the argument fusion in recent works of LFG (Alsina 1991; Alsina and Joshi 1991) is reminiscent of the latter approach.

The reconciliation of monoclausality and biclausality is achieved in transformational theories by referring to different levels of representation. Earlier studies of Transformational Grammar often posit a biclausal deep structure, from which such transformational operations as Raising and S-pruning take place to arrive at a monoclausal surface structure (Kuroda 1965a; Kuno 1973; Shibatani 1973; Inoue 1976b). For Kitagawa (1986), the monoclausality of causatives is represented at S-structure and the biclausality at LF. In contrast, for Baker (1988) and his followers, D-structure universally represents the biclausality of complex predicates, while S-structure may accommodate biclausality or monoclausality depending on the language.[2]

Our analysis has approached the issue of monoclausality and biclausality from a different angle. Based on our working hypothesis mentioned above, we have claimed that, syntactically, Japanese has both monoclausal and biclausal types of passives, benefactives, and causatives. At the same time, in our system, all the complex predicates examined here involve a complex semantic CONTENT structure, independently of their syntactic monoclausality or biclausality. Regarding the biclausality observed in complex predicate structures in general, we have proposed to re-assess the tests which have been considered sensitive to syntactic biclausality. In particular, we have argued that such tests as reflexive binding and adverbial scope do not prove syntactic biclausality but the complexity of the semantic CONTENT structure.

Now let us very briefly review our arguments in Chapters 2 through 5, and recapitulate specific proposals we have made in the course of discussion.

Chapter 2 presented the synopsis of HPSG. We have also set up the assumptions we adopted concerning thematic roles, reflexive binding, and case marking. We have introduced the concept of thematic roles put forward by Dowty 1991. According to this approach, thematic role names such as Agent, Experiencer, Theme, etc. are defined as labels referring to a set of relevant entailments. Agent, for instance, has a large number of entailments such as volitionality, causality, sentience, among others, associated with a Proto-Agent role. One of the crucial features of this approach is that thematic roles are not discrete. The difference between, say, Agent and Experiencer, is a matter of degree; only the former entails causal involvement in the action, but both are sentient.

Conclusion

Regarding reflexive binding, we have followed Jackendoff 1972, Giorgi 1983-1984, Rosen 1989 in claiming that thematic prominence is the key notion in selecting the binder. In our theory, a potential binder is defined as the one with the most prominent thematic role in each soa, where the most prominent role is defined as the one with the greatest number of Proto-Agent Role entailments. So the domain of binder selection is not the SUBCAT feature, which represents the obliqueness of arguments, but the semantic CONTENT feature.

In chapter 3 passive constructions were examined. Following Dubinsky 1989, Kubo 1990, and Terada 1990, we have classified Japanese passives into three types: direct, possessive, and indirect passives. We have agreed with Kubo 1990 and Terada 1990 that direct passives and possessive passives share a significant number of syntactic properties. We have claimed that direct and possessive passives are derived through a lexical rule; they are syntactically monoclausal, and the passive morpheme is a derivational affix. Indirect passives, on the other hand, are syntactically constructed; they are syntactically biclausal, with a sentential complement, and the passive morpheme is a syntactic verb.

Let us start with direct passives. Departing from the formulation of passives in HPSG, we proposed that the direct passive operation creates an embedding structure in the semantic CONTENT feature in addition to the permutation of arguments in the SUBCAT list. The semantic CONTENT feature of the verb stem (or, intuitively, the corresponding active sentence) is maintained as the embedded soa. The higher relation is an underspecified relation, represented as Affect, which is non-causal and non-volitional. By making the direct passive operation involve the embedding of the semantic CONTENT features, the present approach makes a correct prediction concerning the unavailability of direct passives of possessive passives.

We have used the mechanism of coindexing to relate the Affectee role to the non-Agentive argument of the embedded soa, which stands for the situation where, informally, an object argument of an active sentence is promoted to the subject argument of a passive sentence.

The operation of direct passivization changes the organization of the SUBCAT list in such a way that a non-subject argument is promoted to the subject position and at the same time the original subject is dropped off the SUBCAT list, representing syntactic suppression. We have proposed to correlate the argument suppression and the manner of coindexing. Simply put, an argument of a higher soa is to be coindexed with the Ext-Arg of an embedded soa. Except when the Ext-Arg is syntactically suppressed, no other argument of the embedded soa is available for coindexing. The coindexing in direct passives is permissible only under the suppression of the Ext-Arg. Suppressed arguments, i.e., the agent phrases of direct passives, are left out of the syntactic SUBCAT list, and fail to behave like full-fledged syntactic arguments, though they are thematically present (Marantz 1984; Roberts 1986; Zubizarreta 1989; Grimshaw 1990). In Japanese, they are like adjuncts in being marked with postpositions, being omissible, and being unable to bind reflexives. Their thematic presence can be ascertained by their potential for being modified by manner adverbs.[3] They are different from other adjuncts also in optionally receiving dative case. We have stipulated that a default case is available for semantic arguments. So the agent phrase of direct passives receives dative case by virtue of being present in the semantic CONTENT feature, and it is marked with a postposition by virtue of being absent from the syntactic SUBCAT list.

Indirect passives, on the other hand, lack the coindexing characteristic of direct passives. Accordingly they do not involve argument suppression, and do not display the properties related to the suppression of the Ext-Arg. The agent phrase is a syntactic subject of the embedded clause, being able to trigger Subject Honorification and to bind reflexives. It cannot be omitted, nor can it be marked with a postposition.

Possessive passives show syntactic properties similar to direct passives. The lexical rule introduces a new subject argument, and suppresses the argument corresponding to the subject argument of the stem verb. We have claimed that the crucial fact giving rise to the similarity between direct passives and possessive passives is the semantic connection **P** between the (newly introduced) subject and the object argument of the stem verb. Two entities standing in the relation **P** form a network of entailments. The relation A **P** B is defined in such a way that affecting B necessarily entails affecting A. Informally put, B denotes a part (physically or metaphorically) of A. As coindexing in HPSG is essentially an indicator of coreferentiality, the **P** relation leads to an effect similar to that of coindexing. As a simple example, reference to John can include the reference to John's arm, John's personality, or some event for which John is responsible.[4] Because of the **P** relation, the suppression of the Ext-Arg of the embedded soa becomes necessary in possessive passives just as in direct passives.

Chapter 4 analyzed benefactive constructions. We have shown that *te-moraw* benefactives syntactically parallel passives. They consist of three sub-types: direct, possessive, and indirect benefactives. The syntactic properties of each type which are shared by passives of the corresponding type are accounted for in exactly the same way as in passives.

We also called attention to the noticeable differences between passives and *te-moraw* benefactives, which might be taken as counterevidence against our parallel analysis. The differences include morpheme order in Subject Honorification, the ambiguity of adverb scope with indirect benefactives, the obligatory benefactive interpretation, and the optional causative interpretation with benefactives. It has been shown that these differences do not challenge their syntactic parallelism.

As regards morpheme order, we have claimed that the honorific particle *o* is prefixed to the smallest phonologically independent unit.

Concerning semantic properties, we have claimed that the *te-moraw* benefactive relation consists of a totally underspecified thematic relation and a MODAL relation specifying that the subject will be the beneficiary. The former explains why *te-moraw* benefactives optionally convey a causal meaning, which is completely missing with passives. The latter explains why all types of *te-moraw* benefactives obligatorily carry a benefactive interpretation, while the corresponding (though opposite in polarity) malefactive interpretation is obligatory only with indirect passives.

We have proposed that the thematic argument in passives (represented as Affectee in the feature structure) is underspecified, specified only as non-causal and non-volitional. The thematic argument in *te-moraw* benefactives does not even have the non-causal specification. Following Ritter and Rosen 1990, we have assumed that when an argument with an underspecified thematic role is to be related to an embedded event, it can function either as a Causer or as an Experiencer. Recall that in our conception of thematic roles, the roles Causer and Experiencer are simply labels covering a certain set of properties. Causer here is interpreted as the one causally involved in the denoted event. Experiencer is the one not-causally related to the event; it is rather the one who receives some influence from the event. So the subject argument of passives cannot be a Causer, because it is specified as non-causal. It plays the role of Experiencer when it is not coreferential with any argument in the core event. When it is coreferential with a non-Agentive argument in the core event, the role in the core event substantiates the non-causal involvement. The subject argument of *te-moraw* benefactives, on the other hand, can be either causal or non-causal. So it can play the role of Causer or Experiencer (in the indirect type) or some other non-Agentive role (in the direct/possessive) type.

To borrow Croft's (1991) terminology, Causer is an antecedent role, while Experiencer is a subsequent role. That is, the role played by the former precedes the event, while the role played by the latter follows the event. But we have claimed that the difference between Causer and Experiencer is not merely temporal. The crucial point is that the involvement of the former is indispensable for the realization of the event, while the latter makes no contribution to the realization of the event. It follows, therefore, that the referent of the matrix subject of passives (i.e., Affectee) makes no active involvement in the core event, while that of benefactives has the potential for being actively involved in the core event. This account of thematic underspecification in passives and benefactives correctly predicts the difference in the scope of manner adverbs between the two constructions. Particularly, only the matrix subject of indirect passives is not involved in the realization of the core event, and fails to be modified by the manner adverbs. By extending the insights of Oehrle and Nishio (1981) and Kuno (1983), we have also related the non-involvement of the matrix subject of indirect passives, due to its negative specification of causality, to the adversity interpretation, which is obligatory only in the indirect passive.

The last section of chapter 4 examined the other two types of Japanese benefactive predicates, *te-yar* and *te-kure*, to explore the complete system of benefactive complex predicates in Japanese. We have claimed that all three types of benefactives share the MODAL feature as a common denominator, the crucial difference between *te-moraw* benefactives and the other two types being encoded as the specification of thebeneficiary. It is identified with the (matrix) subject in *te-moraw* benefactives, while it is any argument except the (matrix) subject in *te-yar/te-kure* benefactives.

Chapter 5 gave an analysis of Japanese causative constructions, employing the results obtained in the preceding chapters. Japanese causatives were classified first into *wo*-causatives and *ni*-causatives. The former are lexically-derived, monoclausal causatives, while the latter are syntactically-constructed, biclausal causatives. Based on our analysis of direct passives, we have also indentified a third type of causatives, passive-type causatives.

Let us first review *wo*-causatives and *ni*-causatives. Like the passive and benefactive formations, causative formation creates a complex semantic CONTENT structure, irrespective of syntactic monoclausality/biclausality. The lexical rule for *wo*-causatives stipulates that the Patient role of the causative relation is coindexed with the Ext-Arg of the embedded soa; the same coindexing relation is achieved in *ni*-causatives as a property of object control structures (Pollard and Sag 1994).[5] In contrast to the coindexing relation in direct passives/benefactives, the coindexing involved in causatives does not violate the coindexing condition; i.e., an argument of a higher relation is coindexed with the Ext-Arg of a lower relation. Accordingly, no argument suppression is invoked. This accounts for the fact that lexical vs. syntactic causatives fail to display some of the syntactic contrasts shown by lexical vs. syntactic passives, for instance in reflexive binding.

Based on the syntactic parallelism between passives and *te-moraw* benefactives, we have shown that the Causee argument is a passivizable argument in either type of causatives. That is, it is a syntactic argument of the matrix clause, and has a semantic role in the higher relation (i.e., Cause). Data of Object Honorification have further supported the idea that the Causee is a syntactic argument (i.e., object) of the matrix clause.[6]

Based on our analysis of reflexive binding and adverbial scope in passives and *te-moraw* benefactives, we have claimed, counter to Shibatani (1973) and his followers, that the ambiguity of reflexive binding and adverbial scope does not point to syntactic biclausality but to the complexity of semantic CONTENT structure. Accordingly, the data of reflexive binding and of adverbial scope were interpreted as satisfying the predictions made by our analysis of causatives in terms of the semantic CONTENT structure. Our proposal concerning the relation between manner adverb modification and causal involvement correctly predicts that the matrix subject of causatives (the Causer) can legitimately be modified.

The data concerning Subject Honorification and its morphological form were consistent with our analysis of the same issues with passives and *te-moraw* benefactives. The Causee of *ni*-causatives can trigger Subject Honorification by virtue of corresponding to the subject argument of the embedded unsaturated VP. The morpheme order was as predicted, given that the causative *(s)ase* is a morphologically bound morpheme exactly like the passive *(r)are*.

After giving an analysis of *wo*-causatives and *ni*-causatives, we turned our attention to a different type of causative. This type is peculiar in that the agent of the caused event is apparently suppressed syntactically; the agent phrase can be marked with the agentive postposition *niyotte*, can be omitted, and fails to bind pronominals. Based on these properties, this type of causative was compared to *faire par* causatives in Romance languages. These properties are also reminiscent of what was seen in direct passives/benefactives.

We have proposed that the third type of causative coindexes the Patient role of the causal relation with an argument other than the Ext-Arg of the lower relation, denoted by the verb stem. Given our coindexing condition, this coindexing relation has the same effect of argument suppression as direct passives/benefactives. Though we have termed this type of causative passive-type causatives, we do not analyze them as undergoing actual passivization before causativization. The suppression of the lower Ext-Arg, triggered by the coindexing condition, is all that is common to direct passives and passive-type causatives. This directly accounts for the fact that passive-type causatives do not involve passive morphology in spite of the obvious syntactic similarities between them and passives.[7]

One of our main purposes in this study has been to demonstrate the advantages of HPSG as a multi-level, information-based theory. In particular, the claim that linguistic information should be factored out into several co-existing levels has formed the essential undercurrent of our discussion. We believe that this purpose has been accomplished and that the analyses presented in this book have proved the validity of the claim.

Factoring out the information encoded in a language into more than one co-existing level has made it possible to refer to different aspects of linguistic information such as SUBCAT, semantic CONTENT, and so forth, to accommodate complex linguistic facts. Thus, by separating syntactic SUBCAT information and semantic CONTENT information, syntactic monoclausality and biclausality are discussed independently of the complexity of semantic CONTENT structure.

Moreover, encoding information in several independent features has provided a new way to seek a domain to achieve uniformity among different subtypes of a construction, while referring to the differences at the same time. We have suggested three such cases. First, the semantic CONTENT feature serves as the common denominator of each construction: passives, *te-moraw* benefactives, and causatives.[8] Secondly, the MODAL feature of benefactive value is shared by all of the three benefactives, *te-yar*, *te-kure*, and *te-moraw* benefactives. Thirdly, passives and benefactives share everything except the MODAL feature, which is present only in the latter. The shared features are identical, differing only in indices and the value of some of the features.

Notice that the result of our analysis confirms the validity of our working hypothesis that morphological properties and syntactic properties are independent of each other, at least as far as the complex predicates under investigation are concerned. The data of Do-Support and morpheme order in honorification have provided the most direct evidence for this contrast. Moreover, as the attachment of the honorific particle *o* indicates, morphological properties and syntactic properties are not only independent but can also be interdependent.

Thus, the present approach has offered a new way of analyzing Japanese complex predicate structures, and we believe that it has proven to be a promising one. On the other hand, however, there still remain problems and issues which are left for a future investigation. For one thing, our focus has been on the analysis of the system of the three complex predicate structures in Japanese, and we did not attempt to analyze them in a wider context of crosslinguistic studies. Comparison with other languages was given in several points, but no systematic analysis was attempted. Secondly, the interaction between morphology and syntax should be investigated more thoroughly. This has been a very controversial issue, especially so for the past decade. We have concerned ourselves only with the morphemes constituting complex predicates. But the issue ought to be taken up in a more general way involving all types of categories, morphemes, and words. Thirdly, related to the above two issues, the current framework should be extended so that it can accommodate both morphological causatives and periphrastic causatives. This task will involve the question of monoclausality and biclausality across different typological classes of language. This is sure to be a challenging, but fruitful direction to pursue.

Finally, the current model of HPSG (Pollard and Sag 1994) is not equipped with devices to represent, say, thematic prominence or the typicality in terms of Proto-Roles. We have extensively demonstrated the importance of the semantic CONTENT structure in the analyses of reflexive binding, adverbial modification, and others in Japanese, but we were not able to give a very formal representation for such issues. It is essential, therefore, for a future research in HPSG to elaborate more on the representation of the semantic CONTENT structure.

Notes

1. This claim itself will not find much objection. It suffices to point out that most Japanese postpositions have a complex structure, consisting of a genitive marker, a noun, and a case marker, or a case marker and a gerundive form of a verb. See the following examples:

on	*no-ue-ni*	*no*	genitive case
		ue	'up' (noun)
		ni	dative case (or locative)
by	*ni-yot-te*	*ni*	dative case
		yotte	gerund of the verb *yor* 'depend'
against	*ni-taisi-te*	*ni*	dative case
		taisite	gerund of the verb *tais* 'face'

Nevertheless, these units seem to function syntactically as postpositions much like other morphologically simplex postpositions such as *de* 'at,' *e* 'to,' and *to* 'with.' This situation is analogous to the case of English phrasal prepositions such as *in front of*, *in spite of*, *for the sake of*, and many others.

2. Verb incorporation does not in fact make a monoclausal structure. After a verb stem is incorporated into a causative/passive morpheme, the lower clause is still present, headed by traces. Recall also that, as mentioned in chapter 3, for Hasegawa (1988) and Terada (1990), the indirect passive morpheme and the verb stem are incorporated only at PF.

3. Note that this, in return, supports our claim that the potential scope of manner adverbs is determined not by syntactic structure but by semantic CONTENT structure.

4. The definition delimiting the relevant semantic relation is admittedly loose, but we have shown data showing that it indeed has to be loose. Inalienable possession, or even the possessive relation in general, is too narrow to cover the data.

5. Recall that syntactic passives (i.e., indirect passives) do not have a control structure, and no coindexing is involved.

6. The data of Object Honorification, at the same time, proved that the agent phrase of (indirect) passives and *te-moraw* benefactives is not an object of the matrix clause, ruling out the possibility of object control structures for these formations analogous to what is proposed for the causatives.

7. Notice that some of the recent analyses of passives in GB Theory relate the absorption of accusative case by the passive morpheme and the suppression of the (active) subject phrase (Burzio 1986; Roberts 1987; Miyagawa 1989a). In such approaches, the presence of the passive morpheme is indirectly but crucially related to the suppression of the (active) subject phrase.

8. The relationship among passives, benefactives, and causatives is an intriguing issue now particularly for those who seek a deeper understanding and a proper treatment of thematic roles and argument structures. Recently, for instance, Washio (1993) has presented a very interesting analysis cutting across passives and causatives with a focus on the semantic gradation between the two. Assuming the framework of Jackendoff (1990), Washio divides the argument structure into "Action Tier" and "Thematic Tier," and explores the semantic ambivalence of the passive and the causative. He argues that the two share a basic conceptual structure and explains the ambivalence in terms of the notion *affectedness*.

Bibliography

Alsina, A. 1990. Where's the Mirror Principle? Stanford University. Duplicated.

_____. 1991. On Causatives: Incorporation vs. Lexical Composition. Stanford University. Duplicated.

Alsina, A. and S. Joshi. 1991. Parameters in Causative Constructions. *Papers from the Twenty-seventh Regional Meeting of Chicago Linguistic Society*.

Alsina, A. and S. Mchombo. 1990. Object Asymmetries in Chichewa. Stanford University. Duplicated.

Baker, M. 1988. *Incorporation: A Theory of Grammatical Function Changing*. Chicago: University of Chicago Press.

Baker, M., K. Johnson, and I. Roberts. 1989. Passive Arguments Raised. *Linguistic Inquiry* 20: 219-252.

Baltin, M.R. 1989. Heads and Projections. In *Alternative Conceptions of Phrase Grammar,* edited by M.R. Baltin and A.S. Kroch, 1-16. Chicago: The University of Chicago Press.

Barwise, J. and J. Perry. 1983. *Situations and Attitudes*. Cambridge, Mass.: The MIT Press.

Belletti, A. 1988. The Case of Unaccusatives. *Linguistic Inquiry* 19: 1-34.

Belletti, A. and L. Rizzi. 1988. Psych Verbs and Theta-Theory. *Natural Language and Linguistic Theory* 6: 291-352.

Blevins, J. 1989. Constituency in Free Word Order Languages. *Proceedings of the Nineteenth Annual Meeting of the North Eastern Linguistic Societ*: 31-47.

Bloch, B. 1946. Studies in Colloquial Japanese I: Inflection. *Journal of the American Oriental Society* 66: 97-109. Reprinted in *Bernard Bloch on Japanese* edited by R. Miller. New Haven, Conn.: Yale University Press, 1970.

Borer, H. 1986. I-Subjects. *Linguistic Inquiry* 17: 375-416.

_____. 1990. Derived Nominals and Causative-Incohative Alternation: Two Case Studies in Parallel Morphology. Paper presented at the Israeli Linguistic Association, Jerusalem, February, 1990. Duplicated.

Borsley, R.D. 1989a. Phrase-Structure Grammar and the *Barriers* Conception of Clause Structure. *Linguistics* 27: 843-863.

_____. 1989b. An HPSG approach to Welsh: Conception of Clause Structure. *Journal of Linguistics* 25: 333-354.

Bresnan, J., ed. 1982. *The Mental Representation of Grammatical Relations*. Cambridge, Mass.: The MIT Press.

Bresnan, J. and J. Kanerva. 1989. Locative Inversion in Chichewa: A Case Study of Factorization in Grammar. *Linguistic Inquiry* 20: 1-50.

Bresnan, J. and L. Moshi. 1990. Object Asymmetries in Comparative Bantu Syntax. *Linguistic Inquiry* 21: 147-186.

Bresnan, J. and A. Zaenen. 1990. Deep Unaccusativity in LFG. In *Grammatical Relations: A Cross-Theoretical Perspective*, edited by D. Dziwirik, P. Farrell, and E. Mejias-Bikandi, 45-57. Stanford: CSLI.

Burzio, L. 1986. *Italian Syntax: A Government-Binding Approach*. Dordrecht: Reidel.

Campbell, R. and J. Martin. 1989. Sensation Predicates and the Syntax of Stativity. *Proceedings of the Eighth West Coast Conference on Formal Linguistics*: 44-55.

Carrier-Duncan, J. 1985. Linking of Thematic Roles in Derivational Word Formation. *Linguistic Inquiry* 16: 1-34.

Carter, R. 1976. Some Linking Regularities. *Lexicon Project Working Papers, 25 -- On Linking: Papers by Richard Carter*, 1-92. Center for Cognitive Science, MIT.

Cheng, L. and E. Ritter. 1988. A Small Clause Analysis of Inalienable Possession in French and Mandarin. *Proceedings of the Eighteenth Annual Meeting of the North Eastern Linguistic Society*: 65-78.

Chierchia, G., B. Partee, and R. Turner, eds. 1989. *Properties, Types, and Meaning*. Vol. 2. Dordrecht: Kluwer.

Cho, Y.-M. Y. 1985. An LFG Analysis of the Korean Reflexive *caki*. *Harvard Studies in Korean Linguistics: Proceeding of Harvard WOKL--1985*: 3-13.

Chomsky, N. 1957. *Syntactic Structures*. The Hague: Mouton.

_____. 1965. *Aspects of Language* Cambridge, Mass.: The MIT Press.

_____. 1981. *Lectures on Government and Binding*. Dordrecht: Foris.

_____. 1986. *Barriers*. Cambridge, Mass.: The MIT Press.

Cole, P. and J. Sadock, eds. 1977. *Syntax and Semantics*. Vol. 8, *Grammatical Relations*. New York: Academic Press.

Comrie, B. 1976. The Syntax of Causative Constructions: Cross-Language Similarities and Divergences. In *Syntax and Semantics*. Vol. 6, *The Grammar of Causative Constructions*, edited by M. Shibatani, 261-312. New York: Academic Press.

_____. 1977. In Defense of Spontaneous Demotion: The Impersonal Passive. In *Syntax and Semantics*. Vol. 8, *Grammatical Relations*, edited by P. Cole and J. Sadock, 47-58. New York: Academic Press.

Cowper, E.A. 1988. What is a Subject?: Non-Nominative Subjects in Icelandic. *Proceedings of the Eighteenth Annual Meeting of the North Eastern Linguistic Society*: 94-108.

_____. 1989. Thematic Underspecification: The Case of *have*. Paper presented at the annual meeting of the Canadian Linguistic Association. Duplicated.

Croft, W. 1986. Categories and Relations in Syntax: The Clause-Level Organization of Information. Ph.D. dissertation, Stanford University.

_____. 1991. *Syntactic Categories and Grammatical Relations*. Chicago: University of Chicago Press.

Davies, W.D. and C. Rosen. 1988. Unions as Multi-Predicate Clauses. *Language* 64: 52-88.

Dowty, D.R. 1982. Grammatical Relations and Montague Grammar. In *The Nature of Syntactic Representation*, edited by P. Jacobson and G.K. Pullum, 79-130. Dordrecht: Reidel.

_____. 1989. On the Semantic Content of the Notion 'Thematic Role.' In *Properties, Types, and Meaning* Vol. 2, edited by Chiercha et. al, 69-130. Dordrecht: Kluwer.

_____. 1991. Thematic Proto-Roles and Argument Selection. *Language* 67: 547-619.

Dowty, D.R. and B. Brodie. 1984. The Semantics of "Floated Quantifiers" in a Transformationless Grammar. *Proceedings of the Third West Coast Conference on Formal Linguistics*: 75-89.

Dowty, D.R., R.E. Wall, and S. Peters. 1981. *Introduction to Montague Semantics*. Dordrecht: Reidel.

Dubinsky, S. 1989. *The Syntax of Complex Predicates in Japanese*. UCSC. Duplicated.

_____. 1990. Japanese Direct Object to Indirect Object Demotion. In *Studies in Relational Grammar*. Vol. 3, edited by P.M. Postal and B.D. Joseph, 49-86. Chicago: The University of Chicago Press.

Emonds, J. 1990. The Autonomy of the Syntactic Lexicon and Syntax. In *Interdisciplinary Approaches to Language*, edited by R. Ishihara and C. Georgopoulos, 119-148. Dordrecht: Kluwer Academic Publishers.

Falk, Y. 1991a. Causativization. *Journal of Linguistics* 27: 55-79.

_____. 1991b. Case: Abstract and Morphological. *Linguistics* 29: 197-230.

Farmer, A.K. 1980. On the Interaction of Morphology and Syntax. Ph.D. dissertation, MIT. Reproduced by Indiana University Linguistics Club, 1985.

_____. 1984. *Modularity in Syntax: A Study of Japanese and English*. Cambridge, Mass.: The MIT Press.

Fillmore, C. 1968. The Case for Case. In *Universals in Linguistic Theory*, edited by E. Bach and R. Harms, 1-90. New York: Holt, Rinehart, and Winston.

_____. 1977. The Case for Case Reopened. In *Syntax and Semantics*. Vol. 8, *Grammatical Relations*, edited by P. Cole and J. Sadock, 59-82. New York: Academic Press.

Flickinger, D.P. 1987. *Lexical Rules in the Hierarchical Lexicon*. Ph.D. dissertation, Stanford University.

Foley, W. and R.D. Van Valin, Jr. 1984. *Functional Syntax and Universal Grammar*. Cambridge: Cambridge University Press.

Fukui, N. 1986. A Theory of Category Projection and its Applications. Ph.D. dissertation, MIT.

Fukui, N. and P. Speas 1986. Specifiers and Projection. *MIT Working Papers in Lingusitics* 8: 128-172.

Fukushima, K. 1989. A Non-Floating Analysis of "Floating" Quantifiers in Japanese. *Coyote Papers* 7: 11-41. University of Arizona.

_____. 1990. VP-Embedding Control Structures in Japanese. In *Grammatical Relations: A Cross Theoretical Perspective*, edited by D. Dziwirik, P. Farrell, and E. Mejias-Bikandi, 163-182. Stanford: CSLI.

Gazdar, G. 1981. Unbounded Dependencies and Coordinate Structure. *Linguistic Inquiry* 12: 155-184.

_____. Phrase Structure Grammar. In *The Nature of Syntactic Representation*, edited by P. Jacobson and G.K. Pullum, 131-186. Dordrecht: Reidel.

Gazdar, G., E. Klein, G.K. Pullum, and I.A. Sag. 1985. *Generalized Phrase Structure Grammar*. Cambridge, Mass.: Harvard University Press.

Gerdts, D.B. 1985. Surface Case and Grammatical Relations in Korean: The Evidence from Quantifier Float. *Harvard Studies in Korean Linguistics: Proceeding of Harvard WOKL--1985*: 48-61.

_____. 1988. Semantic Linking and the Relational Structure of Desideratives. *Linguistics* 26: 843-872.

Giorgi, A. 1983-1984. Toward a Theory of Long-Distance Anaphors. *Linguistic Review* 3: 307-361.

Greenberg, J. 1963. Some Universals of Grammar with a Particular Reference to the Order of Meaningful Elements. In *Universals of Language*, edited by J. Greenberg, 73-113. Cambridge, Mass.: The MIT Press.

Grimshaw, J. 1987. Unaccusatives -- An Overview. *Proceedings of the Eighteenth Annual Meeting of the North Eastern Linguistic Society*: 245-258.

_____. 1990. *Argument Structure*. Cambridge, Mass.: The MIT Press.

Grimshaw, J. and R.A. Mester. 1988. Light Verbs and θ-Marking. *Linguistic Inquiry* 19: 205-232.

Gruber, J. S. 1965. *Studies in Lexical Relations*. Ph.D. dissertation, MIT.

Guilfoyle, E., H. Hung, and L. Travis. 1992. SPEC of IP and SPEC of VP: Two Subjects in Austronesian Languages. *Natural Language and Linguistic Theory* 10: 375-414.

Gunji, T. 1983. Generalized Phrase Structure Grammar and Japanese Reflexivization. *Linguistics and Philosophy* 6: 115-156.

_____. 1987. *Japanese Phrase Structure Grammar*. Dordrecht: Reidel.

_____. 1988. Subcategorization and Word Order. In *Papers from the Second International Workshop on Japanese Syntax*, edited by W. Poser, 1-21. Stanford: CSLI.

_____. to appear. On Lexical Treatment of Japanese Causative. In *Readings on HPSG*, edited by I. Sag and C. Pollard. Stanford: CSLI.

Hale, K. 1980. *The Position of Walbiri in a Typology of Base*. Distributed by Indiana University Linguistic Club.

Harada, S.I. 1973. Counter-Equi NP Deletion. *Annual Bulletin* 7, Research Institute of Logopedics and Phoniatrics, University of Tokyo. Reprinted in Papers in *Japanese Linguistics* 11: 157-200.

_____. 1976. Honorifics. In *Syntax and Semantics*. Vol. 5, *Japanese Generative Grammar*, edited by M. Shibatani, 499-561. New York: Academic Press.

Hasegawa, N. 1980. The VP Constituent in Japanese. *Linguistic Analysis* 6: 115-130.

_____. 1981a. A Lexical Interpretive Theory with Emphasis on the Role of Subject. Ph.D. dissertation, University of Washington.

_____. 1981b. Lexicalist Grammar and Japanese Passives. *Coyote Papers* 2: 25-40.

_____. 1988. Passive, Verb Raising, and the Affectedness Condition. *Proceedings of the Seventh West Coast Conference on Formal Linguistics*: 99-113.

Henniss K. 1989. 'Covert' Subjects and Determinate Case: Evidence from Malayalam. *Proceedings of the Eighth West Coast Conference on Formal Linguistics*: 167-175.

Higginbotham, J. 1985. On Semantics. *Linguistic Inquiry* 16: 547-594.

Hinds, J. 1973. On the Status of the VP Node in Japanese. *Language Research* 9: 44-57.

Hoji, H. 1985. Logical Form Constraints and Configurational Structures in Japanese. Ph.D. dissertation, University of Washington.

Hopper, P. and S. Thompson. 1980. Transitivity in Grammar and Discourse. *Language* 56: 251-299.

Hovav, M.R., and B. Levin. 1991. Is There Evidence for Deep Unaccusativity in English?: An Analysis of Resultative Constructions. Duplicated.

Howard, I. and A. Niyekawa-Howard. 1976. Passivization. In *Syntax and Semantics*. Vol. 5, *Japanese Generative Grammar* edited by M. Shibatani, 201-237. New York: Academic Press.

Huang, C.-T. J. 1982. Logical Relations in Chinese and the Theory of Grammar. Ph.D. dissertation, MIT.

Hukari, T.E. and R.D. Levine. 1987a. Parasitic Gaps, Slash Termination and the C-Command Consition. *Natural Language and Linguistic Theory* 5: 197-222.

_____. 1987b. Rethinking Connectivity in Unbounded Dependency Constructions. *Proceedings of the Sixth West Coast Conference on Formal Linguistics*: 91-102.

_____. 1988. Liberation and Inversion in GPSG. *Proceedings of the Seventh West Coast Conference on Formal Linguistics*: 159-170.

_____. 1989. Category Antirecursion: Paradoxical Consequences of Gap-within-Filler Constructions. *Proceedings of the Eighth West Coast Conference on Formal Linguistics*: 192-206.

_____. 1991. On the Disunity of Unbounded Dependency Constructions. *Natural Language and Linguistic Theory* 9: 97-144.

Iida, M. 1992. Context and Binding in Japanese. Ph.D. dissertation, Stanford University.

Iida, M. and P. Sells. 1988. Discourse Factors in the Binding of Zibun. In *Papers from the Second International Workshop on Japanese Syntax*, edited by W. Poser, 23-46. Stanford: CSLI.

Inoue, K. 1976a. Reflexivization. In *Syntax and Semantics*. Vol. 5, *Japanese Generative Grammar*, edited by M. Shibatani, 117-200. New York: Academic Press.

_____. 1976b. *Henkei Bonpoo to Nihongo* (Transformational Grammar and Japanese). Vol 1. Tokyo: Taishukan.

_____. 1976c. *Henkei Bonpoo to Nihongo* (Transformational Grammar and Japanese). Vol 2. Tokyo: Taishukan.

_____. 1982. Transformational vs. Lexical Analysis of Japanese Complex Predicates. In *Linguistics in the Morning Calm*, edited by I.-S. Yang, 379-412. Seoul: Hanshin.

_____. 1989. Shugo no imi-yakuwari to kaku-hairetsu (Semantic roles of subject and case arrangement). In *Nihongo-gaku no Shintenkai* (New perspectives in Japanese linguistics), edited by S. Kuno and M. Shibatani, 79-102. Tokyo: Kuroshio.

Ishihara, M. 1991. Lexical Prosodic Phonology of Japanese Verbs. University of Arizona, Duplicated.

Ishikawa, A. 1985. Complex Predicates and Lexical Operations in Japanese. Ph.D. dissertation, Stanford University.

Jackendoff, R. 1972. *Semantic Interpretation in Generative Grammar*. Cambridge, Mass.: The MIT Press.

_____. 1977. *X-bar Syntax: A Study of Phrase Structure*. Cambridge, Mass.: The MIT Press.

_____. 1983. *Semantics and Cognition*. Cambridge, Mass.: The MIT Press.

_____. 1985. Believing and Intending: Two Sides of the Same Coin. *Linguistic Inquiry* 16: 445-460.

_____. 1987. The Status of Thematic Relations in Linguistic Theory. *Linguistic Inquiry* 18: 481-506.

_____. 1990. *Semantic Structures*. Cambridge, Mass.: The MIT Press.

Jacobsen, W. 1982. Transitivity in the Japanese Verbal System. Ph.D. dissertation. Distributed by Indiana University Linguistics Club, Bloomington, Indiana.

Jacobson, P. and G.K. Pullum, eds. 1982. *The Nature of Syntactic Representation*. Dordrecht: Reidel.

Jaeggli, O. 1986. Passive. *Linguistic Inquiry* 17: 587-622.

Johnson, D.E. 1977. On relational constraints on grammars. In *Syntax and Semantics*. Vol. 8, *Grammatical Relations*, edited by P. Cole and J. M. Sadock, 151-178. New York: Academic Press.

Johnson, M. 1987. Grammatical Relations in Attribute-Value Grammar. *Proceedings of the Sixth West Coast Conference on Formal Linguistics*: 103-114.

Joshi, S. 1989. Logical Subject in Marathi Grammar and the Predicate Argument Structure. *Proceedings of Eighth West Coast Conference on Formal Linguistics*: 209-219.

Kageyama, T. 1982. Word Formation in Japanese. *Lingua* 57: 215-258.

Kang, Y.-S. 1985. Case Marking in Korean. *Harvard Studies in Korean Linguistics: Proceeding of Harvard WOKL--1985*: 88-101.

Kaplan, R. and J. Bresnan. 1982. Lexical-Functional Grammar: A formal system for grammatical representation. In *The Mental Representation of Grammatical Relations*, edited by J. Bresnan, 173-281. Cambridge, Mass.: The MIT Press.

Kamp, H. 1984. A Theory of Truth and Semantic Representation. In *Truth, Interpretation and Information*, edited by J. Groenendijk, T. Janssen and M. Stokhof, 1-41. Dordrecht: Foris.

Katada, F. 1991. The LF Representation of Anaphors. *Linguistic Inquiry* 22: 287-313.

Kayne, R. 1975. *French Syntax: The Transformational Cycle*. Cambridge, Mass.: The MIT Press.

Keenan, E.L. and B. Comrie. 1977. Noun Phrase Accessibility and Universal Grammar. *Linguistic Inquiry* 8: 63-99.

Kempchinsky, P. 1988. On Inherent Case-Marking. *Proceedings of the Seventh West Coast Conference on Formal Linguistics*: 203-215.

Kim, Y.-B. 1989. A Fragment of Korean Phrase Structure Grammar. Ph.D. dissertation, University of Victoria.

Kitagawa, C. 1981. Anaphora in Japanese: *kare* and *zibun*, *Coyote Papers* 2: 61-76.

Kitagawa, Y. 1986. *Subjects in Japanese and English*. Ph.D. dissertation, University of Massachusetts.

Koopman, H. and D. Sportiche. 1991. The Position of Subjects. *Lingua* 85: 211-258.

Kroeger, P. 1991. Nonsubject Controllees in Tagalog. Paper presented at the Annual Meeting of the Linguistic Society of America. Duplicated.

Kubo, M. 1990. Japanese Passives. MIT. Duplicated.

Kuno, S. 1973. *The Structure of the Japanese Language*. Cambridge, Mass.: The MIT Press.

———. 1976a. Subject, theme, and the speaker's empathy--a reexamination of relativization phenomena. In *Subject and Topic*, edited by C. Li, 417-444. New York: Academic Press.

———. 1976b. Subject Raising. In *Syntax and Semantics*. Vol. 5, *Japanese Generative Grammar*, edited by M. Shibatani, 17-49. New York: Academic Press.

———. 1983. *Sin Nihon Bunpoo Kenkyuu* (A New Study of the Japanese Grammar). Tokyo: Taishukan.

———. 1987. *Functional Syntax*. Chicago: University of Chicago Press.

Kuno, S. and E. Kaburaki. 1977. Empathy and Syntax. *Linguistic Inquiry* 8: 627-672.

Kuno, S. and M. Shibatani, eds. 1989. Nihongo-gaku no Shin-tenkai (New perspectives in Japanese linguistics). Tokyo: Kuroshio.

Kuroda, S.-Y. 1965a. Generative Studies in the Japanese Language. Ph.D. dissertation, MIT.

_____. 1965b. Causative Forms in Japanese. *Foundations of Language* 1: 30-50.

_____. 1978. Case Marking, Canonical Sentence Patterns, and Counter-Equi in Japanese. In *Problems in Japanese Syntax and Semantics*, edited by J. Hinds and I. Howard, 111-130. Tokyo: Kaitakusha.

_____. 1979. On Japanese Passives. In *Explorations in Linguistics: Papers in Honor of Kazuko Inoue*, edited by G. Bedell, E. Kobayashi, and M. Muraki, 305-347. Tokyo: Kaitakusha.

_____. 1981. Some Recent Trends in Syntactic Theory and the Japanese Language. *Coyote Papers* 2: 103-121.

Ladusaw, W. A. 1985. A Proposed Distinction Between Levels and Strata. Paper presented at the 1985 Annual Meeting of the Linguistic Society of America.

Ladusaw, W.A. and D.R. Dowty. 1988. Toward a Non-Semantic Account of Thematic Roles. In *Syntax and Semantics*. Vol. 21, *Thematic Relations*, edited by W. Wilkins, 61-73. New York: Academic Press.

Larson, R. 1988. On the Double Object Construction. *Linguistic Inquiry* 19: 335-392.

Lasnik, H. and M. Saito. 1984 On the Nature of Proper Government. *Linguistic Inquiry* 15: 235-289.

Lee, I.-H. 1985. Toward a Proper Treatment of Scrambling in Korean. *Harvard Studies in Korean Linguistics: Proceeding of Harvard WOKL--1985*: 190-205.

Levin, J. and D. Massam. 1985. Surface Ergativity: Case/Theta Relations Reexamined. *Proceedings of the Fifteenth Annual Meeting of the North Eastern Linguistic Society*: 286-301.

Levin, B. and M. Rappaport. 1986. The Formation of Adjectival Passives. *Linguistic Inquiry* 17: 623-661.

_____. 1989. An Approach to Unaccusative Mismatches. *Proceedings of the Nineteenth Annual Meeting of the North Eastern Linguistic Society*: 314-329.

Levine, R.D. 1989. On Focus Inversion: Syntactic Valence and the Role of a SUBCAT List. *Linguistics* 27: 1013-1055.

Li, C.N., ed. 1976. *Subject and Topic*. New York: Academic Press.

Li, C.N. and S.A. Thompson. 1976. Subject and Topic: A New Typology of Language. In *Subject and Topic*, edited by C.N. Li, 457-490. New York: Academic Press.

Lieber, R. 1980. On the Organization of the Lexicon. Ph.D. dissertation, MIT.

Maling, J. 1981. The Hierarchical Assignment of Grammatical Cases in Finnish. Brandeis University. Duplicated.

Marantz. A.P. 1981. Grammatical Relations, Lexical Rules and the Japanese Language. *Coyote Papers* 2: 123-144.

_____. 1984. *On the Nature of Grammatical Relations*. Cambridge, Mass.: The MIT Press.

_____. 1991. Case and Licensing. *The Proceedings of the Seventh Eastern States Conference on Linguistics*.

Martin, S.E. 1974. *A Reference Grammar of Japanese*. New Haven, Conn.: Yale University Press.

_____. 1988. *A Reference Grammar of Japanese*. (Revised Edition). Tokyo: Tuttle.

Massam, D. 1989. Part/Whole Constructions in English. *Proceedings of the Eighth West Coast Conference on Formal Linguistics*:236-246.

McCawley, N.A. 1972. On the Treatment of Japanese Passives. *Papers from the Eighth Regional Meeting of the Chicago Linguistic Society*: 256-270.

_____. 1976. Reflexivization: A Transformational Approach. In *Syntax and Semantics*. Vol. 5, *Japanese Generative Grammar*, edited by M. Shibatani, 51-116. New York: Academic Press.

McCawley, J.D. and K. Momoi. 1985. The Constituent Structure of -te Complements. In *Working Papers from the First SDF Workshop in Japanese Syntax*, edited by S.-Y. Kuroda, 97-116.

Mester, R.A. and J. Itô. 1989. Feature Predictability and Underspecification. *Language* 65: 258-293.

Mikami, A. [1953] 1972. *Gendai Gohoo Zyosetu* (Introduction to the Modern Usage of Japanese). Reprint, Tokyo: Kuroshio.

Miyagawa, S. 1980. Complex Verbs and the Lexicon. Ph.D. dissertation, University of Arizona.

_____. 1981. Paradigmatic structures and word formation. *Coyote Papers* 2: 145-162.

_____. 1989a. *Syntax and Semantics*. Vol. 22, *Structure and Case Marking in Japanese*. New York: Academic Press.

_____. 1989b. Light Verbs and the Ergative Hypothesis. *Linguistic Inquiry* 20: 659-668.

_____. 1990. Case Realization and Scrambling. Ohio State University. Duplicated.

Miyara, S. 1981. Complex Predicates, Case Marking, and Scrambling in Japanese. Ph.D. dissertation, University of Massachusetts.

Miyara, S. 1991. On the Insertion of /s/-form *suru* in Japanese. *Gengo Kenkyu* 99: 1-24.

Mohanan, K.P. 1983. Move NP or lexical rules? Evidence from Malayalam Causativisation. In *Papers in Lexical Functional Grammar*, edited by L. Levin, M. Rappaport, and A. Zaenen, 47-111. Reproduced by the Indiana University Linguistic Club.

Mohanan, T.W. 1990. Arguments in Hindi. Ph.D. dissertation, Stanford University.

Nakau, M. 1973. *Sentential Complementation in Japanese*. Tokyo: Kaitakusha.

Napoli, D.J. 1988. Subjects and External Arguments: Clauses and Non-Clauses. *Linguistics and Philosophy* 11: 323-354.

Nerbonne, J., M. Iida, and W. Ladusaw. 1989. Null Heads in Head-Driven Grammar. *Proceedings of the Eighth West Coast Conference on Formal Linguistics*: 276-288.

Nitta, Y., ed. 1991. *Nihongo no Voisu to Tadoosei* (Voice and Transitivity in Japanese). Tokyo: Kuroshio.

Oehrle, R.T. and H. Nishio. 1981. Adversity. *Coyote Papers 2*: 163-186.

Ogihara, T. 1987. "Obligatory Focus" in Japanese and Type-Shifting Principles. *Proceedings of the Sixth West Coast Conference on Formal Linguistics*: 213-227.

O'Grady, W. 1985. Anaphora and Discontinuous Constituents in Korean. *Harvard Studies in Korean Linguistics: Proceeding of Harvard WOKL--1985*: 206-215.

Perlmutter, D.M. 1978. Impersonal Passives and the Unaccusative Hypothesis. *Proceedings of the Fourth Annual Meeting of the Berkeley Linguistic Society*: 157-189.

_____. 1983. *Studies in Relational Grammar*. Vol. 1. Chicago: The University of Chicago Press.

_____. 1984. Working 1s and Inversion in Italian, Japanese, and Quechua. In *Studies in Relational Grammar*, vol. 2, edited by D.M. Perlmutter and C.G. Rosen, 292-330. Chicago: The University of Chicago Press.

Perlmutter, D.M. and P.M. Postal. 1983. Toward a Universal Characterization of Passivization. In *Studies in Relational Grammar*, vol. 1, edited by D.M. Perlmutter, 3-29. Chicago: The University of Chicago Press.

_____. 1984. The 1-Advancement Exclusiveness Law. In *Studies in Relational Grammar*, vol. 2, edited by D.M. Perlmutter and C.G. Rosen, 81-125. Chicago: The University of Chicago Press.

Perlmutter, D.M. and C.G. Rosen, eds. 1984. *Studies in Relational Grammar*. Vol. 2. Chicago: The University of Chicago Press.

Pesetsky, D. 1990. Experiencer Predicates and Universal Alignment Principles. MIT. Duplicated.

Pinker, S. 1989. *Learnability and Cognition*. Cambridge, Mass.: The MIT Press.

Pollard, C. 1985. Phrase Structure Grammar Without Metarules. *Proceedings of the Fourth West Coast Conference on Formal Linguistics*: 246-261.

Pollard, C. and I.A. Sag. 1983. Reflexives and Reciprocals in English: An Alternative to the Binding Theory. *Proceedings of the Second West Coast Conference on Formal Linguistics*: 189-203.

_____. 1987. *Information-Based Theory of Syntax and Semantics*. Vol. 1. Stanford: CSLI.

_____. 1992. Anaphors in English and the Scope of Binding Theory. *Linguistic Inquiry* 23: 261-303.

_____. 1994. *Head-Driven Phrase Structure Grammar*. Chicago: The University of Chicago Press and Stanford: CSLI.

Pollock, J. Y. 1989. Verb Movement, Universal Grammar, and the Structure of IP. *Linguistic Inquiry* 20: 365-424.

Poser, W. 1981. The Double-*O* Constraint: Evidence for a Direct Object Relation in Japanese. MIT. Duplicated.

_____, ed.. 1988. *Papers from the Second International Workshop on Japanese Syntax.* Stanford: CSLI.

Postal, P.M. and B.D. Joseph, eds. 1990. *Studies in Relational Grammar.* Vol. 3. Chicago: The University of Chicago Press.

Rapoport, T.R. 1990. Secondary Predication and the Lexical Representation of Verbs. *Machine Translation* 5: 31-55.

Reinhart, T. 1983. Coreference and Bound Anaphora: A Restatement of the Anaphora Questions. *Linguistics and Philosophy* 6: 47-88.

Reinhart, T. and E. Reuland. 1991. Reflexivity. Duplicated.

Rice, K. 1991. Intransitives in Slave Northern Athapaskan: Arguments for Unaccusatives. *International Journal of American Linguistics* 57: 51-69.

Ritter, E. and S.T. Rosen. 1990. Causative *have*. Université du Québec à Montréal and University of Maryland. Duplicated.

Roberts, I.G. 1987. *The Representation of Implicit and Dethematized Subjects.* Dordrecht: Foris.

Rosen, C.G. 1984. The Interface between Semantic Roles and Initial Grammatical Relations. In *Studies in Relational Grammar,* vol. 2, edited by D.M. Perlmutter and C.G. Rosen, 38-77. Chicago: The University of Chicago Press.

Rosen, C.G. and Wali, K. 1989. Twin Passives, Inversion and Multistratalism in Marathi. *Natural Language and Linguistic Theory* 7: 1-50.

Rosen, S.T. 1989. Argument Structure and Complex Predicates. Ph.D. dissertation, Brandeis University.

Rozwadowska, B. 1988. Thematic Restrictions on Derived Nominals. In *Syntax and Semantics*. Vol. 21, *Thematic Relations*, edited by W. Wilkins, 147-66. New York: Academic Press.

Sag, I.A., G. Gazdar, T. Wasow, and S. Weisler. 1985. Coordination and How to Distinguish Categories. *Natural Language and Linguistic Theory* 3: 117-171.

Sag, I.A. and C. Pollard. 1989. Subcategorization and Head-driven Phrase Structure. In *An Alternative Conceptions of Phrase Structure*, edited by M. Baltin and A. Kroch, 139-181. Chicago: The University of Chicago Press.

_____. 1991. An Integrated Theory of Complement Control. *Language* 67: 63-113.

Sag, I.A., R. Kaplan, L. Karttunen, M. Kay, C. Pollard, S. Shieber, and A. Zaenen. 1986. Unification and Grammatical Theory. *Proceedings of the Fifth West Coast Conference on Formal Linguistics*: 238-254.

Saito, M. 1982. Case Marking in Japanese: A Preliminary Survey. MIT. Duplicated.

_____. 1985. Some Asymmetries in Japanese and Their Theoretical Implications. Ph.D. dissertation, MIT.

_____. 1987. Three Notes on Syntactic Movement in Japanese. In *Issues in Japanese Linguistics*, edited by T. Imai and M. Saito, 301-350. Dordrecht: Foris.

Sells, P. 1985. *Lectures on Cotemporary Syntactic Theories: An Introduction to Government-Binding Theory, Generalized Phrase Structure Grammar, and Lexical-Functional Grammar*. Stanford: CSLI.

_____. 1987. Aspects of Logophoricity. *Linguistic Inquiry* 18: 445-479.

_____. 1988. Thematic and Grammatical Hierarchies: Albanian Reflexivization. *Proceedings of the Seventh West Coast Conference on Formal Linguistics*: 293-303.

_____. 1990. More on Light Verbs and θ-Marking. Stanford University. Duplicated.

Shibatani, M. 1973. Semantics of Japanese Causativization, *Foundations of Language* 9: 327-373.

_____, ed. 1976a. *Syntax and Semantics*. Vol. 5, *Japanese Generative Grammar*. New York: Academic Press.

_____, ed. 1976b. *Syntax and Semantics*. Vol. 6, *The Grammar of Causative Constructions*. New York: Academic Press.

_____. 1977. Grammatical Relations and Surface Cases. *Language* 53: 789-809.

_____. 1985. Passives and Related Constructions. *Language* 61: 821-848.

_____. 1990. *Languages of Japan*. Cambridge: Cambridge University Press.

Shieber, S. 1986. *An Introduction to Unification-Based Theories of Grammar*. Stanford: CSLI and Chicago: University of Chicago Press.

Shimozaki, M. 1989. The Quantifier Float Construction in Japanese. *Gengo Kenkyu* 95: 176-205.

Smith, H. 1990. "Dative Sickness" and Direct Linking. Stanford University. Duplicated.

Speas, M.J. 1990. *Phrase Structure in Natural Language*. Dordrecht: Kluwer Academic Publishers.

Spencer, A. 1991. *Morphological Theory*. Oxford: Basil Blackwell.

Sportiche, D. 1988. A Theory of Floating Quantifiers and Its Corollaries for Constituent Structure. *Linguistic Inquiry* 19: 425-450.

Stowell, T. 1981. Origins of Phrase Structure. Ph.D. disseration, MIT.

Sugioka, Y. 1984. Interaction of Derivational Morphology and Syntax in Japanese and English. Doctoral dissertation, University of Chicago. Reproduced by Garland Publishing, 1986.

Suzuki, M. 1989. A Syntactic Analysis of an Honorific Construction *o ... ni naru*. *Proceedings of the Eighth West Coast Conference on Formal Linguistics*: 99-113.

Takezawa, K. 1987. A Configurational Approach to Case Marking in Japanese. Ph.D. dissertation, University of Washington.

Tateishi, K. 1989. Subjects, SPEC, and DP in Japanese. *Proceedings of the Nineteenth Annual Meeting of the North Eastern Linguistic Society*: 405-418.

Terada, M. 1987. Unaccusativity in Japanese. *Proceedings of the Eighteenth Annual Meeting of the North Eastern Linguistic Society*: 618-640.

_____. 1990. Incorporation and Argument Struture in Japanese. Ph.D. disseration, University of Massachusetts.

Tonoike, S. 1978. On the Causative Constructions in Japanese. In *Problems in Japanese Syntax*, edited by J. Hinds and I. Howard, 3-29. Tokyo: Kaitakusha.

Travis, L. 1984. Parameters and Effects of Word Order Variation. Ph.D. dissertation, MIT.

Tremblay, M. 1989. French Possessive Adjectives as Dative Clitics. *Proceedings of the Eighth West Coast Conference on Formal Linguistics*: 399-413.

Uda, C. 1992. Inflectional Morphology of Japanese: Condition and Trigger of Gemination as Assimilation. University of Victoria. Typescript.

Van Valin, R.D. Jr. 1987. The Unaccusative Hypothesis vs. Lexical Semantics: Syntactic vs. Semantic Approaches to Verb Classification. *Proceedings of the Eighteenth Annual Meeting of the North Eastern Linguistic Society*: 641-661.

_____. 1991. Another Look at Icelandic Case Marking and Grammatical Relations. *Natural Language and Linguistic Theory* 9: 145-194.

Van Voorst, J. 1988. *Amsterdam Studies in the Theory and History of Linguistic Science*. Vol. 59, *Event Structure*. Amsterdam: John Benjamin.

Washio, R. 1989-1990. The Japanese Passive. *The Linguistic Review* 6: 227-263.

_____. 1993. When Causatives Mean Passive: A Cross-Linguistic Perspective. *Journal of East Asian Linguistics* 2: 45-90.

Whitman, J. 1986. Configurationality Parameters. In *Issues in Japanese Linguistics*, edited by T. Imai and M. Saito, 351-374. Dordrecht: Foris.

Wierzbicka, A. 1979. Are Grammatical Categories Vague or Polysemous the Japanese "Adversative" Passive in a Typological Context? *Papers in Linguistics* 12: 111-162.

Wilkins, W, ed.. 1988. *Syntax and Semantics*. Vol. 21, *Thematic Relations*. New York: Academic Press.

Williams, E. 1980. Predication. *Linguistic Inquiry* 11: 203-238.

_____. 1984. Grammatical Relations. *Linguistic Inquiry* 15: 639-673.

Yang, D.-W. 1983. The Extended Binding Theory of Anaphora. *Theoretical Linguistic Research* 1: 195-218.

Yim, Y.-J. 1985. Multiple Subject Constructions. *Harvard Studies in Korean Linguistics: Proceeding of Harvard WOKL--1985*: 101-109.

Yip, M., J. Maling, and R.S. Jackendoff. 1987. Case in Tiers. *Language* 63: 217-250.

Zaenen, A. 1988. Unaccusative Verbs in Dutch and the Syntax-Semantics Interface. Report No, CSLI-88-123. Stanford, CA: CSLI.

Zaenen, A. and J. Maling. 1984. Unaccusative, Passive, and Quirky Case. *Proceedings of the Third West Coast Conference on Formal Linguistics*: 317-329.

Zubizarreta, M.L. 1982. On the Relationship of the Lexicon to Syntax. Ph.D. dissertation, MIT.

_____. 1985. The Relation Between Morphophonology and Morphosyntax: The Case of Romance Causatives. *Linguistic Inquiry* 16: 247-289.

_____. 1987. *Levels of Representation in the Lexicon and in the Syntax*. Dordrecht: Foris.

Zwicky, A.M. 1987. Slashes in the Passive. *Linguistics* 25: 639-669.

Index

aboutness condition, 137, 138
adverb modification
    English passive, 108, 109, 127
    benefactive, 109, 198, 199, 205, 207, 208, 218, 223, 319-321
    causative, 229, 235-237, 250, 259, 262, 269, 272-276, 287, 300, 309, 311
    direct passive, 109, 111, 112, 115, 127, 163, 318, 325
    indirect passive, 127-130, 140, 320, 321
    possessive passive, 140, 141
adversity interpretation, 69, 75-77, 80, 92, 97, 126, 127, 129, 130, 133, 139, 154-157, 166, 174, 175, 205-207, 269, 274, 320
Affect, 108, 112, 142, 144, 169, 190
Affectee, 108, 112, 114, 115, 118, 119, 127, 139, 141, 154, 164, 190, 205, 207, 225, 260, 294, 317, 319, 320
agent phrase
    reflexive binding, 72, 73, 75, 78, 80, 159, 176, 181, 190, 271, 318

case marking, 69-71, 75, 78, 80, 154, 155, 157, 169, 176, 177, 181, 190, 212, 289, 312, 313, 318, 322
    definition of, 157
    OH trigger, 103, 181, 185, 285-287, 325
    omission of, 71, 72, 75, 78, 80, 159, 176, 177, 181, 190, 235, 322
    SH trigger, 73-75, 79, 80, 177, 179, 181, 190, 196-199, 277, 318
Alsina, A., 28, 57, 114, 161, 238, 251, 257, 293, 295, 296, 304, 315
animacy of the matrix subject, 84, 92, 97, 105, 118, 119, 139, 191, 198
argument merger, 2, 224, 238, 246-248, 293, 305, 307, 315
argument-adjunct, 114
aspectual prominence, 58
a-structure, 28, 29, 238, 247, 248
attribute-value matrix (AVM), 3, 7, 8, 13
auxiliary, 1, 5, 174, 209, 219, 220, 223
Baker, M., 2, 24, 27, 58, 81, 93, 96, 112, 121, 162, 163, 238, 243, 246, 305,

351

Baker (cont'd)
    316
benefactivization of causatives, 262, 267-269, 275, 299, 309
binding
    obliqueness (o-binding), 40, 41, 44-47, 49, 61, 317
    prominence, 309
    zibun, 3, 7, 26, 32, 40-54, 61, 62, 316, 317, 324
    benefactive, 175, 176, 190, 208, 218, 221, 321
    causative, 229, 235, 250, 259, 262, 269-272, 275, 287, 300, 311, 321
    passive, 72, 73, 75, 78, 80, 83, 84, 86, 92, 97, 101, 105, 120-122, 138, 151, 159, 160, 166, 235, 321
Bloch, B., 220
blocking effect, 309, 310
Bresnan, J., 18, 25, 28, 47, 57, 81, 82, 113-115, 121, 151, 161
Burzio's generalization, 87-89
Case absorption, 81, 87-89, 104, 145, 150, 183-185, 245, 246, 267, 268, 309, 326
Case Grammar, 25
case marker on the Causee, 230, 232, 234, 235, 240, 241, 248, 249, 252, 260-262, 289, 297, 302-304, 306, 311, 312
case marking alternation
    passive, 67, 70, 74, 84, 86, 92, 97, 98, 101, 119, 120, 138, 144-150, 157, 166, 177, 190
    benefactive, 177, 190
Case Marking Schemata, 36-40, 146, 148
Categorial Grammar, 7, 13, 99
causal chain, 224
    antecedent role, 224, 320
    subsequent role, 224, 320
causative *have*, 200, 206, 224
causative interpretation of benefactives, 199-201, 223, 224, 319
causative transitive, 269, 304, 309
coercive, 230, 231, 234, 235, 237, 240, 249, 258, 262, 263, 265-269, 275, 278, 280, 288, 299, 302, 305, 306, 308. *See also* non-coercive
coindexing
    mechanism, 15, 19, 21, 23, 24, 41, 49, 57
    benefactive, 190, 206, 226, 227
    causative, 252, 254-256, 258, 260, 283, 288, 295, 297-300, 306, 309, 313, 321, 322
    passive, 81, 112, 114, 115, 118, 119, 129, 138, 141-144, 150, 152, 153, 169, 317, 318, 325
coindexing condition, 115, 187
Comrie, B., 19, 229, 289, 293
configurationality, 32, 33, 56

Index

conjunction /te/, 182, 220-223
control structure
    object, 4, 22, 46, 50, 85,
        101, 103-105,116, 180,
        183, 184, 256, 260,
        261, 275, 287, 299,
        325
    subject, 22, 46, 50, 227,
        309
Control Theory, 15, 19-24, 46,
    50, 116, 256, 260, 289,
    299, 306
control verb
    commitment-type, 22, 23,
        57, 227
    influence-type, 22-24, 31,
        47, 57, 116, 256, 260,
        261, 299
    orientation-type, 22, 23
core event
    causal involvement in the,
        206-208, 274, 316,
        319-321
    direct involvement in the,
        127, 129, 130, 139,
        140, 205-208, 274
coreferentiality, 44, 46, 49, 50,
    112, 129, 138, 165,
    205, 222, 227, 256,
    271, 283, 318-320
Croft, W., 31, 224, 320
default case, 39, 40, 148-150,
    253, 306, 318
double direct object constraint,
    240, 303
double-*wo* constraint
    232, 233, 240, 244,
    249, 252-254, 256,
    261, 288, 299, 302,
    303, 307

Dowty, D.R., 12, 24, 25, 29,
    30, 32, 48, 99, 112,
    205, 316
entailment relation **P**, 138-141,
    152, 169, 205, 318
exempt anaphors, 41, 42, 44, 45,
    61, 62
Ext-Arg, 23, 24, 114, 115, 138,
    139, 152, 165, 187,
    255, 258, 260, 297,
    299, 313, 318, 321,
    322
extended demotion, 289, 293
External Argument Reflexivity
    (Principle of), 57
Extended Projection Principle,
    88, 89, 91, 161
faire par causative, 230, 291-295,
    298, 322
Farmer, A., 36, 58, 82, 85, 153,
    237, 238, 240, 241,
    306, 315
Fillmore, C., 25, 28
Fukushima, K., 35, 46, 49, 59,
    62, 103, 165, 225-227,
    257, 303, 304, 306,
    313
Generalized Phrase Structure
    Grammar (GPSG)
    7, 10, 11, 15, 18, 20,
    33, 55, 81
gerundive morpheme /te/, 174,
    194, 220, 221, 223,
    325
Government Transparency
    Corollary, 96, 162, 246
Grimshaw, J., 28, 29, 58, 82,
    13-115, 121, 152, 163,
    318
Gunji, T., 58, 59, 66, 99-103,

Gunji, T (cont'd)
    105, 116, 165, 174,
    176, 180, 181, 185,
    199, 220, 222, 225,
    248, 249, 251, 253,
    262, 263, 275, 287,
    306
Harada, S.I., 234, 235, 240, 261,
    263, 311
Hasegawa, N., 58, 59, 66, 82,
    85, 86, 89, 99, 101,
    103-105, 153, 154,
    159, 161, 162, 325
headed-structure, 9
Head Feature Principle, 11, 13
Howard, I., 66, 83, 84, 120,
    154, 159
Iida, M., 42, 62,
Immediate Dominance Principle,
    15, 16, 33
inalienable possession, 137, 292,
    325
incorporation
    noun, 97-99, 132
    verb, 2, 87, 93, 96, 97, 99,
        104, 105, 162, 181,
        183-185, 238, 243-246,
        267, 268, 305, 309,
        325
Inherent Case, 97, 145, 170,
    246, 267, 268
Inoue, K., 42, 48, 60, 82, 154,
    158, 173, 225, 232,
    235, 238, 267, 306,
    308, 316
Jackendoff, R., 14, 21, 25, 26,
    28, 40, 47, 50, 56, 57,
    108, 306, 317, 326
Japanese Phrase Structure
    Grammar (JPSG), 99,
    162
Kitagawa, C., 48, 50
Kitagawa, Y., 109, 111, 118,
    163, 166, 241, 143,
    262, 267, 269, 270,
    272, 279, 287, 304,
    310, 311, 316
Kuno, S., 36, 42, 57, 58, 60-62,
    66, 69, 72, 73, 77, 82,
    104, 120, 127, 134,
    139, 154, 156, 157,
    159, 160, 165, 169,
    178, 205, 229, 234,
    235, 238-240, 261,
    262, 266, 268, 277-
    279, 304, 310, 311,
    316, 320
Kubo, M., 3, 66, 67, 70, 71, 73,
    74, 76-79, 82, 89-93,
    97, 98, 104, 105, 113,
    118-120, 126, 130-133,
    139, 145, 152-154,
    158-162, 166-168, 178,
    317
Kuroda, S.-Y., 59, 60, 66, 76,
    78, 82, 104, 111, 154,
    156, 158, 159, 163,
    164, 166, 167, 169,
    173, 223, 231, 238,
    269, 287, 304, 310,
    311, 316
Lexical Functional Grammar
    (LFG), 7, 18, 28, 81,
    82, 113, 161, 238, 295,
    315
lexical rules
    mechanism, 18, 19
    English passive, 18, 19, 61
    benefactive, 186-189, 202,
        203, 217

causative, 250, 251, 296, 297
passive, 106, 107, 136, 137, 254
lexicalist, 18, 19, 84-87, 104, 237, 238, 240, 241, 243, 310, 315
Linear Precedence Rule, 35
Locality Principle, 55
Macro-Roles, 25, 30
Marantz, A., 2, 60, 113, 146, 229, 235, 237, 238, 246, 267, 283, 304, 405, 307, 318
marker structure, 56
Miyagawa, S., 36, 60, 66, 71, 82, 87-89, 104, 113, 118, 120, 146, 150, 152, 158, 159, 170, 238, 240, 241, 306, 309, 310, 326
MODAL, 3, 173, 204, 208, 217-219, 319, 320, 323
monostratal, 7
monotonicity, 19, 106
morpheme order, 123, 125, 126, 150, 151, 178, 191-198, 218, 222, 281, 284, 285, 311, 319, 321, 323
morphological causatives, 229, 230, 238, 295, 304, 305, 323
Morphological Nonredundancy (Principle of), 293
morphological word/unit, 126, 151, 195, 315
multi-level, 2, 7, 315, 322
nagara-clause, 110, 111, 128, 140, 141, 163, 164, 166
Nishio, H., 127, 140, 155, 205, 207, 320
non-coercive, 230, 231, 234, 235, 237, 240, 258, 262, 265, 267-269, 280, 288, 299, 302, 306, 308. *See also* coercive
non-uniformist, 66, 82, 84, 86, 87, 101, 104, 153, 154, 231, 233-235, 237, 238, 300
NP-Spec, 131-133, 135, 167, 168
Object Honorification (OH)
benefactive, 181, 185, 222, 224, 325
causative, 260, 275, 283-288, 299, 309, 311, 312, 321
passive, 101-103, 116, 162, 321
obliqueness hierarchy, 40, 44, 46, 50, 54, 62, 224
obliqueness-binding (o-binding), 40-42, 44-47, 49, 61, 317
obliqueness-command (o-command), 41, 44, 45
ordered list, 12, 28, 29
parameter coindexing, 15, 226, 227
parameter identity, 15, 226, 227
passivization
of passives (double passivization), 103, 142-144, 162, 169
of benefactives, 222

passivization (cont'd)
  of causatives, 234, 235, 237, 240, 245-249, 254-256, 260-262, 266-269, 288, 293, 299, 300, 304, 307, 323, 321, 322
P-entailments, 30. *See also* Proto-Roles
periphrastic causative, 2, 229, 238, 246, 305, 323
Perlmutter, D.M., 18, 19, 27, 58, 81, 110
polite causative, 1, 199
Pollard, C., 3, 7, 8, 11, 12, 19, 21-24, 33, 37, 40-42, 44-46, 50, 55-57, 60-62, 73, 82, 106, 108, 112, 114, 122, 162, 165, 171
promotion, 19, 56, 317
protagonist control, 263. *See also* self-controllability
Proto-Agent, 29-32, 48, 53, 54, 112, 118, 121, 151, 164, 205, 271, 316, 317
Proto-Patient, 29-32, 53
Proto-Roles, 24, 29-32, 58, 323
psych predicate, 26, 27, 31, 50, 52, 54, 63, 164, 165
Reflexive Coreferential Constraint, 84, 161
Relational Grammar, 7, 18, 81, 170
resumptive pronoun, 133, 168
Ritter, E., 118, 126, 139, 165, 200, 201, 204-206, 224, 319
Romance causatives, 2, 230, 291, 293-295, 298, 305, 322. *See also faire par* causative
Rosen, S.T., 2, 48, 118, 126, 139, 161, 165, 200, 201, 204-206, 224, 229, 235, 238, 236-248, 259, 261, 262, 267, 268, 291, 293, 304-309, 315, 317, 319
Sag, I., 3, 7, 8, 11, 12, 19, 21-24, 33, 37, 40-42, 44-46, 50, 55-57, 60-62, 73, 82, 106, 108, 112, 114, 122, 162, 165, 171, 257, 260, 306, 321, 323
Saito, M., 34, 42, 58, 59, 155, 168
saturated category, 11, 13, 16, 17, 33, 36, 56, 144
self-controllability, 249, 262, 263, 265, 275, 308
Semantic Principle, 55, 153
semantic role, 3, 80, 112, 115, 118, 121, 139, 157, 190, 919, 200, 204, 205, 218, 321
semantic role assignment, 13, 15, 87-89, 91, 92, 109, 166, 182
Shibatani, M., 127, 214, 229, 232, 234-238, 240, 243, 262, 269, 270, 272, 287, 302, 303, 308, 309, 316, 321
sorted feature structure, 7, 8
sort-resolved, 10
state-of-affair (soa), 23, 57, 108, 114, 115, 119, 141, 142, 187, 190, 206,

Index 357

252, 259, 260, 271, 274, 297, 317, 318, 321
Structural Case, 145, 146, 170, 245, 268, 306
structure-sharing, 10, 11, 15, 55
Subcategorization Principle, 12, 13, 36
Subject Honorification (SH)
   benefactive, 175, 177-179, 190-198, 208, 218, 222
   causative, 235, 260, 275, 277-285, 287, 299, 310, 311, 318, 319, 321
   passive, 73-75, 79, 80, 84, 86, 92, 97, 101, 105, 122-126, 138, 150, 151, 160, 166
subject demotion, 19, 112, 113, 187, 189, 289
subject selection, 25, 26, 31, 57, 63, 113, 164
suppression of an argument
   passive, 14, 82, 88, 114, 115, 118, 120, 122, 138, 139, 150-153
   benefactive, 176, 177, 187, 189, 190, 208, 214, 218
   causative, 248, 271, 273, 286, 291, 292, 295, 297, 298, 300, 306, 313, 317, 318, 321, 322, 326
syntactic word, 5, 120, 150, 179, 187, 194, 195, 276, 277, 282, 299, 315
Terada, M., 3, 36, 66, 67, 70,

71, 76, 78, 82, 89, 93-99, 101, 103-105, 113, 118-120, 130-132, 139, 145, 146, 150, 152, 153, 158-160, 162, 167, 169, 174, 176, 180-186, 205, 223, 225, 234, 235, 243-246, 259, 261-263, 267-270, 275, 287, 304, 305, 307-309, 317, 325
thematic hierarchy, 25-28, 40, 47, 53, 57, 62, 114, 120, 164
thematic prominence, 25, 28, 29, 40, 48, 50, 53, 54, 61-63, 271, 317, 323
thematic relation, 25, 27, 56, 82, 111, 174, 201, 208, 218, 219, 319
thematic roles, 3, 7, 24-32, 38, 47, 56-58, 82, 85-87, 112, 114, 118, 129, 152, 161, 165, 201, 218, 271, 274, 316, 317, 319, 326
thematic roles
   Discrete roles approach, 25, 27-29, 58, 164, 316
   Individual roles approach, 24, 57
   Proto-Role approach, 24, 29-32, 58. *See also* Proto-Roles
   relative position approach, 25, 27-29
thematic/semantic underspecification, 112, 115, 118, 126, 139,

thematic/semantic
    underspecification
    (cont'd), 153, 200,
    201, 205, 208, 219,
    224, 317, 319, 320
token identity, 11
Tonoike, S., 262, 263, 265,
    275, 304, 305, 308
unaccusativity, 26, 27, 29, 58,
    93
unergativity, 26, 27, 29, 58
unification, 7, 10, 19, 106, 116
uniformist, 66, 83, 84, 87, 101,
    104, 161, 164, 231,
    234, 267, 288, 300. *See
    also* non-uniformist
uniformity, 66, 87, 88, 150,
    152, 153, 219, 258,
    300, 322
Universal Alignment Hypothesis
    (UAH), 27
Uniformity of Theta Assignment
    Hypothesis (UTAH),
    27, 58
valency, 1, 68, 175, 211-214,
    219, 225, 229, 238,
    240
valency-changing benefactive,
    214
valency-preserving benefactive,
    214, 279
volition, 30, 31, 52, 53, 112,
    118, 126-130, 201,
    205, 218, 240, 274,
    294, 305, 308, 316,
    317, 319
well-typed, 10
X'-theory, 15-17, 59
Zubizarreta, M.L., 2, 109, 113,
    121, 129, 229, 291-
    293, 305, 318

For Product Safety Concerns and Information please contact our EU
representative GPSR@taylorandfrancis.com
Taylor & Francis Verlag GmbH, Kaufingerstraße 24, 80331 München, Germany

www.ingramcontent.com/pod-product-compliance
Lightning Source LLC
Chambersburg PA
CBHW071757300426
44116CB00009B/1113